Advance praise for *A Life on Fire*

"Kate Barnard was an impressive woman who found her way to advance the cause of Oklahoma Native Americans, women, and the oppressed."
—**CHIEF GEOFFREY STANDING BEAR**,
Principal Chief of the Osage Nation

"Masterfully told, Connie Cronley's popular biography of Kate Barnard will inspire a new generation to learn about the oratory, advocacy, and tenacity of Oklahoma's first Commissioner of Charities and Corrections."
—**PATRICIA LOUGHLIN**, author *of Hidden Treasures of the American West: Muriel H. Wright, Angie Debo, and Alice Marriott*

"An insightful biography of social reform activist Kate Barnard, *Life on Fire* also peels back the curtain on Oklahoma's territorial politics, institutions, political personalities, theft of indigenous orphan rights, and corruption. Connie Cronley writes with grace, humor, and a deft hand of Barnard's fire and ambition, her intellect and gift of oratory, her nervous energy and indefatigable work ethic, her moral core, blind spots, and hubris. The result is a wonderfully compelling read and an important contribution to our understanding of Oklahoma's first female elected official, and the place and the era that bred her."
—**RILLA ASKEW**, author of *Most American: Notes from a Wounded Place*

"The story of Kate Barnard is as wonderful and heartbreaking as the story of Oklahoma itself. In this lively and thoroughly researched biography, Connie Cronley reintroduces us to this woman who embodied so many of the hopes and ideals of the new state, only to be ground down by the betrayal and disillusionment that followed."
—**RANDY KREHBIEL**, author of *Tulsa, 1921: Reporting a Massacre*

"This book is a must-read. The human and political environment of early Oklahoma that Kate Barnard faced was sobering and disturbing. Barnard was tenacious and relentless in alleviating the suffering of children, orphans, prisoners, and the weak and the frail, and in challenging the system that poorly managed them. Sadly, now more than ever, Oklahoma needs Kate Barnards."

— **CHAD "CORNTASSEL" SMITH,** former Principal Chief of the Cherokee Nation of Oklahoma and author of *Leadership Lessons from the Cherokee Nation: Learn from All I Observe*

"Kate Barnard was a woman before her time. She was a leader to the disadvantaged of her era and a true warrior woman."

—**CARMELITA WAMEGO SKEETER,** CEO, Indian Health Care Resource Center of Tulsa

A Life on Fire

A LIFE ON FIRE

OKLAHOMA'S KATE BARNARD

CONNIE CRONLEY

UNIVERSITY OF OKLAHOMA PRESS : NORMAN

This book is published with the generous assistance of the Wallace C. Thompson Endowment Fund, University of Oklahoma Foundation.

Library of Congress Cataloging-in-Publication Data

Names: Cronley, Connie, author.
Title: A life on fire : Oklahoma's Kate Barnard / Connie Jo Cronley.
Description: Norman : University of Oklahoma Press, 2021. | Includes
   bibliographical references. | Summary: "Biography of Catherine Ann
   'Kate' Barnard (1875–1930), progressive reformer and the first woman
   elected to state office in Oklahoma almost fifteen years before the
   ratification of the 19th amendment"—Provided by publisher.
Identifiers: LCCN 2021010541 | ISBN 978-0-8061-6929-3 (paperback)
Subjects: LCSH: Barnard, Kate, 1875–1930. | Women politicians—
   Oklahoma—Biography. | Women social reformers—Oklahoma—
   Biography. | Oklahoma—Politics and government—1907. |
   Oklahoma—Social policy.
Classification: LCC F700 .B373 2021 | DDC 361.7092 [B]—dc23
LC record available at https://lccn.loc.gov/2021010541

For
Angie Debo
Pauline (Polly) Jamerson
Edith Copeland
and
Julia (Julee) A. Short

Contents

Preface

CATHERINE IS A REGAL NAME. It is the name of saints, queens, and empresses. Catherine Barnard was her christened name, but she was known as Kate—a name as short and direct as the woman herself. She was a heroine of the Progressive Era and such a bright star of social reform in the early 1900s that the national press called her "the Good Angel of Oklahoma."[1]

A historian of her time went beyond state boundaries and declared her "one of America's great women," saying she earned her fame as a practical sociologist with "invincible courage" fighting for social justice and economic liberty. Her political career was brief, lasting less than a decade, but at the St. Louis World's Fair in 1904 she caught the prevailing winds of social reform blowing across the nation, and how she soared. Two decades before women could vote, she campaigned for Progressive and labor candidates, helped write the constitution for the new state of Oklahoma based on social reform precepts, and was elected to office herself, the first woman in Oklahoma—and the second in the nation—to hold an elected state office.[2]

Kate was the social conscience of the new "baby state," as it was fondly called, and a champion of the laborer, the imprisoned, the mentally ill, the poor, and especially the children. She campaigned among coal miners and farmers, lobbied in legislatures, and stormed in public and in the press until reform laws were passed and child labor was damned. She never married and was childless herself, but the cause of the child was her foremost mission. What kind of nation are we that we coin wealth from our children? she asked her audiences, as she pleaded with them to keep their children out of the mines, the mills, and the factories.

Kate stumped for William Jennings Bryan (she called him Billy) and was admired by Pulitzer Prize–winning newspaper editor William Allen White and muckraking journalist Ida Tarbell. She was a such charismatic orator that state audiences gathered by the thousands when she spoke, coming by horse and wagon and by train; national audiences rose and cheered her, and President Theodore Roosevelt stopped a receiving line to shake her hand. Samuel J. Barrows, a national authority on prison reform, said Kate taught him "what a single, earnest little woman could do . . . in the life of a state and in the life of humanity."[3]

The press loved her, and national reformers called her a "little dynamo," a modern word at the time, to describe her "marvelous energy" and political successes. Back home, she was the most popular—and the most feared—politician in the state. When she ran for office, she outpolled every candidate except the governor. Yet for all her fame and acclaim, everybody in Oklahoma from governor to newsboy called her "Kate." She never forgot her lowly prairie beginnings, and she remained approachable: "The door of her office in the state house—like the door of her heart—was always open." She dressed plainly and never wore jewelry. "How can a woman wear diamonds in a country where little children starve?" she asked.[4]

A newspaper headline described her as "90 Pounds of Human Dynamite." Kate was tiny, not even five feet tall and never weighing more than ninety-five pounds, but she was fearless and combative. She was the child of homesteading immigrants, a Scots mother and Irish father, and she reveled in bare-knuckle politics. "I am Irish and love a good shindy," she said.[5]

And then.

She made the fatal mistake of trying to help the wealthy Indian orphans of the state, whose properties, allotted to them by the federal government, were being looted in a vast conspiracy of graft—a "cold blooded plot," she said—that reached all the way from Oklahoma to Washington, D.C. At stake was "stupendous wealth," land, coal, gas, and oil valued at multimillions of dollars. Kate's was the only state office with authority to protect them in the courts, and she was the only person with the courage to do it. It was not a cause she chose. Officials from federal Indian agents to the former secretary of the interior petitioned her to intercede. Her battle for Native American children of the Five Civilized Tribes (Cherokee, Choctaw, Chickasaw, Creek, and Seminole), as they were known at the time, and her investigation of fraud among the Osage presaged the infamous account of the Osage Nation murders popularized in David Grann's book *Killers of the Flower Moon*. In a period of unparalleled greed and corruption, Oklahoma Indian fortunes were ripe for stealing, but Kate stood in the way. "Now she has stopped preachin' and started meddlin'," someone local said. It was her downfall. Her colleague Judge Ben B. Lindsey, pioneer of the juvenile court system, saw it for what it was. Kate had become "a power to reckon with," he said. And thus, "She became a marked woman."[6]

The grafters closed in around her. They destroyed her department, and that destroyed her health, her life, and her passionate heart. The looting and swindling and theft and murder for Indian properties went on unchecked. She died at the age of fifty-five, ill, reclusive, and so irascible that some whispered about her mental stability. She died alone in a hotel room, but she died with her fighting spirit intact and saying she intended to recover her health and run for the U.S. Senate.

A crowd of 1,400 men, women, and children overflowed the Roman Catholic cathedral in Oklahoma City for her funeral on a cold February morning in 1930. The governor of Oklahoma and seven former governors were honorary pallbearers. The flag on the state capitol was lowered to half-mast. Newspapers covered the funeral as a major news event, and reporters described her as a pioneer welfare worker, a champion of the needy, an advocate of labor always, and one of the creators of the labor-farmer bloc that controlled the state at the dawn of the twentieth century. The newspaper stories did not mention her last years of sorrow and barely commented on her lost cause on behalf of Indians. That day she was a heroine once again, and the people and press called her "Our Kate."[7]

I first learned about Kate Barnard in the mid-1970s from my friend and mentor, historian Angie Debo. The two women were contemporaries: Kate was born in 1875, Angie in 1890. Angie was a seventeen-year-old rural teacher when she first heard Kate speak, and she described the occasion as overwhelming. She said Kate had a power over an audience that was "completely, absolutely hypnotic." It was a rare power, Angie told me: "Franklin Delano Roosevelt had it, and Aimee Semple McPherson." She remembered that speech and Kate's charismatic personality for the rest of her life. She followed Kate's career as it soared and then as it crashed, destroyed by grafters. Angie came to know a lot about greed and graft herself; she wrote about it bravely in her book *And Still the Waters Run*, the story of the liquidation of the Five Civilized Tribes by the breach of federal treaties and the subsequent criminal activities by social, governmental, and religious organizations to cheat individual Natives of their properties.[8]

I was a young woman of thirty-two when I met Angie (I always addressed her as "Dr. Debo"), and she was an old woman of eighty-five. We were friends until she died in 1988 at age ninety-eight. Angie urged me to write a biography of Kate, who was long dead by then. I was not the only one she encouraged to write about Kate. She guided Edith Copeland and Julee Short with their biographical research and writing about Kate. In the years since then, a couple of scholarly books about Kate have been published. This is the first popular biography of a heroic woman proclaimed as one of "the foremost statesmen of [her] age."[9]

As much as possible, I have told Kate's story in real time, using her own fiery words from the letters, newspaper and magazine articles, and official reports that she wrote; from the partial memoir she left behind, which found its way to the Western History Collections at the University of Oklahoma; from her slightly more detailed diary, acquired recently by the Oklahoma Historical Society; from correspondence sent her by colleagues; and from print media of the day. This brings her off the page, as alive and intense as she was when Angie saw her speak. I was lucky to start my research under Angie's guidance. She directed me to dusty documents at the National Archives and the Library of Congress in Washington, D.C., and to state research sites.

The accepted terminology of Kate's time offers problems for contemporary audiences. Terms such as "insane," "crippled," and "feeble-minded," which were conventional, even official, diagnoses at the time, are painful to modern eyes and ears. Formerly acceptable stereotypes such as "the fighting Irish" are cringe-worthy now, although it was a proud boast for Kate; and casual derogatory terms like "redskin" and "squawman" now make us recoil. The word "Civilized" is no longer used to identify the Five Tribes of eastern Oklahoma. I have tried to use the language of Kate's era sparingly and only in context, often putting the offensive words in quotation marks. And yet, it is unfair to Kate and her colleagues to completely whitewash their language. Mostly they did not intend to be hurtful or unkind, and often their language and viewpoints were advances over their predecessors. Allowing readers to see what they thought and how they talked about it maintains what historian Bernard Bailyn called the honest pastness of the past. We can appreciate what advancements in sensibilities we have made since Kate's time. She would like that because she esteemed advancement and modernity above all.

When I began my research forty years ago, some of the people who had known Kate were still alive and could tell me about her. The more I learned about Kate, the more I understood Angie's admiration for her. The two were mirror hearts. Both women had inviolable convictions, a strong work ethic, and courage in the face of fearsome obstacles. Both chose a career akin to a calling instead of marriage. Biographer Shirley A. Leckie wrote that Angie was determined to live her life according to her own values and principles, whatever the outcome. She learned that, in large part, from Kate's example.[10]

Kate and Angie passed a flame, one to the other, and to many others. They passed it to me, too. Now I am an old woman myself. I am sad that my friend and mentor did not live to read this book, but it feels good to keep promises to people we care about. Angie and Kate both understood that.

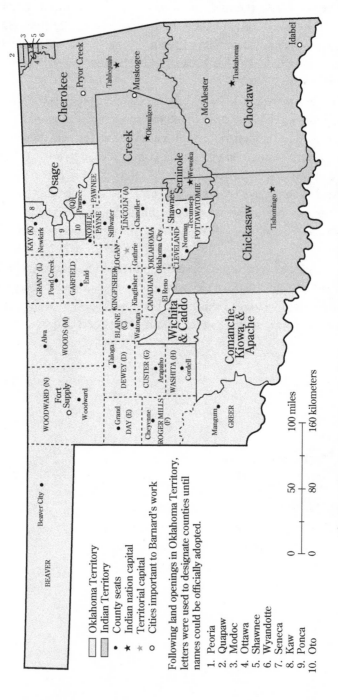

The Twin Territories when the Barnards settled in Oklahoma Territory.
Indian Territory was reserved for the Five "Civilized" Tribes. Map by Bill Nelson.

Following land openings in Oklahoma Territory, letters were used to designate counties until names could be officially adopted.

1. Peoria
2. Quapaw
3. Modoc
4. Ottawa
5. Shawnee
6. Wyandotte
7. Seneca
8. Kaw
9. Ponca
10. Oto

Oklahoma Territory
Indian Territory
County seats
Indian nation capital
Territorial capital
Cities important to Barnard's work

CHAPTER ONE

A Winter Childhood

K ATE WAS PROUD of the Irish ancestry she shared with her father. She liked the term "the fighting Irish" and said that was where she got her fighting blood for political frays.

She did not talk about her mother's Scots heritage, but it was such a powerful influence, she chose a lifestyle completely opposite that of her mother. Kate's maternal family name was Shields (sometimes spelled Shiells), and they were hardy settlers who emigrated from Scotland to Canada West, now known as Ontario, for the free land grants. They were established in frontier Canada by 1825 among a scattering of other white settlers, French fur traders, and missionaries. The land was fertile for wheat and barley, but it was a hard geography for pioneers. Even governmental descriptions admitted that it was "a very distant place" of long, cold winters with "sudden and violent storms" blowing off Lake Huron.[1]

Kate's great-grandparents, Robert and Rachel Shields, were among an extended Scots Presbyterian clan of farmers who cleared land and built homes in the forested area. They were part of the British immigrant wave, especially Scots and Irish, beginning new lives in a new place. Kate's grandparents, Robert and Jane Laing Shields, followed that lifestyle, living in a log cabin with their ten children. Their oldest child, born in 1845 and named for her grandmother, was Rachel. She would be Kate's mother.[2]

When Rachel was nineteen, she married thirty-six-year-old John Mason, also a Presbyterian born in Scotland, and they continued a farming life. They, too, lived in a log house, spun their own wool, winnowed their own wheat, and tapped their own trees for maple syrup. They soon had two sons and, in the family tradition, named them for parents and grandparents. The two Mason boys were Robert, named for Rachel's father, and John, named for Rachel's husband and father-in-law. Rachel's life stretched before her as straight and predictable as a good furrow.[3]

Two events changed her life completely. Rachel had been married only three years when her husband died. Suddenly she was widowed with two small sons and a farm with more cattle, sheep, and swine than she could manage alone. Her life was toppled even more when an economic depression hit the area and drove a wave of Canadian settlers south to newly opened territories in the United States. In 1868, some of the Shields clan— including twenty-three-year-old Rachel and her sons—moved to the brand-new state of Nebraska. They followed the same dream that had lured settlers to the continent since the 1700s: private ownership of land. The Homestead Act of 1862 offered 160 acres of free land to a man or woman at least twenty-one years old who lived on it for five years and paid fees of about eighteen dollars. Rachel's parents and three brothers staked homestead claims in southeastern Fillmore County. Some lived in sod houses while they began planting hundreds of fruit trees as part of a federal tree cultivation program for the vast, arid grassland known as the Great American Desert.[4]

In Canada they had endured fierce storms and long winters. In Nebraska they faced the brutality of the Great Plains, where the weather veered from droughts to floods to blizzards. The biggest contrast to the timbered lands they had left behind was the flat landscape, a place of desolate emptiness—no trees until pioneers arrived bringing seeds, seedlings, and birds of flight. The wind was a constant force, blowing, pulling, pushing, and tearing. Strong winds snapped fence posts and drove prairie fires with a fury.[5]

In addition to the torment of the weather, incessant Indian wars erupted around them. Territorial conflicts exploded among the Nebraska Indians indigenous to the area: Pawnee, Sioux, Cheyenne, Crow, Arapaho, Comanche, Kowa, and Osage. Some tribes, especially the Pawnee, Otoe, and Omaha, were generally peaceful toward encroaching white settlers, but the Sioux were more volatile, especially to pioneers trespassing across their hunting grounds on the Oregon Trail. In 1873, five years after the Shields family arrived, the last great war between Indian tribes and settlers was fought in Nebraska. That same year, a mighty Easter storm lasted two days, destroying lives and property. Then, in the fall, the Panic of 1873 marked the beginning of a six-year national financial depression. These misfortunes culminated in a natural horror worse than all the other hardships, one of the most calamitous phenomena in western history. Over seventeen years, seven invasions of grasshoppers hit the area with a devastation not known before or seen since. The worst grasshopper invasion in Nebraska was in 1874, six years after Rachel and her extended family arrived.[6]

Millions of grasshoppers suddenly filled the sky in a solid mass, stacked the ground four inches deep, and destroyed every living plant. Children screamed in terror, and cattle brayed helplessly as the insects crawled over them. The voracious grasshoppers devoured entire fields of wheat, corn, and vegetables. They ate the leaves off of young fruit trees and consumed curtains, clothing, and food in cupboards. They attacked everything made of wood: furniture, fences, kitchen utensils, pitchfork handles, and horses' harnesses. Ponds, streams, and open wells, brown with grasshopper excrement, were unfit for use. Chickens, turkeys, and hogs were bloated from eating grasshoppers and tasted so strongly of the locusts that they were inedible to the settlers. The destruction was thorough. Some farmers were poverty stricken overnight, and pioneers sold or gave away their land claims. One departing pioneer drove a wagon with a sign reading "Eaten out by grasshoppers. Going back East to live with wife's folks." Rachel and her family must have rued their decision to settle in this land of Old Testament plagues.[7]

Kate grew up hearing stories about the legendary grasshopper attacks. In 1908, on her way to address a national conference, she wrote a friend about her clothes for the occasion: "I will be true to my pedigree and wear a verdant suit of grasshopper green."[8]

In September 1874, amidst these calamities, Rachel remarried and changed everything about her life, from religion to her livelihood. She chose John P. Barnard, not a Scots Presbyterian but an Irish Catholic, and not a farmer but a railroad surveyor, land speculator, and sometime lawyer. Unlike the Shieldses, whose family history can be documented for generations, nothing is known about Barnard's background except what he said about himself, and much of that was fiction. Barnard claimed, even on the marriage license, that he was born in Mississippi to Terrence and Ellinor Barnard. Kate would repeat this story: "My father was a Mississippi slave owner, and when the [Civil War] swept all of his fortune away he went to Oklahoma to retrieve his fortune. He saw much poverty before doing so." Later, she changed the story of his heritage and said that he was born in Cork, Ireland, and came to America as a babe in his mother's arms, "fleeing English persecution and the potato famine caused by ruthless English landlords." Whichever version is correct, with immigrant parents, Kate was a first-generation United States citizen.[9]

Both Kate and her father rewrote details of their personal histories with the skill of a novelist. She wanted the world to see her father as she saw him—more honorable, more noble, and more admirable than he was. After his death, she discovered that even she did not know the whole truth about his life. Probably, Barnard was either born to or raised by Terrance and Eleanor Trainor, Catholics who immigrated to Canada from Ireland. A relative was named Barnard Trainor, and it is highly possible that Kate's father appropriated the given name to rechristen himself John P. Barnard. He presented himself as a southern gentleman and an adventurer who had known life on the Canadian frontier. If Rachel had known him in Canada, she would have seen the birthplace discrepancy on the marriage license. Maybe she didn't care. Maybe she knew why he had reinvented his history. It was a place and time when creating biographical facts was easy. A new identity for a new life in a new country? Why not? It is easy to imagine Barnard as a handsome dreamer who charmed Rachel with romance and blue-sky plans. Perhaps she was not deluded. After the misfortunes of Canada and Nebraska, perhaps she wanted to change her life, too, and marrying Barnard was the easiest way to do it.[10]

He was thirty when they married and Rachel was twenty-nine, although she fabricated a bit herself on the marriage document and listed her age as twenty-seven. Just eight months and eight days after the wedding, their daughter was born May 23, 1875, in Alexandria, Nebraska. In late June, the baby was christened Catherine Ann Bernard [sic] in the nearest Catholic church, St. James in Crete, Nebraska. Kate's Irish godparents bore the lilting names of Michael Flaherty and Catherine Conway. In Rachel's family, namesakes stretched back through generations like a chain, but Catherine Ann, Kate for short, was not a Shields name. It was a name from her father's Irish family and friends. From the moment of her naming, Kate's life was charted by Barnard adventures. What she got from the plodding Shields clan was a dogged, head-down work ethic. The combination of Shields determination and Barnard ambition gave her the personality she would need for the tumultuous career that lay before her. She believed in change and new beginnings; it was in her bones.[11]

Barnard bequeathed his daughter the coloring known as "black Irish"—blue eyes, black hair, and apple-red cheeks. She also inherited an Irish talent for language and storytelling. Kate's flair for the dramatic propelled her to success as a riveting orator.

When Rachel and Barnard met in Nebraska, he was helping to build the Union Pacific railroad. Railroad surveyors were explorers who crossed the frontiers first, in multiple waves of railroad building, and behind them towns and communities sprang up like green gardens after a spring rain. The area was becoming the nation's corn belt, and wheat was soon to follow, transforming the region into the breadbasket of the world. Barnard was no farmer, so what he saw on the frontiers was opportunities for merchants and land speculators, more glamorous work with quicker returns. Just a few months after Kate's birth, the Barnards moved south across the Nebraska border to Kansas. They were a family of five: Barnard, Rachel, infant Kate, and Rachel's two sons, ages eight and ten.[12]

East-central Kansas was no escape from the perils they had known in Nebraska. It was equally inhospitable, with bad weather, grasshoppers, and Indian massacres. In 1875, the year the Barnards arrived in Kansas, U.S. soldiers killed a Cheyenne band about one hundred miles west of their new home, and three years later the Natives killed settlers in retaliation.[13]

The Barnards chose the prosperous young city of Kirwin as the best place for a young family to begin a prosperous life. It was the largest town in Phillips County, with a thousand residents, two newspapers, and businesses from blacksmiths to billiard halls ringing the town square. Barnard became a businessman with a butcher shop, and during the county fair he operated a restaurant and entered a sorrel horse in a trotting race. More befitting his aspirations, he also set up a realty office: J. P. Barnard, Real Estate Dealer. He accumulated a sizable amount of city property, some of it bought in Rachel's name and likely with her money, and five hundred acres of ranch land in five counties. His Christmas gift to Rachel the first year of their marriage was the deed to a city lot. Barnard's realty work was a profession of marginal repute. A Salvation Army prayer of the time asked special mercy for "liars, thieves, gamblers, prostitutes, and real estate agents. O Lord have mercy on their souls and teach them the better way."[14]

Despite Barnard's questionable profession, the family fortune was growing, and the family began to grow, too. In 1877, when Kate was a toddler of two, Rachel became pregnant. Rachel's mother had borne a child every two years for twenty years, and Rachel herself had given birth to three healthy children. Still, childbirth was perilous in the nineteenth century, and infant mortality was alarmingly high. The leading causes of death were measles, consumption, and childbirth. One year alone, more than half of the thirty-five deaths recorded in Kirwin were children under the age of five.[15]

The hardest winter in memory hit Kirwin that year. The storm that began on January 15 was "the worst storm ever known in this part of the State," according to a local newspaper. "It commenced Monday morning about two o'clock. . . . During the entire day the wind blew the snow so that a person could not see ten feet in any direction. Several of our citizens were lost when but a few rods from a house or building."[16]

Three days later, as the Barnard home was still gripped by the blizzard, Rachel died in childbirth. The baby died a few days later. Mother and infant were buried in the frozen Kirwin Cemetery. The afternoon of the funeral was icy, but a large crowd turned out for the burial of the young mother, the local newspaper reported, to extend "heartfelt sympathy" to the widower "and his family of children." Kate was not quite three years old, but the stark image of Rachel's snow-covered grave haunted her for the rest of her life. Winter and death run like bleak threads through her public speeches. "My mother died when I was so young that I cannot even remember her face." For Kate, winter was a synonym for a motherless child, "when the wind sighs and whistles and moans around the gables of your house; when the sun veils its face . . . , and the whole aspect of nature is drear, cold and dismal."[17]

Graves in the Kirwin Cemetery are marked with stone angels, praying hands, and other traditional images of mourning. Rachel's is the only tombstone carved with a weeping willow. She had come to the flat prairies from a land of water and woods. During her life, Barnard gave her city property. In death, he gave her a stone tree on that treeless Kansas prairie.[18]

Rachel's death destroyed the young family. Barnard never recovered his promising new start on life. In a matter of months, he dressed the children

Rachel's grave on the Kansas prairie with the weeping willow
tombstone. Photograph from the author's collection.

in new clothes and new boots and sent them to Nebraska to live with their
Shields grandparents. He began selling off the property he and Rachel had
acquired and paid the Shieldses for room and board for Kate and her half-
brothers. Rachel's father was appointed guardian of her sons, but the
grandparents were old and worn out by hard work in hard climates. Kate
lived with them for only a year. When she was four, Barnard brought her
back to Kirwin. The Shields family melted away; some died, including her
grandfather most likely, and others gave up on the heartless Great Plains
and moved west. Rachel's two sons eventually lived in California. More by
fate than by choice, the Shields family abandoned Kate. When they were

gone, she had nobody to talk to her about her mother or to tell her stories about Canada or Scotland. All she had was her father.[19]

Years later, Kate talked to the public and the press about her mother, who lay "in a cold, northern graveyard," and her father, who loved his dead wife too much to remarry. "It was one of those old sweet romances," Kate said, "the 'true loves of long ago.'"[20]

Actually, when Kate was six years old, her father did remarry, but it was another of his misfortunes. Barnard was thirty-six in 1881 when he wed eighteen-year-old Anna Teresa Rose, the oldest daughter of a large Prussian emigrant family of farmers. They were married in Germantown, Kansas, by a Roman Catholic priest, filed a claim for a forty-acre farm, and soon had a son they named Frank. The couple divorced two years later. Some said it was conflicts over Kate that broke up the marriage. Anna remarried twice and changed the baby's name from Barnard to her final married name, Krohlow. The marriage and the son became Barnard family secrets. Barnard did not maintain contact with his son, and Kate said, "I was never allowed to know this boy."[21]

Barnard was a man often befallen by bad choices or bad luck—"tremendous cataclysms," Kate said—and his life began to plummet. The community sympathy expressed at Rachel's funeral was gone. In 1882 a neighbor reported him to authorities for failing to fulfill the residency requirements on a homestead claim, and he lost the property. Four years later, a local newspaper reported a salacious story about Barnard making persistent advances to a neighboring farmer's wife while the man was out of town. The woman had to use a boiling tea kettle to "drive the dirty dog out of the house." The newspaper continued, "this was not the first time Barnard had been accused of similar action toward decent but unprotected women," recalling another case a few years earlier. Things got worse. The woman's husband pressed charges, a fight erupted between the two men, and Barnard drew a revolver. This was a public disgrace even in the rough young state of Kansas.[22]

Barnard resumed work as a surveyor and was gone for most of the next several years. When he was in Kirwin, he lived at a hotel. "My mother's sons were brought up by my Grandma Shiell [sic] while I drifted the world with my father," Kate said. Barnard was the one who did the drifting; Kate stayed behind, boarding with families in a small town where secrets had no place to hide. The 1870s and 1880s were years of agricultural depression, and she said it was a combination of continued drought and business reverses that left her father a poor man at age forty-five. He preferred "honor and poverty" to bankruptcy protection, she said. She omitted the part about scandal, but surely that was another reason he left town. Barnard's surveying trips were longer and farther away. He sent Kate a picturesque letter from Montana saying he was writing "from the mouth of the Tongue River." Once, the local press reported "a vague rumor afloat" that Barnard had been summoned to President Grover Cleveland's mountain retreat in New York to discuss a post office for Kirwin. Every time he went away, Kate was afraid he would never return. In fact, Barnard was once reported "killed by Indians while coming home from the Hills," and a week passed before the story was found to be untrue.[23]

Kate was a lonely girl who often stood on a rise outside town and watched the trains in the distance. Author Mari Sandoz, another Nebraska native who had a hard pioneering childhood, might have been describing Kate when she wrote, "The underprivileged child . . . is interested in social justice and in the destruction of discrimination between economic levels, between nationalist levels, between color levels, and so on." It is no wonder that Kate gravitated to these very subjects as a career. She had an intense sympathy for anything small and hurting—a hungry child, a mistreated dog, a stray kitten. "The least appearance of suffering or sorrow rang a keynote to the loneliness and desolation in her own heart," a friend said. She found her calling as both a ministering angel and an avenging angel. The twin tendencies grew from her orphaned childhood, a time when "she cried herself to sleep, many a lonely night, because other children had mothers to love them and she had not." Kate herself said, "I wanted someone on earth for a blood relative." One of her greatest fears was "drifting sick and alone among strangers." The tragedy of Kate's life is that it was not a fear, it was a prophecy.[24]

The "dirty dog" scandal tarnished Barnard's reputation, but that is not what ruined him financially. He was a victim of time and place. By 1889, Kansas was a busted state. The decade had begun with a boom of land speculation and bumper crops, but droughts led to massive crop failures, and historic blizzards finished the job. Banks failed, businesses closed, and some fifty thousand settlers streamed out of the state. Barnard was one of them, heading south to the newly opened Oklahoma Territory.

The area was occupied by the Creeks and Seminoles until pressure from thousands of white intruders, railroad interests, and subsidized newspapers influenced Congress to push the tribes into selling their lands to the United States government so it could be offered to homesteaders. Indian Territory, the adjacent land to the east, was still reserved for the Five Civilized Tribes, as they were known then.[25]

The public race for free land in central Oklahoma Territory took place April 22, 1889. It was one of the most colorful episodes in western history, a great horse race known as the Run of 1889. Almost two million acres, some twelve thousand homesteads, were thrown open for public claim to those who could get there first. Thousands of people lined up at the Kansas border trying to claim them. The "89ers" held high pioneer standing among white Oklahoma residents, and although Barnard was not part of the race, he was close enough to enjoy the associated glory. Not long after the Run, he staked a claim in the city of Kingfisher, Oklahoma Territory, a former stagecoach stop along the Chisholm Trail traversed by great cattle drives from Texas. A second land run opened the Unassigned Lands to non-Indian settlement, and the area attracted a smattering of Black settlers, most from Kansas, where they had relocated after leaving the old Confederacy. Immigrants, especially Czechs, Germans, and Germans from Russia, poured in and transformed the prairie grasslands into the buckle of the wheat belt. Barnard was not interested in farming wheat or any other crop; he wanted town lots. The county was the site of a slugfest of legal land fights, and the following year he lost title to his Kingfisher city lot in a lawsuit. His small law practice in Kingfisher failed, too. Barnard said he had arrived with thirty-five dollars, and after his business setbacks, he was so broke he had to borrow money to pay for his room and meals. Once again, he went back to working as a surveyor.[26]

Kate was fourteen when her father left Kansas, and she did not see him at all during the two years he spent in Oklahoma Territory scrambling for land and another new start. Before he left her behind, he wrote an inspirational message in her autograph album: "Let Faith, Hope and Charity be the theme of your whole life and when temptation lures you to forsake either of the three great Christian principles, remember our Saviour Jesus Christ died on the cross to redeem sinners. Your loving father, (Signed) John P. Barnard." He signed his full, formal name in elegant penmanship complete with swirls and flourishes. Kate cherished the inscription with its noble sentiments. "My love for my father, and a desire to help the poor, became the two great dominant factors of my life. . . . It is the strength of character inherited from that great pioneer which enables me to forego love, home, and other material pleasures, and become a Voice to those who suffer." Justice was a passion with him, she said. "He never broke a promise. He hated a lie. He never conversed on frivolous subjects." These were traits she vowed to develop in herself.[27]

Kate was a poor half orphan, but she did not shrink into meekness humbled by her condition. On the contrary, she was an extrovert who liked to take charge and stand center stage. Kirwin's new two-story school was a showplace in the county, and Kate flourished there as a student. She made excellent grades and was never absent or tardy. Her shining talent was public speaking. She won Sunday school prizes for memorizing the Ten Commandments and the Sermon on the Mount, and at school programs she recited essays and poems.[28] She was articulate and had such a good memory, she spoke without notes. She was comfortable on stage with a magnetic presence, and audiences responded to her. She liked that, too. When Kate discovered her power as a public speaker, she found the key to her future.[29]

Kansas's turbulent politics swirled around her. She saw revolutionary political concepts such as the Women's State Suffrage Association campaign for the right for women to participate in school, bond, and municipal elections. This was interesting, but she was more intrigued by what the men were doing and how the farm and labor parties were growing in strength. When she was sixteen, Kate watched the Farmers' Alliance become one of the most powerful influences in the state by joining forces with labor to become the Populist Party and the champion of the common man. The experience was burned into her political sensibility. Fiery Populist orators stumped the state warning farmers about the evil of big business and "money power" conspiring to ruin them. One of the most forceful Populist speakers was Mary Elizabeth Lease, a former Kansas schoolteacher whose family farm was lost in an economic depression. She challenged farmers to "raise less corn and more hell." Although reporters had invented that quote, Lease adopted it as her own, saying, "It was a right good bit of advice."[30]

These politics, whipped with fervor, were part of everyday conversation in Kirwin. They seeped into the bedrock of young Kate's own belief system and persona. Years later, she returned to Kirwin to deliver a speech, and a veteran newspaper reporter wrote that "her address brought back most forcibly to the writer's mind the political turmoil and upheaval of the late 80's and the early 90's in Kansas . . . when Mrs. Mary Ellen [*sic*] Lease [was] such a power and force in the politics of this state. Much of [Kate's] address was an almost exact counterpart of the addresses we used to hear in those days when the Farmers' Alliance was drifting into Populism."[31]

Kate was almost seventeen when her father returned. He was forty-six, and Kate was shocked by his appearance—"the careworn countenance, the furrowed brow, the faded eyes and silvered hair." He was so aged, she barely recognized him. They visited Rachel's grave one last time, both weeping; then they left Kansas forever. This time, they left together. This time, like a storybook's ending, her father came to take her away with him.[32]

For their first year in Oklahoma Territory, they lived in a Kingfisher boardinghouse. Then they moved to Oklahoma City, about fifty miles away. Kate saw the city as it exploded into existence. On the morning of the '89 Run, Oklahoma City was a sleepy little Santa Fe railroad station with a few tents and campfires around it. By sunset, ten thousand people were camped there, and buildings went up as fast as boards could be hammered together. That first day, settlers opened stores, started banks, set up doctors' and lawyers' offices, and published newspapers. When Kate and her father arrived there a couple of years later, Oklahoma City's population had stabilized at about five thousand, but the bustle and building continued. The city's energy and sky-is-the-limit attitude suited Kate's personality.[33]

She was enthralled by St. Joseph's Cathedral, under construction in the heart of the city. Kirwin had not had a permanent Catholic church, only visiting priests. In Kingfisher, the Protestant owners of the Barnards' boardinghouse were alarmed at Kate's Catholicism and warned her about the pope and the Church. Kate now reveled in her Catholic faith, attending mass regularly and fervently. For the next two years she attended the

Catholic school across the street operated by Sisters of Mercy nuns. Kate later embellished her parochial schooling and said she had spent several years in a convent. Sometimes, if the audience was right, she said her father had sent her there because she was unruly. That was not altogether an exaggeration, because she was too headstrong to be a demure daughter, as her father discovered in an incident with a white dress.[34]

Kate was going through a pious phase, enamored with self-sacrifice and charity. Being Kate, she added a splash of self-dramatization. Barnard bought her a new white dress for a special school event, but when a classmate died and Kate paid a sympathy call on the family, she was stricken at the sight of the mother mourning twice, once for the daughter who had died, and again because she could not afford to buy a dress for her child to be buried in. In her short life the girl had known hardship, the mother cried, and even in death she could not have one luxury. Impulsively, Kate gave the mother her own new white dress for the burial and wore an old dress for the school program. Barnard was furious, but Kate stood her ground. She would not enjoy fine clothes while a poor mother cried about a dead girl in a worn dress. On such stories as this, legends are built.[35]

In July 1893, Barnard made yet another effort at homesteading. He registered 160 acres of former Kickapoo-Pottawatomie reservation, the last of the unsettled lands being opened to the public. It would not have occurred to him to harbor concern for the Natives he and others were displacing, any more than Kate's ancestors had thought about the First Nations of Canada or the Nebraska tribes. To them, this was progress for the nation and personal opportunity for settlers, all sanctioned by the federal government. To secure the title to the land, Barnard had to fulfill two requirements: establish permanent residency on the claim and make improvements to the land. He had failed twice to prove a homestead claim, and he was determined to succeed this time. Kate could be the solution. She could be the permanent resident on the claim while Barnard was working in Oklahoma City or away on surveying business.

The residency would have been a challenge for a strong man or for a family, and it was even harder for a young woman living alone. Oklahoma Territory was suffering some of the worst weather in history, a drought that would be unequaled until the Dust Bowl of the 1930s. Barnard's claim was only twenty miles outside Oklahoma City, but to Kate it seemed on the edge of nowhere. The closest town was Newalla, and with little more than a general store and a blacksmith shop, it stretched the definition to call Newalla a town. The earth in that part of Oklahoma is a distinctive color, as red as a wound, and although the Barnard claim was flat enough for farming, the land is clay, fit only for grass, grazing, and the native gnarled blackjack trees, which are not fit for much of anything. Barnard had no interest in farming the land himself; he wanted the 160 acres as an investment. At least the property had a stream. Between two large oak trees, hired hands built a two-room house with a lean-to kitchen, a barn, and an outhouse. They also bored a well and dug a storm shelter against the very real threat of tornadoes. This satisfied the homestead requirements for making improvements on the property.[36]

The homestead gave Kate a panoramic view of Oklahoma's spectacular sunsets—gaudy purple and crimson one evening, nursery pastels the next—but she did not care to look at scenery. She longed for people and progress. She missed the bustle of Oklahoma City and the Catholic cathedral. On the homestead she was isolated and alone. All she could see in any direction was empty sky and rolling land. What is more, she had a fear of snakes, scorpions, and centipedes, so she spent most of her time inside. She had no interest in domesticity, either; her days were spent reading and fretting. A few neighbors lived nearby, but she could not visit because she had no horse for transportation. Her only companion was a St. Bernard dog. "Those were times of desperate poverty for all Oklahoma pioneers," Kate said, "and often the best my father could send me was fat side meat, navy beans, and cornmeal."[37]

A common hardship for women on a plains homestead was loneliness. "I tell you girls you may think you are lonely sometimes," a young Oklahoma Territory homestead girl wrote, "but if you want to know how you feel when you are lonesome, you must move away from your friends to a new country and be by yourself nearly all day. It seems to me sometimes as if there is no one in the whole world that cares anything for me and I just can't stand it any longer." That was what Kate's two years' residency were like. Patience was never her virtue, but at nineteen, waiting was agony for her. "I felt the creative years of my life slipping away," she said. "In the blossom and bloom of life—forced into idleness."[38]

Once she was away from the homestead, she was proud of her accomplishment and boasted about it. It gave her credibility among the other settlers in the territory. She could not resist exaggerating the experience, saying she had been a little girl of only twelve living alone in the woods, in a "shanty." Actually, the house had eight-foot ceilings, and although it was small, it was built so solidly, even to its plank floors, that the original structure was still a residence almost a hundred years later. Whatever the reality, to Kate it was a shanty in the wilds.[39]

In August 1895, Barnard won the title to his homestead free and clear. He installed tenants on the farm and brought Kate back to Oklahoma City. Kate, now twenty, was eager to go. Back in the city, Barnard advertised his services in the fields of law, loans, and real estate. He ran for elected office and served as Oklahoma County surveyor from 1898 to 1902, but his career never succeeded as he hoped. In 1904, at age sixty-three, he ran for police judge in Oklahoma City, but was not elected. He was reappointed Oklahoma County surveyor for a few months in 1906. By then, both his health and his career were in decline, just as Kate's life was beginning to soar. She was always saddened by the opposing trajectories of their lives, and she tried to help him even as her ambition pulled her on her own course.[40]

With the homestead ordeal happily behind her, she was ready to start her adult life. The life she wanted was an extraordinary choice for a woman of the time. Almost all young women on the plains in the 1800s married, but Kate was not like most young women. She made a decision while still young never to marry. Her sentiments were well known, and she avoided anything resembling flirtation or courtship. "She wouldn't have anything to do with the boys," recalled a girlhood acquaintance. In contemporary sensibilities, people would leap to the conclusion that Kate was homosexual, but there is no indication that she ever fostered intimate feelings for another woman. Her work became so engrossing, she had little social life and few friends of either sex. She preferred the association of professional colleagues. Perhaps the Shields family was one reason she did not want to become a wife and mother. Kate had seen what farm life on a desolate land had cost her mother and her grandmother—drudgery, premature aging, and early death. A few women of her time might have worked at jobs before they married, and wealthy married women might have done volunteer work for clubs or churches, but traditionally, almost all women married, and after marriage they did not work for wages outside the home.[41]

This decision not to marry marked Kate as an oddity all of her life. Some puzzled or gossiped about her unmarried status. A few suggested that her appearance, her tiny size, and her aggressive manner were the reasons she remained single. She was about five feet tall, never weighed more than a hundred pounds, and wore a size three dress. Almost everyone who met her commented on her high energy and intense focus. Most people found her petite size and dynamic personality a delightful combination, but not everyone agreed. "She is very small and not very attractive," said one man who knew her. Some were put off by her forceful personality and outspoken manner. Even an admiring friend described her as "an ardent woman who spoke with much command of herself."[42]

She considered herself so "small and plain," she rarely agreed to be photographed. "I am a crank on the subject," she said. The few existing photographs show a serious, unsmiling young woman with pretty features, big, expressive eyes, a broad mouth, and dark, strong brows. "Her eyes were a deep beautiful blue," Angie Debo said, "so deep they often looked black in photographs." Kate wore her thick black hair in a soft chignon—sometimes tied with a bow—at the nape of her neck. In photographs she is strikingly lovely, almost the image of a demure coquette, but Kate was neither demure nor coquettish. She was not being coy when she said, "I am a very plain little woman and not attractive in any way. I have none of the usual weapons that some women use to an advantage." That was the image she had of herself. She did like fashionable clothes and big hats in the style of the time. "She never wore tailored clothes," said Mabel Bassett, a colleague. "Hers were always fussy and feminine." This suggests a poor country girl overdressing to go to town. Later in her career Kate dressed more simply, but whatever the style, she was notoriously untidy, with strands of hair flying out of the pins and combs of her heavy chignon. "I saw her well-groomed only once," Bassett said, "when she spoke at a territorial teachers' meeting." Kate looked like what she was—a young woman in a hurry. As her fortunes improved, she bought velvet dresses from her favorite dressmaker in Oklahoma City, black satin shoes from Denver, and accessories in Baltimore. She kept a list of dressmakers and shops in Philadelphia (street suits) and New York (lace dresses and English twills) and French

Bernard. Kate

Kate usually dressed plainly in dark colors, but she liked fashionable clothes and big hats. Early in her career, they were feminine and fussy. Photograph courtesy Oklahoma Historical Society.

milliners in Denver and Boston, but those indulgences were years away, and even then she still threw them on hastily, without much attention.[43]

More likely, Kate never married because she chose to devote herself wholly to a professional career. Angie Debo modeled her life in many ways on Kate's lifestyle and said if she had divided her energies between wife/mother and work, both efforts would have been diminished, so she elected to be single. Kate never said anything as introspective, only that she wanted an occupation. She had few choices, primarily the Church or the schoolroom. She was intrigued by the nuns, so distinctive in the territories, and she identified with their lives of self-sacrificing work for others. Kate's compassion was one of her most distinctive features. It burned like a flame, Debo remembered. Still, there is no record that Kate ever expressed interest in becoming a nun. She was too independent. The vow of obedience would have been a challenge for her.

So she decided to become a schoolteacher, a lofty profession in the territories, where schools were few and education was a precious thing. She spent her time on the homestead preparing to take the teacher certification test, studying with books she already had and under the direction of her father. In 1894, when she was nineteen, Kate left the homestead long enough to take the teaching examination. Not only did she pass, she earned a second-level certificate. Many teachers worked with only a third-level certificate. With her teaching credentials in hand, she began searching for a position. She wrote to schools, she corresponded with teachers' associations, she pressed her father to ask if anyone knew of a school that needed a teacher, all without luck.

The Panic of 1893 began a seven-year national economic depression and what Kate called "universal poverty." Oklahoma Territory suffered additionally from droughts, crop failure, and high unemployment. This grim economic climate was a bleak time for an aspiring teacher like Kate. Bad luck and misfortune seemed to afflict both Barnards.[44]

CHAPTER TWO

The Searching Years

TEACHERS WERE IDOLS in territorial communities. "They walked in grandeur among us," said Angie Debo, a territorial student herself. As a teacher, Kate would join other professionals—ministers, merchants, and lawyers—who were shaping the developing land. If only she could find a school job.[1]

After almost a year's search, another anguished year of seeing her dreams put on hold, she got a job in a one-room rural school in 1896, much humbler than the schools she had known in Kirwin or Oklahoma City. The school's term was six months, and her salary was $25 a month, respectable pay in those lean times when the average daily wage for a railroad engineer was $3.34, and a farm laborer during harvest earned $1.20 a day. She boarded with a family nearby, walked to school early to build a fire for heat, stayed late to sweep the floors, and taught all grades. Her daily attire was a long full skirt, high-button shoes, and a black apron to protect her clothing from the chalk dust and coal stains. At last, she was beginning the life she wanted.[2]

Her second year as a teacher, Kate got a better school with an eight-month term and a higher salary. After a third year, she quit teaching in the spring of 1898. Years later, she opened her address to a county teachers' association with the wry remark "Once, I had the misfortune to be a school teacher." Kate's personality was not suited to teaching. She lacked the patience the job required; she disliked living in small, rural communities; and most of all, her ambition suffocated in a one-room school. Her dreams overflowed the little *McGuffey's Primer*. "She was driven by an urgent need to find an outlet for her unusual talents and energies," researcher Edith Copeland said astutely.[3]

Back in Oklahoma City and living with her father, she enrolled in business school to study typing and shorthand, skills of speed that suited her. To the end of her life, she typed her private letters, and her personal papers included notes in precise Gregg shorthand characters. Barnard expected his daughter to be their housekeeper, and she did prepare some of their meals, but cleaning ladies did most of the housework. Wherever she lived, Kate's rooms were as untidy as her dress. Her rooms were strewn with clothes; belongings were piled on furniture and under the bed; books and papers were stacked everywhere.[4]

Barnard's selection of an Oklahoma City home was an odd choice for a man who prided himself on his real estate expertise. He bought a yellow five-room house on Reno Street, a district on its way to a lurid reputation for saloons and gambling dens. Not far from the Barnard home were the city's most prosperous brothels. Kate passed saloons on her way to and from her business school classes. Reno Street became so notorious, it was featured in a book about Oklahoma City titled *And Satan Came Also*. It had been a working-class area, but the neighborhood deteriorated out from under them, Kate said. If so, it was yet another bit of bad luck for her father, and he had plenty of it. The Schlitz Saloon and Beer Garden was just across the alley from the Barnard house, and Kate developed a special hatred for the place. It rent the night with raucous noise and split the early morning with gunshots and shrieks. "No one can sleep in this block," she complained.[5]

Stenographers were in high demand, so once she completed her classes, Kate had no trouble finding secretarial work, but she had considerable difficulty keeping the jobs. She was easily bored with routine clerical work and quick to suggest changes in procedure, speaking in a tone that was abrupt, even curt. She liked to do things her way. A friend was diplomatic when he said she "displayed executive propensities." An employer was blunter: "She wanted to run the whole show." Kate changed jobs frequently in the next few years. She worked for a law firm and for a land company, valuable experiences for her political education because in both offices she saw hand-rubbing lust for the millions of acres owned by Indians. Native minors owned fifteen million acres in Indian Territory, three-fourths of all Indian lands, but they were restricted by law from selling it, and leases had to be signed by their legally approved guardians. A constant topic of discussion was how whites could remove the federal restrictions and gain control of the profitable Indian properties. "They were vitally interested in Indian-owned land," researcher Copeland said.[6]

Both Kate and her father were devout members of the Democratic Party. Barnard's campaign slogan when he ran for county surveyor was "The Laboring Man's Friend." His elected post was not a high-ranking position, but it gave him entree into the party. The Barnards were among the political underdogs in the Republican-dominated territory. Political patronage began with the president of the United States, who appointed the territorial governor, and trickled through hundreds of appointed offices down to notary publics. For Democrats squirming under the Republican yoke, the Territorial Legislature, elected by the people, was an oasis of democracy. The legislature employed a handful of clerks for stenographic work, and Kate was determined to be one of them for the 1902 legislative session. She had worked for a lawyer named Mont Highley, and she went to him for advice.

"I told her the way to get the job would be to write a little note with her qualifications and to say she wanted a job with the Legislature and to put a copy of this note on the desk of every senator," Highley said. Kate followed his instructions, got the job, and moved thirty miles away to Guthrie, a Victorian city on the prairie and the territorial capital. She lived in a boardinghouse and was one of five clerks for the Seventh Territorial Legislature's three-month session, January through March 1902. She volunteered for extra work, typing committee reports or taking minutes, and gained a reputation as an eager, hard worker. She did not socialize, partly because she worked compulsively and partly because she was socially insecure. She thought the other stenographers considered her "old fashioned."[7]

Like her father, she was not interested in the art of small talk. Politics is what interested Kate. In Guthrie she studied the legislators, watching how alliances were formed and lobbying was conducted. She paid particular attention to Henry Asp, a Republican and a powerful railroad attorney for the Atchison, Topeka and Santa Fe Railway, "the lifeline of Oklahoma's commerce." She noted that he had a "pocket full of railroad passes, smiles for the women, caresses for the children, and a long arm controlling jobs from Oklahoma to Washington." Railroad interests and the federal administration dominated the lives of people in many ways: railroad fares and freight rates, tax assessments, inspections, available jobs, Indian land openings, and mineral and timber rights. Just too damn much power, folks said. Not to mention heartless. The railroad industry was one of the most dangerous in the nation, but it had no comprehensive workers' compensation laws. In the 1890s, a quarter of a million railroad workers were injured on the job, and more than twenty-five thousand were killed. Kate saw Asp as a smooth politician and everything the Democrats disdained.[8]

The legislators' major interest was achieving statehood, and an opportune event seemed to be the upcoming World's Fair, officially named the Louisiana Purchase Exposition, to be held in St. Louis, Missouri, in 1904. They voted appropriations totaling $61,000, an astronomical sum at the time, to create an exhibit at the World's Fair to show the world the progress and possibilities in Oklahoma Territory. The exhibit would need someone to staff it, a secretary/publicist in today's definition, and almost five hundred applications poured in for this glamorous job. Kate was determined to be the one chosen; in fact, she applied for the job a year before it even existed. She thought the key to the appointment would be Fred Wenner, the territorial governor's private secretary. She hounded him so relentlessly that he called her a pest, but Kate ignored his disapproval. "I finally promised her the job just to get rid of her," Wenner said.[9]

In 1904, at age twenty-nine, Kate stepped off the train in St. Louis into the fairytale spectacle of the World's Fair, which would be her home for the next eight months. Expositions of the nineteenth and twentieth centuries were a combination amusement park, museum, and education symposium. Compared to the Paris Exhibition of 1889 and the Chicago Exposition of 1893, the St. Louis World's Fair was acclaimed at the time and for decades afterward as "the greatest exposition in history." Straight from the Oklahoma prairies, Kate must have gasped at the magnitude, ten acres of remarkable beauty and carnival atmosphere. The exposition's "radiant glory" was its magnificent illumination by electrical light. Back home, Kate lived with light from kerosene lanterns, open fireplaces, and gas. Electrical lighting was a rarity in the territories, and here it surrounded her. At night, with thousands of electric lights, the entire exposition twinkled and glowed liked a magical kingdom.[10]

Kate dived into her work with an abundance of confidence, mailing promotional materials and maps, reporting names of Oklahoma Territory visitors to the St. Louis press, and answering letters of inquiry about travel and accommodations. She even listed her St. Louis home address (912 North Garrison Ave.) and phone number (Kinlock 538-A), inviting people from home to "look me up when you are in St. Louis." One of her responsibilities was writing dispatches from the fair for an Oklahoma City newspaper. "You will learn more here in two weeks than in two years at school, or in a trip around the world," she wrote in her first article, signing it "Catherine Barnard," befitting the solemnity of her responsibility. It was the only time in her public career that she used her formal name.[11]

Indian Territory had an exhibit, too, unpretentious and severely plain, with displays of Native American basketry and the trunk of an old Seminole execution tree pocked with bullet holes. It was the Oklahoma Territory Pavilion that captured fairgoers' attention. The two-story Spanish building was pretty, but what excited interest was the territory itself, with its phenomenal growth. From 1890 to 1900, Oklahoma Territory's population had mushroomed by 543 percent, a boom comparable only to a gold rush. The West was clearly the future of America, and "the most interesting part of the wonderful new West is represented by the pleasing Oklahoma building," the fair's guidebook said. This admiration was just what the territorial legislators had hoped for. Kate understood the Oklahoma exhibit's intangible appeal and explained it in her newspaper articles. "We exhibit our push, pluck, intelligence, and energy. We make a specialty of something called Western hospitality." Fairgoers called the Oklahoma exhibit "the Exposition baby," she wrote the folks back home. They consider it "the most prodigious infant the world has ever seen."[12]

The exhibit's success fueled Kate's ambition. She hounded the fair's administrators for more responsibility, driving them to exasperation as they advanced her from one office to another. The end of the line was Charles M. Reeves, secretary to the president of the fair. Kate wore his patience paper thin. "They passed her off on me," he grumbled, "and I'm about to move out of town." Fred Wenner, who had secured the job for Kate, said, "She wanted to be head of everything and couldn't get along with anyone."[13]

At first, Kate was as awestruck as the rest of the sightseers joining what she called "the giddy throng" that rushed from one exhibit to another. She confessed that she stole "a big chunk of wood" from President Roosevelt's log cabin in the North Dakota exhibit. She saw interesting new foods, including a hot dog and an ice cream cone; the world's largest Ferris wheel, which carried two thousand people at a time to a height of 250 feet; wireless telegraphy; and a "mysterious substance" called radium with exhibitions of the "medical miracle" named X-ray. One of the fair's celebrities on the Pike, the mile-long strip of entertainment, was Oklahoma roper Will Rogers. She met John Oskison, who was visiting the fair with his friend Rogers; both had grown up near Claremore in Indian Territory. Her path would cross Oskison's again several years later at significant points in her career. Geronimo was there from Oklahoma, too, signing autographs in the Apache Village and selling souvenirs he had made himself. Kate was never particularly interested in the arts, but here she attended musical concerts and even took guitar lessons.[14]

Her serious nature prevailed, though, and she assured the newspaper readers back home that she was "making good use of my opportunity to broaden my intellect and become a more useful worker for the world." Life is not a playground, she wrote solemnly, and that is why she was drawn to the educational aspects of the fair, with its exhibits of modernity. Social reform was in the air in America of 1904. The dream of rural homesteads turned out not to be the utopia it was imagined to be. The industrial revolution had promised a better life, but what it brought was rampant urban growth with social problems of massive proportions; intolerable working conditions in mills, mines, sweatshops, packinghouses, and railroad yards; and almost inhuman living conditions in city tenements, where disease, namely tuberculosis, was epidemic. In industries, factories, and mines, the average work week was fifty-nine hours, but eighty-four-hour weeks were not unusual in some industries, such as steel. The average rate of pay was less than ten dollars a week. Sixty percent of the adult male working population did not earn enough to support their families, so they put their children to work. Child labor meant that children by the thousands were employed ten or twelve hours a day, and their jobs were among the most dangerous and lowest paid in the nation.[15]

A handful of mighty industries emerged from the 1800s—Standard Oil, the Great Northern and Union Pacific railroads, United States Steel, the Armour meat company—and they produced magnates of wealth and power. In sharp contrast, by the early 1900s, fifty million Americans were living at or below the poverty level, without adequate food, shelter, or clothing. This prompted a spontaneous sense of justice for the lower class and for workers. A spirit of reform called the Progressive Era, roughly from 1902 to 1917, involved socially conscious reformers and progressive politicians. The new president, Theodore Roosevelt, was among them. Kate was at the right place at the right time to be part of this revolution. She embraced it with both arms and her whole heart.[16]

Reform was in the air in Oklahoma Territory, too. William Allen White, the influential newspaper editor from Emporia, Kansas, joked about it when he spoke at a meeting of newspaper editors in Guthrie: "Everybody is engaged in reforming someone else. The preachers are reforming the newspapers, the newspapers are reforming the politicians, the politicians are reforming the railroads . . . [a] bulldog of reform" chasing its tail. Despite his witty cynicism, White himself was a convert to progressivism. At age twenty-eight he met Roosevelt and heard in his own heart "the first trumpet call of the new time that was to be." Kate and White were close in age, kindred spirits, and from neighboring states, so their lives were destined to cross.[17]

At the World's Fair, Kate saw social reform exhibits from New York, Boston, Minneapolis, and elsewhere, blue-ribbon work displayed in a space the size of four city blocks. Some three hundred educational conferences attracted national experts. The most acclaimed gathering was the week-long International Congress of Arts and Science. Kate persuaded Oklahoma's territorial governor to appoint her as a delegate so she could attend. Hundreds of social science authorities addressed the congress, but only four of them were women. One of those was Jane Addams, the legendary social worker and founder of Chicago's Hull House. Begun only five years earlier, Hull House was the headwaters of social reform issues such as juvenile courts, immigrant issues, women's rights, public health and safety, and child labor reform. Kate was in the audience to hear Addams deliver the prestigious closing address.[18]

Addams praised the government's efforts to care for the criminal, the poor, the defective, and the child, especially through the new juvenile court system, but the machinery of the cities had broken down, she said, "groaning under the pressure" of industrialism and "multitudes of immigrants." The nation saw the problems but was motionless with timidity. Recent Chicago stockyard strikes had proved that the unions, not the government, were concerned with the people's need for shelter, employment, and bread for their children. Addams quoted Browning and Aristotle, referred to Mary Wollstonecraft Shelley's *Frankenstein* (likening the monster to "hideous politicians"), and cited contemporary professors, economists, and "criminals whom I knew." She finished her speech to thunderous applause.[19]

Kate was mesmerized. She was seeing a plain, matronly woman hold an audience spellbound by championing the common man, then bring that audience to a tremendous ovation. Kate so believed in destiny that the word became a regular part of her vocabulary. She said she would write her autobiography one day with the title *A Woman of Destiny*. On that bright Saturday afternoon at the World's Fair in St. Louis, Kate, not quite thirty years old, found her destiny, and it was social reform.[20]

Kate had a powerful urge to help people, especially children in want and families in poverty. Analysts might say she was an orphan trying to rescue herself. Social reform answered this need on a large scale because the goal of social reform was to rescue the entire nation. Additionally, social reform solutions were described as scientific, a word that appealed to her, and a word that to her was the opposite of the term "old-fashioned."

Kate did not fit the mold of a social reformer. She was not born to a prosperous family like Jane Addams. Her interests were not quite the same as those of prominent women reformers like Lillian Wald, Florence Kelly, or Julia Lathrop. Neither was she an advocate of women's suffrage. Most of the notable reformers Kate would meet would be eastern, Protestant, and well-educated men with professional and financial stature. Kate was the opposite: Catholic, female, western, skimpily educated, and without financial or social attributes. How did she presume to make a career in social reform? Because she wanted it and she was determined to do it.

Kate began an immediate self-education in social reform using the city of St. Louis as a living laboratory. Ultimately, she would read extensively in the field of reform and collect a sizable library on the subject, but she always preferred firsthand research: "No man can deal intelligently with life until he first understands how all classes of men live and under what conditions they make their daily bread." Kate had never seen a city even a fraction of the size of St. Louis, the nation's fourth-largest city with a population of almost six hundred thousand. The city was a leader in quality of life for the industrial working class, and economists called the streets of South St. Louis "one of the unsung wonders of the world." Charities flourished there. One of the best was the St. Louis Provident Association, which had begun by providing care for orphans after the Civil War and for the needy from the Panic of 1873. Social workers came from across the nation to study the revolutionary methods of director W. H. McClain. The St. Louis Provident Association became Kate's model for her own charity work in Oklahoma Territory, and McClain became her mentor. Their admiration was mutual. "I am proud of the little girl I started in the work," he wrote to her. The pupil had far exceeded the teacher, he told her. When McClain died a few years later at age fifty-nine, his obituary in the *St. Louis Globe-Democrat* described him as "one of the most widely known philanthropic workers in America," noting further: "It is believed his death was hastened by overwork." Seven months earlier the newspaper had urged this city hero to retire or take a prolonged vacation lest he become a victim of extreme overwork, strain, and sympathy. That could have been a forewarning to Kate.[21]

One research adventure in St. Louis became a Kate Barnard legend, and she told the story herself many times. It illustrates her fearless, straightforward style. She walked into a St. Louis newspaper editor's office and said, "I am Kate Barnard of Oklahoma, and I expect to make a career. I am interested in poverty and crime. I want to cure them. Please send me to the slums in St. Louis to look into the matter." The editor was surprised by the serious woman who stood before him, so small and youthful. At first glance, people guessed her to be about sixteen years old. He assigned a reporter to show her through the city's poorest districts, where she was shocked to see widespread hunger, poverty, unemployment, and squalor.

She urged the reporter to spare no details in the story he would write describing the city's poor. Muckraking journalism, the forerunner of investigative reporting, was the journalistic arm of the Progressive Era and just blossoming into vogue. That St. Louis newspaper story enraged local politicians and the citizenry. This was hardly the image they wanted to present to the tourists of the world. The reporter was fired, but a new reform movement was begun in the St. Louis slums.[22]

Delighted with the stir she had caused, Kate went back to the editor and asked to see more. "Why don't you clean up Oklahoma?" he asked. She was shocked and said she had not seen pauperism there. "He said, 'Miss Barnard, you live on Reno Street which is one of the streets near the slum district of Oklahoma City. If you will sit at your parlor window any afternoon, you will see a procession of barefooted children, slatternly women and shamblin' men pass in a constant procession.' I went home and sure enough I saw what he said was true."[23]

The idea of applying social reform to Oklahoma Territory had not occurred to Kate. "I thought I had to leave home and go to large cities to work." Like a penny clicking into a slot, she realized that a new state would need enlightened social workers as much as businessmen, farmers, and teachers. Sometimes the right person looms up on the horizon, she later told an aspiring social worker. "Map out a plan that will fit local conditions and then go to work." Kate assumed she was the right person, and she began mapping out a plan for her role in creating the new state of Oklahoma.[24]

<hr />

When the World's Fair closed in December 1904, Kate returned to Oklahoma having made two discoveries that would change her life. One was her devotion to social reform, and the second was the acquaintance of Hobart Huson, an itinerant journalist who taught her the power of the press. In a couple of years, he would become the most important person in her life. "His advice proved to be the keystone of my career," she said.[25]

The Oklahoma exhibit at the World's Fair was not alone in touting the possibilities of the Southwest lands for development and immigration. Railroads, with hefty profits to realize, were full-throated boosters, and none was more enthusiastic than the St. Louis–San Francisco (Frisco) Railway. The Frisco System Land and Immigration Association sponsored free railroad excursions through Kansas, Missouri, Oklahoma, and Texas for hundreds of agents and newspaper writers. Its *Frisco System Magazine* was filled with head-swimming descriptions of the luxuriant landscape, bountiful harvests, lush orchards, and pleasant weather with cool breezes in Oklahoma Territory, where "crop failures are unknown." The publication described a bucolic country that no Oklahoma resident would recognize; it was certainly not the homestead of Kate's experience. According to the railroad magazine, besides the fields of corn, wheat, oats, and alfalfa—all flourishing with "plenty of rain"—there were rich oil and gas fields, asphalt, and timber. Land was cheap and prosperity was guaranteed in this "wonderland for every class of people." This meant white people. Indians, if they were mentioned at all in the publication, were referred to as "squaws" or "redskins," who sometimes were industrious and peaceful, but often were lazy and broke. New areas for settlement were opening in Oklahoma Territory. Even in Indian Territory, which was restricted to Native Americans, land could be purchased and leases obtained, sometimes from dead Indians. The mighty oil fields of the Creek and Osage nations, "of such inestimable commercial value," were dangled like gumdrops before readers. Even if Kate had read the magazine's description of oil land and Indians, she would have given it little heed. She lived in Oklahoma Territory and had little interaction with Native Americans.[26]

Hobart Huson would have read them, though, because he was the magazine's circulation editor when he and Kate met in St. Louis. Kate was a young woman afire with energy and potential; Huson was older and looking for a new start. He was learned, erudite, and charming; Kate was hungry for opportunity. She was from the golden land of Oklahoma Territory; Huson had seen something of the world and bore the scars of it. They came together in a fusion of ambition and hope.

From January to March 1905, Kate was again in Guthrie, one of six clerks working for the Eighth Territorial Legislature, but with newfound confidence. After the legislative session, she moved back to Oklahoma City, where she hit town fired with reform zeal. She got a stenographic job in the office of City Attorney Gus Paul, but her tenure there was short and stormy. Paul hired what he considered "a modest little black-haired woman." At first, Kate worked "diligently and enthusiastically" and inspired her boss as an "extravagantly busy little woman." Then she began to expound on her theories of reform in general, and for Reno Street in particular. Reno Street was a crime district that corrupted the city's youth, she said, and tempted the poor to squander their earnings. The brothels should be closed, and the saloons should be made to obey the law. The worst offender of all, she said, was the infamous Schlitz Saloon and Beer Garden.[27]

The city attorney was dumbfounded. The meek little woman had suddenly become "sagely self-assertive." Her timidity had disappeared, and in its place was "clerical independence theretofore unwitnessed." At first he ignored her, but Kate expounded about Reno Street and the Schlitz Saloon until he fired her, officially citing her refusal to work overtime and on Sundays. She appealed her case to the city council—appealed it "exhaustively," official minutes reflect—taking the opportunity to tell the council about city government's responsibility to the poor, about Reno Street, and about the Schlitz Saloon and Beer Garden. When she finished, the council upheld the city attorney's decision. Kate's dismissal stood. A colleague consoled her: "They thought they had you beaten, but they only inspired you to work harder." Kate would have said they ignited her fighting Irish nature.[28]

Whether it was coincidental or deliberate, her stand for stricter laws for gambling houses and saloons was politically well timed. That July, Oklahoma City hosted a large convention on the absorbing subject of statehood, which was close to becoming a reality. Oklahoma Territory was eager for issues that would showcase it as a place with a modern populace worthy of statehood. Social reform was just such a unifying subject. Kate stepped forward as a knowledgeable advocate of reform.

In its mere sixteen years of existence, Oklahoma City had developed severe problems of poverty and unemployment. Even worse, there was no effective system for relief. Churches, women's clubs, and the Salvation Army tried to help the aged, the ill, the unemployed, and dependent women and children, but the need was growing faster than the aid. A Methodist minister suggested that a single efficient charitable organization would be more effective than scattered efforts, and the best choice was the United Provident Association, a ministerial alliance that was in need of reorganization. The Retail Merchants' Association, weary of funding various charitable efforts, agreed. Kate touted her knowledge of the St. Louis Provident Association and became the new matron, or director, of the United Provident Association of Oklahoma City (which she and others always shortened to Provident Association), at an initial salary of $25 a month.

She went into action immediately, even before her job was official, by hiring a horse and livery to tour Oklahoma City's rag towns. She inspected shacks and tents and found them populated with "a small army of shivering" and famished people. She saw ill, half-naked babies crawling on dirt floors, and children unable to attend school because they had no shoes or warm clothes. November was already cold, but Kate knew that these people would suffer even more when winter really settled in. "I thought of my own mother in a cold grave and thanked Heaven for her better lot."[29]

Print was the sole news medium of the era, and local newspapers wielded an almost unimaginable influence, especially in the territories. Kate used what she had learned in St. Louis about the influence of the press and wrote an article for an Oklahoma City newspaper describing what she saw: "Mrs. Johnson and ten children in an old tent needing clothes; Grandma Brown ('colored') in an old shack, daughter insane, little granddaughter with no clothes for school; Mrs. McKee, destitute, down by the dump pile, husband sick four months, two children ages three and four." She appealed to the public for help. In her naiveté, Kate asked readers to deliver contributions directly to the poor, or, if they preferred, to leave them with her. Not surprisingly, most chose the latter option.[30]

It was cold and rainy the day after her newspaper article appeared, but the weather did not dampen the public response. "I was perfectly overwhelmed by the results," Kate said, probably exaggerating when she stated that "almost 100 people came in wagons, buggies, and on foot with contributions. Ten thousand cast-off garments were dumped in my little five-room house." A woman delivering a basket of groceries to the Barnard home found her on the phone calling everybody listed in the city phone directory, asking for still more help. She wrote another newspaper article documenting the success of her appeal. She thanked "the women's clubs, society ladies, the business men, the photographer," the livery barn, and others. The response had proven, she wrote, "what anyone can accomplish by hard work, courage, determination, and the cooperation of the press and the public." This would be Kate's formula for success throughout her career.[31]

While the United Provident Association board was still talking about reorganization, its new matron had single-handedly launched a successful program and publicized it. One reason she succeeded, Kate often said, was that she went right to work. That was the advice she gave people wanting to start a charity organization: "Don't wait. Go right in."[32]

Kate's father was not as happy with her success. He came home from work to find that his house had been turned into a charitable society, filled with old clothes, baskets of food, sacks of flour and sugar, loaves of bread, and boxes of coal and firewood. Kate described his reaction succinctly: "He stormed." Barnard insisted that everything be moved out of the house immediately. He would not have the poor knocking on his door day and night. Kate stood her ground and told him the donations were staying, even if it meant she would have to build an office in the back yard to hold them—and she then set to work to do just that. She solicited donations of building materials, monetary contributions, and volunteer labor to construct a two-room office behind her home and pushed the men to work at night by lantern light to finish the job quickly.[33]

A month after Kate had taken charge, the United Provident Association was operating on a larger scale than any charitable organization in the city's history. It was clothing and feeding the poor, and it had money in the bank. Kate transformed the organization completely, and it would live on long after she was gone. Poor children were her first concern. She wanted to give them more than used clothing—"Rags ruin self-respect," she said— and she wanted to teach them social responsibility. At Christmas she had a party in her back yard for 150 poor children. She persuaded businessmen and society women to collect toys and to fill baskets with oranges, apples, nuts, and popcorn. She made a little speech: "When you are grown up and have lots of money and are rich like the people who sent these presents to you, how many of you are going to make a Christmas for all the little boys and girls in your town?" The children cheered their answer.[34]

Despite her success, Kate had bigger ideas for the charity, and she did not wait for approval. One day she visited the poorhouse, a shocking thing for anybody to do, much less a respectable woman. She described her visit in another newspaper report. The poor, she wrote, arrived "covered with filth and vermin and so infected with loathsome diseases, they are scrubbed in hot water and disinfectant and their bedding burned." The popular view was that poorhouse residents, like prisoners, deserved their fate. Kate had modern ideas: "The fault lies with all of us." Next, she went to the police court, a filthy basement full of loud, drunken prisoners. She was on a mission to rescue wayward slum children confined there with adults. She paid the youths' fines or bail, took them to her home to be fed and clothed, then found them housing and jobs. She reported this in the newspaper, too. Her visits to the poorhouse and the police court were inspired by stories in a St. Louis newspaper about investigations and a new theory of reform replacing punishment.[35]

Kate's bold actions disturbed the women she called "society ladies," and they censured her, questioning whether these children were worthy of her help. "Are they worthy?" was Kate's incensed retort. "A child's destiny is the world's destiny. All the world suffers when a little child suffers." The simmering differences between Kate and the club ladies erupted publicly when she tried to block the renewal of the liquor license of her nemesis the Schlitz Beer Garden. She said the saloonkeeper was a "monster who prostituted his genius to a wicked cause." The ladies gasped at her use of the word "prostituted," and the incident flamed into a minor scandal, with newspaper stories and letters to the editor. Her friends and her board rallied to her defense. "She does not even use slang," they insisted. Kate explained it away to a colleague: "You know how impulsive I am." Unfiltered might be a more accurate description.[36]

She nurtured the support of the Woman's Christian Temperance Union, the Anti-Saloon League, the Suffrage Club, and newspaper society columnists such as the *Daily Oklahoman*'s Edith Johnson. These were women who could support her work—but from that time on, Kate never completely trusted club ladies of society, and she never forgot the sting of their disapproval. When she was asked how to organize a charity, her advice was, "Get as few women in your organization as possible. Interest the men. They are the ones who have the money."[37]

The United Provident Association board and the local press praised her, saying she had accomplished more than a dozen ordinary persons could have in such a short time. During the day, she collected, sorted, and distributed materials to the needy. At night, she kept records of her work and wrote articles for the newspaper. She wrote about a little boy, the sole support of his mother and young siblings, who had been killed by an automobile. All Kate could do was help with his funeral and provide used clothes for the family. She wrote about a sick man living in a river-bank dugout, and about a destitute old man trying to walk fifty miles to the county poorhouse.[38]

Kate thrived on her accomplishments and drove herself to do more, routinely working fourteen hours a day. She saw such monumental need among the people, the emotional strain on her was as draining as the physical work, and in 1906, after several months of this schedule, she collapsed. Her doctors diagnosed her illness as pneumonia, or maybe a bad case of hay fever, and insisted on complete bed rest. Kate called it complete nervous exhaustion. This became a pattern throughout her working life: she drove herself with unbridled energy and emotion until she became physically ill and was confined to her bed for days, and later for weeks. Eventually, recovery would take months.[39]

Even on bedrest, she continued to work, but she began thinking beyond hands-on charity, looking instead for permanent solutions. She decided the best way to eliminate poverty and its resulting lines of cold, hungry children at her door was to address issues of education, labor, and wages. "In my effort to do something for humanity, I was drawn into politics." She began by becoming involved with organized labor to raise wages, which she saw as the best way to help the working man and his family. Her father, who had campaigned for office as labor's friend, was a strong influence.[40]

Kate was not only involved with labor, but with her customary all-or-nothing enthusiasm, she became extremely involved and joined everything at once. In 1905 she helped found an Oklahoma City chapter of the Women's International Union Label League, urging women to buy only union-made products, and became its recording secretary. She was the only unmarried officer, the *Daily Oklahoman* noted. In 1906 she formed the Oklahoma City Child Labor League, which became affiliated with the National Child Labor Committee. It was the first such group in the territories. She and the league's president, Mrs. D. M. Thorpe, then organized women to form leagues in other towns, and those groups joined forces with the Federation of Labor in campaigning for like interests.

In 1907 she founded Federal Union No. 12374 for unskilled laborers in the slums, and thus became active within the Oklahoma City Trades and Labor Assembly. Under her leadership, the union become influential in city politics, especially the mayoral election that year. She expanded her involvement beyond the city to the bigger Oklahoma Territorial Federation of Labor. As a member of the American Federation of Labor, she persuaded 158 unskilled laborers to join, and found them employment building city streets and digging sewers. Then she campaigned to raise the wages of Oklahoma City street workers from $1.25 to $2.25 a day. When the carpenters were on strike and union financial aid was insufficient, Kate asked permission to speak at a union meeting. "Men, I know that you and your families are suffering," she said. "If you will come to me yourselves—don't send your wives or children—and bring me your union card, I will help you." She offered them loans based on their union cards. All but one man repaid her.[41]

To widen her influence even further in that predominantly rural territory, she joined the Farmers' Union, too. In only two years, she became influential in organized labor, won the loyalty of working men and their families, and was positioned to rally large delegations from the Child Labor Leagues, the Union Label Leagues, and the Territorial Federation of Women's Clubs to support her social justice causes. She had accomplished far more than the expectations of a local social worker and demonstrated her skill in recruiting, influencing, and organizing large groups of people. She had developed political muscle, and she was ready to use it.

In St. Louis she had learned what cities were doing in regard to public health and sanitation, so she supported those interests in the territory. She worked in the clinic founded by the new Epworth University, which became Oklahoma City University, and she was secretary of the first state board of the American Red Cross formed in Oklahoma. Her later inspections of state institutions would always include reports on sanitation facilities, medical care, and food for the patients.[42]

Kate's burst of benevolent work was successful but ultimately disappointing to her. Charity, she decided, was "the weakest of weapons with which to combat the problems of poverty, crime or disease"; temporary relief for the poor was "like pouring water into a sieve." Even the unions could not be the solution. What was needed instead of bandages was prevention in the form of legislation—wise laws to prevent poverty, to protect the weaker, and to provide opportunity.[43]

The Oklahoma Enabling Act of June 1906 declared that Oklahoma Territory and Indian Territory would enter the union as one state, so statehood was in sight. That meant that a state constitution had been written and laws drafted. Here was an opportunity to prevent societal ills from taking root. Kate saw this as a once-in-a-lifetime chance to "shape the destiny of the new state." She longed to be involved, but at age thirty-one, she had collapsed in exhaustion and despair. In a flash of inspiration, she knew what she had to do. Following her own advice, she mapped out a plan, got out of bed, and put her plan into action.[44]

CHAPTER THREE

Fledgling Reformer

STATEHOOD SPELLED for me the one word—Responsibility." Kate was serious. She believed that reform laws were critical to prevent child labor and that she was key to implementing them.[1]

The burden was great because she also believed that everybody in the territories was "young and ignorant of statecraft," unprepared to write a constitution and state laws. She felt confident about her own credentials because as a charity worker she had done "social research for the cause of poverty," and as a member of the labor union she had come "face to face with certain ugly social facts." Still, she was overwhelmed by the enormity of the task ahead until she had a brainstorm: if the people and the legislators knew about sweatshops, factories, child labor, and tenements, they would see the need for social legislation. With public sentiment in place, Kate said, "the politicians always fall in line." She took her plan to Roy Stafford, editor and owner of the *Daily Oklahoman*, a newspaper that had printed her articles from the World's Fair and the Provident Association. Stafford was tall and thin, about her age, and equally ardent about the Democratic Party.[2]

Kate proposed that Stafford finance a trip for her to gather information about labor conditions, child labor in particular. Along the way, she would persuade leading social workers to write articles for his newspaper. He agreed at once because he believed that publicizing reform issues would help the Democrats create a progressive state constitution. Their disingenuous public explanation for the trip was that Kate would study philanthropy to improve the efficiency of the United Provident Association. Kate

secured letters of introduction from Republican territorial governor Frank
Frantz and from the mayor of Oklahoma City. When she arrived in St. Louis
in the summer of 1906, that city's mayor welcomed her and arranged visits
to bagging factories, cement mills, fertilizer companies, box factories, and
steelworks. It was a guided tour of human misery.[3]

Kate saw children as young as ten working twelve- and fourteen-hour
days in laundries, sorting coal in coal dust so black that they wore lamps
on their caps at noon, and in fertilizer and lye factories with acrid air that
burned her nose and throat. Tuberculosis was a primary medical concern
in the early 1900s, claiming the lives of 150,000 Americans every year. The
cause was not known, but after touring St. Louis factories, Kate was convinced that workplaces with unhealthy air were "homes for tuberculosis."
Inside cement factories, she saw enormous machinery so hot it glowed.
Thirty men had died from the heat in Missouri's cement factories before
the position of state factory inspector was created. Now, workers could go
outside every two hours to breathe fresh air and to lower their body temperature. This was considered a victory for labor.[4]

One sultry August day, she toured a shop that renovated feathers and
found young girls working in stifling heat and breathing air so "putrid
with decaying animal matter from the feather ends" that it gagged her.
"Yet all the windows must be closed lest a current of air smother the workers in heaps of feathery down." Children working in glass factories spit
blood from breathing glass dust. In a drug company, she asked the floor-
walker why he stared so intently into the faces of the girls working there.
"These girls are bottling arsenic," he said, and he was watching for early
signs of arsenic poisoning. "When their lips turn white, I take them out
for air." In a bagging factory where two hundred girls sewed burlap bags at
frenzied speed, Kate discovered that noise—the roaring sound of sewing
machines—was another wretchedness of factory work.[5]

The notorious child labor of the cotton mills touched Kate's heart
more than anything else. She saw "long rows of . . . thin-chested, stoop-
shouldered, . . . leadened-eyed" children with machinery pounding at an
ear-splitting level, the temperature sweltering with hot steam, and the air
dense with lint. She would re-create these cruel images of child labor
scenes so vividly that audiences of thousands were hushed and riveted to
her words, then ask rhetorically, What kind of nation are we that coins
wealth out of the life of its young?[6]

The notorious use of child labor in the cotton mills touched Kate's heart more than anything else. Photograph courtesy National Child Labor Committee Collection, Library of Congress, Prints and Photographs Division.

Kate gathered child labor statistics to report back home: "Two million children . . . are wage-slaves in our country. . . . Eighty-two thousand are breathing the lint of cotton mills. . . . Eight hundred and three are working with acids and breathing the fumes of the bleachery and dye-works. Five thousand three hundred and sixty-five are breathing pulverized glass. Eleven thousand four hundred and sixty-two are steeping their systems in the nicotine of tobacco factories, and forty-two thousand are breathing the dry dust of the coal-breakers." She said it was "inhuman" and "unchristian" that the government had no minimum wage and no maximum hours. Women were paid less than men, and children were paid as little as fourteen cents a day.[7]

Kate also sought out examples of St. Louis's charitable successes and what she called "scientific statecraft." One of her most important meetings was with Mary Perry, who introduced her to a new concept—the Missouri State Conference of Charities and Corrections, an organization for charity and reform workers to meet and discuss their work. It inspired Kate to expand her own citywide charity work to a state level. "Miss Perry gave me the idea of a State Charity Department," she said.[8]

From St. Louis, Kate traveled to Chicago, the capital of social reform, where she toured Jane Addams's famous Hull House and Judge Julian W. Mack's juvenile court, a new way of disciplining wayward youth. She met the staff of the National Conference of Charities and Correction. Her public relations instincts told her that its magazine, *Charities and the Commons*, later renamed the *Survey*, could be useful to her. She attended some sessions at Graham Taylor's School of Civics and Philanthropy, the first school to train social workers, and at the University of Chicago she heard lectures about public, municipal, state, and federal charities. She met Dr. Hastings H. Hart of the Illinois Children's Home and Aid Society.[9]

From Chicago she went to New York, where she was reacquainted with John Oskison from Indian Territory, now a respected writer for the *New York Evening Post*, and Roland B. Molineux, a noted penologist who had been convicted of murder, confined on death row, but subsequently pardoned, and who now wrote and lectured on prison reform. She called on the National Child Labor Committee headquarters and met Owen Lovejoy, Samuel McCune Lindsay, and A. J. McKelway. En route home, she stopped in Denver to meet Judge Ben B. Lindsey, who had written Colorado's juvenile court laws in 1899, and who would provide the model for Oklahoma's juvenile court system.[10]

Another young woman so new to social reform might have been hesitant about approaching such prominent figures, but Kate not only readily confessed her inexperience, she used it to her advantage. "She was captivating and convincing," said former University of Oklahoma professor Jerome Dowd, who came to know her well, and she impressed the reform leaders with her passion to help humanity. For Kate, this was not a sightseeing trip with social introductions. She conscripted the reformers into a national network of professional colleagues, and in some cases close friends. She asked a lot of them, and most responded generously.[11]

The trip fanned Kate's sense of mission to a "burning desire" to improve conditions for children, workers, and the poor. She returned home feeling that city charity work was limited and as stifling to her as being a teacher in a one-room school. The only way for her to effect change was to have more power and influence, and the way to accomplish that was to become a politician. She took this big step in a little town in Indian Territory where the Shawnee Convention was making plans for statehood. Representatives from Oklahoma Territory and Indian Territory met together there to draft political platforms and to nominate candidates who would write the state constitution.[12]

This conference was a meeting of the Twin-Territorial labor unions, the State Farmers' Union, and four railroad brotherhoods. Kate called it "a working man's convention." They planned to follow the advice of American Federation of Labor president Samuel Gompers: "Elect labor's friends and defeat labor's enemies." A guest speaker at the convention was the celebrated Irish labor agitator Mother Jones, seventy-six years old and revered for her work to help coal miners, textile workers, and child labor. Dressed in black with her tidy bonnet, Mother Jones looked like a grandmother, but she was a tough firebrand with a gift of showmanship who could out-swear any miner. Her war cry was "Pray for the dead and fight like hell for the living." Working people idolized her. In St. Louis, Kate had heard the voice of intellect in Jane Addams's speech; she heard fire from Mother Jones. Kate's political speeches would be a blend of both styles. She added her own talent for stirring emotion. She could fight like hell, too.[13]

Kate capitalized on her labor connections and attended the Shawnee Convention as a delegate from the Women's International Union Label League. She immediately began to command attention and maneuver her way into leadership. She made her first public speech there, advocating for compulsory education and child labor laws, and people took notice. Convention chairman Jesse Dunn saw how the audience leaned forward, agreeing with her fervent belief in organized labor. He was one of the first to recognize her influence among labor, and he drew her into the all-male inner circle of Democratic politics. She liked the place. She became a member of a board that produced a list of mutual interests for labor and farmers known as the 24 Demands—and she herself wrote three of them. One made education compulsory, the second prohibited child labor, and the third reflected her devotion to labor unions with a fellow servant's law that made employers liable for work-related injuries.[14]

The 24 Demands supported a political system of progressive concerns for the new state: labor's demand for the eight-hour workday, health and safety laws for mines and factories, and the appointment of a mine inspector, a labor commissioner, and a corporation commission. Kate was whole-heartedly behind these requirements. Additionally, she supported the farm-ers' demand for a liberal homestead exemption law and a commissioner of agriculture. She endorsed the initiative and referendum, a new phenome-non, that would allow a designated percentage of voters (eventually deter-mined to be 5 percent) to propose or suspend legislative measures. Kate and Dunn bargained like horse traders. She already had some labor unions and the women's labor leagues behind her; she added to that clout by secur-ing the Catholic bishop's endorsement, which controlled eight thousand votes. In return for delivering these votes, she asked that the conference adopt her planks for child labor, compulsory education, and one other spe-cial wish of hers—establishing a state department of charities. All of the other planks from the coalition of farmers, labor, and coal miners had been proposed earlier and elsewhere. This charity department was the conven-tion's one unique contribution to the final Democratic platform. It would be the humanitarian arm of the state government, established to super-vise and inspect all state eleemosynary institutions. It carved Kate's name in history.[15]

Convention leaders then formed an elite lecture bureau to go on the stump to campaign for the labor-endorsed candidates and to explain the 24 Demands to the populace. Only four speakers were selected, and Kate was one of them. The other three were the most powerful labor leaders in the territory, all Scots or Irish; Kate was both. Peter Hanraty, always known as Big Pete to distinguish him from his son Little Pete, was a miner and founder of the Twin-Territorial Federation of Labor. J. Harvey Lynch, a plas-terer, was secretary-treasurer of the Oklahoma State Federation of Labor. Jack Britton, a coal miner and respected labor leader, was a tall man, quiet and slow to anger, but dangerous when crossed. Kate, tiny, fearless, and fiery, brought her dedication to the Democratic Party and social reform.[16]

This rustic foursome launched an ambitious speaking campaign. They had only two months until the election. Kate was not campaigning as a candidate herself, and women could not vote, but she gave 125 speeches supporting organized labor and decrying the horrors of child labor. She went from town to town, sometimes alone and sometimes with candidates, traveling by bumpy horse-drawn carriage and open-windowed trains to arrive windblown, dusty, and covered with soot. She spoke from wagon beds and wooden platforms, on street corners, in school buildings—anywhere a crowd could gather.[17]

Kate became one of the most popular speakers in the territories. She was charismatic on the speaker's stand, possessing a natural gift of speech as some people have a gift of song. Public speeches were popular entertainments of the day, with audiences gathering in great numbers from isolated farms and ranches, small towns, and the mining communities. Kate informed the people, even when her facts were tenuous, and she enthralled them with speeches throbbing with sentiment, emotion, and sincere passion. She was the voice of their conscience and of their longing, and she spoke with a heartfelt fluency that most could not articulate. The rapport was mutual and strong. "I build my addresses from the inspiration of the audience," Kate said. She was particularly popular with the British and Irish. Some of the mining towns' populations, especially Polish and Italians, could barely speak English, but they recognized her as one of them; she did not put on airs. She was simply Kate, and the people trusted her.[18]

Always she described how the progressive laws would benefit children—"God's little ones," she called them. The initiative and referendum would "guarantee equality of opportunity," labor laws would protect workers who were family breadwinners, a homestead exemption would help build homes—it was all for families and children—but especially she championed compulsory education and child labor laws. She told the crowds about going down into the mines herself, to see where the children worked. She found "the little children down in those inky passages, forgotten by the bright outside world, down, down, down, where no grass grows, no birds sing, and no flowers bloom." Reform legislation would give them a better way of life, she told her audiences; thus they should vote for the men who supported compulsory education and the end of child labor.[19]

In Ardmore, a railroad town at the southern border of Oklahoma Territory, Kate and Harvey Lynch were featured speakers at an elaborate Labor Day celebration. Despite heavy rains, a crowd of three thousand gathered in the public park for barbecue and speeches. A newspaper reporter summarized Lynch's speech but reported what Kate said in detail. "My heart goes out to the 1.7 million children who are denied school

Kate went down into the mines herself to see the inky depths where the child miners worked. Photograph courtesy National Child Labor Committee Collection, Library of Congress, Prints and Photographs Division.

privileges and who are forced to work in the factories of the United States," she told the audience. The hope for the children, she related, lay in a state constitution of reform. "I have always maintained that the people's hearts are true and you will do the right thing when properly appealed to."[20]

Her speeches were colored with biblical references in the fashion of the day, and she knew what effect she had when she asked, "What would our Savior say, he who said 'Suffer the little children to come unto me,' if he came to earth tonight and saw those little children enslaved in child labor?" She delivered her message in a voice like a crystal bell. Angie Debo was a young schoolteacher when she heard Kate speak several times, and it was so memorable that seventy-five years later she remembered Kate's distinctive voice, "a piercing sweetness [that] carried with no effort. She had a power over an audience that I have never heard equaled."[21]

When Kate spoke to an audience, she sometimes emphasized her fragility, lifting a slender arm as she said, "I weigh only ninety pounds, but as long as God lets me live"—she repeated the phrase like a vow—"as long as God lets me live, I am going to use all the strength I have to help these children."[22]

Not long after the Shawnee Convention, two men with political courtship on their minds called on Kate in Oklahoma City. They were ambitious Democratic leaders from Indian Territory looking for a strong ally in Oklahoma Territory, and they recognized Kate's growing political stature. One was Charles N. Haskell, fifty-six, stocky, and dynamic, with a successful career in law, business, and no-holds-barred railroad promotion. Haskell had come from Ohio, where he had failed in races for state senator, congressman, and governor. He did not intend to fail in politics again. He wanted to be Oklahoma's first governor, but his railroad association was a handicap; he needed Kate's influence with labor. Kate sized him up as an "astute politician" equaled only by Henry Asp. They were "the two colossal brains of the state." Kate and Haskell formed an immediate bond.[23]

The man who accompanied Haskell was Dr. J. H. Stolper. Born in Swentzian, Russia (now Poland), he was employed by several large coal companies, which gave him sway over the miners, especially the foreign born. His personal stationery listed degrees from multiple universities in Europe and the United States, and he claimed credentials as both an attorney and a physician. Stolper was thirty, a year younger than Kate, but with an authoritative presence that made him seem older. He was tall, with dark, curly hair, a thick moustache, and an accent that some mistook for

Italian. His formality of dress and polysyllabic vocabulary gave him the air of a proud peacock. He once irritated Jane Addams by appearing at a social reform conference wearing a top hat and white gloves. Kate was impressed with Stolper's education and courtly manners, but he would become a costly associate for her.[24]

———∽———

When the votes were counted in November, it was a Democratic landslide. "Sister Kate," as she was known within labor organizations, was so proud of the accomplishment that she wrote Samuel Gompers, another national leader she had recruited as a colleague, describing the campaign strategy and victory: "Only twelve Republicans were elected [as delegates] to the Constitution [sic] Convention and ninety-eight Democrats." Even with this overwhelming majority, the Democrats were not guaranteed a progressive constitution. Republicans were determined to write a more conservative document.[25]

The national press converged on Guthrie in November 1906 for the opening of the Constitutional Convention. It was the era when newspapers and magazines were the heartbeat of American culture, reporting history on the hoof. Frederick Upham Adams wrote in the influential *Saturday Evening Post* that this convention would be as significant in national history as the Philadelphia convention of 1786 that drafted the United States Constitution. President Roosevelt and the federal government were watching closely, too, because what happened here could have far-reaching consequences. Oklahoma could become the first state founded on issues of social concern with a supportive government. Or, if the delegates wrote a more conservative constitution, the Progressive movement would suffer a defeat.[26]

Kate attended the Constitutional Convention not in any official capacity but as an interested observer as matron of the United Provident Association. She certainly was not a delegate with voting privileges, but she intended to wield influence nonetheless. She insinuated herself by offering her secretarial services, sometimes paid and sometimes voluntarily, to different delegates and committees. She researched laws in other states, helped draft planks for the constitution, and lobbied the delegates one on one with the vehemence of her progressive passion. Primarily, she was there to remind many of the delegates that her stump speeches had got them elected, and now was the time for them to vote her planks into the constitution. She was confident that she could get "the boys" to vote her way.[27]

She stayed close to Big Pete Hanraty and other Democratic labor leaders, and since her ties with the farmers were more tenuous, she worked to demonstrate her support of farm interests. When the members of the Farmers' Union paraded through the city wearing straw hats and overalls, Kate marched with them in a sunbonnet and a long calico skirt. As the Constitutional Convention began, not everybody was taking her seriously. "Around Convention Hall," wrote researcher Edith Copeland, "politicians and reporters regarded her as picturesque. Very few recognized her as powerful and astute." Kate would change that before the convention was over.[28]

One of her activities at the convention became historical lore. Kate took her meals at Mrs. Van Vorhess's boardinghouse, where she learned that Henry Asp was calling a secret caucus of Republican delegates one night at the Royal Hotel to write their own version of a constitution. Kate persuaded her roommate, the daughter of the Oklahoma City marshal, to join her, and the two climbed out on the hotel's porch roof to eavesdrop. They were soon discovered, and Kate was furious—not because they had been found out, but because they were chased away before she heard anything of value to report.[29]

The Constitutional Convention convened at 2 P.M. on Tuesday, November 20, when convention president William H. Murray rapped the gavel and said, "Delegates will take their seats. Loafers and lobbyists will get out." That included Kate, who was relegated to the visitors' gallery. She was not pleased that Murray was elected president. Although he was a Democrat, in the power play between labor and farmers his election was a victory for the Farmers' Union. She was placated that her friend Hanraty was named vice president. Her political admirer Haskell was considered the real power.[30]

In the next few months, the delegates built a state from scratch. They wrestled with major issues, but they also spent an inordinate amount of time on minor issues, such as designing the state seal and coining county names to honor one another. Kate listened to every debate as she waited for her special issues to come to the floor. She had plenty of time to observe "Alfalfa Bill" Murray in action.[31]

She saw a tall, lean farmer and self-educated lawyer with a drooping moustache. Murray was a former schoolteacher and had been an unsuccessful candidate for political office in Texas before coming to Indian Territory. At thirty-seven, he was a "gawky, overbearing, unkempt, and eccentric" white man who gained status and property by marrying Mary Alice Hear-rell, a teacher and part Chickasaw. This marriage entitled Murray to citizen-ship and land in the Chickasaw Nation. In the vernacular of the day, a newspaper described him as a prominent "squaw man," which was a "pejo-rative and offensive" term for "a white man who improved his lot by inter-marrying." (This was not an uncommon union. Lee Cruce, who would become the state's second governor, was also an intermarried citizen of the Chickasaw Nation.) The delegates respected Murray's knowledge of consti-tutional law and his sharp mind, but his manners were so roughhewn, the press described him as crude. Later, Murray became known for his trade-mark white cotton suits, looking every inch the southern colonel, but at the Constitutional Convention he was unkempt and not too clean. Kate said that his hat had sixteen grease spots to the inch, his britches had never known a crease, and his shoes were innocent of shine. Guthrie gossip whis-pered that his table manners were so bad, he was asked not to frequent the Royal Hotel. He was not the only unpolished man in the territories. A fed-eral judge there was known to eat a head of lettuce like an apple.[32]

Kate and Murray disliked one another from the start. He had a Victorian attitude toward women, opposed women's suffrage because he believed it was unladylike for women to vote, and considered women in political office an abomination. He was also a vocal advocate of separate rights for Blacks, whom he called Negroes in the terminology of the time, and said the idea of equality was "entirely false"—they should be relegated to jobs as "porters, bootblacks, and barbers, and [in] many lines of agriculture." At the conven-tion he spoke at some length about "pushy Negroes." Blacks were a decided minority in Oklahoma Territory, slightly over 8 percent of the population, but Murray was not alone in his Jim Crow proclivities. Haskell was the dele-gate who sponsored the constitutional mandates for segregated schools and railroad facilities and the disfranchisement of Black voters. "Make no mistake," Frederick Upham Adams reported from the convention, "Okla-homa is of the South, and though . . . the colored brother may vote—if he cares to—he . . . must keep his place." Kate took no public position on segre-gation, but she was more racially tolerant than many of her territorial col-leagues. She said in a private letter, "Personally, I wish to see the white, black, red, yellow, and all the races of the world excel mentally, morally, and physi-cally, but my Utopia is a long way off and I am dealing with environments and people who do not see as I do."[33]

Prohibition was a subject of long debate at the convention. Carrie Nation, the hatchet-wielding opponent of saloons, had moved to Guthrie from Kansas to influence the delegates to write prohibition into the new constitution. Kate was more liberal on the subject and advanced in her thinking. She thought liquor was a bad influence on youth, but she regarded alcoholism and drug addiction as conditions that could be treated and cured.[34]

Women's suffrage was one of the earliest issues on the convention agenda, and it resurfaced throughout the long proceedings, but it was linked to racism, which condemned it to defeat. Haskell opposed suffrage because his wife did. Kate stayed out of the women's vote debates, but she later said that if the suffragists' lobby had taken her advice, they might have succeeded. "I volunteered advice, but they thought they were right and went their own way—and failed." Although she was a member of the women's suffrage organization in Oklahoma City, Kate did not campaign for women's right to vote. She said she respected the wishes of her father, a southern gentleman who abhorred the idea of women at the polls. She explained repeatedly that she was so involved with her own reform measures, she didn't have time to take on suffrage.[35]

The most contentious issue between Murray and Kate was not racism, prohibition, or suffrage; it was child labor. Murray's sentiments lay with farmers, who worried that child labor laws would prohibit them from using their own children in the fields. Since child labor was the issue closest to Kate's heart, it was inevitable that she and Murray would clash. They were two combustible personalities with strong opinions and short fuses.[36]

As the convention progressed, Kate revamped her initial idea for a state board of charities into a more extreme version. She had come to believe that boards tended to oppose reform and whitewash problems instead of correcting them. Rather than a board, she now preferred a single elected position—a commissioner of charities and corrections. An independent elected commissioner would have more authority and be free to act "in case of abuses and scandals." It would be the enforcement arm of reform. This office, along with the child labor and compulsory education laws, became known at the Constitutional Convention as "Kate's planks."[37]

Kate was a natural lobbyist, and before long, with her persistent pest personality, she knew every delegate by name and where he stood on every political question. She identified the future leaders, and she knew the losers. When the convention got down to the business of discussing propositions for the constitution, child labor was virtually the first one submitted. It was a monumental honor when Kate was invited to address the entire convention on the subject on December 5. Hanraty led a small contingency of labor delegates who escorted her to the platform. Nobody in the room missed the connection: Kate was labor's friend.[38]

She had only thirty minutes to speak. It was not the largest audience she had addressed, but it was the most important. She looked like a schoolgirl that day, wearing a dark, full-skirted dress with leg-of-mutton sleeves. With the power of an eyewitness, she described what she had seen in the factories and sweatshops. One listener said that Kate was so youthful, he had to pinch himself to believe that she had personally observed such scenes of misery. She asked the convention for compulsory education, for a state factory inspector, and for a state commissioner of charities and corrections to inspect prisons, asylums, poorhouses, and other institutions. Most importantly, she asked the delegates to prohibit child labor in Oklahoma. "Don't crush the children of the poor in the mills of toil," she beseeched them in her clear, musical voice.[39]

Her speech was recorded as "one of the most notable events of that historical convention." When she finished, the attendees burst into applause. Delegates gathered around her pledging their support. Kate had filled the gallery with groups of women from the Oklahoma City Anti-Child Labor League and the Women's International Union Label League. They cheered, too. A veteran newsman watching from his press desk put down his pen and remarked that her appearance had been well staged. He recognized political finesse when he saw it. He was Hobart Huson, the journalist from St. Louis. They came together professionally like two magnets. She was going somewhere, and he could help her get there.[40]

Nobody knew it yet, but he was becoming her most valuable ally. Kate's unfinished memoir gives him the credit for the Department of Charities and Corrections. "The Idea was born in HIS brain," she wrote, capitalizing words for emphasis. "I drafted the bill, took it before the Constitutional Convention, made the plea before this body which drove it through; took the stump and popularized the Idea . . . BUT the Idea for the Department originated in Hobart Huson's brain. Without that Idea, I should never have achieved my Life Work."[41]

Coinciding with the convention's deliberations, the Oklahoma City newspaper articles that Kate solicited from experts began to appear. They hammered on reform topics: John Spargo of the National Child Labor Committee; J. C. A. Hiller, Missouri state factory inspector; A. J. McKelway, assistant secretary of the National Child Labor Committee; Jane Addams, writing about the need for compulsory education; Luther Burbank, the great horticulturist, proposing a new concept of state and national aid. Almost every article in the series acknowledged Kate's role "working in the interest of child labor legislation." This exposed the true nature of her summer "research trip," revealing her not as a kindly charity worker, but as a conspiring political activist. It blew up into a minor scandal.[42]

Personal attacks on her began. A whispering campaign and a vitriolic letter to the editor from the Woman's Christian Temperance Union charged that Kate was unqualified to be matron of the United Provident Association—she lacked "judgement and common sense," she was too young, she associated with a "dreadful" police matron, and she had collected her salary while traveling the previous summer. This became a pattern. The more success Kate attained and the more publicity she received, the more critics snapped at her heels like little dogs. There was gossip about her. Mabel Bassett, another Oklahoma woman in public service, said that Kate was unconventional and different from most women. "Her thinking was fast, her ideas were advanced, and she was a woman in politics." Some people appreciated her independence and strong will, while others were put off. She called men by their first name, and she was friendly with common laborers. All in all, Kate preferred working with men. Just because they "give a bundle of cast-off clothes," women felt called on to interfere and criticize, she said.[43]

---∞---

The Constitutional Convention continued for months, making slow progress. As one debate dragged on, Clem Rogers, the oldest delegate at age sixty-eight and the father of cowboy humorist Will Rogers, said in frustration, "It would have been a godsend to the Convention if they hadn't sent so many lawyers here." Kate kept pressing to get her issues heard on the floor, and finally she was again invited to address the convention. This time when she discussed child labor, she spoke directly to the farmers. She knew that forty-three farmer delegates were about to revoke their promise and vote against the child labor proposition. "If you farmers don't vote for child labor, I hope in the fall of the year when your cornstalks are dry and dead and rasping and bare, that God turns those cornstalks into the skeletons of little children and shakes their dry bones at you." Kate's macabre speech brought action. Her child labor plank was introduced and passed unanimously. Her other planks, compulsory education and an office of co mmissioner an d charities and corrections, were adopted on March 7. Her new national colleagues provided models for the first two planks; she and Huson wrote the third one.[44]

Not everyone was charmed. A Guthrie Republican newspaper editor took potshots at the delegates who had fallen under the spell of this "little ninety-six pound bunch of nerves," meaning brashness, and who scared them with "her great influence with the union l abor party." The newspaper admitted, however, that Kate controlled more convention votes than any man in either party.[45]

As the Constitutional Convention plodded on, Kate saw an opportunity to rally national support for the proposed constitution. She asked Territorial Governor Frantz to appoint her as a delegate to the National Conference of Charities and Correction meeting in Minneapolis that June. He agreed as long as she paid her own expenses. "I had only $200 in the world," Kate remembered years later, "saved from my $50 a month salary as matron of the United Providence Association, but I took this, bought a ticket and arrived in Minneapolis to learn that nobody ever appeared before this conservative body except those on the program." The program was r igidly set, but she found W. H. McClain from the St. Louis Provident Association in the crowd, and he helped her get special permission to speak. It was not a prominent place on the program, but it opened the door a crack to a national audience.[46]

At the Minneapolis conference, she was a reform fledgling s peaking t o 1,700 seasoned experts. She asked for their wisdom, because in Oklahoma, "We are young. We are inexperienced." She told them that she had sought advice from reform experts and that their advice had been woven into a reform constitution. "We have fought for your measures until we are sick and weary and worn with the struggle." At this, the audience broke into cheers. "Men and women stood up and waved handkerchiefs and hats at me." She had to wait for the commotion to die down before she could finish.[47]

Kate had wooed them and won them, and now she called for action. National pressure was being brought to bear on President Roosevelt to veto the constitution. "The whole Republican party is clamoring for its defeat. Help us in the pulpit and in the press. Write your congressmen, your political leaders, and the President himself. Will you help us?" Kate beseeched the conference. This technique had worked for her among audiences in the territories, and it worked at this national convention in Minneapolis. A sea of hands went up.[48]

"Stand up," Kate said, "stand up and be counted," and the entire conference stood cheering and applauding. "I stood for nearly an hour receiving congratulations and assurances that each would write or wire or see the President in person." The conference attendees, who had clapped with feeble politeness when introduced to this unknown little woman from the West, now pounded their hands together with what one newspaper called "ringing applause and real enthusiasm." Her speech lasted just five minutes, but in that scant time she sprang from obscurity to national recognition.[49]

The newsmen were enchanted with Kate. Hers was the best address of the conference, the *Minneapolis Tribune* declared, describing her as "sweet and dainty as a wild flower, and as refreshing as an Oklahoma breeze." The press scrambled for interviews, and she painted a beguiling biography as a "motherless girl," convent-educated, "in a hard, cold world." Her sad childhood made her yearn with "her whole heart . . . to save other girls and boys from the same hard fate."[50]

Kate did not captivate everyone at the Minneapolis conference. "She is impossible," some murmured, "aggressive. High falutin'." No matter. She had accomplished what she had come to Minneapolis to do. After the conference, Child Labor Committee secretary McKelway himself went to Washington and told the president that he had not seen the national conference so stirred in fifteen years. The president replied that he had received almost two thousand telegrams and letters on Oklahoma's behalf. Still, the national Republican organization pressured the president not to admit another Democratic state to the union and threw its massive weight behind the fierce Oklahoma campaign.[51]

————∞————

Women's suffrage failed to win the Constitutional Convention vote, but in an extraordinary recognition of Kate, the office of commissioner of charities and corrections was designated as a post to be held by either sex. It was the only Oklahoma state elective position that could be held by a woman, and it was generally understood that the office "was made for Kate Barnard" in appreciation for her support of Democratic candidates and the Democratic Party. For years she was assumed to be the first elected state officer in the nation. Kate could not vote, but she could hold office. She deserved it, the leading Oklahoma City newspaper reported: she was "the one woman who has done more than any other to protect the interests of children in Oklahoma." "It almost took my breath away when I found out that I was considered the logical person to be the first commissioner," Kate said. She always insisted that she had gone to the convention with no personal ambition, "not a single thought" of entering politics. The following month, Kate resigned from the United Provident Association, accepted a gold medal from the Oklahoma City Chamber of Commerce in appreciation for her work, and announced her candidacy for the office of commissioner of charities and corrections.[52]

Finally, after eight months in the writing, the constitution was finished in July. At fifty thousand words, it was the world's longest constitution: longer than most novels, ten times as long as the Constitution of the United States. The document made news, not because of its amazing length, but because of its prevailing reform sentiment favoring labor and the common people against corporate power. The initiative and referendum attracted particular attention. This constitution, creating a working man's state, was a socialist's dream come true, a national magazine rhapsodized. Frederick Upham Adams wrote that he had witnessed "not merely the birth of a new State [but] the birth of a new kind of a State." Samuel Gompers said it was the most progressive constitution existing on the American continent. British ambassador James Bryce called it "the finest document of human liberty written since the Declaration of Independence" and gave special credit to Kate for her contributions. Republicans denounced the constitution as "freak legislation." Kate and the other Democrats rejoiced and stood fast with the slogan "Let the people rule."[53]

Writing the constitution was the first step. Now it had to be ratified by the people in a popular election that would also choose state and local officials and members of Congress. The election was set for September 17, only two months away, so the campaign was off with the speed of a quarter horse. Kate was in it from the starting bell, deeply involved in party politics.

Two Democratic contenders were vying for governor. Kate considered Haskell the stronger candidate, but S. O. Daws, president of the Farmers' Union, had the popular vote. If both were nominated, they would divide the vote, and the Republicans would surely win. Yet neither would withdraw. The situation was at a stalemate.

Haskell called Kate and asked for her help with the labor bloc. He promised that if he was elected governor, her labor planks would become law during his administration. In return, he wanted her to get Daws to pull out of the gubernatorial race. At the Shawnee Convention, Daws had swung the votes of seventy thousand organized farmers to join labor and include Kate's "three precious demands" in the final 24 Demands. "How could I bite the hand so generously extended to me?" Kate asked herself. She anguished and prayed, but there was her own campaign to consider also. Which man could help her more? She made her decision, met with Daws, and persuaded him to retire from the race and swing the farmer-labor group to Haskell. It was the end of Daws's political career, and he died in poverty. Every time Kate saw his "stooping shoulders and hopeless eyes," she remembered her role in his dead-end life. Remorse is the price for a steely political heart.[54]

The Democratic Central Committee capitalized on Kate's talent as a vote getter and scheduled her for almost fifty speeches. It was unusually hot and dry that summer, with temperatures over 100 degrees and a drought settling in. She often spoke in two or three towns in the same day, traveling by train, interurban car, and horse-drawn wagon. The heat stretched into September, a cruel month in Oklahoma: the calendar may say autumn, but the temperature says summer. The sun burns the grass and parches the earth, dust is layered over thirsty trees, and people are worn down by the heat. In this heartless weather, Kate went on the stump wearing the fashions of the day—long skirts brushing the dry ground, her waist rigidly constricted with whalebone, and necklines high and tight. By day's end, her high-topped shoes were thick with dust. She pushed on with the zeal of an evangelist. In one town, she talked so intently with the local official who met her train that she did not notice when her suitcase broke and her underwear began trailing down Main Street. The embarrassed man did not know whether to help her retrieve the garments or politely cover his face with his hat. Kate never stopped talking as she gathered up the underclothes herself.[55]

Kate did more than campaign; she launched a crusade. She gave forty-four speeches, and with every speech, her fame grew. "I was acknowledged the strongest speaker and the best vote getter in the state," she said. An announcement that Kate Barnard was speaking would draw a crowd of up to eight thousand, a phenomenal number in the sparsely populated territories. Farm families traveled twenty miles by horse and cart to hear her. Her speeches were uninhibited as she attacked the Republicans: "This constitution is so fine that if I knew of a man opposed to it, I would spit on his grave." Future state governor Henry S. Johnston took her aside and urged more restraint. She thanked him for his advice, but when an audience in solid Republican country resisted her arguments, Kate lost her temper and threatened them with a strike. "Vote the constitution down if you dare, and I'll call out every miner in the coal districts. Then what will you do for coal this winter?"[56]

Often, Kate would step onto the platform after other candidates had spoken for several hours and in the scorching summer's air hold the audience enthralled for ninety minutes or more. In farming and cattle country, she talked about mortgages, homestead exemptions, high interest rates, bank failures, and the novel concept of a bank commissioner. Oklahoma would be the first state to enact a law for the full protection of depositors, she said.[57]

When she talked to labor audiences, she told them about bills that would guarantee safe working conditions and the eight-hour workday. She denounced the "millionaire coal barons" who were trying to defeat laws requiring mine inspections and emergency exits. Her audiences knew that the Indian Territory coal mines were the most dangerous in the nation, yet if a man was injured on the job, he was thrown on charity. She denounced the mines that objected to building protective sheds or scaffolding for workers' safety: "I believe that the mine owners should provide for the men crippled in their service just as the railroads do," she said. Her audiences understood the reference to railroad injuries. The year before, 9,703 railway employees and passengers had been killed and 86,008 injured in accidents, collisions, and derailments.[58]

The weather wasn't the only thing that was hot. The campaign was heating up, too. She was stumping in Hobart, in southwestern Oklahoma's cotton and livestock land, when Republican gubernatorial candidate Frank Frantz and his entourage marched into the crowd with two brass bands, four automobiles (a rarity at the time), and a procession of about three hundred men. Frantz had scores to settle with Kate. She had persuaded him, a Republican appointee, to endorse her national trips to stir up people against the Oklahoma Republicans. The Democrats were still laughing at him.

"I had about 3,000 people listening to me," Kate would remember, "and he attempted to drown out my speaking with brass band clamor." The scene was bedlam for almost two hours. "It would not have taken more than a word to have precipitated a riot." Kate challenged Frantz to join her on the platform, but he left town on a freight train instead.[59]

Some of the more ferocious campaign battles were fought deep in the coal-mining area. Kate was stumping in Henryetta when the situation grew dangerous. She had just begun to address an audience of about two thousand when her opponent and his loud, boisterous party arrived and tried to break up her speech. He made a stinging remark about women in politics, and the miners answered back angrily. The two groups were on the edge of violence as coal miner Jack Britton stepped forward. He was a "huge" man, Kate noted, with a "mighty frame, broad shoulders, and big, sinewy hands," but he spoke softly: "The speaker has been invited to help the miners with their legislative program. The miners respect women and expect their outside guests to do the same." In a voice intensely calm, he asked Kate's political opponent to vacate the premises. "They vacated," Kate said, and she continued her speech. "In that wild moment," she remembered later, Britton's unruffled and "quiet dignity" prevailed.[60]

She was stumping in the mining district when a mine explosion killed twenty-five miners. She told this story to her audiences with horrific detail—the fire leaping up through the mine's single entrance, the smell of burning flesh, and a desperate wife trying to throw herself into the mine as three small children clung to her and sobbed. Public emotion was so strong that town officials asked her not to speak in a town where one of the mine officials lived. She went anyway. When told that no public hall was available, she spoke on the street corner. During her speech, the mine owner pushed his way through the crowd and stood directly in front of her. He folded his arms and silently dared her to accuse him of negligence. The crowd shuffled nervously, looking from Kate to the mine owner.[61]

Kate paused, then pointed directly at the mine owner and said in a firm voice, "The diamonds you are wearing in your shirt-front were bought with the blood of fifteen men who were burned to death in a mine which you own, because you would not spend the money to provide two entrances. You made their wives widows; you made their children orphans; you are responsible to Almighty God for the long, weary lives of poverty and ignorance which they face; and if the people of this state of Oklahoma will elect me to the office which I am seeking I will change such conditions, not only in your mine, but in all others."[62]

It was about this time that the people adopted a new nickname for her. They began calling her not just Kate, but "Our Kate." She knew this: "Many referred to me as the spiritual life of the statehood battle."[63]

In late August, the Republicans called in their strongest national figure, Secretary of War William Howard Taft, who was slated to be a presidential candidate the following year. In early September, the Democrats retaliated and summoned William Jennings Bryan, who would run against Taft for the presidency. Bryan arrived by chartered train during the last few days of the campaign. In Tulsa, five thousand people listened to Kate until his train pulled in. Bryan—Kate called him "Billy"—had come to ask the people to vote for the constitution, telling them, "It is not only the best constitution in the nation, it is better than the federal constitution."[64]

That summer, Kate spoke in almost every sizable town in the territories, then crowned her whirlwind tour with a final open-air speech in Oklahoma City on the eve of the election. She was welcomed like a heroine by the crowd and the press. When the votes were counted, both the constitution and the Democratic Party had won by dominating majorities. The progressive constitution was approved by a ratio of five to two, and not only by Democrats but by many Republican voters as well. Haskell was elected governor by 137,579 votes to Frantz's 110,293. Kate not only won her race for commissioner of charities and corrections, she had the second-highest number of votes of all the Democratic candidates. Only Haskell had received more votes than Kate.[65]

"To a large extent, the success of the Democratic party has been due to her efforts," the Oklahoma press reported. She had secured child labor, compulsory education, and the office of commissioner of charities and corrections in the new state constitution. National figures noted her influence. "Of course, there are other reasons for the victory of the Democrats," said McKelway from New York, "but Kate Barnard was several reasons herself. She was thoroughly trusted by the two largest classes of voters, the farmers and the labor union men, and she was the favorite [Democratic] speaker." The election victory proved to Kate that the progressive issues she championed were the will of the people. Their hearts beat with hers. Kate reciprocated: "I loved the people."[66]

Jack Britton went back to mining coal. So did Peter Hanraty, who lost both legs in a mining accident. J. Harvey Lynch was sentenced to the penitentiary, convicted of check forgery and "trouble with some girls in Kansas," Kate said vaguely; "blackmail," Huson explained. Newspaper editor Roy Stafford became a successful candidate for state senate. Haskell, Murray, and Kate went on to elected office, destined to meet again in political climates both fair and foul.[67]

That October, the drought broke with heavy rainstorms. It was the wettest October on record. Oklahoma weather is as extreme as it is fickle, but Kate soon learned that weather is not the only thing fickle in Oklahoma. Fellow politicians can be strong contenders for the title.

CHAPTER FOUR

Miss Commissioner

NOVEMBER 16, 1907, was a spangled Saturday, with weather made to order for a celebration. Thousands gathered in the streets of Guthrie that crisp morning to ring in statehood and to inaugurate the first elected state officials, including Kate as Oklahoma's first commissioner of charities and corrections. The crowd waited for the signal from Washington that President Roosevelt had signed the proclamation declaring Oklahoma the forty-sixth state of the union. The day crackled with anticipation, as if a gift were about to be opened.

The president was expected to sign the proclamation at 10 A.M. Eastern Time, but he dallied over his morning mail and signed it several minutes late. "Oklahoma is now a state," he said flatly. The news was telegraphed to Guthrie, where a man rushed out into the street and fired a pistol into the air.[1]

The steps of Guthrie's Carnegie Library were adorned with flags and pompon chrysanthemums. To commemorate the union of the Twin Territories, a symbolic wedding ceremony united a beautiful Cherokee woman called Miss Indian Territory and a cowboy called Mr. Oklahoma Territory. Governor Haskell in his frock coat led a two-mile parade to a public barbecue in the park. Dancing and merriment stretched into the night. Some tried to drink the saloons dry before the new prohibition laws closed them at midnight.[2]

That morning Kate dressed in a new brown velvet dress and waited with her father for their parade carriage. They waited for an hour watching as smart carriages and sleek horses called for other officials. Kate gaped at the old buggy that finally stopped for her, so feeble that she thought it would collapse when she climbed aboard. Once it was in motion, the buggy's upholstery snowed softly on the humiliated Barnards.[3]

As she ascended the library steps, the audience cheered her and called out, "Kate! We want Kate!" But the governor did not bring her forward to speak to the people. She stood quietly throughout the ceremony, then she and her father hurried to the statehouse to see her office. Another disappointment awaited her there. "Since I was the only woman state official—and frail—I supposed innate courtesy had assigned me space on the first floor." She was wrong. They finally found "a tiny pigeonhole" on the third floor next to the men's toilet. "I expected happiness when I reached the State House," she wrote, but what she got was "a hole in the wall with foul odors." She was so insulted, she threatened to lay the matter before the Federation of Women's Clubs as an outrage upon public morals. Eventually, state officials took action. They did not move her office, but they did move the men's room.[4]

At the inaugural ball that evening, the women sparkled in diamonds and finery. Mrs. Haskell wore a dress imported from Paris, and Miss Indian Territory wore a lace dress cut in the new princess style. Kate wore a softly shirred white silk dress and no jewelry. Each newly elected state official led a dance, and when Kate's turn came, she chose her father as her partner. Their victory waltz was a bittersweet celebration of pride and regret. He was a man of political ambitions whose daughter had outdistanced him.[5]

Kate believed that the inferior office and the shabby buggy were deliberate insults by Haskell and Murray. She poured her anger, and her sense of worth, into the details of setting up her office. She fussed when the seal for the office was delayed, when there was trouble with a shipment of stationery, when her name was misspelled on a rubber stamp, when the union label was missing from her official letterhead, and when the Remington Typewriter Company sent her a faulty typewriter "entirely unfit to use." An ink company addressed her as "Gentlemen" and she snapped, "I believe that I am the only woman holding an elective state office in the United States." These were little vexations compared to her outburst about a forthcoming book of state officials' biographies: "I insist that my page come in its proper official sequence after that of the governor. Under no circumstances will I tolerate it if a two-by-four representative like Bill Murray is given precedence over an elected State Officer."[6]

The First Legislature convened December 2, 1907, and met for six months, accomplishing an extraordinary amount of work. Murray was

Kate's official portrait as the newly elected commissioner of charities and corrections in 1907. Photograph courtesy Oklahoma Historical Society.

elected Speaker of the House, moved to tears by the honor. "This is the happiest moment of my existence!" he said. Kate was not weepy; she was all business and grimly determined to see bills for organized labor, compulsory education, and child labor passed into state law. She planned carefully. As she wrote Samuel Barrows, "I have been watching the rise and

Kate (*in dark dress*) was as small as a child. Photographed here with the state labor leaders she called her "boys" and an official Labor Department stenographer, she is flanked on her right by Commissioner of Labor Charles L. Daugherty and on her left by miner and Federation of Labor leader Peter "Big Pete" Hanraty. *American Magazine*, October 1908, 590.

fall of the different legislators and trying to find out who is the strongest member of either house."[7]

The legislature did not approve the Charities and Corrections Act establishing her office until March 23, so for several months she devoted herself to legislation and lobbying. She saw that a reformatory and probation bill and a compulsory education bill were introduced in the legislature and passed. The compulsory education bill required at least three months' school attendance a year for all healthy children ages eight to sixteen. Legislative work was fast paced and often fiery. Laws were passed, bills were defeated, and causes were lost or won at a racing speed. "No other Oklahoma legislature has ever considered so many matters of equal importance," a historian declared.[8]

Kate's duties, as prescribed by the state constitution, included the entire system of public charities and corrections, which meant examining the condition and management of all prisons, jails, almshouses, reformatories, reform and industrial schools, hospitals, infirmaries, dispensaries, orphanages, and asylums; making recommendations for their operation; and providing a full written report each year to the governor. To accomplish all of this, she had the assistance of one stenographer. With a staff so small, "You can't do it as it ought to be done," the chairman of the Missouri Board of Charities and Corrections wrote her. He had a staff of seven people.[9]

The enormity of the work did not dampen Kate's enthusiasm. What upset her was that her department's appropriation was delayed month after month. She grew anxious about the report due from her department in October. Since she had no funds, she could not conduct inspections, and until she could inspect, she had nothing to report. She suspected the funding delay was political sabotage, but she did what she could without funding. In April she organized the first State Conference of Charities and Corrections in Guthrie to generate grassroots support for social progressive and labor bills. She began jail inspections by touring two county jails nearby.

Her salary would be fixed by law at $2,500 a year, and one of the first things she did after taking office was cut it to $1,500. The gesture was meant to exhibit frugality, but it did not endear her to other elected officials, and within a year she regretted the rash action and asked to have it restored at the next election.[10]

Another action was even more reckless. Without authority or funding, she hired Hobart Huson to be her assistant commissioner. If later she ever realized the full price of this folly, she never acknowledged it. Their relationship was a source of speculation. Whispers persisted that she and Huson were lovers, but nobody ever came forward with proof. Kate lived such a public, scrutinized life that her political opponents would have been quick to reveal evidence of a personal scandal. Kate dismissed the notion of any amorous relationship with anybody. "I had no time for romance— and no inclination." Her friends said her only love was her work. She always lived in a hotel or a rooming house within walking distance of her office, and she had no outside interests beyond her work.[11]

Kate described Huson as her most valued friend, lavished him with praise, and generously shared credit with him. She hired him at the same salary as her own; she even bought a cemetery plot for him close to those she bought for her father and herself. When they began working together in 1908, Huson was fifty-two and Kate was thirty-three. He was five feet ten and stocky with brown eyes and thick brown curly hair, and was described as "a damned good-looking man." Women were drawn to him. He was Kate's opposite: patient, methodical, well educated, and well read. He tempered her impetuousness; she personified his dreams of glory. His background in journalism and railroad work made him an efficient press agent and aide in planning her complex travel schedules by rail, arranging press interviews and speaking engagements, and booking her hotel accommodations. She relied on him to conduct departmental business when she traveled outside the state. He provided organization for the office and corralled her fearsome energies, sometimes in a rather patronizing way. "I am doing all I can to keep Miss Kate's efforts all in one general direction," he wrote an acquaintance. "By this means she accomplishes something."[12]

It is easy to see how Kate admired him, even idolized him. To her, he was the epitome of experience and culture, her unofficial private tutor. His personal library numbered about five hundred volumes, including extensive collections about the Civil War and leather-bound sets of classics that he transported in specially made boxes the size of coffins with handles at the sides. Next to her father, Huson was the most important man in Kate's life, and his influence was enormous. She relied on his political insight because he was "an old Tammany man from New York" and said, "he was my tower of strength in the wild political storm." Huson told Kate he had worked for a string of newspapers in Chicago, New York, and New Orleans, as well as "every large paper of the Southwest." He said he was a southerner and a member of the United Sons of Confederate Veterans, and that he had come to Oklahoma to escape southern prejudice on "the Negro question."[13]

"He was one of the noblest men who ever lived," Kate said. Others did not agree. One of Kate's friends who frankly disliked Huson was Jerome Dowd, a sociology professor at the University of Oklahoma: "He was no good at all. He cared for her work only for what he could get out of it." Dowd did not see charm in the man; instead, Huson struck the professor as "a quiet, plodding, unsentimental type." Some were offended at Huson's get-rich-quick schemes and his attempts to borrow money or secure financing from Kate's associates. His proud discourses repelled some people. "I am a great lover and admirer of high art," he wrote one of Kate's professional colleagues, and went on to expound about Venus de Milo. Whatever their individual idiosyncrasies and faults, Kate and Huson combined their strengths to form an effective team. She said she depended upon him "entirely" on all legislative matters, and said that he not only suggested bills, he wrote many of them: "He drafted six of thirteen measures my department helped to pass in the [First] Legislature." With Kate as the star and Huson supporting her, they shaped Oklahoma statehood and they made history.[14]

There was much about Huson's past that Kate never knew. He was one of five children and the black sheep in an established family of lawyers and statesmen in Rochester, New York. His father, Calvin Huson Jr., had established a brilliant career as an attorney and politician while still a young man and seemed a certainty for election to Congress until the Civil War intervened. He was watching the First Battle of Bull Run, the Union term for the battle, as a sightseer, not a soldier, when he was captured by Confederate troops and imprisoned in the notorious Libby Prison in Richmond, where he contracted typhoid and died at the age of thirty-nine in 1861. Huson's account of family history differed. He maintained that his father was a volunteer aide to Confederate general Nathan Evans, and that he was wounded at the First Battle of Manassas, the Confederate term for the same battle, and died three days later at Richmond. Huson, four years old when his father died, developed a lifelong obsession with prisons and collected a small library on the subject.[15]

Emulating his father, Huson began to read law while still in his teens, but as a young man he became embroiled in a scandal that ruined any chance of a career in Rochester. "I'll tell you the story as it was told me," a Huson relative said years later. Legal documents support her story, that in 1879 Huson promised marriage to two young women at the same time. When one of them became pregnant, he quickly married the other, and the first woman then pressed charges. He was jailed and indicted by a grand jury. The marriage was annulled, and he was forced to marry the pregnant woman. He abruptly left town and both women.[16]

By 1890 he was in Texas, married to a widowed music teacher and the father of two sons and a daughter, when a series of tragedies befell him. A newspaper he had founded in Denison, Texas, failed; their three-year-old daughter died; and he suffered a hip injury in a railroad accident that would leave him with a limp and pain for the rest of his life. He left his family behind and worked at odd jobs, barely able to pay for the humblest room and board. When his wife tried to locate him, his neighbor advised her to forget him, saying, "He can't support a good dog." About 1901, he abandoned his wife and sons for good, saying he did not want to be a burden to them. Four years later, he met Kate in St. Louis.[17]

Huson took pains to show Kate his strengths and to hide his failures. Kate did not pry. She did not know that he was estranged from his wife and children. "I often marveled that such a man should remain single, but association with my secretive father taught me never to seek confidence where it is not volunteered." In many ways, Huson and Kate's father were alike, men of secrets and shadowy pasts, loquacious dreamers with big plans. Throughout her career, Kate tried unsuccessfully to obtain appointments for both of them. Both men were relegated to living in her shadow.[18]

Kate was busy throughout the First Legislature's session, involving herself with bills in four categories: the child section (juvenile court, child labor, and compulsory education), the penal section (adult probation, a reformatory with indeterminate sentences, and a court of parole), what she called the "defective" section (care and treatment of the "insane," the "feeble-minded," and epileptics), and the labor section (factories, state employment offices, mining bills, and the eight-hour workday). "So you see I am busy," she wrote a friend. "This is a new state and all the laws are to be enacted."[19]

She lobbied, but she also wrote some of the bills, calling on national experts to help with authorship and then come to Oklahoma to shepherd them through the legislature. Hastings H. Hart came from Chicago as the authority on orphanages. Dr. Alexander Johnson of the National Conference of Charities and Correction came from Philadelphia to discuss the care of the feeble-minded (the accepted description of the time). For the juvenile court bill, Judge Julian Mack of Chicago provided data, and Judge Ben Lindsey of Denver, the leading authority on juvenile courts, traveled to Guthrie several times to help write the bill and to address the legislature. Some of these men became more than Kate's professional colleagues; they became her fans. "Never have I known a more devoted and determined champion of human rights than Miss Kate," Lindsey said years later. And yet, he noted an ominous foreboding that had shadowed her successes. "She became a power to reckon with, a dangerous obstacle in the way of privileged and selfish interests in politics. So her every victory in legislation was a nail in her coffin for defeat."[20]

Samuel "June" Barrows, U.S. representative from Massachusetts, creator of the International Prison Congress, and the leading authority on prison reform, helped Kate design the state's penal system. He counseled her to promote the indeterminate sentence, a range of time such as five to ten years instead of a fixed period, to encourage rehabilitation. This would put Oklahoma ahead of any state in the union, he said. Then he paid his own way to come to Oklahoma several times to speak to audiences and legislators. "I am sorry that I have no funds at my disposal to defray your expense," Kate apologized. When he left after one of those trips, Barrows wrote Kate from the train that it was difficult to say goodbye to the "baby state." He adopted the tone of a fond uncle: "You have taught me what a single, earnest little woman could do. What a factor she might be in the life of a state and in the life of humanity." He referred to her as a "dear little dynamo" because that "describes your marvelous energy."[21]

The one subject paramount to Kate was the child labor law. She solicited help with it from Owen Lovejoy, general secretary of the National Child Labor Committee in New York. "I need a law formulated by you which has been reviewed by members of your national committee and found to be without flaw," she said bluntly. Lovejoy sent her the documents, but she lost them, blaming a "careless chambermaid" while she was ill. Kate told him to send them again, which he did, and then he arranged for A. J. McKelway to travel to Oklahoma to help her write the bill and push it through the legislature.[22]

McKelway's work with the National Child Labor Committee had influenced the public conscience toward reform. In 1903 the first child labor laws were passed by Alabama, Kentucky, North and South Carolina, and Texas, but only after bitter struggles. Now it was Oklahoma's turn.[23]

McKelway spent several days in Guthrie, addressing both branches of the legislature. To Kate's great surprise, the bill began a troubled trip through the legislature. The leading opposition came from farmers, led by Kate's nemesis Speaker Murray, who agreed that child labor should be forbidden in mines and factories, but not in farming, where it was needed for cotton

picking and the harvest season. Neither should the commissioner of charities and corrections assume the role of a child's parents. Providence watches
over Indians, drunk men, and children, Murray was fond of saying.[24]

Kate worked to bring the bill to a vote, and sixteen times it was first on
the calendar, but each time Murray filibustered until it sank to the bottom
of the list. By then it was late May, and the First Legislature would adjourn
in a few days. In desperation, Kate appealed to Governor Haskell for help.
He intervened, and the child labor bill finally came up for debate, but the
Speaker and a handful of his cohorts "shot the bill into fragments [with]
amendments, amendments to amendments, and substitutions [trying to]
kill it," Kate said. The debate lasted five hours, labor against farmers.
Kate's ace in the hole was H. S. P. Ashby, who at seventy years old was still
the best orator in the legislature, nicknamed "Stump" for his golden voice
in campaign stump speeches.[25]

Murray's allies tried to sabotage Ashby's address by plying him with
prohibition liquor. Kate knew it and went searching for him. "I found
Stump rather dizzy, told him I was depending upon his eloquence to save
the children of the poor, and took him into a cafe for strong coffee." The
opposition was hurling invectives as she led him to his seat in the legislature. Tall, bony Ashby, "aged and poor but regal as a king," Kate said,
struggled to his feet, swayed slightly, and gathered himself to speak. He
did more than take the floor, Kate said: "he took wings and soared." His
arms were outstretched, his eyes were aflame, and his voice blazed with
holy fire. Word spread throughout the corridors and offices that Ashby
was setting the House aflame. People poured into the assembly room to
hear his extemporaneous soliloquy. He spun a canopy of shining oration
over the gathering, and when he finished, it floated softly over admirers
and opposition alike to hold them in silence. Kate heard a clock tick. "I
have never witnessed anything that produced such psychic terror," she
said. "There won't be another speech like it in the history of Oklahoma."
The vote was called, the bill carried, the House stood adjourned, and the
legislators rose respectfully to let Stump Ashby pass by.[26]

The child labor bill also passed the Senate and went to the governor for
his signature, but as Oklahomans of that era said, school ain't out till the
big kids spell. Kate had outmaneuvered Murray, and he was being "twit-
ted on all sides for being thrashed by a girl," she gloated. He demanded
the governor's veto, and Haskell pledged it. When Kate learned this, she

immediately went to see the governor. "People have said that I have some persuasive ability," she wrote later, "[and] I exercised that to the utmost, as well as every bit of tact, ingenuity, knowledge of the horrors of child labor, and Irish blarney." Barrows had seen Kate in action and said, "Her personal power is phenomenal." Kate unleased its full force on the governor, but nothing moved him. He vetoed the child labor bill.[27]

Kate was stunned: "I never counted that four or five determined and adroit men could run counter to this large majority." Even editor Roy Stafford could not persuade Haskell to sign the bill, but he did what he could to bolster Kate's ego and her political influence. In story after story, the *Daily Oklahoman* praised her as the most remarkable woman in the state and labor's incorruptible champion, adored by the masses for her work for the betterment of the human race.[28]

This was not her only legislative defeat that session, but it was the most bitter. Bills for a juvenile court, a prison system, and care and treatment of the "insane" were withdrawn, postponed, or voted down. Some were so pale with compromises that Kate did not grieve at their demise, but she was genuinely shaken by the failure of the child labor law. "I worked day and night for the passage of this measure. I interviewed individually each of the 154 men in the First Legislature. I am at a loss to know why my child labor bill was vetoed. You might as well ask the wind, or the birds of the air, or the fishes of the sea."[29]

She had successes, vigorously supporting eighteen bills and succeeding in getting fourteen of them enacted into law. "I wanted to establish an inebriate asylum, too, and had a fine bill drawn up, but when I spoke of it I was reminded by the legislators that we have Prohibition and we're not supposed to have any drunkards." Consequently, an institution for inebriates would be a great joke. Kate disagreed. "In my charity work, I have had a great deal to do with drunkards and dope fiends. I believe they can be cured as any other disease can be."[30]

The defeat of her child labor bill outweighed everything else. She blamed herself. She had stretched herself too thin with efforts for other bills. Even worse, she had been traveling when the bill was introduced, and it was left in the hands of "unlettered farmers and laborers [who] were no match for parliamentarian debate." Even a physician had stammered in debate "like a big schoolboy." Without her driving the bill, they were out of their depth.[31]

Kate was embarrassed to think about campaigning in the upcoming fall election. "How can I go on the stump?" she asked Stafford. "How am I to meet the voters when they ask me why we protected the cattle from ticks, why we protected insects, bugs and toads, but did not protect the Oklahoma child?" She wrote tides of letters to her national reform allies, bravely reassuring them of her resilience. "In passing my hands over the wounds received in my legislative battle, I find that I am not so badly hurt after all," she wrote to one, and "I am already putting on my armor for another conflict." "I am not moping or holding my hands," she wrote another. "I am still militant and belligerent. I am Irish and have the traditional love of a shindy."[32]

She received reams of letters of consolation and encouragement, reminding her that reform crept at its own slow pace. "Don't be discouraged if it takes four or five years to get your bills through," wrote John Glenn, the director of the Russell Sage Foundation in New York, an organization dedicated to improving living and working conditions among the working class. Barrows advised her, "Be more patient. Reforms must go slowly. It is only by persistent effort that any can be brought about." Her national colleagues also cautioned her—lectured, even—to slow down and take better care of herself. She should rest after such an arduous effort and prepare for her next campaign, Barrows wrote. She must be prepared for these disappointments, Judge Lindsey told her: "Take it as a compliment to your work and to the strength and power that come to you from the people." He gave her a warning: In her battles for humanity, she would become dangerous to the enemies of the people. She would become a marked woman.[33]

Kate solicited their counsel and assistance on legislature, but she ignored the personal advice and continued to push herself with growing fatigue and stress. Her assistants complained about the "nerve wracking" pace she set. Her office was a maelstrom of "organized confusion," with visitors knocking at her door and Kate, her stenographer, and Huson all typing at once as they attacked piles of correspondence and planned trips, speeches, and lobbying strategy.[34]

———✖———

The target of Kate's wrath over the child labor bill's defeat was Speaker Murray, and her anger toward him had deep roots. Early in the legislative

session, Murray saw her on the floor of the House talking with a representative and called for the clerk to read aloud the law prohibiting lobbyists on
the floor. It was clear that he meant Kate. She hurried to the balcony flushed
with indignation. Members of the House followed after her to apologize.
The incident grew into rumors that Murray had ordered her from the
House floor with insults and vile language. Murray was attacked on all
sides for ungentlemanly behavior toward a lady, damning criticism in 1908.
The incident blackened his reputation for years, and he was denounced as a
"dirty, foul-mouthed politician unfit to represent the grandest state in the
Union."[35]

Their next skirmish was the House debate in May on the appropriation
for Kate's department. Murray told her that he did not consider her office
important enough to support more than one stenographer and a small
expense fund. The day the appropriation was debated, he left the chair and
took the floor, where he made his position public. To Murray's surprise, a
storm broke as representatives rose to denounce his motives, to praise
southern womanhood, and to eulogize Kate. Stump Ashby called her the
"Good Angel of Oklahoma." Murray's own brother-in-law made a strong
speech in her favor, and the leader of the Republican minority declared
that she belonged to the unfortunate—white and Black and red looked to
her for relief—and called for $10,000 more than she had asked for. Murray
did not know it, but seventy-eight legislators had visited Kate's office in
the preceding days to pledge their support. She had organized them to
deliver a series of speeches, and they complied, one after another, from the
floor. They recited, Kate reported proudly as a former teacher, "with the
precision of a school entertainment."[36]

When the vote was called, the legislature voted 104 to 5 to appropriate
her department $1,000 more than she had requested. "Everybody has been
laughing at Murray for the outcome of his fight with a woman," Kate
crowed. "The boys always stand by me. No woman has more or truer
friends. To use a western term, Bill Murray was literally skinned alive and
the wounds salted."[37]

There is another western expression that perhaps Murray knew: If you
wait long enough, your enemies will come into your gunsights. Murray
waited. A month later, the child labor bill came before the legislature, and
he took aim. Kate might have claimed astonishment at the bill's defeat, but

she was shrewd enough to know that it was Murray's victory in the political war between them.

The appropriation for Kate's department was finally approved on May 9, shortly before the legislature adjourned on May 26, and she was able to begin investigating the state's institutions. "Now I am forced to do twelve months' work in the hot weather of June, July and August," she fumed. "This is a terrible outrage to perpetrate on a frail woman like I am and one who is spending her life's forces on mankind." She was not exaggerating about her frail health; she had been sick in February and again in April.[38]

The state primaries would be held in August, with a national election hard on their heels in November. The air was heady with politics. This would be Oklahomans' first opportunity to vote nationally since achieving statehood. Kate was attuned to national politics and wrote Samuel Gompers that William Jennings Bryan's election was of double importance "because the next president will probably have the appointment of four supreme court judges."[39]

She was excited about the upcoming elections, yet admitted, "I don't know how I can stand another summer campaign." Kate was not running for reelection herself, but she was committed to helping the Democratic Party and her faithful friends and allies. She knew her value in the campaign. "You provide the politics and I'll provide the sentiment," she told another Democrat as they planned a joint appearance. She wanted to rally support for bills for child labor, a juvenile court, adult probation, and homes for the insane. Perhaps most delicious of all, she wanted to wage "bitter and acrimonious war" against Alfalfa Bill Murray.[40]

While delivering campaign speeches that summer, she also inspected state institutions. Her health began to show the effects, and by July she was physically ill, "greatly distressed in mind and body." Huson described her condition as "a complete nervous breakdown." Her energies were at their lowest, but Kate was in demand more than ever. "In good health she can make two speeches a day if the distance isn't too great," Huson replied to a request for a speech from Kate. She tried to preserve her energies by keeping her speeches to an hour in length. "Still the temptation to talk longer always comes when you know that a thousand or more people have come long distances to hear you," she confessed. And come they did. "It is because I make warfare in favor of my friends and against my enemies that these great crowds gather in this hot weather."[41]

Despite her fatigue and illness, her prowess on the stump was as great as ever. An article in *American Magazine* reported that the state's Republican candidate for governor had wisely avoided debating her, and if any Republican candidate did appear on the same platform, he left before Kate began speaking. The candidate for attorney general, however, challenged Kate to a debate, and "after she finished speaking, they not only hooted the other speaker from the platform, he was literally laughed out of the state and is now somewhere in Alaska."[42]

A man wrote to tell her about the spellbinding effect her speech had had on him and his wife, saying they had sat "until the small hours of night" talking about the experience with New Testament allusions. "If you had said, 'Come, go with me,' we would have followed you. We believe that God works through individuals that evils may be checked and that great wrongs righted. We believe you [are] inspired and called by Him to do the grand and noble work that none other but one inspired could do." Kate kept the letter for the rest of her life.[43]

She produced more fireworks that summer than a Fourth of July celebration, culminating in what she called a little "hair pulling with Bill Murray." During the campaign, their supporters tangled in fistfights and physical skirmishes on city streets and in hotel lobbies. She lambasted Murray all across coal country with powerful speeches attacking his opposition to bills for compulsory education and child labor. She relished speaking in support of a senator whose opponent was Murray's brother-in-law, and she pressed her attack into Murray's farming country. Defying rumors that his supporters would pelt her with rotten eggs if she appeared in Tishomingo, his home town and the capital of the Chickasaw Nation, she gave a rousing speech there and left unscathed. "I suppose you read in the newspapers how I flayed him," she gloated in a letter. By August, when the two adversaries met at the Lincoln County Farmers' Union picnic, Murray said that he was sick from the attack made on him, and Kate said that he looked it.[44]

When the smoke cleared and the primary election votes were tallied, Kate had won the day. She was especially gratified that the candidate she supported had defeated Murray's brother-in-law. Telegrams of congratulations poured in to her, and Kate declared it a "splendid victory," but other politicians, including the governor, criticized her for her aggressive campaign. The Democratic Party chairman called her "interfering, interposing, unbecoming, and undemocratic." Kate was nonplussed. "I believe I have done the state some service," she said.[45]

The battle between two of the state's most powerful Democrats was a topic of discussion for years. Huson wrote letter after letter replying to inquiries about it. "Miss Barnard comes of Irish stock," he explained. "If anyone fights her, she will fight back, but she is generous by nature and when the fight is ended, she quits."[46]

The reason Kate was out of state when her child labor bill was introduced in April was that she was speaking at the annual meeting of the National Child Labor Committee in Atlanta. Word had spread about her remarkable work in the "baby state," and she was in demand as a speaker, becoming known as the "consummate politician" in Oklahoma. Her Atlanta speech was Kate at her most lyrical. She said she was saddened to learn that in beautiful Georgia, "where the roses and magnolias bloom and where hearts are warm and sincere and sympathetic, . . . little human beings are hidden away in factories." By contrast, out west a new civilization was being built, and Oklahoma was caring for its children by passing wise legislation. She hoped to replicate her success in Minneapolis and leverage national influence against Oklahoma's governor and legislature. The Atlanta convention did pass a supportive resolution, but regrettably it had no effect in Oklahoma. Kate's child labor bill failed the following month.[47]

In June she was in Richmond to address the National Conference of Charities and Correction. In Atlanta she had been poetic; here she was direct. "I drove a wedge into that solemn body," she said. "I told them that for thirty-six years they had been meeting annually discussing causes of poverty and still groping in the dark." To her, the answer was clear: "The basic cause of poverty is wages and the question of labor. The Conference was aghast." Kate told the 2,300 delegates in her straight-shooting style that in the West "we are willing to learn. We live for the future."[48]

One of the most stirring speeches of Kate's career was at the International Congress on Tuberculosis in Washington, D.C., in late September. Nineteen

Oklahoma delegates accompanied her. President Roosevelt was president of the conference's American sector. "We're going to visit Teddy," Kate wrote J. H. Stolper, one of the delegates. Kate's speech was titled "Industrial and Social Causes of Tuberculosis and Preventative Measures in Oklahoma," but she did not let the formality of the title impede her. As usual, she extemporized: "I have never committed a paper to memory." When a full copy of a speech was needed for publication, Huson wrote it from Kate's notes, but his text could never capture the impact or passion of her delivery.[49]

In 1908, tuberculosis was the nation's leading cause of death, killing an estimated 150,000 people a year in the United States. Kate discussed the dreaded disease from her unique perspective, with Dickensian details of the overcrowded, overworked, underpaid workforce. She told the startled international audience that the way to stamp out tuberculosis was to correct the conditions that fostered the disease—the "squalid and unsanitary conditions" in factories, sweatshops, and slums. Adequate wages and shorter hours would enable employees to afford wholesome food and develop healthy bodies to resist the ravages of tuberculosis. Kate's speech was a highlight of the conference. "Ten thousand scientists rose and cheered," she said with evident joy of accomplishment. "Roosevelt stopped a receiving line to congratulate me." Kate was blazing like a comet. She spoke at national conferences and wrote articles for national news magazines (*Good Housekeeping*, the *Survey*, the *Independent*) and for the state's important *Sturm's Oklahoma Magazine*. She granted interviews to the nation's largest newspapers and magazines.[50]

She gained such a reputation as a public speaker that in October 1908 she was asked to help with the national election. She did not boast, but she was aware of her merit. "I am the only woman in the world to go on the stump" for presidential candidate William Jennings Bryan, she said. She made speeches for him in Illinois, Indiana, and Ohio, ten days "of the hardest kind of work." She was happy to do it and told Samuel Gompers, "If I can help elect a President and a Congress friendly to labor, I am more than willing to do so." She wrote a Boston reform colleague, "I have very roseate hopes. It is my nature."[51]

She returned to Oklahoma to give twenty-one more speeches for state candidates. Her speaking schedule reads like a railroad conductor's call.[52] When the national election returns were in that November, the Democrats had suffered a crushing disappointment. Kate had campaigned hard and hopefully, only to see her rosy dreams wither in defeat. From her office window in Guthrie, she watched the Republican victory celebration in the streets below, complete with noisy crowds, marching bands, waving flags, and clattering carriages hung with bunting. She sat alone at her desk and typed letters of condolence and dismay.[53]

She wrote Bryan, "I presume I am the only woman in the nation who went on the stump for you. I went there for the sake of principle and I would go there again." She told him that she was baffled at the sounds of celebration she was hearing. "Just what they are cheering over, I do not know. It may be the 15,000 starving children in the city of Chicago. It may be the millions of unemployed working men in the United States. It may be the ten million underfed, poorly clothed and badly housed people in America. Or it may be the working man's empty dinner pail."[54]

She tried to rally Bryan's spirits, and her own, with her indefatigable courage: "Nothing is ever settled until it is settled right." She shared her real feelings of disappointment with U.S. senator Thomas Gore from Oklahoma. "I went all the way to Illinois at Gompers' request to help Billy Bryan and I feel very bad over the results." Finally, her despair could not be contained, and like a river topping its banks, she wrote a labor worker in Washington, D.C., "All we can do is struggle and struggle with and for the toiling, suffering masses and if they in their ignorance do not accept our help, we are not to blame. Why are they driven into the hands of their enemies? May God understand the reason."[55]

When Bryan lost the election, a deep grief fell over Kate. She suffered another physical collapse, this time more serious than before, and she lay in a dim sickroom for weeks. Five months of campaigning and public speaking across Oklahoma and in six states had taken a heavy toll, but she had been doing much more than give speeches. Simultaneously, since April, she had conducted her first inspections of state jails, mental hospitals, and orphanages. The campaigns exhausted her, but the inspections broke her heart.

CHAPTER FIVE

The Good Angel

K ATE'S JOB AS COMMISSIONER, as mandated by law, was to inspect the state's institutions. She would do more than tour the jails, hospitals, and orphanages; she was determined to transform them with the same social concern ideals she had pushed into the state constitution and touted in the campaign speeches that had helped get her elected to office. These were the ideals that national journalists had said made Oklahoma not just a new state, but a new kind of state. Now was the moment of opportunity. This was Kate as the Good Angel.

Once her department's appropriation was approved, she began investigations with fervor. By the end of the year, in the space of six months, she had personally visited 123 county jails, poor farms, orphanages, and city jails, as well as insane hospitals, as they were called then, and schools for the blind and deaf. Huson inspected sixty-five other jails, and together they visited sixty-one of the state's seventy-five counties established at statehood (two other counties were added in 1910). They inspected some state institutions more than once.

Kate was both professional and compassionate in her investigations. Her fundamental criteria for facilities were humane treatment and safe, sanitary conditions. She wanted Oklahoma to adhere to the latest methods for reforming prisoners and caring for mental patients. She wanted even more from orphanages; there she wanted a nurturing atmosphere and job training. She expected to find temporary and barely adequate facilities from territorial days, but she was outraged to discover such primitive conditions for prisoners and sickened at the treatment of mental patients. She slashed through the state's institutions, heralded for her work by the weak and suffering, but accumulating adversaries in her scorched-earth path. When institutions' administrators were recalcitrant and resisted her directives for change, she did not politely plead and request that offenses be corrected. House Bill No. 348, the legislation that defined her position, gave her a big stick, and she used it with all the authority of her office. Kate had the power to grant or revoke certificates, to order facilities closed, and to ask the court to prosecute and punish by law the officers of offending institutions.[1]

All of the institutions she inspected needed improvement, and most needed major changes. She began with the hospitals for mentally ill patients. When she first inspected them, she uttered a sentence that became legend: "Hell has reigned here undisturbed for ten years."[2]

The state's two hospitals were dissimilar in construction, but Kate found both to be "revolting" and no more than "legalized barbarism." The first hospital, centrally located in Norman, consisted of one large brick building and several frame buildings "more or less out of repair." It was operated by the professional Oklahoma Sanitarium Company. The second hospital was established in May 1908, when the legislature approved the Western Oklahoma Hospital for the Insane, and some four hundred patients from Norman, many in tears, were herded onto a special train and sent to Fort Supply, an abandoned army barracks of thirty-six buildings isolated in the western part of the state.[3]

Even before she set foot inside the hospitals, Kate knew what she was likely to see. She had received letters from former patients, relatives of patients, and even attendants testifying to the ill treatment at both places. "I saw them kick and abuse a colored man till he died the next day," a former patient wrote her. "I saw a woman attendant whip some girls with a large rubber hose. Oh, it was Hell on Earth. We were fed like dogs and part of the time were kept on bread and water."[4]

The bedding at Norman was "nothing more or less than a great, big bag of straw," an attendant told her. "In raining or damp weather, it is wet straw and damp blankets for covering. They do not even have a nightgown but are put to bed naked. If patients soil their bed in the night, the condition stays," and their lower limbs would become raw and painful.[5]

Kate replied with empathy and vowed to change conditions for the unfortunate patients in state care. She began her inspections of mental hospitals in mid-October 1908 and visited them repeatedly over the next few months, sometimes for days at a time, at other times making surprise visits. Her inspections were not superficial. Whenever she appeared at a hospital, "I literally turned it upside down," she said. She walked the wards with attendants, scrutinized the conditions of the buildings, observed the patients, and tasted the food. She made specific suggestions for improvement: the installation of skylights in a women's violent ward "to relieve the darkness which makes the place unwholesome and unsanitary," and a coat of white paint "to cheer the place up." She detailed instructions to the attendants: use thermometers, not their hands or elbows, to check the water temperature for bathing patients. Mostly she concentrated on the treatment—and mistreatment—of the patients. She saw attendants who were ignorant and cruel, hospital directors who were either unqualified or uncaring, buildings that were obsolete, and physical restraints that were barbarous.[6]

She printed the findings of her inspections in her *First Annual Report of the Commissioner of Charities and Corrections*, written for the governor and the Second Legislature, but she went far beyond that and became a muckraking journalist herself, writing an article for a national magazine and publicly condemning the hospitals' management. She wielded her typewriter like a blunt object. "As a rule, I have found physicians in charge of state and county institutions for the insane incompetent and careless." It was not that the attendants were inexperienced; the problem was the experience they had. "Every one of the attendants whom I have evidence against for cruelty has come from the state asylums of Kentucky, Alabama, Arkansas, and Texas." When she caught an attendant choking a patient at the hospital in Norman, he defended himself by saying he had first-class references, and everywhere he had worked, the patients were handled in this way. "Male attendants, calling themselves 'hospital bums,' make a business of traveling about the country, working in asylums, hospitals and similar institutions," Kate wrote. "Tuberculous and syphilitic patients [are] herded with others not already so infected; straitjackets, irons and unpadded dark cells [are used in] the treatment of violent patients; choking, beating and starving [are] administered indiscriminately for infractions of discipline." Her intention with this article was to sway public opinion and to influence state legislators to reform action. Kate viewed the press as a tool for her benefit.[7]

Her understanding of mental health, advanced for Oklahoma in that era, was based on her own research. She visited five of the "finest U.S.

hospitals and one in Canada," where she saw hydrotherapeutic baths, electric massage, and other modern methods of treatment. Oklahoma would do away with mechanical restraint, she promised. "I am making a fight to place our institutions on this high plane."[8]

She lamented the public's popular ignorance of mental health. "There is an illness of the nerves and brain which we term insanity. [Yet] we cast these sick people into prisons (which we term asylums) and there forget them." Kate declared war and vowed to get the patients in state care the protection and treatment they deserved. The patients and their families were grateful to have her as a defender, but her public criticisms did not endear her to the hospitals or to embarrassed state officials, especially the politicians who appointed the hospital administrators.[9]

At Fort Supply, she directed the management to construct four additional wards, another kitchen, and cement walkways. She was concerned especially about the heating in the buildings. Each fifty-foot ward housed fifty patients but had only two coal stoves, so the heat was poorly distributed. "An insane person is a sick person," Kate told the hospital superintendent with labored patience, "and no one would think of placing a sick relative near a red hot stove where the temperature alone would make a well person ill. Neither would they place them on a bitter cold day in a room without fire."[10]

She worried about the danger of fire at the Fort Supply hospital. Instead of coal stoves, she recommended that a heating plant be installed immediately to provide uniform, economical steam heat. Otherwise, she warned, "'Tis only a matter of time until a holocaust will happen." Her concern was not unfounded. A prairie fire had destroyed a number of the hospital's buildings the previous spring, and improperly installed chimney flues would cause another fire the following year.[11]

Kate wrote directly to Governor Haskell, telling him, "I am appalled at the conditions I found there." Unfortunately, the Fort Supply hospital superintendent, Dr. E. G. Newell, was a Haskell political appointee. Someone who knew the superintendent described him as a man who chewed liberal amounts of black tobacco, talked loquaciously about himself, and said he had no experience in asylum work—"a statement I never have doubted," the acquaintance said dryly.[12]

Kate also wrote to the state's attorney general about violations of labor laws at the Fort Supply hospital. The attendants reported for duty at 5:30 A.M. and worked until 8:00 P.M., assisting patients in dressing, washing, eating, and similar tasks. Not only did the attendants work a fifteen-hour day, in violation of the state's eight-hour-day law, but they were required to sleep in the wards where they were on call to tend to the needs of the patients.[13]

Despite Superintendent Newell's connection with the governor, Kate "severely criticized and reprimanded" him on the spot and also lectured the attendants. Back in her office, she continued blasting Newell with commands. She sent him a copy of a letter from the superintendent of the Manhattan State Hospital for the Insane, the largest institution in New York, which she considered "the best institution in America," and instructed him to read it several times, "because I intend to base our future reform work [in mental hospital care] upon this man's opinions." She enclosed a questionnaire to be completed by nurses, attendants, and supervisors "right away" in order to "stir your employees up to a larger sense of their duty and a better realization of the scientific information which they should possess."[14]

She was not finished. "I would especially call your attention [to the New York] characteristics of a good hospital, [primarily] a proper medical spirit marked by a spirit of kindness. Second, conscientious, capable supervisors, nurses, and attendants. Third, lack of mechanical restraint, except in protective sheets, baths, etc. And fourth, kind, intelligent, tactful nurses."[15]

She was particular about the food served to orphans, patients, and prisoners in Oklahoma's institutions. "In modern insane hospitals," she wrote, "...a regulated diet of milk, eggs and nourishing food is provided to rebuild shattered brain and nerve cells."[16]

Yet, for all her efforts to learn about up-to-date scientific treatment of the mentally ill, Kate was working in an era when there was only a nascent understanding of mental health. A journalist of the time later wrote, "the mentally ill were regarded as lunatics and potentially dangerous." The emerging concept of curing patients was new. The barbarous conditions she saw were commonplace, and knowledge of mental disorders was crude. She asked Superintendent Newell to list the causes of insanity for the Fort Supply hospital patients, and he replied in terminology standard for 1908: syphilis, 2; ill health, 3; heredity, 43; inebriates, 12; old age, 8; overwork, 2; morphine and cocaine, 3; obscure causes, 5; mental worry, 3; injury to brain, 7; idiots, 1; imbeciles, 6; unknown causes, 10; self-abuse, 2; epilepsy, 16; criminally insane, 1; sunstroke, 2; cigarettes, 2; not insane, 3; and menopause, 1.[17]

Even by these broad definitions, not every patient at the state's two hospitals was mentally ill. A person identified as a public nuisance, aged, or indigent could be declared "insane" by an examining board and sent to a hospital. Physicians reported that an adult child who wanted control of a parent's property could easily get an "old, crotchety man or woman declared insane."[18]

Punishment and restraint were the familiar treatments; locked cribs-— wooden boxes about the size of coffins, with slats for sides—were used for punishment at both mental hospitals. So were leather wrist-to-waist restraints. Kate was adamant that these be eliminated. She wrote Newell, "I spoke in sixty counties in the campaign and everywhere assured the voters that we had abolished the cribs and dungeons and beatings and strangling and tortures of the old Republican regime." About a month later, a man appeared at her office and swore an affidavit alleging continued cruelties at the Fort Supply hospital. She wrote the superintendent again, ordering that brutalities were to be stopped at once. "Will you please call your attendants together as I did the evening I was there and forbid any corporal punishment stating that patients are never to be kicked or beaten or have used upon them soapy towels for strangulation, etc."[19]

The state's other mental hospital, a three-story former school in Norman, was a dark and foreboding place. A large coal stove in the center of each corridor provided heat, so here, too, fire was a constant concern. In its favor, the Norman hospital operated on the cottage plan, the system Kate preferred, in which patients were divided by categories of medical diagnoses of the time: epileptics, imbeciles, and idiots. She noted that Superintendent A. T. Clark subscribed to the "sun cure," which consisted of plenty of fresh air and sunshine. On fine days, inmates were taken outside to "take exercise or sit in groups" in the shade of a "fine grove" of trees.[20]

What Kate actually felt for Superintendent Clark was contempt. "He is a carpetbagger, a druggist, and not a doctor." She believed that both he and the company that employed him were more interested in the hospital's profits than in providing medical care. Conditions were so bad that after her first inspection of the Norman hospital, she was pale and "shaking as with a fever," a colleague observed. Kate wrote directly to Clark and documented what she had witnessed. "I was shocked to find that you confined your hopeless, sick insane in cribs. That you tied them with straps and chains or shut them into bare rooms with no blankets or bedding, nor heating, and nothing but bare floors and hard walls." She lectured the superintendent as if he were a backward student. Mental patients were not convicts, she told him. "In modern hospitals they are recognized as sick—mentally sick—that's why the sanatorium is called a 'hospital for the insane.' Taxpayers and Christian civilization expect that the helpless inmates sent there will receive hospital care." Modern hospitals, she added, used baths, hot and cold packs, massage, and electricity to care for their violent patients. Hospital attendants did not whip or stomp their patients. When Superintendent Clark replied that funds were insufficient for more scientific care, Kate persuaded the legislature to appropriate an additional $200 a month per patient for more advanced care. She sent Huson to do a follow-up inspection to check on improvements, but none had been made.[21]

A year later, Kate re-inspected both mental hospitals herself. She was enraged at what she saw. Her letter to Newell at Fort Supply must have burned the postal carrier's hands. He was to "employ immediately" the full quota of thirty attendants, she wrote, and to replace the old doors in the cells with screens. "I hope you already have the extra stoves in wards Eight and Three that I recommended." She told him that she would be back in about ten days to see if this had been done, and she wanted to know what had been done about the nurses working fifteen hours a day.[22]

What Kate saw at the Norman institution was even worse. The attendants were so ill-informed, they did not know how to take a patient's temperature, she reported, and she instituted weekly education sessions. As she had predicted, a fire occurred, destroying, among other things, some of the heating stoves. Kate went to see the situation for herself. The new heating system had not yet been installed, and neither had replacement stoves been ordered. The day was very cold, and she found patients huddled around one stove in each ward. Water pipes and sewers were frozen.

Kate ordered the new stoves herself and did not leave the hospital until they were installed.[23]

Whether out of stupidity, indifference, or stubbornness, the Norman hospital superintendent and attendants flatly ignored her directives. She confronted Superintendent Clark's defiance by sending him a list of orders to be carried out "immediately," including the installation of two stoves in each ward. Violent patients were not to be secluded in cells without heat. "It's so damp and cold it would make a normal person insane."[24]

She enumerated to him some of the brutal situations she had observed:

"Mr. Springs from Wagoner: hands fastened to side with leather handcuffs and chains in a bare, unpadded room without even a blanket. Human offal on floor."

"Samuel Thompson of Frederick: locked in a crib." When Kate told the attendant to let him out, the attendant looked through the slats and asked the patient, "Will you be good now?"[25]

Even the Norman hospital's records were inadequate. "A black girl inmate, reported dead five years ago, seems to be alive," Kate told the superintendent.[26]

Kate was tenacious and unrelenting, both in person and by mail, as she pushed the superintendents to change. She hectored Superintendent Clark with visits and letters, but he remained steadfast in his defiance. Even the normally restrained Huson described the exchange between Kate and the hospital superintendents as "one of the most terrible battles I have ever seen." Finally, Kate wrote the Norman hospital's Superintendent Clark, "I do not believe you a fit person to manage a hospital for the insane and I therefore demand your resignation." Otherwise, she would be "compelled under the law to act." Clark did not go easily, and, true to her word, Kate had him fired with a handful of affidavits of cruelty that she threatened to present in court.[27]

She went to the hospital herself and told Dr. D. W. Griffin, the resident physician, "I'm firing Clark and putting you in charge and the first thing you do is burn the cribs." She and Griffin had the cribs, stocks, chains, dungeon doors, and handcuffs dragged out into the yard in front of the administration building. Kate wrote, "I stood by and saw them chopped up with axes" and set afire. She watched as the great bonfire sent shadows dancing across the hospital. The Norman for-profit hospital became a state-owned institution, and Griffin, who was considered to be kind and humane, made improvements at the facility. He personally chiseled the word "insane" from the great iron entrance gate because he thought it was disrespectful.[28]

More relief for the state's mentally ill patients was on the way. Kate learned that the Board of Trustees for Insane Asylums, a separate state board appointed by the governor, was planning to build a third hospital in Vinita, in the northeast corner of the state. She wrote the board immediately, asserting her authority. "I have an actual as well as moral right to inspect the plans since this institution will come under the inspection of my department."[29]

The Eastern Oklahoma Hospital for the Insane at Vinita was established in 1909 and opened in 1913, built on the cottage plan that Kate liked. Dr. F. M. Adams was appointed hospital superintendent, with Dr. Edwin Williams as his assistant. Both were recognized for their innovative treatment of mental illness. Kate inspected the new hospital and declared the lighting, heating, and sewage systems "among the best in the state." However, she noted "serious mistakes" in the new building's construction, notably the "inexcusable" placement of the windows with the lower sill five feet above the floor, so that patients could not see out. "I cannot understand what could have led to such an unfortunate blunder," she said. "These poor people are shut off from the landscape and deprived of sunlight. It transforms the 'hospital' into a prison. It made me heart-sick to think of the years and years to come in which 300 people will suffer daily. This mistake should be remedied at once." She had other recommendations: a larger library, craftwork and amusements for the patients, one trained nurse in charge of every ward, and flowers growing in the windows. And finally, because she wanted the hospital to have a homelike atmosphere, she said, "I would like to see bird cages filled with good songsters in each ward. I noticed the pathetic way in which the patients caressed and petted an old cat in one hospital ward."[30]

She kept a sharp eye on all three mental hospitals throughout her time in office. Advancements were never fast or easy, even after the competent Dr. Adams took charge of the new Vinita hospital. One of Kate's inspections there was so fraught with unfortunate experiences, it was almost comical. Adams wrote her a follow-up report: "We have plenty of water now, less flies, and [are in] a great deal better condition than when you inspected us some days ago." Also, "[we] have returned six of the nine men that escaped while you was [*sic*] here and think I have two more located."[31]

One day soon after a climactic battle at the Norman hospital, which had roiled for almost fifteen months, Kate's eyes were unnaturally bright, Huson noticed, and her face was flushed. "That night she went to bed with a high fever," he said, "and we all thought it was smallpox." She had just inspected a jail and detention camp outside Oklahoma City where 350 patients lay ill and dying of the disease. Kate's condition was exhaustion, the doctor said; "nervous prostration," Huson said. She was confined to her bed for six days. She attributed the cause of her "nervous strain" to the conditions she discovered at the hospitals. When she returned to work and answered letters, she apologized for her delay in replying: "I have been so overwhelmed with work overhauling the two hospitals for the insane, I have not had a single minute for private correspondence. Today I am lying in my office taking medicine. I am very frail in health and do not know whether I will weather the gale or not, but you may rest assured of one thing, that as long as Kate Barnard lives, she will do everything in her power to relieve the distress of helpless humanity." It would be tempting to dismiss this statement as exaggeration, and although Kate was dramatic, she was also a literal person. She did not glow with dreamy hopes; she burned with intensity and action. She was literally using all of her power and more physical stamina and health than she had. She continued her work by sheer willpower.[32]

As soon as the public learned about Kate's institution inspections, the floodgates of pent-up need broke, and she was deluged with requests by letter and in person. The people beseeched her for help on every imaginable subject. She was everybody's advocate, ombudsman, and best friend.

Neighbors wrote to report that they could hear a little boy "kept in a room without clothes for three weeks at a time on bread and water" begging for something to eat. A woman said she could no longer care for her grown daughter who had epilepsy and wanted to find a state home for her. A man asked for help with his mother-in-law, and Kate had to tell him that "there is no place in Oklahoma" to take care of an eighty-six-year-old woman who was blind, deaf, and senile. Italian miners, too poor to hire

Kate wore little jewelry and famously said, "How can a woman wear
diamonds in a country where little children starve?"
Photograph courtesy Oklahoma Historical Society.

attorneys, petitioned her to investigate a local employer for illegally gar-
nishing wages. A nun, addressing her as "Dearie," asked her to urge a
young priest to take better care of himself. The nun was writing Kate, she
explained, "because I have heard so much of your kindness."[33]

People appeared in person at her office door in Guthrie, including a man
who had been sent by county officials. He was ill, and the county commissioners had assured him that Kate would send him on to Kansas City for the
surgical treatment he needed. Since she had no discretionary funds for such
expenses, Kate took money from her purse to pay his fare back home.[34]

The heartbreaking stories kept coming. A lawyer wrote her about "the
sad case" of a thirteen-year-old girl he described as a "dope fiend and moral
leper" and wondered where she could be committed. Huson investigated
and learned that she was epileptic, syphilitic, and pregnant. After the girl
was placed in a facility, Huson wrote sharply to her father about his having
allowed her "to run loose and become the victim of the lust of soldiers" who
had supplied her with cocaine and liquor. When the father wrote repeatedly
complaining that Kate had not enforced laws to protect his daughter or
prosecute the soldiers, Kate lost her patience and replied with a blistering
letter. "Why do you first neglect your daughter and then appeal to me after
the damage is done and then refuse to take the advice I have given you? I
have sympathy for your sorrow, but nothing for your neglect. Now don't
write any more letters to this Department until you have taken the advice
we have already given you as I have not time to fool with people who . . . do
nothing. I am overworked and have about 40,000 helpless on my hands."
She wrote more kindly to the lawyer, a former bank robber named Al J. Jennings. "I know something of your past and it moves me . . . that you will
take this interest in this poor girl. I wish there were more men in Oklahoma
like you." She invited him to attend the next state Conference of Charities
and Corrections. Kate and Jennings stayed in communication. He became
active in politics and eventually ran for governor.[35]

Kate was not unsympathetic to the plight of the girl. When asked about
help for a fifteen-year-old girl described as mentally deficient and "shame-
fully mistreated" by her foster father, who then abandoned her among
strangers, Kate had to reply, "We absolutely have no place for girls, good
or bad, in the state." Pitiable letters crammed her mailbox. A man asked
how to treat himself for tuberculosis since the state had no sanitarium; a
woman wrote asking how to organize a consumers' league; a justice of the

peace inquired about the legality of a pigeon shoot with tame pigeons; and a ladies' committee wanted to know if free school textbooks were available to children of miners on strike. "I have encountered much hard feeling because I could not do everything," Kate wrote a labor friend.[36]

Huson saw how Kate was pressured. "The woman suffrage people are after her good and strong," he wrote. She spent considerable time either dodging the question of votes for women or explaining her position. "I know that a great many of our women of our state think that I ought to drop my work and take sides with them in this struggle for suffrage, but I do not think that I am capable of assuming any more load than I am now carrying." Again and again she pointed out that suffrage was not within the jurisdiction of her office. "I am more interested in saving the poor, destitute, blind, deaf, and insane than in securing the vote for women." Everyone had her own life work, she said, "and when I chose mine, I knew that it would take all my time and would not allow me to belong to literary societies, reading clubs, or suffrage leagues." Although she knew suffrage firebrands, she saw little popular demand for the vote. In her observation, only one woman in twenty wanted the ballot. Yet not all women were followers, she said, citing the "magnificent exceptions of Florence Nightingale, Clara Barton, Jane Addams, Julia Lathrop, Mary Richmond, and Lillian D. Wald."[37]

Kate was sadly aware of the enormity of the tasks before her. In November 1909, she responded to a man who had written her asking for help, telling him, "My health is in a terrible condition, so bad that it threatens my future work. I am positively sick and worn out with the helpless people in the 325 institutions of the state who are depending on me. I need three times the help I have to get all the work done." This was only one year after she had begun her inspections.[38]

All the while she struggled with the intractable mental hospitals, Kate continued her inspections of the state's city and county jails. She knew that Oklahoma was operating with temporary, overcrowded "cheap jails," and she had expected jail conditions to be primitive, but what she found was beyond her imagination. She saw godless places, scarcely fit to be animal shelters, much less accommodations for humans. The jail inspections launched her into a mighty campaign for penal reform.[39]

This was Huson's special interest, and it is easy to hear his voice in her ear, urging her to action. "The present day [penal] systems of America are a curse to the Nation," Kate declared. She denounced "the punitive and politically controlled systems and internal management of our prisons and penitentiaries" as a failure. The country had spent a billion dollars the previous year "for the detection and punishment of crime," but "what do we do to prevent crime?"[40]

Her inspection diary of county jails relates one horror after another:

July 1: "This jail contained three cells. No beds or bedding, no water pails or slop buckets, no stove, not a vestige of furniture of any kind, except an old filthy mattress which lay on the floor." Prisoners were "fastened to a ring in the wall" with a log chain.

"What provisions have you for furnishing food?" Kate asked.

"We don't have any plan," the marshal answered.

"What if the prisoner gets thirsty?"

"I reckon they don't get thirsty."

When she lifted a corner of the rotten mattress, mice and rats scattered across the floor, "much to the Marshal's delight." Kate was not amused.[41]

July 27: "Inmates present, 21. Dilapi[d]ated frame building. Comfortable capacity of jail, 11. Sewerage, none. Fire protection, none. Air, suffocating. Prisoners in semi-darkness. Three tiny windows supply the only light and air for 21 men. . . . Eight bunks for 21 men. Floor, filthy. Most of the prisoners sleeping on floor. Five buckets of night slops had not been emptied at 3 o'clock in the afternoon and into the hot July air they poured their reeking stench."[42]

Kate was appalled at the number of innocent people she found jailed. Of the 5,711 people incarcerated in all the state jails, only 834 had been found guilty in courts and given sentences. "So, nearly 5,000 men, women and children thrown in our wretched jails" were innocent, she reported.[43]

Concerned citizens and officials wrote her constantly. One county sheriff described his own jail as a "hog pen" and asked her to urge the county commissioners to make improvements. A man asked her to investigate another county jail where twenty-six prisoners were "packed like sardines in one room about 16 × 28 with scarcely room to lay themselves down," including a fifteen-year-old boy who had "been in that filthy place for 10 days without any charge filed against him."[44]

Of the sixty-one county jails that Kate and Huson inspected, twenty-five had electricity, ten had gas, and the rest were lit by lamps or lanterns. Only twenty-three had sewage systems, forty-one had running water, and fifty-five used night buckets. At one county jail, she found a bulldog named Pat patrolling the hallway. The dog was on the payroll.[45]

The city jails were worse. Kate visited one "dirty, dark cell" located in the rear of the fire department's horse stable. To inspect it, she had to step around piles of horse manure and pools of horse urine, which rendered the jail foul with odors in the sweltering August air. "The horses in the fire department are much better housed than these hapless men," she reported. She toured a one-cell city jail so susceptible to fire that she was frightened. The dry frame building was surrounded by a wooden fence, yet at night the jailer locked the inmates in. "Who cares if we burn?" the prisoners asked her. "We're only working men."[46]

As she had with the hospitals, Kate fired off orders to the jailers: paint the walls and whitewash the buildings, boil the bedding and scrub it at least once a week, enlarge the windows, provide night buckets and drinking water, build a platform for the beds. She set a deadline for the improvements and returned to see that they had been made on schedule.[47]

She wrote her first official departmental report of jail inspections with restraint and diplomacy, withholding the names of most cities and explaining that her report was intended "to arouse a wide-spread interest and inquiry" into jail operations, and "not for the purpose of giving unpleasant publicity." Only in her personal letters did she describe the horrors of filth and disease she found in her inspections. She wrote directly to jailers, judges, county attorneys, boards of commissioners, justices of the peace, and other authorities detailing unsatisfactory conditions and changes she wanted made. "Do some thorough cleaning and disinfecting around lavatories and bathtubs in cells, white wash walls," she wrote to one county commissioner. "I have explained repeatedly the necessity of having a jail with a separate cell for the sick," she wrote the worried father of an incarcerated "poor boy." In her annual report, she invited lawmakers who wanted to know the plain truth to visit her office and read her inspection diary for themselves. "This Department is simply eyes and ears for you lawmakers. When we make a true report of actual conditions, our duty is done. The responsibility is then shifted to you." Kate wrote Samuel Barrows in New York that Huson had "raised his hands in horror" at her official report "because I used the phrase 'you law makers' and my report read like a personal address to them. However, I can not be bound by conventionalities." This was Kate in her truest colors, personal and direct.[48]

Kate used her department's annual report to patiently explain her revolutionary theory of modern penology to the skeptical audience of Oklahoma legislators. "A jail should be simply a place of detention for accused persons who are unable to give bail," she wrote. Ideally, a speedy trial should follow, with either acquittal, probation, or sentence to "a State Reformatory, where they will be usefully employed, or the penitentiary." Without remedial efforts, Kate said, jails were merely "schools of crime." No matter how bad conditions were in territorial days, she assured the legislators, the state was poised for a new prison system.[49]

In actual fact, Commissioner Kate was not content to be the eyes and ears of the lawmakers, and she did not turn over the responsibilities to them. Sometimes she sought out city or county officials—a sheriff, mayor, county commissioner, or justice of the peace—and demanded an explanation, lodged a complaint, or issued a reprimand. In one city, she called a mass meeting of the citizens, reported conditions at the jail, and "secured a promise from the ministers of the city that they would hold Sunday services at this place." She wanted total community responsibility and involvement.[50]

If these methods did not bring results, Kate threatened to go to the press and to the public with her findings. Local officials retreated at that prospect, but Kate encountered anything but universal cooperation. However well-intended city or county officials might be, her improvements were costly, troublesome, and embarrassing to them. Kate wrote city jail officials in Tishomingo, Murray's home town, "Your jail is so tilted it's about to fall over." Moreover, "I was told while I was there that a man had been locked in a building with a hog. I am loath to believe this is true." How Murray must have burned to hear about her criticism of his town's jail. The mayor wrote back: "Will say in reply that if you take care of your own business, we will certainly take care of ours."[51]

When Kate took office, her primary concern was the state's orphans and needy children. By her estimate, 60 Oklahoma youth were in jails for misdemeanors, 60 more were in the Lansing Penitentiary in Kansas convicted of serious crimes, and 225 should have been placed in a state industrial school instead. "I appeal to the Spirit of father love in your hearts," Kate said to the legislators, "to give us a State Industrial School."[52]

National consultants such as prison authority Hastings H. Hart told her it would take at least three years to reform Oklahoma's institutions, but slow and patient was not Kate's style. "How I wish I could do everything by one stroke, but I have not only the prisoners, but the insane, the feeble minded, the epileptics, the blind, and the deaf to look after." When the magnitude of the job seemed to overwhelm her, Kate thought of herself with some sympathy and much fact as "one frail, little woman trying to be brave." She was not hearty, but she was more than brave—she was fearless. While she was confronting city and county jails one by one, she designed a plan to force state officials to take immediate action for penal reform. It would be sensational.[53]

CHAPTER SIX

The Avenging Angel

OKLAHOMA HAD NO PRISONS of its own because before statehood, the Twin Territories had contracted to confine prisoners in Kansas. Oklahoma Territory sent its prisoners to the Kansas State Penitentiary at Lansing, paying forty cents a day per inmate. Lansing was a complex of state industries and private businesses—a coal mine, a twine factory, a brickworks, and a furniture plant. The manpower of 1,300 convicts, about half of whom were from Oklahoma, made the penitentiary a lucrative concern. It was so profitable that in July 1908, Warden William H. Haskell (no relation to Oklahoma governor Charles N. Haskell) boasted that the Lansing prison's industrial income was a near-record surplus and in excess of $100,000.[1]

The touted profit made Kate suspicious. She had heard rumors of cruelty at Lansing, and former inmates had told her that the penitentiary was "a relic of the 'Dark Ages'" where prisoners were mistreated to the point of torture. She was particularly influenced by Ira N. Terrill, who had an ironic history with Lansing. As a member of Oklahoma's First Territorial Legislature, Terrill had voted for the Lansing prison contract. Then he killed a man in a homestead claim dispute, was convicted of murder, and found himself imprisoned there. When he was released in 1906, he devoted himself to giving illustrated lectures about Lansing prison brutalities.[2]

The First Oklahoma Legislature had appropriated $50,000 to return the prisoners to Oklahoma and prepare to build a state penitentiary, which would fall under Kate's jurisdiction of inspections. She was anxious to establish her authority in the state's penal system and to demonstrate her knowledge of prison management in order to lay the groundwork for her bigger goal, which was penal reform in Oklahoma. She did it with an exposé that excited great public attention.

Monday, August 17, 1908, Kate lined up with the crowd at the penitentiary in Lansing, paid the ten-cent admission fee, and joined a tour. After she had seen the prison's "show places," she presented her card to the warden and said she wanted to make a thorough investigation. The warden was aghast, as was the prison's Board of Directors, who happened to be meeting that day. They called her a spy and said she had no authority at a Kansas institution. "I am commissioned by a million and a half Oklahoma citizens to investigate this penitentiary," Kate said. "I shall do my duty here, unless I am forced from this institution."[3]

The prison authorities sputtered and fumed, but Kate was allowed to investigate. She spent several hours in the mines, where she saw broken roof supports threatening a cave-in and miners lying flat on their backs to work in a twenty-two-inch vein of coal. "I, myself, as small as I am, had to get down and crawl through many of these passages," she said.[4]

At the time of her inspection, 562 men and 13 women from Oklahoma were incarcerated in the Lansing prison. About 450 prisoners worked in the mines, most of whom had no previous mining experience. Even novice miners were punished when they failed to make their quota of three cars of coal a day. Kate learned that sixty boys from Oklahoma under the age of seventeen were imprisoned at Lansing, including a pale, slender seventeen-year-old she found shackled to the iron wall of a dungeon for failing to meet his quota of coal. In another dungeon, she discovered a sixteen-year-old boy who had been manacled to the wall for eight hours. She castigated the guard and went to the warden to protest.[5]

The guards tried to keep Kate from speaking to the Oklahoma prisoners, but in the mines, some incarcerated men managed to tell her about "revolting and unspeakable crimes" being committed there and about prison punishments. One miner stepped out of the darkness and whispered, "See the water hole, girl, for God's sake see the water hole." When she asked the warden about it, he denied the existence of anything known as a water hole. She did see the infamous crib used for punishment, fourteen dungeons with handcuffs on the walls, and the inadequate, often inedible, food served to prisoners. Miners were fed only "two pieces of Bologna sausage, three inches long," along with "plain bread and tomato and pea soup." She managed to speak for a few minutes with three of the

Oklahoma prisoners in the prison's office, but only after a "lengthy, stormy [personal] conversation" with the warden.[6]

Kate left Lansing to visit the federal penitentiary at Leavenworth, Kansas, where Indian Territory had sent 323 prisoners before statehood. She found it to be a model institution, worthy of its reputation as one of the best in the country.[7]

In September she gave Governor Haskell a written report of her Lansing inspection. He ignored it. In December she repeated her charges in her annual report for the Second Legislature, asserting that the Lansing punishments were brutal, inhumane, unnecessary, obsolete, and flagrant violations of the Kansas statutes. The governor was dragging his feet on building the new penitentiary, and dismissed her reports as exaggeration, and her as a sentimentalist. "Kate would like to see the prisoners kept in rooms and fed and treated as if they were guests at the Waldorf Astoria," he scoffed. State officials would not act on her request for an official investigation of conditions at Lansing, so in December Kate went directly to the newspapers and publicly released her charges. The Department of Charities and Corrections was becoming known as the "hell raising department."[8]

Her press releases ignited a public outcry. People bombarded her with letters urging her to rescue the Oklahoma convicts, and some state officials swung their support to her call for an investigation. Penal reform was a national interest, so news spread of Kate's Lansing charges. The national progressive publications *Charities and the Commons* and the *Survey* wrote about it. An author in California sent her a copy of his book about prison reform. In contrast, a hostile Kansas press attacked her and "roasted you to a finish," a Lansing inmate wrote to tell her. Kansas governor Edward W. Hoch went on the defense and demanded vindication, and Oklahoma governor Haskell was forced to reverse his position. The two governors agreed to appoint a joint committee and hold an investigative hearing at Lansing in January.[9]

Kate began a correspondence with William Allen White, the acclaimed newspaper editor in Emporia, Kansas, asking for his support. Her motives were pure, she told him, and she had a special affection for Kansas, where she had spent her childhood, and where "my mother has lain sleeping in the Kansas soil for twenty years." She explained that her five main objections were the prison's food, tasks, guards, mines, and punishments, which were in violation of Chapter 99, Article 30, Sections 7701 and 607 of the General Statues of Kansas of 1905. She also told him she knew that his newspaper, the *Emporia Gazette*, had called her a muckraker in a derogatory manner.[10]

White sent her an apology and confessed his "lamentable ignorance" of Kansas prisons. He apologized especially for the muckraking accusation in his newspaper. "I was in New York and I am ashamed of it. The man who wrote it knew nothing of my admiration for you and my faith in the justice of your cause. [That writer] was a drunkard until he came to this job." He followed her investigation closely, wrote about it, communicated about it with the Kansas governor-elect, and made a tour of the prison himself with his wife.[11]

Kate set about finding reliable witnesses willing to provide testimony or affidavits to substantiate her accusations. She found them, but it took considerable begging and cajoling to persuade some of them to testify. One of the strongest witnesses was Dr. Gid Breco, who had killed another doctor in a dispute and was convicted of manslaughter in the third degree. He served three months at Lansing before being pardoned. While incarcerated, he worked in the prison hospital and treated many victims of the crib and water cure punishments. He also kept a journal. Another effective witness was Dr. D. S. Ashby, brother of the golden-throated orator Stump Ashby, who had served seven years in Lansing for manslaughter and since his release had established himself as a physician in Amarillo, Texas. Kate also found Joe Runnels, an ex-policeman from Guthrie, who had been convicted of manslaughter and was out on parole; she persuaded Governor Haskell to pardon him so that he could testify without fear of repercussion. Runnels had been a "straw boss" in Lansing, a prisoner in charge of other prisoners, whom he tortured under orders.[12]

Early in January, armed with a stack of affidavits, Kate traveled to Lansing to appear before the joint committee. She was accompanied by six witnesses, whom the Kansas press labeled "Kate Barnard's band of murderers," as well as the five Oklahoma committee members appointed by Governor Haskell, Oklahoma attorney general Charles West, and Huson. The governor requested that Dr. J. H. Stolper from Krebs join the group as an expert witness on penal reform. Stolper was the physician/lawyer who had been with Haskell when they called on Kate after the Shawnee Convention and asked her to stump the state for the Democrats. Now he was back in her orbit and would stay there with both success and shame.

Although the Oklahoma governor and Stolper himself shared a lofty opinion of the doctor's credentials, the Kansas committee did not, and they refused to let him testify.[13]

Kate and the Oklahoma contingent stepped off the train into a climate of fear and anger. The Kansas air hissed with rumors about Kate: that she had a husband who was a convict; that her assistant, Huson, was an ex-convict; that she herself had been a prisoner at Lansing. As the Oklahoma group neared the prison, they heard inmates cheering Kate from the cell-block. The shouting was so loud that prison officials feared a mutiny and ordered a double force of armed guards to march four hundred inmates to their work in the mines. Arming the guards was a telling gesture; firearms were carried inside the prison walls only in cases of great emergency. The Lansing penitentiary was a tinderbox, and the nervous prison officials knew it: this was, indeed, a great emergency.[14]

The five-member committee appointed by the Kansas governor was joined by representatives from the Kansas State Penitentiary Board of Directors and Kansas state senator J. T. Reed, who acted as defense counsel for the prison warden. The Oklahoma attorney general served as prosecutor. The investigation was structured like a courtroom proceeding, with evidence presented and witnesses called to testify and be cross-examined, but the hearing did not proceed smoothly. It proved to be, Kate said, "quite spectacular and exciting at times." She provided much of the excitement herself.[15]

Kate was the only woman present at a hearing filled with men, some of them anxious, some resentful, some defensive. The room pulsed with male ego and anger. The focus, however, was on Kate, the little woman commissioner from Oklahoma, who was solidly confident of her authority and sure of her facts.

The Oklahomans began by questioning Warden Haskell and Deputy Warden Jim Dobson about the organization and operation of the prison. Personally, Kate felt amiable toward the warden, a man who seemed to be dedicated to public life, although it became clear during the hearing that he knew nothing about mining and almost nothing about prison management. The deputy warden was another story. He was a big man, at least two hundred pounds, with a reputation for brutality.[16]

The Oklahoma prosecutor asked about the prison's chain of command, discipline, and punishment. Then he focused on the prison mines. "Does sodomy occur in the mines?" he asked plainly. It did, the warden said, and if it was consensual, the men were "ringed." He explained the penalty: "They had rings put in the foreskin of their penis," a "humane" punishment that was "not painful particularly."[17]

"Did it ever occur to you that possibly such men were insane?" the Oklahoma prosecutor asked. "I don't think they were of high mentality," the warden replied, but "I don't think they were insane." Sodomy was against the law, and homosexuality was so taboo, it is not surprising that some ascribed it to a psychiatric disorder.[18]

In his turn on the stand, the deputy warden was also quizzed about "ringing." Wasn't it "just like putting a ring in a sow's nose," the Oklahoma interrogator asked, "and don't all men find it debasing?" "Some of them have gotten so far down the scale they don't care anything about the debasement," was the reply. The deputy warden explained that ringing was also done to stop masturbation, and so was circumcision. "We have seen a good many boys that were very near degenerates" from "a bad case of masturbation," the prison official said, but ringing or circumcising "would stop that, and they would grow up and be pretty good boys." This line of questioning was not designed to shock; it reflected Kate's genuine concern for Oklahoma's young prisoners, who were being forced into mines where they might be victimized.[19]

The Kansas prison officials were asked about the danger of sending a young boy (seventeen, eighteen, or nineteen years old) into the mines to work with stronger men. Yes, they agreed, sodomy was a possibility, but "sometimes you need them in the mines." Besides, the only Lansing prisoners between the ages of sixteen and twenty-one were from Oklahoma. Kansas laws prohibited the courts from placing young Kansas citizens in prison, and the warden refused to accept any prisoners from Oklahoma under the age of sixteen. "I don't think a boy of 18 should ever be sent to the penitentiary," he said, "but as long as you send a lot of children here, what are you going to do with them?" His testimony unwittingly supported Kate's own case for the need for a reformatory and industrial school in Oklahoma.[20]

———∞———

The heart of Kate's charges was that the prison's punishments were not only excessive, they were "cruel and unusual," inhumane treatment prohibited by the U.S. Constitution. Kansas senator Reed challenged her report, and Kate sprang to her feet outraged, saying that her veracity had never been doubted before. "Please don't make a stump speech here," the senator said. Kate slammed a stack of papers on the table and said, "Here is my evidence—twenty-three affidavits. Is that enough?"[21]

What the Oklahoma committee saw as bordering on torture, the Kansas authorities portrayed as customary correction. The warden said the crib was used primarily on prisoners who were "insane" or "quarrelsome." The water cure—waterboarding in today's terminology—was "the best punishment that has ever been devised," the deputy warden testified. "[It] is quick and short and the fellow dreads it. . . . Turn the water on him [for a few minutes] and that wilts him at once. He wilts and says he will be good. It might take days in a blind cell until his system was all deranged." The Oklahoma prosecutor asked, "Don't you know that the object of the water cure is to produce the effect of drowning on the man?" The deputy warden disagreed. The object, he said, was "to make the man behave himself." Kate asked about the force of the water: "How far could you throw that stream of water?" "Fifty or sixty feet," was the answer. "How near were you to the men's faces?" she asked. "From six inches to six feet," was the reply.[22]

Kate's affidavits of brutal treatment were read into evidence. One man's statement described being in the crib for twenty-four hours, lying on his stomach with his hands shackled together, his feet shackled together, and his hands and feet then drawn together behind him until his body was bowed backward like a crescent moon. "I was insensible when removed. I was taken to the hospital and it was two days before I could walk." One of the most damning affidavits was from Dr. Gid Breco, who had not been punished himself but had witnessed the crib and the water cure, and he had treated the prisoners after those punishments. Some men, he said, were left with permanent physical damage. Some died from the punishments.[23]

Ira N. Terrill, the former prisoner who now gave illustrated lectures about brutality at the Lansing prison, signed an affidavit of his eyewitness accounts of sadistic punishments. He had seen a prisoner, "Antonio Brown by name," knocked into a tub of scalding water, where he was burned so severely that "the skin and flesh fell off his body, and Brown died from the scalding." Terrill's affidavit said that he had "personally complained of the beating, maiming and murdering of prisoners" to Oklahoma territorial governor Frank Frantz, Oklahoma governor Haskell, Kansas governor

Hoch, and the Kansas legislators, and to the people at large in both states in public addresses in various cities. It was Kate who finally listened to him, and it was largely because of his complaints and her inspection that the hearing was taking place.[24]

The affidavits were powerful testimonies, and to reinforce them, Kate stood in person before the committee relating what she had seen and heard during her inspection of Lansing. The Kansans attempted to portray her as gullible and idealistic. They tried to discredit her credentials and her witnesses. At first, she was patient but persistent. She said that as commissioner she had visited prisons in Atlanta, Georgia; Richmond, Virginia; and Little Rock, Arkansas. She was quizzed about her experience or special study of prison work, and she was asked sarcastically to explain her theory of penal reform, "so that the state of Kansas and officials of this institution may have the benefit of your knowledge."[25]

Kate was angry by this point, but she responded by reading a prepared statement, "Exhibit O," a document entitled "Oklahoma Penal System: Some Suggestions as to an Ideal Penal System," with recommendations for a tax-supported penal system and guidelines for prison administration, courts, a penal code, a classification of offenses, indeterminate sentencing, and probation. She cited some of the nationally known professionals she had consulted, predominantly Samuel J. Barrows, as well as the best penitentiaries and the best wardens in the United States, and told them what she had learned about the difference between a bad prison and a good prison. A bad prison, she said, was one whose main purpose was punishment: "The chief aim is to break the spirit, to degrade, to extinguish every spark of manhood in the prisoner. Men go out of such a prison worse than when they entered." Conversely, "a good prison" was one that "strives to reform and upbuild the character of the prisoner, to the end that he can reenter society . . . a better man physically, mentally and morally," with only a small chance of relapsing into crime.[26]

The Kansas officials listened to Kate's theories of modern penology with little interest and much impatience. Their questions and her answers quickened with speed and temper. Emotions in the room built and then crested.[27]

"Is your private secretary an ex-convict?" a Kansan asked her.

"The gentleman probably has a better education than you have and seen more and he isn't an ex-convict," Kate replied.

Huson was sworn in to refute the rumors. "Have you ever been charged with a crime? Ever [been] convicted of any crime in any court?" he was asked.

"Never," Huson lied. Perhaps he remembered his youthful grand jury indictment as a legal charge but not a conviction. Besides, who present was to know about that unpleasant affair in Rochester so many years before?[28]

Kate left the stand exhausted and sat resting her forehead on her hand as subsequent testimony continued to give accounts of prisoners stripped and beaten until they were senseless, and of degradations so foul they were omitted from the record.

Then Kate's witnesses took the stand. Dr. Ashby testified about the punishments he had both received and seen. He was a colorful witness, and it became clear that he had been a colorful prisoner. Ashby showed the scars from his prison punishment and told about other injuries he had suffered while incarcerated at Lansing: he had lost two fingers in an accident at the twine factory and had a crippling leg injury from an accident while working in the pump house. The doctor was as rebellious on the stand as he had been in the prison. "During your imprisonment wasn't you constantly in trouble with different prisoners and the officers and doctor and everybody else?" the Kansas interrogator asked. "Do you remember of calling one of the cell house men a dirty, cowardly bastard?" And hadn't he "written obscene language on the library books?" Ashby replied that it was his own book and it was a joke: "When I am dead bury me face down, so these Kansas screws can bury me without kissing my face." It is likely he did not say "bury" twice, but used another word too obscene to print at the time.[29]

The star witness was Joe Runnels, the former Guthrie policeman who had served five years of a twenty-five-year sentence for manslaughter, and was out on parole. He had been responsible for the care and punishment of Lansing's "crazy and incorrigible." Kate had been reluctant to introduce him as a witness because he was "such a willing monster" she was afraid his testimony might backfire, but she took the chance and he took the stand. He described administering punishments—the crib, beating with a short hose, the water cure—until "they have begged to be shot."[30]

The highlight of the hearing was when Kate had handcuffs, chains, mitts, muffs, and a hose used for whipping brought into the room, and Ashby volunteered to illustrate the "irons" punishment. He lay face down on a table as Runnels fastened his feet and hands together with steel shackles and drew them together behind the doctor's back. "Within a minute of this torture," Kate said, "the veins filled and stood out dark blue on Dr. Ashby's face, while every muscle of his arms and legs seemed ready to snap. A great silence fell in the room." Even the prison officials looked appalled and conscience stricken. And then the chairman of the prison's Board of Control laughed. Kate whirled on him and said, "Sir, you are a disgrace to civilization." He replied with such a "disrespectful, brutal answer" that both sides of the committee erupted. It was almost, Kate reported, "a physical war." With men on their feet shouting and on the verge of fisticuffs, thus ended the second day of the hearing.[31]

The next day, the proceedings concluded quietly and without flourish. The Oklahomans were humiliated that they had sent inmates to be subjected to such treatment, and the Kansans were ashamed that such cruelty had taken place under their oblivious noses. Nobody, not even Kate, was jubilant in victory.

The Oklahoma committee returned home and submitted an official report on "the gravest indictment against the prison," dominated by the goal of making money, which led to barbarous punishments. The Lansing penitentiary stood as a "warning never to allow a political board to be in control of its prisons [or] its warden." The committee to a man declared that "Miss Barnard was correct in substance and in effect in all of her charges." The Kansas committee recommended an entire reformation of the prison, with all forms of punishment to be abolished. Lansing prison officials from the warden on down either resigned or were removed from their positions. Most Kansas newspaper accounts of the Lansing investigation were less than laudatory, and one said the affair was a tempest in a teapot. However, William Allen White wrote in the *Emporia Gazette*, "The substance of the report on the penitentiary is to the effect that the warden hasn't done anything to be ashamed of, but he shouldn't do it again." The editor wrote Kate that he intended to continue to pursue the subject of the Kansas penitentiary because "I am in no way persuaded that the truth has been found." What is more, "I shall make it my business in so far as I can to see that the recommendations are carried out." He added,

After Kate's inspections of Kansas penitentiaries and Oklahoma's state
institutions, she was called the "Good Angel" of Oklahoma; but her Department
of Charities and Corrections became known as the "hell-raising department."
Photograph from the author's collection.

"I may call upon you from time to time for help," although he did not want his intentions publicized. Kate printed the transcription of the entire hearing, complete with affidavits and testimony, in her department's second annual report. It comprised 101 pages of seven-point type.[32]

Mere days after the hearing, starting January 15, 1909, Oklahoma began taking its prisoners out of Lansing. They rode on a special chartered train of seven coaches, described in the press as "the biggest train load of 'bad men' ever hauled at one time in the history of the United States." They were removed during a winter blizzard rather than stay one single day more in Lansing. Oklahoma's contract with Kansas prisons expired January 31 and was not renewed. The state's Second Legislature passed a bill prohibiting the use of convicts as contract labor, and it is still law in Oklahoma.[33]

Kate had gone to Lansing with a mission, and she had accomplished it. The sensational prison exposé and the resulting publicity influenced the state legislators and the public toward prison reform. She hurried home with an ambitious agenda. The Second Legislature was in session. Kate had urgent business with the lawmakers and new institutions to build.

CHAPTER SEVEN

Bearing Witness

"I HAVE BEEN WORKING on a very interesting human document," Kate wrote a colleague, "namely my *Second Annual Report* to the Governor and Legislature. I believe it will be a great eye-opener." In addition to the inspections, Kate was constitutionally mandated to write an annual "full and complete report of the operations and administration" of her office, and "such suggestions as said Commissioner may deem suitable and pertinent."[1]

Kate considered this more of an opportunity than a cursory task. She was determined to make her annual reports unique documents that would be "a revelation of what can be done in a short time toward scientific and kindly treatment of the deaf, mute, blind, insane, the prisoners, and the orphan children of the state." She reported what she was doing, why she was doing it, and what yet needed to be done, which meant passing laws and providing funding. Kate's annual reports did much more than capture her yearly inspections of state institutions. They are colorful narratives interspersed with tables of data. She laced together statistics and numbers with human details and first-person observations. She added philosophy for good measure. Each year she put a copy of her remarkable report on the desk of every member of the Oklahoma State Senate and House of Representatives.[2]

Kate was the only state officer so mandated. No printed report was constitutionally required from the commissioner of labor, the insurance commissioner, the chief mine inspector, or the Board of Agriculture. The state examiner and inspector was required to publish an annual report of state and county treasurers' books and accounts, and the commissioner of the

Land Office had to issue semiannual reports on the moneys and actions of school land and public land transactions, but neither of those officials produced work that had the flavor or fullness of Kate's annual reports. She took to heart the dictate "full and complete," and she exercised to the extreme the directive to make suggestions. In Kate's interpretation, the word "suggestions" meant the one and true way, which was her way. In her mind, it was the enlightened way.[3]

Kate's annual reports were as unique as her personality. They describe her inspections and capture her passion for her work, and they stand as eyewitness accounts of the young state emerging from the frontier. History was being made on the ground, and Kate and her small staff were social anthropologists in the field. The reports are, indeed, interesting human documents. Her first annual report, submitted in 1908, was the shortest, at under one hundred pages, but then, as she noted with considerable pique, it covered only six months' work because the legislature had delayed her appropriation. After that, they grew longer and more detailed, until by 1912 her fourth report was more than four hundred pages long, about the size of Edgar Rice Burroughs's popular novel *Tarzan of the Apes*, which was published that same year.

───────⚭───────

She gave the lawmakers an unfiltered look at the raw young state and its most helpless citizenry. She was sure that if they saw what she saw, they would believe in reform as she did, not only because it was the right thing to do, but because it was the most practical. "The present-day [penal] systems of America are a curse to the nation," she wrote. "Crime is the heaviest burden the tax payers, the State and the Nation have to bear. It cost our Nation five billion dollars last year." She could not resist the opportunity to add drama: "And it leaves a trail of ruined homes, wrecked lives, lost souls and bleaching skeletons wherever it lays its bloody fingers. . . . The jails of Oklahoma should be a matter of grave concern to all thinking Oklahomans."[4]

She assured the struggling institutions that depended on her of her efforts to help them. "I am working all over the state to get a statewide political organization which will stand for more liberality toward the charitable institutions of this state," she wrote ever hopefully to the superintendent of the School for the Blind, "and I think in the next Legislature I will be in a position to get better appropriations for the work you and I represent." Often her optimism was unrewarded.[5]

Kate was so verbal, she probably would have written detailed reports of her work whether or not it was required. With her eyes on her mission, she wrote her yearly reports with fact and for impact, reprinting laws that had been passed that were pertinent to her department, and reminding the legislators that these were the law of the land and that she was authorized to enforce them. She included drafts of bills she hoped would become law, such as for a court of rehabilitation and for a comprehensive approach to the care and treatment of the insane, both to direct the lawmakers' attention to her goals and to nudge them out of hidebound notions. It was an "old idea that insane people are possessed of devils," she wrote. In print and for the record, Kate was shepherding the legislators toward the high ground, and she used every resource she could. When author Theodore Dreiser asked her who might be interested in his pamphlet about antiquated orphan homes, *Where 100,000 Children Wait*, she replied, "I am going to overwhelm you," and sent him the names of all of Oklahoma's legislators.[6]

She reminded them that creating a new state department like hers was not easy, and that it was unique: "no other state has a department exactly similar in scope and work." She was doing innovative work and explaining it as she went in reports that were sometimes lecturing, and often impassioned. Her reports were her pulpit, and in them she sermonized her reform crusade to the audience of elected governmental officials. Just as a preacher has favorite scriptures, her chosen issues were prisons, mental hospitals, and orphanages, and she hammered these home with numbers and theories. She praised the lawmakers for what they had done, and in the next sentence pushed them to do even more.[7]

She reported the conditions of city and county jails in detail, not only as a moral issue for "all thinking Oklahomans," but as a heavy burden on taxpayers. "We who study these questions of crime come to a terrible realization—namely; that many prisons are so bad that society sins worse in committing a man to one of them, than the man who has sinned against society." With patience that did not come naturally to her, she explained that the causes of criminal behavior were disease, physical degeneracy, weak will, poor family training, lack of education, neglect, poverty, and a bad environment. From the time she took office, Kate said that she would take as her standards "two of the best prisons in America . . . west of the Mississippi," the Minnesota State Prison at Stillwater and the U.S. Penitentiary at Leavenworth, Kansas, because "the aim of both of these institutions is to make better men of their convicts" through "the idea of character building, not revenge."[8]

She liked demographic information, so the section on the new state prison at McAlester in her 1912 *Fourth Report* identified inmates by county of origin, term of imprisonment, crime committed, nativity, age, occupation, and religion. With respect to occupation, most were classified as farmers (518), and many were common laborers (244), although there were also an upholsterer, an undertaker, a mail carrier, an oil driller, and a capitalist. The majority had been born in Texas (303), Oklahoma (299), Arkansas (119), and Missouri (101). A handful were from foreign soil, including one from as far away as Newfoundland.[9]

The State Training School one year enumerated its thirty-nine boys by "age of boys when committed," "counties received from," "state born in," "nationality of parents," and "offense committed." Thirty of the thirty-nine had been arrested more than once; fifteen had no father living and thirteen had no mother living; twenty had no religion; twenty-four had used cigarettes before commitment.[10]

Her penal institution reports listed the use of tobacco smoked, chewed, or both, not out of prim disapproval, but because it was a violation of the Anti-Cigarette Law passed by the First Legislature. Selling or giving away cigarettes and cigarette papers or bringing them into the state for any purpose was a misdemeanor. It was a law on the books but not enforced, and Kate noted that "men and boys seem to purchase cigarette paper without hindrance." Of the 5,711 prisoners in county jails in 1908, 4,013 were listed as addicted to tobacco. Neither, she observed dryly, were there any arrests or convictions for selling cocaine, opium, and other drugs: "No effort [is] made to prosecute the Druggists for selling the dope." The new state had good intentions and high standards, but it passed more laws than it could enforce.[11]

———— ∞ ————

Kate explained that modernizing the state's mental hospitals was an agonizingly slow process because it had started from such a low point and had so much ground to make up. Caring for mental patients in the state and at state expense was a foreign concept to the lawmakers. The last territorial legislature before statehood had adopted an appropriation bill in which it was declared that "imbeciles and idiots" were not to be kept at territorial expense but were to be paid for by the counties that sent them to the hospital. After statehood, patient numbers swelled when a large number from Indian Territory were brought back from St. Louis and institutionalized at the state hospital in Norman. Considerable expense lay ahead, Kate warned grumbling taxpayers and legislators.[12]

Another problem contributing to the growing number of patients in Oklahoma's mental hospitals, she wrote, was the state's lax admission requirements. The Fort Supply hospital superintendent strongly recommended that this be remedied with a new law establishing a period of legal residence for individuals before they could be admitted to the hospital. "In several instances," he said, newcomers to Oklahoma had been "going back to their home states and getting insane relatives, and bringing them here and committing them to our hospitals the next day after they have arrived."[13]

Some years she detailed the demographics by category at the Hospital for the Insane at Norman. In 1910, the 1,105 patients were identified by race (white or "colored"), age, nativity, occupation, and form of disease. The forms of disease as classified by the hospital superintendent were mostly variations of melancholia. Occupations included 129 farmers, 127 housewives, 97 laborers, 11 blacksmiths, 8 teachers, 5 merchants, 2 each realtors, soldiers, painters, and printers, and 1 each cook, jeweler, nurse, telephone operator, and newspaper reporter. Presumably this indicated that mental illness was no respecter of occupation or status. Or it was merely curious information.[14]

Always, always in her annual reports, Kate championed children, "the State's most valuable asset." As a candidate, she worked for child labor laws and compulsory education. As commissioner, she advocated for juvenile court laws, training schools for delinquent youth, and institutions for children with special needs. "The Problem of the Child," she wrote in her first report, "is a Social Problem, . . . a Financial Problem, . . . [and] a National Problem, because the Nation exists only for the present and future child." The state's immediate problem was "the wayward child," "the feeble-minded child," "the blind, deaf or mute child," and "the child of the poor." Her heart went out most tenderly to the poor children. "What shall we do with the Child of Poverty to enable it in the world's great struggle, to have a fighting chance?" she asked repeatedly.[15]

Kate's era was unhampered by confidentiality, and her reports included personal details about people in state institutions that are informative but shocking to contemporary eyes. She printed the State Orphan Home's listing of each orphan by name, age, and analysis of mental and physical well-being:

> Albertson, Edna—Female; age 14; fifth grade; digestion and assimilation good, strong and robust; fair intellect; obedient and reasonably industrious.
>
> Bristow, Fardly [one of three Bristow siblings in the orphanage]— Died Sept. 17th of tuberculosis of the bowels.
>
> Dunkerson, Willie—Male; 10 years of age; first grade; impoverished condition of blood; poorly developed; mind a little below the average; easily managed; no serious illness, but never thoroughly well.
>
> Silversmith, Pearl—Female; 5 years old; seems to be brighter than any of the Silversmith children [six Silversmith siblings were in the home]; excellent health.
>
> Welch, Nancy—Female; 15 years of age; Cherokee; first grade; mind slow and plodding; exceedingly neat in person; careful and faithful in performance of duties; strong and robust; obedient to the slavish point.[16]

Kate delivered unvarnished truths in her annual reports. Her department discovered that orphanages and foundling institutions received children and infants without having them examined for infections or "contagious trouble" and reused clothing without disinfecting it, resulting in an outbreak of measles from the contaminated clothing.[17]

In her reports, Kate tried to assess the scope of the state's present and future needs. The School for the Blind at Fort Gibson in Muskogee County might be able to secure additional housing for a total of seventy-five pupils, she reported in 1908, which was woefully short of the need. "Facilities should be provided for a school [of the blind] population of at least 400," she wrote. Two years later, she offered calming news about the advances in medical care: only "25 per cent of all the blind children in all the blind schools of this country are unnecessarily blind," she reported, because of a discovery made twenty-eight years earlier, that using a 2 percent solution of silver nitrate in a newborn infant's eyes prevented ophthalmia neonatorum (conjunctivitis of the newborn). The advancement she predicted was slow in coming, and in 1912 she reported that "eye troubles," meaning eye disease and blindness, were the primary physical problem of students at the Murrow Indian Orphans' Home in Bacone. Her mail also brought pleas from parents asking for help with their "crippled children." The scope of the need was unknown. "There are no statistics to tell how many crippled children there are in the state," she reported in 1908. And no facilities existed to help them.[18]

Kate gathered whatever numbers she could collect to predict what services would be needed for the growing state population. Oklahoma's population of 1,414,177 in 1907 grew to 1,657,144 by 1910, more than double that of 1900 and an increase of 540 percent since 1890. And it was still growing. It was impossible to project precise future needs. "There are practically no statistics as to the number of Orphans and dependent children in the State," she wrote in 1908, but from very incomplete information she calculated that about 942 were either in institutions or with families awaiting placement or adoption. She was deluged with letters from "poor broken down widows" frantic to find homes for children they could not care for, and from families wanting "girls large enough to 'act as nurse girls, or to help in the kitchen.'" These were poor people in "a desperate struggle to make a living," with too many mouths to feed and not enough hands for the work of basic subsistence. As for the state's penitentiary needs, Kate anticipated that Oklahoma's population would reach 2,000,000 in the near future, and therefore "we must arrange to handle and care for 1,600 convicts." Mental institutions could anticipate that one thousand out of every one million persons would be afflicted with nervous and mental diseases, and with Oklahoma's rapid growth, these statistics supported the need for more hospital facilities.[19]

Lest her readers despair at the overwhelming need that lay ahead, she offered consolation where she found it. Eight counties had poor farms or poorhouses in 1908, but "when Oklahoma establishes all of the institutions deemed necessary by the most progressive states, poor houses and poor farms will not be needed" because "the imbeciles, idiots and feeble-minded will be cared for in schools for feeble-minded. The aged will be taken care of in an institution established for that purpose. The children will be placed in the orphan homes, and cripples will have a state colony." The language is harsh to contemporary ears, but the state's heart was caring. Specialized institutions would be far better than poor farms, where the helpless were thrown all together.[20]

Kate wrote most of the early reports herself in language that mirrored her public speeches and often pulsed with the passion she was feeling. Huson urged her to adopt a more professional style, but she would not move away from her direct and personal narratives. Her annual reports harangued, lectured, and explained what a jail or a mental hospital should do and be while they revealed the state's primitive policies and conditions. She printed Norman superintendent Griffin's infuriated description of how mentally ill patients were committed to the hospital. It was wrong, he said, that officers "were taking from the sick bed a mentally sick man or woman, in many instances taking them to the county jail, throwing them in among some of our worst criminals . . . , there to lie unnoticed, uncared for, and . . . unfed, . . . then to be taken into open court to face a jury as a criminal while hundreds of the curious gaze on." He believed that "in every county there should be a [three-person] committee, composed of a physician, lawyer and layman, and when a case of insanity should be reported to this community they should go quietly to this home, there make their examination, and if the person is found to be a fit subject for one of our institutions, then take him directly from his home to the institution." As patients were conveyed to the hospital, they often were brutally treated by officials. "Imagine, if you please," Kate wrote in 1912, "an officer who is generally an able-bodied man, putting irons, handcuffs and the like upon a little emaciated woman in the neighborhood of 60 years of age, who is scarcely able to walk, and strapping a gun upon himself, boldly (?) setting out to convey this sick woman to a hospital! She needs the attention of a nurse and a doctor, not an officer. . . . There are many such cases." She repeated that insane persons were not criminals, but in order to be committed to the hospital, they were arrested on the charge of insanity and judged by a commission of men who knew little or nothing about mental disorders. What the state needed to do was repeal the old insanity laws inherited from Arkansas and Kansas and adopt new legislation.[21]

Kate reported any positive development as a cause for delight, such as a new training school for nurses at the state mental hospital in Norman with the advanced concept of including female nurses. Superintendent Griffin said that women attendants in male wards were a calming influence. "The patients . . . are quieter and more contented. . . . Especially when physically sick do the men appreciate the presence of a woman nurse. Even disturbed cases of maniac depressive insanity show the softening influence of women nurses." This experiment crashed disappointingly a year later when the nurse training school had to close because of a new state requirement that nurses have a high school diploma. Progress seemed to be a dance instead of a forward march. As Kate explained, "Oklahoma is a new state, and all of its institutions are in their infancy."[22]

Many of the institutions' crises echoed the needs of the state itself. Water was always a primary need. Kate recorded the struggles of hospitals, jails, and orphanages to get a source of clean water to drink and enough water for cleaning, and she wrote of their struggle for an operational sewage system. She found and reported improvement, scattered and seldom as it might be. The least note of progress was cause for celebration. In a state where passable roads were not commonplace, Kate delighted in the penitentiary warden's report in 1909 that convict road crews had been able to build nine and a half miles of wagon road. The work was "practically completed to the extent of making a first class country road."[23]

As her department grew slightly, other staff voices joined hers in the reports: Stolper, with his legal terminology, Latin phrases, and self-praise; Huson, who provided steady, factual accounts; and eventually a young doctor, R. C. Meloy, who inspected jails and hospitals and wrote concise reports with matter-of-fact numbers, although he could be evangelic, too, with informative discourses about nutrition. He wanted the prisoners in city and county jails to have a diet containing "carbonaceous and nitrogenous articles . . . necessary to maintain the average adult in a healthy and normal condition," but he "regret[ted] to say that authorities take very slight, if any, interest in anything looking towards the betterment of conditions for the prisoners." He wanted the authorities "to furnish prisoners three [meals] a day with wholesome food and in sufficient quantities" as required by law, instead of only one meal a day as some did.[24]

Kate's annual reports summarized and they detailed, including the transcripts of her Lansing prison investigation and testimonies from Indian orphan estate cases her department litigated. She wrote departmental reports, public speeches, magazine articles, and press releases to inform, to persuade, and to guide her state to progressive reform. Above all, she bore witness.

CHAPTER EIGHT

A Force to Be Feared

WHILE KATE WAS IN LANSING, Oklahoma opened its second legislative session on January 5, 1909, committed to "moral reform," and set to work as busy as a hive of bees. The lawmakers would convene for only three months, so Kate hurried home to get some of her own bills passed and support several others. All the while, her fight with the mental hospitals was roiling, and she continued her investigation of other state facilities. "I am making desperate efforts to get better conditions for our insane and our orphan children," she told an Oklahoma newspaper, "but these filthy jails keep me employed until I am worn out, both body, mind, and soul."[1]

Weary or not, she was becoming the state's best-known citizen. She gave speeches to national audiences, she wrote articles for national publications, and she collected admirers with every activity. As *American Magazine* prepared to print a glowing article about her, the famous investigative journalist Ida Tarbell wrote Kate that her story was a "stimulating tale of achievement." The trailblazing journalist went on, "I hope someday to have the pleasure of meeting you and talking over Oklahoma with you." This was high praise from the fearless reformer who had taken on Rockefeller and Standard Oil in her 1904 exposé about business monopolies. It was Tarbell's articles that inspired President Theodore Roosevelt to coin the phrase "muckraker" in reference to her, Upton Sinclair, Lincoln Steffens, and other critical journalists.[2]

Kate was "justly called the 'Joan of Arc of Oklahoma,'" reformer and author Warren K. Moorehead wrote. "Of slight figure—even frail—she is possessed of lion's courage and is a most direct, forceful, and dramatic speaker." Nobody from Oklahoma was quoted in the national press more than Kate. She read her press clippings for what they were—hyperbole. "Many of the newspaper and magazine articles about me are very highly colored and overdrawn," she said. She valued them because they called attention to her work, which to her was "such a serious thing."[3]

Kate could have made a career as a public speaker. She was offered contracts to become a professional speaker for both the Chautauqua circuit and the Lyceum Bureau, two enormously popular public education and lecture series. She declined. Her personal modesty attracted as much praise as did her passion for her work. The press often commented on her reserved attire, saying she dressed more plainly than the clerks in the statehouse. A reporter asked her why she never wore jewelry, and her answer became fable: "How can a woman wear diamonds in a country where little children starve?"[4]

Her celebrity did not ensure her legislative success. Even as her star ascended outside the state, at home she was gathering detractors and outright enemies with her scalding criticisms of state institutions, her strident pressure for reform, her demands for additional funding, and her confrontational take-no-prisoners style. Yes, the state had voted for progressive reform, but it was turning out to be troublesome and expensive. As the most popular politician in the state, Kate could hold the growling opposition at bay as she plunged into the second legislative session, but it clamored at the gate.

She focused her legislative agenda and her energy on "correcting our vile prison system" with groundwork laid by the Lansing investigation. "The fact that people cannot understand the difference between a reform institution and a correction institution causes me no end of trouble," she wrote a constituent. "It is a perfect nightmare." She wanted a new state penal system with three kinds of institutions: a penitentiary, a reformatory, and a correctional school with youthful inmates divided by age and convictions.[5]

Her immediate goal was the passage of a juvenile court bill, one of the first bills to be considered by the Second Legislature. The juvenile court was a hallmark of the Age of Reform. Child welfare reformer Hastings H. Hart and jurist Harvey B. Hurd founded the juvenile court in 1899 in Chicago, stressing reform over punishment. Kate had first learned about this concept in St. Louis at the World's Fair, where she became acquainted with the work of Denver's Judge Ben B. Lindsey, popularly known as "the father of the juvenile court," who established the first juvenile court in

Kate made frequent trips to New York and elsewhere for speaking tours and
research visits to mental hospitals and penitentiaries.
Photograph courtesy George Grantham Bain News Service photograph
collection, Library of Congress, Prints and Photographs Division.

Colorado in 1903. The concept, radical at the time, designated offenders
under the age of sixteen as delinquent instead of labeling them as criminals and sentenced them to probation with a suspended sentence. If the
youths complied successfully with the court-imposed conditions, they
were not charged with a crime. This approach called for a substantial
change in mindset and a moral awakening, asking the states to handle
youthful offenders with care and intelligence instead of punishment and
revenge. Kate embraced this caring approach and did not hesitate to contact the personable Judge Lindsey for help. He, in turn, did not hesitate to
respond. He was a small, balding man, rather elfish in appearance, with a
big moustache and bright eyes. The two formed a close relationship that
lasted the rest of Kate's life.[6]

This was the second time at bat for Kate's juvenile court bill. During the First Legislature in 1907, she had persuaded Lindsey to draft a juvenile court bill and secured funding from the Russell Sage Foundation to pay his expenses to travel to Oklahoma to champion it. His fervor matched her own as he addressed the legislators. "Oklahoma has placed before the world the greatest constitution of the age," he said, "and now she has the opportunity to draw up and put into operation the best juvenile court law." To Kate's sorrow, the bill died on the last day of the legislative session as the calendar ran out. She vowed not to let that happen again.[7]

She set up a plan of action as detailed as a general's battlefield strategy to guide the juvenile court bill through the legislature. She began by enlisting her old friend Roy Stafford, newspaper editor and now a state senator, to introduce it. She offered Stafford her help, her advice, and the considerable data she had gathered.[8]

"Esteemed Friend," she wrote him, using an address she favored. "My whole heart and soul is set on the passage of your bill. Depend on me to get you all kinds of help from the outside to bring the House in line." Stafford accepted both her opinion, which he considered valuable, and her aid. "Dear Kate," he replied. "Command me whenever I can be of service to you."[9]

Stafford introduced the juvenile court bill January 12, while Kate marshaled an enormous letter-writing campaign to support it. In February, when the bill came up for consideration, she made a speaking tour to the state's five normal schools (teacher colleges) and two universities, urging hundreds of students to write three letters each—one to their father, one to their state representative, and one to their state senator—supporting its passage. The letter to the fathers asked them to also write a senator and a representative. Every letter her office received about juvenile delinquents received her standard reply: "Tell your senator. Tell your representative." Soon the legislators were drowning in mail. "Miss Kate, what do you want?" one senator finally beseeched her. "I'll vote for anything you want, but for God's sake stop this flood of letters. I got 500 in Monday's mail." By March, the juvenile court bill and Kate's mail campaign were rushing toward the finish line. "See the members of the Senate and have them ready to vote for it on Friday," Kate directed Stafford. "I am going to land most of the letters in the House and I hope your bill will be there at the time these letters arrive."[10]

Kate followed the drama of the bill's tortured trek from her sickroom, where she was recuperating from what she described as nervous prostration, but in the final days of the legislative session, the bill was in such troubled waters that she had to get out of bed and rescue it from almost hourly peril. Once, the bill got caught in a conflict between Stafford and the Speaker of the House. Four days before adjournment, it still had not passed the Senate and reached the House. Then Kate learned of a freeze plan: no new bills, including hers, would be considered in either house after March 8. The day of the deadline, she contacted Stafford to warn him of this and urged him to haste. While he went into action, Kate begged Senator H. S. Blair, the father of her departmental stenographer, Estelle, to get the bill before the Senate. He succeeded, and it was then referred to the House Judiciary Committee.[11]

Two days before adjournment, the bill still had not been reported out of committee. Kate went before the committee and pleaded with them. About noon the day before adjournment, she got a tip that the actual physical copy of the bill had gone astray. She went in search of it and found it with the Committee on Municipal Corporations, of all places. In one hour, Kate talked personally with more than half the members of the House, asking them to use their influence with the committee chairman. At last, the House Judiciary Committee reported the bill favorably at 5 P.M. the day of adjournment. Kate then got to the steering committee and asked for a special order to be called at 7 P.M. Another effort to sidetrack the bill sprang out of the bushes—an amendment to change the age limit for criminal prosecution—and Kate fended off this ambush by securing pledges of support from seventy-five House members.[12]

At 7:30 P.M. the bill finally passed the House, but with two amendments, which meant another conference committee at 8:20 P.M. Kate "flew to the House and back to the Senate" and arranged for the conference committee to report the amended bill as soon as it was passed by the House. At 8:45 P.M., the bill passed the House. Luckily, Kate had friends among the clerks in the engrossing room, and she got a final copy of the bill printed by 10:30 P.M. and sent it to the Senate. The lessons she had learned as a clerk at the Territorial Legislature about one-on-one lobbying and cultivating staff friendships served her well. The Senate approved it at 11:55 P.M., five minutes before adjournment. Governor Haskell grudgingly signed the bill on March 24. He had lukewarm enthusiasm for juvenile courts, but he needed the support of

Stafford's newspaper. Whether accidental or deliberate, the bill's labyrin-
thian journey was not unusual. A book of legislative shenanigans, said former Oklahoma Senate President pro tempore Rodger Randle, would be as
thick as a Sears catalog. "The Kansas City papers dubbed me 'The Little
Dynamo' for [my] work on the last day of the Legislative session for
juvenile law," Kate wrote in a letter. The effort took its toll. "I am confined
to my bed as a result of overwork on the bills," she wrote Stafford. It was
worth the effort to her. "Juvenile Court is the most important [aspect] of a
child's education next to that of a good parent," she wrote a constituent.
Kate was not entirely satisfied with the bill because it had been so heavily
amended; still, she wrote Judge Lindsey, it was better than no bill at all.[13]

The law went into effect June 11, 1909. "The effort left me prostrate,"
Kate wrote prison reform colleague Samuel Barrows in New York. "Men
may be very strong, but they seem to lose all their grit when the supreme
moment comes." Sadly, Barrows did not see her letter of success because he
had died two weeks before she wrote it. Kate was hit hard by the news of the
death of this wise counsel, reliable friend, and the man who had told her to
call him Uncle June. She had not even known he was ill, and suddenly he
was gone, leaving an unrepairable hole in her life.[14]

She soon found that her legislative victory was a hollow one. Kate had
her juvenile court law, but enforcing it across the state was another matter.
A Tulsa District Court judge proclaimed the juvenile court law "the greatest law ever enacted by mankind," saying that it "immortalizes Kate Barnard in Oklahoma forever." This judge was among the enlightened few,
because the law sat solidly but sullenly on the books while county courts
and county commissioners largely ignored it. Some county commissioners opposed the fifty dollars a month salary for a required probation officer; some county judges did not understand the jurisdiction distinction;
and others simply refused to appoint probation officers.[15]

Within a year, Kate assigned the ubiquitous Dr. J. H. Stolper, newly
employed in her department as attorney, to intervene in juvenile cases. He
attacked the work with vigor, some success, and considerable frustration.
In case after case, county after county, he found judges violating the juvenile law. In one county, a four-year-old boy was found living in jail with
his father, who was charged with murder. By law, the child could not live
in the jail. Stolper had him sent to the state orphanage. In another county,
a ten-year-old full-blood Indian boy was convicted by a justice of the

peace, not a county judge as specified by law, and confined with adult convicts. This constituted two violations of the law—jurisdiction and confinement with adults. Stolper had the boy released and personally delivered him to members of his tribe. In yet another county, three juvenile boys, ages twelve to fifteen, were charged with burglary, tried in Superior Court, and sentenced to two years in the State Training School at Pauls Valley. Here were three violations of the law—jurisdiction, the charge, and the sentence. Stolper had the sentence dismissed and the case set aside, and then he represented the boys in the Juvenile Court.[16]

The most notorious case Stolper represented, the one he considered his greatest victory, involved four boys who were charged with murder in the first degree and were being held in the county jail without bail. The case escalated to questions of criminal jurisprudence, challenging the constitutional powers of the state legislature and the United States. In essence, the entire juvenile court law was on trial. Stolper prevailed, and stated to the District Court judge that the boy, "guarded as a murderer when he entered the court room . . . , walked out only as a bad boy under the loving protection of Kate Barnard."[17]

Kate herself witnessed how the juvenile law was ignored. While inspecting a county jail in Oklahoma City, she found eight boys, ages eleven to fifteen, in cells with adult men. She spent all afternoon confronting the jailers, the county attorney, and the county judge. "After all my efforts to pass a Juvenile Court law, I find the richest county in the State unaware that there is one. The law has been in effect for over a year, and it is beyond me why you do not know about it." Days later, another problem arose when a ten-year-old Black boy charged with stealing a bicycle was put in a cell with white boys, which was illegal in a segregated state.[18]

Kate was such an advocate of the juvenile court system, she encouraged juvenile probation officers personally whenever she could, invited a man to come to Guthrie for a couple of days to talk about his duties, and wrote a woman to assure her that a woman could hold the office. "Some of the most successful probation officers in the U.S. are women," she told her. Kate struggled for years to enforce her wonderful new juvenile court law, including a case before the State Supreme Court in 1912, which held in her favor that commissioners were required to pay a probation officer. Stolper and Kate came to believe that the juvenile law was imperfect, that probation officers should be under the jurisdiction of the commissioner of charities and corrections, and that the state needed separate district juvenile judges. Oklahoma may have been dragged into the progressive world of a juvenile court, but much of the state did not like it and would not stay there. "Oklahoma has a splendid penal system—on paper," Kate noted dryly.[19]

———∞———

"Miss Barnard was not talking through her hat," a newspaper announced. Her validated Lansing investigation resulted in legislative bills in March to build a state prison at McAlester. Kate believed the appropriation for construction and maintenance, about $556,000, was much smaller than needed; she and Huson estimated that a first-class prison could cost about $2 million. She attributed the meager appropriation to two things: a lack of public understanding of a modern penal system and rumors that a prison coal mine would be opened. McAlester was in the heart of coal-mining country, and a prison mine would be competition to the professional mines. "This [rumor] came very near losing the penitentiary in McAlester," Kate said. Much of the workforce building the prison was comprised of able-bodied prisoners, a policy supported by Kate, who believed in keeping people in all state institutions busy. She vehemently opposed convict labor as a profit-making endeavor for the prison, but she liked to see inmates and orphans alike occupied, especially learning skills that could lead to self-sufficiency. She hated idleness. "Every young man and woman upon arriving at the age of 21 should be able to make a living for themselves if necessary." The process of building the state penitentiary languished on at a snail's pace. Besides the actual construction problems, staffing at the facility was another issue, most notably with the first warden. Kate invited herself to be in the middle of it.[20]

She was in regular communication with the nation's leading penal authorities, who respected her as a professional colleague. Warden Henry Wolfer of the Minnesota State Prison sent her photographs of a new prison being built in Minnesota and asked her opinion. She corresponded with the convicted murderer turned author Roland Molineux, whom she had met in New York after reading his book about penal reform, and they began a discussion about the new concept of a public defender. Kate admired Molineux and considered him "next to Samuel J. Barrows, the greatest penologist of our nation." Occasionally, Huson inserted himself into communications from her department, and it is easy to see his efforts to influence Kate's thinking. "I hold very advanced ideas on prison reform," he wrote a man in New York. "I like the Swiss, French, and Mexican forms of court procedure."[21]

At home, however, she knew that at best she was misunderstood, and at worst she was dismissed as a novice or a nuisance. "All are amateurs here," she wrote Wolfer, "and while I have been able to get eight bills through the Legislature, yet I am sure that I am considered more theoretical than practical because I give utterance to advanced ideas that I have absorbed from you, Warden McCloughry," and Barrows.[22]

Amos Butler, president of the American Prison Congress and one of the country's top penal experts, asked Kate to meet with Oklahoma's new prison warden and encourage him to join the national prison organization. She was eager to comply and described the disheartening meeting to both Barrows and Warden Wolfer. The new warden, Charles E. N. Coles, appointed by Governor Haskell, was "a strong husky individual entirely without prison experience," she wrote. He was, however, full of self-confidence and self-satisfied with his credentials. "Imagine my dismay when he told me that he had spent two weeks at the Lansing prison studying prison management and instead of learning anything at [the upcoming prison association conference], he could probably teach the members something." The warden rejected her offer of letters of introduction to go study other prisons. She said he was so full of self-assurance, "he couldn't wear his hat and walked so straight he tilted backwards."[23]

Her disappointment with him was soon resolved, but not as she had expected. He died suddenly two weeks later. Kate told Barrows that she was "a strong believer in the intervention of providence in particular cases," and this appeared to be one of those cases. Prison wardens were dropping right and left. About the same time the Oklahoma prison warden died, Lansing's notorious deputy warden "fell down dead on the streets of Kansas City," Kate wrote a former Lansing inmate. "For those of you who believe in the justice of God, it will seem like retribution for a monster of cruelty."[24]

———— ∽ ————

Kate was an exceedingly loquacious person, so torrents of words poured out of her office in the form of reports and letters to an eclectic span of correspondents. She detailed accounts of her work to professional colleagues, and she wrote warm personal letters to constituents and prisoners in a folksy style. She received a steady stream of letters from prison inmates, their families, and their sweethearts imploring her to help with pardons and paroles.

Most of her replies were kind and understanding, but not always. "I remember your case perfectly as I was living in Oklahoma City at the time," she wrote one penitentiary inmate, "and I regret to say that many people living there still believe that you are guilty." She scolded a woman asking for the release of a man convicted of burglary. "Your letter shows nothing but selfishness. You are in love with this man and you think that because you are, he should be released just to please you."[25]

Sometimes she did try to help. One Christmastide, she wrote the Oklahoma prison warden asking for a three-month parole for a sick inmate so he could be tended to, and perhaps cured, by his mother and sisters. "I have known Tom's family and have attended school with his sisters. I have always felt that his mind was unbalanced at the time he committed the deed." The deed was murder.[26]

She was a hands-on reformer who kept in touch with the men incarcerated at the McAlester penitentiary. Many of her letters were advisory. Some were comforting: "Your mother is well and getting along all right. I had a talk with her over the phone this morning." A few were harsh, as to a prisoner who was being punished. His father had traveled five hundred miles to seek Kate's help, but when she called the warden, she learned the punishment had been administered because the young man refused to work. She blasted off a chastising letter to the young prisoner: "Jim, I am ashamed of you. I, a poor orphan girl, have risked my position and everything to try to help you boys and then you would eat bread furnished by the poor tax-payers of the state, many of whom pick cotton at a cent a hundred pounds to pay their taxes, and then you refuse to work. No man, Jim, or woman either, should eat unless they work." She signed the letter "Your True Friend."[27]

She tried to answer all of their letters, but she asked one inmate to explain to other prisoners that she had not yet replied to them because she was "positively sick and worn out with the helpless people in the 325 institutions of the state who are depending on me." The prisoners cherished her. One of them sent her a small book "carved from the slate taken from the Lansing mines as a small token of esteem from him and others to whose aid you came like an administering angel from heaven." Kate kept it on her desk as a daily reminder of her efforts on behalf of the Oklahoma prisoners. She kept their letters, too.[28]

Penal reform became her consuming interest of the moment, overshadowing other issues. She repeatedly investigated the new prison being built and always examined the menu, sampled the food, checked the bedding and sewer system, and paid special attention to the heat. She made sure the inmates had blankets and mattresses. Kate could not bear for people to suffer from the cold. "I am now even accused of neglecting the orphan children for the prisoners of the state," she wrote an inmate at McAlester. "You can see I get the worst of it all the way around. Someday, I may leave this department and give my whole time to looking after the boys down there."[29]

The child labor bill, which had been such a disappointment to Kate in the First Legislature, passed both houses without debate by the end of February. Alfalfa Bill Murray was not there to oppose it, which was likely a significant factor. Long after Kate's death, a labor historian wrote in praise of Oklahoma's child labor law: "Few laws have been of such vital importance to Oklahoma."[30]

The juvenile court and child labor laws were the brightest lights of the legislative session for Kate. Much of the time she watched in frustration as legislators scrambled like contestants at a pig catch trying to secure funding for their pet projects. "Senators and representatives, anxious to achieve glory and secure institutions for their home towns, are introducing bills calling for every conceivable institution," she observed. Most of the dubious institutions were not needed, and she called them "puffery." Kate was disgusted by it. "Except for the child labor bill, nothing is being done for the poor, the unfortunate, and the children of the poor." She despised the contest, but she understood it. Every state institution meant prestige and a payroll for Oklahoma towns. She scorned some of the proposals because they interfered with her own plans. Kate was part of the legislature's free-for-all herself and had bills introduced for a school for the deaf, a state orphans' home, separate state training schools for white and Black boys and girls, a school for the blind, a state reformatory, and another hospital for the mentally ill.[31]

⁂

In addition to the penitentiary being built, Kate's plan for penal reform included two facilities for youth who violated the law: a reformatory for young first-time offenders and a state training school "for children needing correction." This was standard in most progressive states, she said.[32]

She was not talking theoretically about the need for separate facilities. She told lawmakers about the number of citizens who appealed to her for help and what she had experienced herself as part of her investigations. To illustrate the need for separate facilities, Kate told of pleading with a justice of the peace who refused to release a ten-year-old boy on probation, saying he was "hopelessly bad." She visited the child in his cell among eighty-seven men, four of them convicted murders. She reached through the bars and patted the boy gently on the chin. "What are you in here for, Sonny?" she asked. At her touch, he burst into tears and told her his story. His father had died three years earlier, and his mother washed clothes from morning until night to care for him and his three younger siblings. Left to fend for himself, he had fallen in with a gang of boys. The stern law of Oklahoma had put him in jail, Kate said, where he was "learning to pick locks and blow safes and murder men." This is why the state needed a state industrial school for reform and education, to separate young offenders and unmanageable youth from the jails and penitentiaries Kate called the "dens of vice."[33]

She wanted a children's police court and described accompanying a fourteen-year-old girl and two other children to the Police Court in Oklahoma City, a crowded and dirty basement room thick with tobacco smoke where three long benches of accused—"drunken men and fallen women"—awaited their turn before the judge. It pained Kate that her young wards heard the details of the seamy cases before theirs. A prostitute attacked the man who had brought charges against her and "clubbed him to the floor with her fist," Kate said. The judge and attorneys jumped into the fray, and the children screamed in terror.[34]

Letters poured in to her from a caring citizenry asking for her help with "wayward" youth. A sheriff asked her to find a home for some children who had been badly raised and were living in the fields and stealing "something fierce." "The children would make good citizens if given a chance," he said, but "they say they prefer to stay in jail instead of going home as their parents are awfully mean to them." Moreover, he said, "Their parents are also thieves."[35]

A minister inquired whether there was any state institution that would care for an eleven-year-old orphan boy "just as smart as he can be" but undisciplined. "I think he will make a smart man, if he is taken in hand at once."[36]

A county judge wrote her asking about a fourteen-year-old boy who had "drifted here in search of a home," driven from his family home by a drunken, abusive brother and now accused of burglarizing a residence. "The boy is fairly intelligent and speaks and writes both German and English. I am at a loss to know what to do with this lad . . . as there is no reform school. . . . The County Commissioners are willing to pay the expense of transporting him to any place where he will be taken care of, and the prosecution is willing for him to go. Kindly let me hear from you by return mail."[37]

A sick widower, "a cripple" who was "not able to work," wrote asking Kate what to do with his fifteen-year-old son, who was gravitating toward bad company. Some of the letters told her about girls in need of protection from abusive stepfathers or corrupting influences.[38]

Her reformatory bill lurched through the legislature. The Senate's version was splendid, Kate said, "one of the best reformatory bills ever written," and no wonder, because "it was drafted by Samuel J. Barrows," who had "visited this state and understood the conditions here." Even so, the bill was reported unfavorably by the committee, and legislators annoyed Kate by urging her to combine a training school for juveniles with the reformatory for young criminals. "I refused utterly to listen. I refused to be a party to mixing children with criminals of any age." Lawmakers mangled the final reformatory bill beyond Kate's tolerance; the age was changed to twenty-five, and the sections on indeterminate sentencing and parole were gone. This rendered it no more than a "side show," she said.[39]

Kate was continually frustrated that the legislators, the public, and even the press did not understand the difference between a reformatory and a penitentiary. Eventually the parsimonious lawmakers voted a small appropriation for a state reformatory in Granite—"because the western part of the state wants an institution of some sort"—and some temporary buildings were constructed there in 1910 for 117 youthful offenders. In the first six months of operation, only 13 boys escaped, which everybody considered a success.[40]

The state training school issue vexed her mightily because a fight for its location between two towns stalled construction for months. The final choice of Pauls Valley was an odd location for a boys' correctional school because the town had a reputation for lawlessness and violence. Gunfire was so frequent there that Main Street was nicknamed Smoky Row. As delays dragged on, Kate quarreled bitterly with the school's Board of Control, which, she said, "has utterly failed to grasp the idea of what a modern training school is or should be." She wanted it built on the cottage plan, similar to the modern boys' school she had seen near Rochester, New York, but she was fighting old notions. "Every town, as soon as an institution was established, wanted a great big, red brick building." She claimed a right to direct the design because "the bill was drafted in my office and put through and made a law by my effort and if it had not been for my work during the last few days of the session, the bill would have been lost entirely. I will not sit by and see money which I have lobbied from legislatures and tax payers spent on old, obsolete ideas."[41]

She was particularly frustrated with the state training school because it was her own pet project, according to Huson, who had a special interest in it himself: he wanted the job of superintendent. Overlooking the fact that he had abandoned two sons in Texas, this was the job of his dreams— shaping boys' character and molding a boys' training school with his passion for reform and his lifelong study of the subject. He wrote an obsequious letter of application and persuaded Kate to endorse him. "No one in Oklahoma has a wider knowledge of institutions than he," she said. "He does his work quietly, modestly, and effectively." So much so, she said, that people tended to underrate his ability as an organizer and politician. "I have not done as much for him as I could because it would be very hard to replace him in my office." Their letters were to no avail. Huson was not offered the position.[42]

The person chosen for the job was a man named E. B. Nelson. "He is a young man with a fair brain and good executive ability, but he had not ever visited a training school nor read upon the subject. Immediately upon his appointment I made things so red hot for him that he spent several weeks visiting institutions in Colorado, Kansas, Missouri, and Illinois." She came to admire Superintendent Nelson and his work. Sadly, her amiable relationship with him did not hold. A couple of years later, conditions were so bad at the training school that Kate's department instigated a two-day investigation-cum-hearing on the school that turned hostile on both sides. Stolper, testifying as a physician about the health effects of unsanitary conditions at the school, spoke in a tone as arch as a cat's back. Nelson protested: "It's not fair. The Department of Charities and Corrections swoops down on me without any previous notice and I have no time to prepare or have a lawyer present at the investigation." He said he did not know what Kate wanted and did not care; he took his orders from his board. Kate gave him a pictorial education pamphlet entitled *From Flies and Filth to Food and Fever*.[43]

Most administrators thought they were doing the best they could, so naturally, rebukes from Kate's office rankled. Stolper made matters worse. As departmental inspector and attorney, he was sharp with his criticisms. His tone and his arrogance provoked people. Antagonism festered among the chastised officials of jails, hospitals, schools, and orphanages, and they complained to their friends and state representatives. People began to think that Kate, Huson, and Stolper were getting too big for their britches.

Kate was impatient, but her department's inspections and reports did result in improvement in the state's institutions, although it was slow and sometimes nominal. The worst institutional disgrace emerged at Taft, where the state's Industrial Institute for the Deaf, Blind, and Orphans of the Colored Race was severely overcrowded and underfunded, receiving about half the per capita appropriation of the white orphanage at Pryor Creek. The frantic Taft superintendent begged Kate for help, saying that the children were starving. She reported the Taft conditions to the legislature but evidently did not take more direct action. Perhaps she knew it was futile. Oklahoma was a white supremacy state and unlikely to spend much sympathy or money on the Black orphans.[44]

<hr />

When the second legislative session closed its wild ride on March 12, Kate inspected her bumps and bruises and was generally pleased with how well she had not only survived but prevailed. "Eight bills—six from this department—have been passed and are in the hands of the governor for his signature." She listed her triumphs: "A splendid child labor law, a simple but effective juvenile court law, an industrial school for boys (already signed), a school for the feeble minded, and an adult reformatory bill now needing only the Governor's signature. And we have a penitentiary." The only bad feature of the penitentiary was that it had two-man cells instead of single cells. "The question of money has triumphed over the moral welfare of the convicts."[45]

She did not get everything she wanted, but she got a lot. There would always be next year and new plans. Kate had plans to protect women and girls. She wanted a law that made wife desertion a felony, an industrial school for wayward girls under the age of sixteen, and a court of rehabilitation for released convicts, "to help them find jobs and start outside with more than $5 and a cheap suit of clothes." She was as satisfied as Kate could be. In just two years, she had lobbied for a total of twenty-two bills that had passed into law.[46]

In March, as soon as the Second Legislature closed, she went immediately to New Orleans to address the Southern Conference on Uniform Child Labor Laws. She was so tired, Huson said, it was not one of her better speeches. She returned to Oklahoma to convene her Second Annual Conference of Charities and Corrections at the end of April.[47]

And then her world broke apart.

For months, her father's health had been in decline. He suffered from recurring attacks of a severe skin disorder, diagnosed tentatively as erysipelas (a bacterial skin rash), but it may have been cancer or something else. Additionally, a passenger train wreck the previous spring had left him with internal injuries. He sought traditional medical treatment and, in the custom of the times, also tried the recuperative powers of sulfur water or radium springs in spas, going from one sanitarium to another seeking a cure. Mineral Wells, Texas, was the site of such a spa. The expense of his illness was a financial drain on both him and Kate.[48]

Kate struggled with financial concerns. That spring, she told an Oklahoma City political campaign that she was unable to donate money because she and her father had so many expenses from sickness. Instead of a cash contribution, she said she would spend two or three days actively campaigning for the candidates.[49]

In late April, Kate received a telegram summoning her to Mineral Wells. Her father had taken a turn for the worse. Huson went with her to

Texas. Kate's father died May 8 at the reported age of sixty-seven. Kate was shattered, so grief-stricken she could not get out of bed. Barnard's death was the ultimate abandonment. It orphaned her again, but this time with chilling finality. This time she was truly alone. There was no one to come riding in from the west to rescue her as her father once had done. Her grief was so intense that she could not function, and sometimes she behaved so irrationally that Huson worried about her sanity. He took charge and did a masterful job. He witnessed J. P. Barnard's last will and testament, collected the bills, accompanied the body back to Oklahoma City, and made elaborate final arrangements for not one but two services. He engaged the undertaker; ordered the casket, the carriages for the funeral procession, and the band of musicians who accompanied it to St. Joseph's Cathedral, where a requiem mass was said; purchased the cemetery lot in Fairlawn, Oklahoma City's Catholic cemetery; and arranged thirty masses for the dead. The epitaph on Barnard's tombstone read: "Every good deed of my life I dedicate to him and my one ambition is to live a life worthy of his name. Kate Barnard." The words, like many of Kate's accomplishments, would fade with time. Both funeral services in Oklahoma City were well attended, according to newspaper account., which conferred on him the honorific title of "Judge" J. P. Barnard, saying he left behind "Miss Kate Barnard, [his] only child and living near relative." That would prove to be the newspaper's innocent but embarrassing inaccuracy.[50]

When she was finally able to write letters, Kate confided, "I am broken in health and my heart is consumed with grief. I do not know whether I will ever be my old self again. I do not know whether I will ever be able to continue the good work I have begun." She wrote letter after letter saying she was so "plunged into grief" that she felt her work was nearly done. Her work was not done; her work was now all she had in her life. But she was right about her broken heart: she never fully recovered from her grief.[51]

When Barnard's estate was probated and his last will and testament were made public, it became open knowledge that he had a son, Frank P. Barnard, to whom he had left "the sum of five dollars and no more." Everything else, both property and personal items, he had left to "my beloved daughter," Kate. The news of Barnard's second marriage and a living son was a bombshell to people, exciting gossip and tittering. "Kate was very bitter about it," historian Edith Copeland wrote. She had sanctified her father and publicly praised his old-fashioned romantic love for her mother in what was now revealed to be a humiliating sham.[52]

Some good news did surface. While going through his papers, Kate learned that Barnard had siblings (or half-siblings or adopted siblings), including Rose Trainor Barker in California and John Trainor in Michigan, both of whom had been born in Canada. This supports the theory that her mysterious father was a Canadian and not a southern slave owner.

The news of these newfound relatives delighted her. She set out to find her family members, traveling first to Atwood, Kansas, to reconnect with her half-brother, now named Frank Krohlow as a result of his mother's remarriage. It was not a happy reunion. "I gave them money and presents but they continue to hold me responsible and to hate me for a divorce which occurred when I was eight years old!" Frank, bitter or greedy or both, contested Barnard's will, embroiling Kate in a legal fuss.[53]

For four months after Barnard's death, first with Kate's bereavement and then while she was traveling out of state, Huson served as the virtual commissioner of charities and corrections. All the while, he was dodging troubles of his own. A committee from the Senate traveled to San Antonio, Texas, found Huson's sons, and apprised them of their father's whereabouts. What prompted this committee's quest to ferret out details of Huson's past? Did his application for the training school superintendent's job send people to check on his background? Was it displeasure with Kate and her investigations? Fear of her power? Probably all of that, political opposition intensified by personal animosity. Kate revered Huson, but he rubbed other people the wrong way. Kate's popularity with the people, especially miners and labor, was undisputed, but she was gathering enemies. A growing concern about her involvement with the estates of Indian orphans was gaining traction. Whatever the reasons, the wolves were circling.

As soon as she was well enough to travel, Kate embarked on a demanding, almost desperate, travel schedule. She went north on the advice of her physician, she said, escaping the hay fever problem that came with

Oklahoma summers. In June she went to Buffalo, New York: "My health is very bad, but I feel I must represent Oklahoma at the National Conference of Charities and Corrections." Her presence there was subdued. Then she went to Michigan for a tender meeting with her newly discovered relatives, finding, as she had so longed, "someone on earth for a blood-relative." From there she went to Quebec, to the summer home of Samuel and Isabel Barrows, where the widow was grieving her husband's sudden death. Broken hearts, like magnets, seek other broken hearts for consolation, and the two mourning women comforted one another.[54]

Kate was out of the state until October. She gave addresses in Boston, then traveled to New York, where she was a guest of Lillian Wald at Wald's Henry Street Settlement and spoke to an association of neighborhood workers. She visited the large University Settlement, which served Jewish and Italian residents of the Lower East Side and was then called the Ghetto, renewing an acquaintance with Cherokee Nation–born John Oskison, who worked there part time while building a career as a writer and editor with the *New York Evening Post*, the magazine *Collier's Weekly*, and other publications. She spent some time with James Graham Phelps Stokes, an early supporter of the University Settlement, and his wife, union activist Rose Pastor Stokes. Both Stokeses were avid socialists, and when they chastised her for not joining the Socialist Party, Kate summarized her work philosophy in a statement as clear and cold as ice: "I have chosen to be an opportunist and get what I can for the poor from the Democratic party." If any were tempted to dismiss Kate as an emotional moral crusader, this remark clarifies her intent. She wanted laws to help the poor, the weak, and the helpless, and she wanted individuals and states to honor those laws.[55]

Huson accompanied her on part of the trip east, venturing with either defiance or denial onto the home turf he had left in scandal. In New York City he even introduced her to his sisters, who were evidently models of discretion and never mentioned his blackguard past. Kate would say that she did not know about his abandoned family in Texas until years later. Perhaps she never knew about his youthful romantic indiscretion in Rochester, and perhaps his sisters did not know at the time about the Texas family. Everybody was exceedingly discreet.

One reason for her New York trip was to tour the Ward's Island Asylum, a Gothic structure that had been reinvented as Manhattan State

Hospital to treat mentally ill patients with modern methods. Kate was gathering information for her efforts to reform Oklahoma's mental hospitals. The hospital investigations she had begun the year before were now reaching their climax. In May, a former patient claiming to have been mistreated at the Norman hospital went there with a gun and killed both the offending attendant and himself. Kate returned to Oklahoma to see her conflict with the mental hospitals peak in December with front-page headlines. She denounced the Fort Supply hospital's brutal treatment of patients, and the superintendent responded angrily. Concerned relatives of patients and former patients inundated her office with letters. The brouhaha reached a crescendo in a meeting of "violent discussions" between Kate and the Supply hospital's board of trustees. By the beginning of the following year, the superintendent was finally forced from office, just as the top administrator at Norman had been, and both facilities began to implement the changes Kate required. Reform was not immediate, but slowly the hospitals improved. Kate continued to inspect them regularly to monitor the changes.[56]

Kate's tumultuous year of 1909—legislative work, personal heartbreak, professional conflict, and extended travel—mercifully concluded, leaving her tired, depressed, and wondering if she would be able to continue her work. She did continue. She even launched new crusades, but not with the full firepower of before. From this time on, Kate fought battles valiantly, but with a heavier heart, and never again with youthful joy for a good shindy.

Nevertheless, a new shindy, one so great that it would become all-consuming, was rushing toward her. It was not a fight she would have chosen for herself; she was pitched into it. As soon as she assumed office in 1908, she had received a chilling letter from the state's revered blind U.S. senator, Thomas Gore, calling her attention to "certain important political matters" that he wanted to discuss with her. The subject was "one of the gravest existing evils—the rapid dissipation by unscrupulous guardians of the lands of Indian orphans." Senator Gore wanted Kate involved, he said, because she would be "more influential than any other Democrat in the state." He recognized that the graft was already so enormous, so established, and so accepted that it would require a long process of strategy and planning. Kate could not take it on at the time because she was embroiled with jails and mental hospitals, but she had vowed to address it in the near future. That future had now arrived.[57]

CHAPTER NINE

The Last Shindy

K ATE CLAIMED THAT SHE HAD PLANNED every step of her career, but she had never planned on working with the "Indian Problem," as it was known. This was not like child labor and compulsory education, the reform issues she had championed from the beginning. It was not like the prisons, mental hospitals, labor unions, and orphanages she had come to advocate.

She had certainly not planned to get involved with the estates of Indian orphans. She was requested to do it, begged, even, by people who had witnessed how the state's Native children were being victimized. Who are these children? she asked.

Kate would find many Indian orphans in the state's orphanages, but that was not the beginning of her involvement with Native minors. As she told the story, soon after she took office, "I heard of three 'wild' children in the woods near one of our cities. On investigating the matter I found three little children, sleeping in the hollow of an old dead tree. . . . Their hair was so matted that we had to cut it from their heads." The children owned valuable land allotted to them by the federal government, but their parents were dead and they were on their own, unattended and uncared for. After six weeks of inquiry, she located their legal guardian, who was "charging exorbitant prices for their schooling and other expenses, yet he himself did not know where the children were." They were "drinking from a nearby stream, and eating at neighboring farm-houses. . . . Their 'guardian' had fifty-one other children under his protecting care."[1]

She would discover "scores of little Indian children" in the state's orphanages, all of them on tribal rolls and owners of lucrative land allotted to them by the federal government, but their estates were disappearing at an alarming rate. Unscrupulous professional guardians drained their assets and left the Indian orphans impoverished, to be cared for at taxpayers' expense. She reported this in her first annual departmental report in the fall of 1908, but she took no other action. It was but one of many problems she found in the orphanages, a ragtag operation of facilities in various stages of mismanagement and need.[2]

The orphanage investigations touched Kate's heart more than any others. When she visited orphanages, she met old ghosts of loss and abandonment. She wanted to give the state's orphans more than clean, safe dwellings. She wanted to give them substitute homes, with warmth, security, and comfort. The word "home" recurs again and again in her orphanage reports.

The care of orphans was the subject of some controversy, or as Kate phrased it gingerly, "the problem of what is best for the orphan remains a most perplexing one." The prevailing preference was to place orphans in good Christian homes instead of institutions. In Oklahoma, about 342 orphans were in the state's institutions in 1908, but some 600 were lodging with families. A handful of denominational orphanages provided temporary care until private homes could be found. Two exceptions to this policy were the Oklahoma Orphanage at Oklahoma City, with its mission to educate and train children to become missionaries, teachers, and church workers, and the Murrow Indian Orphan Home, founded by the Choctaw and Chickasaw Nations expressly to care for Native orphans. Forty Indian orphans were housed in the Murrow Home, and sixty others had been rejected that year "owing to lack of room." Kate estimated that three hundred Indian children qualified for placement.[3]

About half of the state's institutionalized orphans were in the Whitaker Orphan Home at Pryor Creek in the northeast corner of the state, an orphanage Kate found so superior, she believed it could become a national prototype. The Whitaker orphanage was opened in 1897 by W. T. Whitaker and his wife, who had eleven children of their own. At first they took in only non-Indian orphans from Indian Territory, caring for them in their own home, but after the Cherokee Orphan Home burned in 1903, they began accepting Cherokee orphans. Pryor citizens bought the property, along with forty surrounding acres, in 1908 and gave it to the state. The First Legislature designated the orphanage a state institution for white children under the age of sixteen, but it was still popularly known as the Whitaker Home. The state constitution defined the white race as all persons except those of African descent; therefore, Native children were eligible for the state home. The orphanage housed 125 children in nine buildings, and taught them agriculture and gardening. Kate had the highest praise for Superintendent Whitaker: "He is kind, patient and gentle, and the orphans all love him. He rules the institution by love, and makes a real home for these little waifs."[4]

The Whitaker Home was unusual because it cared for a child until the age of twenty-one unless a good home was found with "a regular legal adoption." The caveat of legal adoption is where Kate jumped into the orphan issue. The argument against orphanages was that they developed dependent adults without a means of livelihood, who were likely to be a continued drain on the state. It was far better to place an orphan with a family, but that did not equate to legal adoption. Kate found that people who adopted very young children usually wanted a child to love, but most others wanted an older boy or girl only as free labor. Kate adamantly opposed placing children with families unless it included adoption with inheritance rights, an education, and a trade. Orphans put Oklahoma at the crossroads of reform. Kate envisioned a new role for the state, demonstrating to the nation that a state government could be as protective and caring as a great parent.[5]

In addition to the Whitaker Home, she found another enlightened orphanage at a privately financed widows' and orphans' home at Sand Springs, nine miles west of Tulsa. It was founded and operated by the philanthropist Charles Page, who had made his money from oil and gas wells in Indian Territory. Kate described Page as "a man of large wealth, and larger heart, [who] cares for Tulsa County's poor, friendless and helpless." When Page was eleven, his father died, leaving his widow to raise seven children by scrubbing clothes. Young Charles dropped out of school to help support the family and resolved that if he ever had money, he would use it to help widows. The Page Home in Sand Springs was the realization of that resolve.[6]

Facilities like the Whitaker and Page homes were rare. Kate was more likely to see the kind of conditions she found at the orphans' home in the town of Cornish, where she investigated allegations of cruel and unusual punishment and saw that they were appallingly true. "I found that little children had been tied up in tow-sacks and hung up on ladders and that in some instances, buckets of cold water had been thrown over them while they were in those sacks. I found that many had been shut into an air-tight and water-tight circular washtub which contained from two- to three-inches of water, and that they had been turned around in this tub, coming out cold, drenched to the skin, nearly suffocated and greatly frightened. Several very small children had been shut into a black cellar with the skeleton bones of an old cow and were frightened. Some had been whipped with leather straps." She saw an epidemic of "sore eyes"—probably trachoma, a bacterial eye infection that causes blindness—and "vile sores" that appeared to be contagious. It was cold at the orphanage, and she directed the distribution of two suits of underwear for all children and new mattresses two inches thick. Kate was so concerned about the cruelties that she took away with her two children, John and his sister Bernice, and installed them at the Page Home.[7]

Local Cornish residents reacted angrily. One wrote in an affidavit contesting Kate's allegations and actions that the home was "like a large, private family, except more children." The matron was splendid and the children loved her, a neighbor said, and the punishments were not so bad. "By the time Miss Barnard raises as many children of her own as I have, she will find other methods of correcting them herself than the switch." The orphanage matron was replaced, but the neighbor thought the wrong person had been discharged and that Kate ought to be recalled from office. "The people here think she was wanting advertisement, a personal political boost." For every single improvement Kate effected, two seeds of criticism were sown.[8]

In the broad category she called the "Child Problem," Kate encountered youth who were blind, deaf, "mute," mentally ill, physically incapacitated, and "wayward," in the vocabulary of the era. The "wayward" category included "that large class of young women and girls, who have been betrayed, and led astray," and who had become "friendless girls" and "fallen women" (euphemisms for females who were sexually active). They were cared for in a piecemeal fashion in several rescue facilities with names such as the Home of Redeeming Love for Erring and Betrayed Girls. "These girls sometimes remind one of a scared, hunted animal," Kate wrote. When she and Huson investigated the shelters, they discovered heinous conditions in many of them and an alarming informality of operations. They were dismayed to see maternity homes adopting out newborn babies without recordkeeping or court action, and private orphanages accepting children without the ability to provide proper care. As the territories teetered into statehood and modernity, the citizens struggled to care for one another. They were doing the best they knew how, but often the well-meaning service was woefully inadequate.[9]

Despite her initial enthusiasm for the Whitaker Home, officially the Oklahoma State Home, within a couple of years conditions and management there deteriorated, until Superintendent Whitaker was replaced in 1909. Two other superintendents then came and went in quick succession before A. L. Malone was appointed to the position in August 1910. It is amazing that he did not grab his hat and run like the others. Not only was the orphanage bedlam, but he clashed immediately with Kate's department. The new superintendent reported to her that he found "almost insurmountable difficulties and . . . practically unsolvable problems" at the home. This was no surprise to her, based on her investigations and the letters she had received, and it would take some time to resolve the issues. Even two years later, Kate would learn that for a while the children in the orphanage had been fed discolored pork, which made them break out in sores, and when the pork was gone, they had nothing to eat except cornmeal dishes, mostly fried mush until the lard ran out. They all drank water from an old tomato can because they had no drinking cups. "Many mornings the children cried with the cold," a report to her department noted.[10]

People distressed about the children's care wrote Kate steadily with complaints and appeals. A widower said that he had put his five children in the orphanage only to discover that all the children there were "ragged, dirty, [and] unkempt" except on days the board of trustees visited. He asked Kate's help in having his children returned to him.[11]

In 1910, conditions at the orphanage were at a nadir, and as if that were not bad enough, while Kate was out of state delivering a speech in 1910, Stolper and Huson bungled a relationship with the frustrated new superintendent. The two were now boon companions, such close friends that Stolper named his first daughter after Huson—Freda Hobarta Stolper. Both men were overtired, overstressed, and at their worst when they barged into the orphanage separately but equally ham-handed and insensitive.[12]

The timing could not have been worse when Huson showed up to make an inspection. Superintendent Malone had been on the job barely six weeks. It was the day of the funeral for a child who had died during an epidemic of typhoid fever at the orphanage, and when Huson arrived, the superintendent and most employees were at the cemetery. Three other children had also died of the disease, and there was "much sickness" among the children. Two boys had run away, afraid they, too, would catch typhoid and die. In the superintendent's view, Huson was not only unsympathetic with the situation, he "took positive delight at the confusion. He condemned, criticized, complained at everything," the superintendent wrote Kate. When they most needed his encouragement in this hour of bereavement, "his every sentence was to impress them of inexperience, incompetency, and mismanagement."[13]

Huson told the orphanage matrons that he intended to give up his present position as Kate's assistant commissioner because the salary was too low, and that he wanted the orphanage superintendent job for himself, although he would likely take a railway position. Furthermore, he told the matrons that they did not dress well enough. Matrons at other state institutions, he said, wore silks and satins every day. In short, the superintendent wrote Kate, Huson was "odious to the children of the Home" and to the staff.[14]

At about the same time, Stolper blew the top off Kate's tenuous relationship with the orphanage. In his job as inspector that year, Stolper flexed his expertise as a physician and refused to certify five of the fourteen hospitals he inspected and four orphans' homes, including the State Home at Pryor Creek. He even threatened to close some of them for good. After that, he returned to the State Home in his role as attorney for Kate's department, demanding and imperative. This was the fragile situation when Kate began to look into the issue of Indian orphans there.[15]

Earlier that year, a superintendent at the orphanage had pleaded with Kate to take "vigorous action" on behalf of its Indian orphans, many of whom were Cherokee. "It is a serious matter," he told her, "especially when the property is of considerable value and has fallen into hands of the Professional Guardian class." She had already received a similar request from Senator Gore in Washington. Dana H. Kelsey, the federal agent in charge of Indian affairs in the state, also had asked her to help with the "shocking pillaging of unrestricted [Indian] children" being bled dry by their legal guardians. And James E. Gresham, a special assistant to the U.S. attorney general, wrote asking to meet her on a "matter of much concern to Seminole minor Indians." These men all knew she was the only state official with authority to look after the orphans' interests, and what is more, she was the only one with the courage and compassion to do it. She was ready to comply, but she did not know that this would be her greatest shindy.[16]

First, she needed to know how many Indian children were in state care. The Pryor Creek orphanage had admitted 145 children in the period from August through November 1910, and after releases, escapes, and deaths, 130 orphans remained. These included 103 white children, 11 full-blood Indians, and 16 children of "Indian extraction," or mixed blood. Twenty percent thus were Indian orphans, and some of these children became Stolper's first probate cases. It was the very beginning of Kate's work with the Indian Problem, tentative work in uncharted territory.[17]

For information on his first case, Stolper telephoned the orphanage collect—telephoning was still rare in Oklahoma, and expensive—but the superintendent refused to accept the charges. The incident exploded, with Stolper's threatening him with court action, fines, and imprisonment. The superintendent reminded Kate that both she and Huson had said that Stolper was "the biggest egotist and bombast in all the country and that you yourselves could at times hardly stand him." Kate tried to put the wings back on the fly with a flurry of letters and a personal visit to the orphanage. In a six-page letter, she assured the wounded superintendent that Stolper "is one of the most competent men I have ever met, but like all people of extraordinary ability, he has his shortcomings and perhaps his one fault is that he is exceedingly direct and abrupt and perhaps a little too forceful." Perhaps he was even "a wee bit over zealous" in threatening legal action, she wrote the chairman of the orphanage board, who had become embroiled in the kerfuffle. She sent Stolper a mild letter of rebuke. "I never saw a man that could accomplish more in a short time than you, but you are a perfect piece of dynamite when you get started." They were all "working longer hours than the state requires of us," she comforted the superintendent, and she and Huson had been "worried to a point of mental distraction for two years" about the State Home. She was also worried about money. "We are now without funds and without help, we must absolutely stop work until after the General Session [and new legislative allocations]."[18]

Kate dived into the Indian Problem. To secure her authority over Indian children's legal affairs, she set her sights on pushing a bill through a special session of the legislature to be named "the next friend to all orphans and minors." The lawmakers promptly set their sights on her. Just the year before, the legislators had waved the flag of moral reform, but a thin wind had moved in. Tight-fisted lawmakers were wary of elected officials financed by taxpayer money and weary of services that cost more than they expected. Kate had to fight off a bill that would have cut Huson's position under the guise of an "economy measure." It was a sign of things to come.[19]

To answer her own question about the Indian orphans—Who are these children?—she went to see Dana Kelsey, a man in his early thirties with the big responsibility of Union agent. He was the liaison between the Department of the Interior and the Five Civilized Tribes, as they were referred to at the time—the Choctaw, Cherokee, Creek (Muscogee), Chickasaw, and Seminole. Kelsey was based in the town of Muskogee in the Creek Nation and supervised 126 employees in fifteen district agencies scattered among the tribes. The offices were in Vinita, Nowata, Sapulpa, Okmulgee, Muskogee, Westville, Tahlihini, Hugo, McAlester, Holdenville, Atoka, Madill, Ardmore, Pauls Valley, and Chickasha. He had plenty of detailed data for Kate, and his information shocked her.[20]

Not only did the Indian children own land allotted to them by the federal government, but they also received cash disbursements. They were wealthy, vulnerable, and at the mercy of their legal guardians. It was those legal guardians who were culpable in the theft of their properties. Kate told Kelsey that under the laws of Oklahoma, she was authorized and duty bound to appear as next friend for orphan children, especially in state institutions. She vowed to take all steps necessary with the guardians and the county courts "to preserve these children's estates intact for them so that they will have the means of making a living when they become of age." Kelsey pledged the full support of his federal office. He and his district agents were the men who could provide Kate with the information she needed for legal recourse. She directed Stolper to prosecute "without fear or favor."[21]

Like many state officials elected from the West Side, formerly Oklahoma Territory, Kate was ignorant of Five Tribes conditions and said so herself. She was about to step into the East Side, the forty counties that constitute the former Indian Territory, and she would find it to be a very dark place.[22]

How it got to be so dark is a story that stretches back to the Indian Removal Act of 1830 and President Andrew Jackson's policy that relocated the Five Tribes from their ancestral homes east of the Mississippi River. The tribes were bribed, tricked, and then forced at rifle and bayonet point to cede their lands to the United States government and migrate west to the unsettled territory that became Oklahoma. This forcible removal became known as the Trail of Tears, an infamous trek with a catastrophic loss of life; 25 percent of the Cherokees, 45 percent of the Creeks, and probably 15 percent of the Choctaws died of disease and starvation either during or because of the march. U.S. Poet Laureate Joy Harjo, a member of the Muscogee (Creek) Nation, calls it "America's Holocaust."[23]

After some of the Five Tribes allied with the Confederacy during the Civil War, a punitive United States government took back the western half of their land, which became Oklahoma Territory, and opened it for homestead settlement. This is the sun-spangled land that drew John P. Barnard and his daughter Kate. The federal government's professed intent was to assimilate the Indians into the majority white population and persuade them to adopt a homesteading lifestyle. The Five Tribes were left with the eastern area, consisting of 19,525,955 acres, roughly the size of Maine or South Carolina. White settlers pressed so hard for more land that the federal government caved in to their demands, breached the treaties that guaranteed the Natives sovereignty "as long as grass grows," broke up tribal governments, allotted lands held communally by the tribes to individuals, and opened surplus land for lease or sale.[24]

Allotment was a complicated, unworkable system. The Five Tribes included full-bloods, mixed-bloods (progeny of Indians with whites, Blacks, or Indians of other tribes), and freedmen ("Negroes" in the terminology of the day), who had come west with the tribes either as slaves, intermarried, or designated tribal citizens. The Indians were allowed to sell some of their allotments under a complex policy that varied according to tribe and blood quantum. An exploding white population that outnumbered the Indians five to one circled the Indians hungrily, eager to buy their surplus allotments or lease their timber, agricultural, and oil rights. But at what price? Average Indians, especially full-bloods, were so inexperienced with real estate and business transactions of this type that even kind white people searched a thesaurus to describe them—innocent, simple, primitive, ignorant, helpless.[25]

Indian allotments were exempt from property taxes, and the young state wanted more land that could be plowed and taxed so that more roads, schools, bridges, and towns could be built. Individuals wanted personal gain. Indian properties offered both, so Oklahoma politicians pressed to terminate federal bureaus and remove restrictions on the sale and lease of Indian lands. The Act of 1908, passed just as Kate took office, did just that, removing about 70 percent of all the allotments from restrictions of alienation (which prohibited the transfer and possession of Native property) and placing the Indians under state probate, in this case the county courts. Tribal leaders and officials responsible for Indian affairs argued against it vehemently. M. L. Mott, the hardworking attorney for the Creek Nation, protested to Congress, saying that Indian interests could not be served properly by local interests of the white population dazzled by the riches within reach. He was ignored. According to Kate, the Oklahoma delegation in Washington "clubbed Congress into submission on the theory of 'states rights' and everybody south of the Mason Dixon line supported them." Muskogee, the unofficial capital of the East Side, celebrated the 1908 Act for a week.[26]

The state's probate courts now had almost complete control of Indian estate administration, and this offered enormous opportunities for exploitation by hungry land buyers. Freedmen and mixed-blood allottees were the first victims. "Sixty days after Congress removed the restrictions from the Creek freedmen, not one of them had an acre of land or a dollar of money to show for it," Creek chief Moty Tiger said.[27]

So began what Angie Debo called "an orgy of plunder and exploitation probably unparalleled in American history."[28]

———⊷———

This was the climate of epic avarice awaiting Kate and her vow to save the properties of Indian orphans. She and her small, imperfect staff did not stand a chance.

Stolper charged into court and began filing cases, urged on by Kate and with Huson's steady assistance. They soon found that they stood virtually alone. Stolper met some county judges who were sympathetic to the Indian minors and supportive of his work, but he found others who were unethical. Graft had spread to include politicians, schools, farmers, real estate dealers, attorneys, and officials at the county, state, and national level.

Kate saw it for the calamity it was. "Within a year," she wrote, "the wholesale robbery of Indians and Indian orphan children was so great, *Everybody's Magazine*, had an article entitled 'Oklahoma's Shame.'" The nation no longer admired Oklahoma as a prodigious baby state, but saw it as a place of graft and fraud of Indian properties.[29]

People did not deny the graft. A county judge being prosecuted for conspiracy involving land belonging to Seminole minors and freedmen testified that he had campaigned for office on the platform of getting Indian titles extinguished and passed to white ownership; this was his policy while in office, and it would be his policy if he ran again.[30]

Kate could grieve the horrifying number of victimized adult allottees, but it was never her intention to right the entire allotment system. Her authority was limited to Indian orphans in state institutions, and at first she stayed within those boundaries. Stolper began with the case of three Indian siblings, Bertha, Fannie, and Sadie Brown, in the Oklahoma State Home at Pryor Creek. A man purporting to be the Brown orphans' guardian had mismanaged their estates and then sold them, leaving the children not only with nothing, but indebted to him for almost forty dollars plus guardianship fees. Stolper prevailed, and the county judge praised him and Kate for their "fearless and patriotic" action. This initial success seemed to bode well for Kate's work with Indian orphans.[31]

Even so, she soon saw the magnitude of the job before her and the limited resources of her department. "I did not realize the great amount of work that would be heaped upon this office," she wrote in her annual report in 1910. "I knew little about court costs or necessary preparations for presenting a case in court." By her own estimation, thousands of Indian orphans were in the hands of incompetent or improper guardians. Stolper began to complain publicly that he was overworked—"doing the work of a dozen men"—and underpaid (earning $1,200 to Huson's $1,500), with no staff of his own. Furthermore, his heavy workload in Kate's department was cutting into time for his private practice. He was still embroiled in the recalcitrant juvenile court cases, and now with Indian orphans, he was appalled at the number of cases Kate wanted him to take to court. Sometimes it was too late to rescue the orphans' holdings, but with information from Kelsey's district agents, he was seeing positive results. Six months after beginning work, Stolper reported that he had intervened successfully in court as next friend in 137 Indian orphan cases, won all of them, had dishonest guardians removed, and restored more than $500,000 in money and land to the children. Two years later, he wrote a U.S. representative from Oklahoma about his "manly fight" on behalf of the Indians, "helping something over 40,000 Indian minors."[32]

News of Kate's involvement with Indian orphans quickly reached Washington, D.C., and at first, congressmen from Oklahoma voiced their support. U.S. Representative Charles D. Carter applauded "'that fearless defender of the weak and helpless—Miss Kate Barnard,' . . . and her 'equally capable and enthusiastic' assistant, Dr. Stolper." U.S. senator Robert L. Owen telegraphed that he was "thoroughly in sympathy with your idea of protecting the Indian orphans" and lamented "the enormity of the frauds perpetrated upon orphan children."[33]

This is a curious message in view of Owen's own position as an adamant advocate of removing restrictions from Indian lands. Part Cherokee and a former member of the Dawes Commission, which had dissolved tribal land-ownership, the senator had built his ranch fortune in Indian Territory by dealing with Indian lands. His dealings with Cherokee allotments resulted in an investigation by the Board of Indian Commissioners and subsequent lawsuits in which many of his contracts were ruled illegal and invalid. Kate was learning that Oklahomans at home and in Washington, D.C., held conflicting sentiments about Indian allotments. They claimed to favor protection of Indian orphans' properties, but thought differently about lands available for sale or lease that belonged to adult Indians and freedmen.[34]

Stolper was not the only one who was overwhelmed by his workload. "I'm afraid Our Kate will kill herself with overwork," Samuel Barrows wrote

Roland Molineux. Barrows had been concerned about Kate since he met her. Yes, he admired her "marvelous energy" and was such a fan of hers that he hung her photograph over his desk. He praised her for her dedication and accomplishments, yet in the same breath he warned her about overwork and urged her to get plenty of sleep, prepare to encounter obstacles, and "leave a little to be done in the future." Barrows was not alone in noting her habit of working too much. An Oklahoma newspaper wrote, "Why doesn't somebody introduce a bill to prevent Miss Barnard laboring so hard? There i sn't a 15-year-old boy anywhere who i sn't huskier than Miss Kate and there isn't anybody who works as hard."[35]

Kate was aware that her work style was intense. She relished it. "I am by temperament not fitted for the slow and systematic way of doing things. I am too impulsive and too nervous to wait. I plunge in, demand, and make a rapid organization of all forces. This is my way of doing business and it has proved very successful for me."[36]

In addition to state inspections and legislative work, Kate packed the year with national travel and speaking engagements, followed by retreats to hospitals, sanitariums, and spas to regain her health. Today, this pattern of manic work followed by physical collapse likely would be diagnosed as bipolar disorder. In February 1910 she went to Des Moines to address the Farmers Grain Dealers Association, and to New Orleans to speak at the National Editorial Association, a speech that Huson called "the greatest triumph and recognition of her work, yet." But in March she was too unwell to attend the National Conference of Charities and Correction in St. Louis, a telling concession to her health because this organization was of paramount importance to her. In April she answered a plea from labor unions and went to Memphis to join child labor advocate Florence Kelley, where they spoke at the Southern Conference of Textile Manufacturers in "a fierce battle for child labor law."[37]

Kate returned to Oklahoma to convene the Third Annual State Conference of Charities and Corrections, where she and Huson sensed some dimming public enthusiasm for reform. Then she retreated again to a sanitarium in Colorado for six weeks. As often as possible and for as long as possible, she fled Oklahoma summers for cooler climes. "I may go to Canada and if there were a railroad to the place, I would go to the north pole—anywhere to leave this hot weather b ehind." An underl ying health condition seemed to be growing more severe than her seasonal allergies.

She had to return to Oklahoma in July because she had a heavy state speaking schedule ahead of her.[38]

Since 1910 was an election year and Kate was up for reelection, she conducted a "short but spirited campaign," giving twenty-three speeches in twenty-one days. Governor Haskell was not running for reelection, in part because he was one of a group of prominent men from Muskogee who had been indicted for conspiracy to defraud the Creek Nation. Kate supported gubernatorial candidate Lee Cruce, a banker and intermarried citizen of the Chickasaw Nation, whom she considered "a splendid man." On the campaign trail she clashed again with Alfalfa Bill Murray, who had come out of a short-lived political retirement with sharpened ambitions. Once again, their feud made front-page newspaper headlines. In the wake of her attack, Murray lost the primary, with 40,166 votes to Cruce's 54,262. Murray had gone down to "inglorious defeat," Kate reported gleefully. She outpolled them both with 72,386. These were all male votes; women still did not have the franchise, so Kate couldn't even vote for herself.[39]

In September she went again to Des Moines to speak at the United Brotherhood of Carpenters and Joiners, and later wrote a gossipy letter to her miner friend Little Pete Hanraty, now living in Seattle, telling him, "I brought farmers and laborers together for the first time in the history of the state. I think some good will come from it."[40]

With the fall election in sight, Kate launched "my usual whirlwind campaign," twenty-seven speeches in twenty-one days. She added a new issue to her campaign that year: Indian children. She was the only candidate on the stump talking about Indians, and the only elected official in the state making a serious effort to protect them against graft. The Republican platform ignored the subject entirely, while the rest of the Democrats expressed only a pious wish for the protection of minor Indians from grafters and blamed "'the deplorable condition resulting from misgovernment' of Indian affairs in Oklahoma by the Republican national administration."[41]

Kate was now talking about Indian children with the same passion she had used in describing child laborers working down, down, down in the inky mines. "The skinning and robbing of the Indian children of the Five Civilized Tribes has been going on for twenty years and has to be stopped," she wrote Douglas Henry Johnson, governor of the Chickasaw Nation, "and I am now engaged in a tremendous effort to stop it. I told the story of the wrongs of your little children all over the state in my campaign in forty-nine counties," promising to prosecute all offenders, and "everywhere they cheered to the echo." However, her health was so bad, she told him, "I may not live my term out, but while I live, I want to stop this terrible outrage." There could be no greater epitaph on a tombstone, she said, than "Here lies one who protected the helpless orphan children of his state."[42]

The "systematic plundering of Five Tribes allottees" dominated the first twenty years of Oklahoma statehood, Debo wrote. The smaller reservations on the West Side of the state were victimized, too, but to a more limited extent, probably because they had fewer resources to steal. "Historians have been inclined to pussyfoot in this field of Indian exploitation, but nobody who ignores it can understand Oklahoma politics." Furthermore, she wrote, "To know Oklahoma, one must know oil." Indians and oil were a tragic combination.[43]

Kate triumphed in the November election, winning reelection with more votes than Cruce got for his gubernatorial victory. She was still the most popular Democrat in the state. The town of Tecumseh even named its school for her. She must have rolled her eyes when she saw that it was just the kind of structure she deplored—a two-story red-brick building.[44]

For the second inaugural ceremony, the new governor served buttermilk instead of the traditional punch or wine. This frugal beverage was an omen of governmental cost cutting to come. Cruce had been Kate's partner on the campaign trail, but if she thought that meant they were allies in all things political, she was wrong. He was a tall, handsome man with sentimental eyes, a high-minded businessman with no experience in politics except for three years as regent for the state university. Many saw him as an amateur now sitting in the governor's chair. He wanted the state to be run like a business, and he focused on finances, which led to ruinous budget slashing. Kate soon felt the effects of the new governor's well-intended methods of administration.[45]

CHAPTER TEN

Wolves!

THE WORK WITH INDIAN ORPHANS was becoming a burden on Kate's department, but instead of pulling back, she wanted broader authority so she could intervene on behalf of all Indian minors, not just those in institutions. This was a righteous mission and a professional mistake.

When the Third Legislature convened in January 1911, she had a bill introduced that would provide for a public defender to work in her department. Kate was a veteran when it came to finessing bills through the legislature, but this time she faced an impenetrable wall. Underlying opposition was bitter, unleashing grudges long buried and new resentments just surfacing. Kate said it was "a battle royal which lasted sixty days and nights," dominating the legislative session.[1]

Some lawmakers voted nay on economic grounds, with a slap at state officials like Kate. One said that "tax-ridden, poverty-stricken people" ought not feather the nests of salaried officers. He was right about the hard times. A two-year drought had left the state with its driest year of the century. Crops failed, unemployment was growing, money was tight, and the economy was so bad that more people than ever were seeking admittance to the state's overloaded institutions. All of this inclined the lawmakers to governmental budget cutting, so creating any new office would have been difficult, but for Kate to add a public defender to her department was impossible.[2]

A major reason for opposition was Kate's staff. Some people did not like Huson, but they despised Stolper. A senator from the East Side said it baldly: "The reason I am opposed to the bill . . . is that there is a moral certainty that Miss Kate Barnard will appoint Doctor Stolper to be the Public Defender. Doctor Stolper is dangerous in such a place. He is a fanatic. When he goes after something . . . you can neither pull him off, coax him off, reason with him or buy him off or do anything with him."[3] Stolper considered this high praise.

Stolper was ridiculed for his zeal. A story circulated that he was suspicious of a $750 charge to the estate of a deceased Creek man for a coffin. The undertaker explained that he had been instructed to provide the best. Stolper had the grave opened, inspected the casket, and admitted it was superior. Still, he was not without admirers. Frederick S. Barde, a respected reporter, wrote that he was "engaged constantly in a battle with graft and graft of the worst kind—graft that seeks to rob orphans, widows, minor children, and persons of unsound mind in direst poverty." His history of fighting graft was exactly why some people did not want him as public defender.[4]

Kate knew that "interest[s] friendly to unscrupulous guardians [would make] every effort to defeat said bill." Senator J. B. Thompson supported it because he recognized the magnitude of the Indian minors' monies at stake and said, "Never in the history of the world have so many minors possessed property." They owned "approximately one-third of the realty in [the] vast area" of the former Indian Territory, Indian agent Dana Kelsey reported; it was an unparalleled condition and "an unprecedented probate situation," he said. Oklahoma led the nation with the largest number of minors with estates of their own. The state had about sixty thousand Indian minors with land valued at $130 million. Much of the land was rich with timber, coal, and asphalt. In the next couple of years, the value of oil alone would be approximately $25 million.[5]

Senator E. M. Landrum denounced the bill for the same reason. "It is unfortunate so large a portion of the state's population is of Indian blood. I almost wish that the Indians could be wiped off the earth since they have been a bone of contention since Columbus landed." Yet another lawmaker voted no on the basis of practicality; with only one attorney, Kate's office would barely scratch the surface of the Indian minors' estate problems.[6]

The press came to Kate's defense, supporting what they termed "Kate's Bill," which would give her the right to intervene and protect the rights of all Indian orphans. When it became apparent that Governor Cruce intended to veto the bill, her friends in the Senate slipped what Kate called a "joker" into the appropriations bill, adding $2,500 to her department for legal services. Those extra funds gave her the money to hire Stolper as general attorney, a de facto public defender.[7]

Kate was everywhere that spring, and everywhere she was became a battlefield. The legislative battle had barely cooled when she became embroiled in a community fight over a new water supply system for Oklahoma City. She took a stand not as commissioner but as a taxpayer and a humanitarian on behalf of the poor, and opposed the recommendation of Dr. Alexander Potter, identified as a hydraulic engineer from New York. Kate questioned his credentials and claimed his proposed dam would pollute the Canadian River, exposing people to dysentery and typhoid fever. The debate became so violent that citizens assaulted the water engineer in a hotel lobby, a public meeting turned into a brawl, and Kate was sued for slander. This time the press did not support her, so she took on the fight alone and distributed hundreds of handbills titled "Death in the Water." Kate triumphed. The voters defeated the bond issue she opposed, and Stolper defended her in the damage suit, which was dismissed with prejudice at the plaintiff's expense.[8]

Kate was a fighter, but she could also be a peacemaker. The Oklahoma City streetcar union went on strike in March 1911, generating such anger and fear that officials stationed sharpshooters around the city. Union negotiations broke down, and some three thousand people gathered in front of the Lee-Huckins Hotel clamoring to hear from their new governor. Cruce sized up the sensitive nature of the situation, handed brief remarks to an attorney to read on his behalf, and left. The crowd began calling for Kate, who was known to be a member of the American Federation of Labor and a friend of the working man. She stepped out onto the balcony and spoke to the crowd, advising them to remain calm and to "keep a close watch on those who might commit any act of violence." The crowd quieted. Three days later, the strike ended and streetcar service was restored to the city.[9]

Kate involved herself in Arizona's and New Mexico's crusades for separate statehood, wanting to help them implant social reforms in their new constitutions. She asked Samuel Gompers in Washington, D.C., to send people to organize the workers there and to demand legislation to help the working people, just as she had done in Oklahoma.

Kate, a tiny figure on the balcony, calms the crowd during the Oklahoma City streetcar strike in 1910. She typically addressed audiences of this size and larger while campaigning. Photograph courtesy Oklahoma Historical Society.

She volunteered to make five or six speeches in each of the two states, paying her own expenses, "as a free-will offering to the cause of justice and humanity."[10]

Meanwhile, Stolper said he was "absolutely swamped" with Indian cases. The number of Indian children in orphanages surprised him, but the number of Indian minors in the state with their estates in jeopardy was staggering. Why were there so many Indian orphans? Tuberculosis, mainly, especially among the full-bloods living in isolated areas. Some thirty-six thousand restricted Indians lived in remote areas with few roads, families crammed together in one- or two-room dilapidated cabins with unsanitary conditions that bred disease, especially tuberculosis and trachoma. Henry Purchase was an example. He was the head of a family of nine living deep in Cherokee country. Eight members of his family died of tuberculosis within one year. The surviving heir was Edward, a minor. The administrator of the boy's estate provided medical care that kept him alive until he became of age and could sign over a deed to his property. Then he was returned to his rural home, where he was left to die of tuberculosis himself.[11]

Union Agency superintendent Kelsey and his district agents were the workhorses behind Kate's efforts for Indian orphans because they provided the information essential for her legal cases, but this small band of men was entirely inadequate for the magnitude of the work they were assigned to do. The preceding year, they had handled $10,702,624.27 for more than 12,000 Indian accounts, distributed per capita payments to more than 60,000 members of four tribes (excluding the Creeks), written 72,700 disbursement vouchers, made 29,000 remittance entries, and dealt with almost 30,000 oil and gas leases. Small wonder, then, that Kelsey wrote Kate asking for assistance with the Indian children's estates. The district agents' workload was so heavy that they could spend only a small part of their time on probate work; but to their discredit, they made not a single request to have guardianship abuse investigated.[12]

In fairness, the district agents were at the mercy of the cooperation of county judges, and some of the judges so resented their involvement that they refused to allow the agents into their courtroom. The forty county judges in the East Side had their own problems. In addition to their other work, they were swamped with the probate of tens of thousands of Indian minors; the infrastructure was totally inadequate to administer the minors' estates. Then, too, county judgeships were elective positions and subject to the influence of constituents, some of whom wanted access to Indian properties; yet nothing excuses the fact that county judges often were the threshold for the graft.[13]

Indian minors were required by law to have a guardian to manage their legal affairs, and parents or other relatives were often considered unacceptable because they either did not speak English or did not seem to understand the business of landownership and leasing. "Incompetent" was the term of description for the allottees and their relatives on deeds and legal documents. County judges then approved professional guardians, sometimes relatives and often not. This flung open the door to temptation and created a new profession. Professional guardians were the scourge of the Indian minors. "They are not guardians, they are wolves, wolves!" cried the Right Reverend Theodore Payne Thurston, the Episcopal bishop of

Oklahoma. Guardianship arose as a profession either because the courts were overburdened and the use of guardians was an easy solution to bloated dockets, because the people who were chosen for this role were supporters of county judges who rewarded them with plum guardianship appointments, because the guardians gave kickbacks to the judges, or because of a combination of these factors. "In two [out of] three cases the biggest crooks and grafters are attorneys who are acting as guardians for a good many Indian children," Kelsey reported. Warren Moorehead, a member of the U.S. Board of Indian Commissioners, summarized the situation: "Covetousness overwhelmed Eastern Oklahoma."[14]

The development of oil and gas fields in eastern Oklahoma, Kelsey observed, "attracted a small element, comparatively, who, like vultures, with . . . white interpreters and agents acting as their eyes and talons, reach out to take advantage of every opportunity to catch the ignorant full-blood and defraud him of his property." Debo described the episode more vividly: "scrambled hell and violence" and "thunder and greed." Greed was rising as fast as a flooding river, and it was about to overwhelm Kate. Honest citizens willing to help were skeptical of her success. Kelsey said the state's population was indifferent; Kate said the public lacked conscience. Some mixed bloods and even a few full bloods were complicit, but by far the majority of grafters were white people who did not swindle one another, but who felt no compunction about defrauding Indians out of their property. Today the term "grafter" invites scorn and refers to a dishonest person who cheats another, but then a land "grafter" was an acceptable, even proud description of someone who dealt in Indian land. "These men called 'grafters' are not such bad fellows," a court clerk said, testifying before a Senate committee investigating misdeeds related to allotments in the Chickasaw Nation with its rich agricultural lands. "They spend a lot of money in getting these allotments made to these ignorant Indians. . . . I think it is right that these people called 'grafters' should have a chance to get their money back and a lot more along with it."[15]

It was common practice for unscrupulous people to become minors' guardians or administrators and then drain their estates, but Kate's department gaped at the many ways Indian minors were being swindled out of their properties. The easiest ways were forgery, false impersonation, and manipulating an allottee to sign a deed or lease for a fraction of its value. Sometimes guardians sold the property for one-tenth of what it was worth, and if restrictions prevented outright sale, they stripped it of its mineral rights and pocketed most of the royalties. Always they charged exorbitant fees. Nationally, the fees of natural guardians for Indian children were 3.1 percent, but professional guardians in Oklahoma charged 19.3 percent of the amount handled. Stolper wrote for the department's *Fourth Report*, "In many cases attorneys fees, court costs and the cost of the bonds as well as the guardian's fees and expenses amount to nearly two-thirds and often three-fourths of the total amount of the estate." From his experience, Stolper surmised, "The policy of guardians through the State of Oklahoma seems to have been to sell everything that the minor has." Consequently, "when the minor reaches majority he has nothing left."[16]

Grafters plumbed the depths of human creativity to invent ways to scam the Indians, including perjury, bribery, embezzlement, defrauding, forgery, underpricing, loans without adequate surety, and malfeasance in office. Their most extreme method was murder. A dozen elderly Choctaw allottees were poisoned to death with carbolic acid soon after naming land grafters in their wills, and two Creek freedmen children were dynamited in their sleep once deeds were forged to their oil property valued at $250,000 in the fabulously rich Glenn Pool oil area.[17]

Later writers were cautious about naming offenders, but Moorehead was not one of them. Writing in real time in his 1914 book *The American Indian in the United States*, Moorehead quoted from official records and was not shy about identifying both victims and perpetrators. Kate's annual reports named names, too, in detailing the Indian orphan cases that Stolper prosecuted. Sometimes the reports included the printed testimony from hearings to show the extreme gullibility of the victims and the heartlessness of the grafters.

Two popular schemes used to swindle the minors were kidnapping and marriage; Stolper confronted both. Abduction, a sly form of kidnapping, was commonplace: just before young allottees came of age, they were taken away or induced to leave the state—"spirited away" was the euphemistic term often used to diminish the crime—and kept under constant supervision. On the day of their majority, they were pressured to sign documents to lease or sell their land; then they were usually free to return home. The Indian Office in Washington notified Kate about the interstate case involving a young Creek freedman named Malinda Davis, and Stolper went to court to rescue her property.[18]

Two men had persuaded Malinda to go with another young Creek freedman to Huntsville, Missouri, promising them "a hog-killing time," all expenses paid. Other young freedmen couples were there, too. Malinda was kept there for three weeks, provided "a right smart" amount of beer, and watched every day and night until she turned eighteen and signed a deed conveying both her homestead and surplus land to two white men for fifty dollars, which she spent on clothes. She testified that she did not know exactly what she had signed, something "to clear up my land," and that she had been threatened with jail if she did not sign.[19]

Usually, the minors were taken to neighboring states—Texas, Missouri, or Arkansas—but the case of a Creek minor named Marcus Covey was remarkable for the distance he was taken. Marcus disappeared in late 1911, just as oil was discovered near his allotments. His parents were neither ignorant nor helpless Indians, and they were frantic to find him. His mother contacted the secretary of the interior, and his father, a member of the Masonic fraternal organization, asked the Masons' help in finding the boy. The Secret Service searched for four months and finally found Marcus in Southampton, England. "He was sent there by one Thomas Gilcrease," the Secret Service agent reported, and was found "in company with a hired lieutenant of Mr. Gilcrease's." Gilcrease, part Creek himself, became one of the state's most famous oilmen and philanthropists. The celebrated Thomas Gilcrease Institute of American History and Art in Tulsa, now known familiarly as Gilcrease Museum, was established to showcase his extensive art collection.[20]

Charles Page, the philanthropist Kate so admired for the widows' and orphans' colony he had founded and financed, was another oilman who apparently committed unprincipled acts to acquire oil leases. He was charged with employing agents to abduct Indian women, whom he then claimed to have heroically located and returned to Oklahoma. Their leases were his reward. An Oklahoma newspaper reported instances of Page bribing officials, pressuring witnesses, fictionalizing testimonies, and hiring enforcers to strong-arm opponents. He knew how to do it because in his home state of Wisconsin he had been a chief of police and then an operative with the Pinkerton Detective Agency.[21]

Revered state benefactors like Gilcrease and Page rarely have their oil fortunes linked to shady dealings. Their subsequent good works smoothed the rough edges of history. The late Indian law historian Rennard Strickland was clear-eyed but coy on the subject: "In Oklahoma, you don't build beautiful museums or buildings or cities without oil, and in Oklahoma you don't get oil without Indians." He might have been paraphrasing Honoré de Balzac's famous dictum "Behind every great fortune there is a crime."[22]

Social anthropologist and author Garrick Bailey is blunter: "Oklahoma was the last frontier, the last place white men could steal from Indians and get rich. The city of Tulsa was built on corruption and exploitation of Indian resources." Tulsa historian J. D. Colbert agrees. His research of Creek property documents has unearthed "sad and tragic examples of early Tulsans, now considered esteemed founding fathers, who stole and murdered Creek Indians to get their lands." One conspiracy emanated from Tulsa City Hall and the then mayor, John Simmons. Four "untimely deaths" of Hickory family members who were Creek allottees and their court-appointed guardian opened the way for a new guardian to sell lands that ultimately became Tulsa's famous Brookside area, Maple Ridge district, and the Gathering Place park.[23]

Another popular way of separating minors from their property was through a contrived marriage. Minor allottees were males under the age of twenty-one and females under eighteen, but if they married, a state law declared them to be adults. Some bogus marriages took place in a real estate office so the deed could be signed immediately.

Stolper represented Theodore Grayson, an eighteen-year-old Creek freedman, in just such a case. Theodore would have liked to marry a young Indian named Amanda, but his Creek uncle joined forces with some white men who had plans of self-interest. As Kate reported, "We found one Indian boy with valuable oil land. They wished to secure a lease, so they married this minor boy to a colored woman of bad character. The next day, finding that the marriage had been made in the wrong county, they took this boy over to another county and married him to another colored woman of equally questionable moral standing, and were then able to transfer his lease."[24]

Theodore's testimony in the subsequent court hearing reveals a young man of pitiable vulnerability. His uncle had told him "he could get me some money, but . . . the only way I could get any money I would have to get married." In the first marriage, Theodore said he met a woman named Ada at the train station when his uncle took them "to secure some licenses." A white attorney took them to a Black justice of the peace, who refused to perform the ceremony, saying "he wouldn't marry no boy like me to a woman like that." So the attorney found a white justice of the peace who performed the marriage, had the deed signed before a notary public, and gave Theodore one hundred dollars and the woman fifty dollars. Then, the boy testified, "I and Ada and [Uncle] Steve . . . went on down to a colored store there named Elliott Brothers," where "I bought me a suit of clothes and give Steve thirty dollars." Then "we went on down to a restaurant and ate and . . . got on a train [and came home]." He never saw the woman again. The swindle hit an unexpected bump when the attorney discovered that Theodore was listed on the Creek rolls under the name Frank Bruner, so the uncle had him go through the process again and married him to a different woman.[25]

The hearing was decided in Theodore's favor, and Uncle Steve was jailed. In a letter of questionable compassion, Stolper wrote the commissioner to the Five Civilized Tribes that the boy "is almost feeble minded . . . and should be placed in some school or institution."[26]

The Oklahoma Supreme Court finally declared contrived marriages illegal in 1910 after Governor Haskell complained about them to the legislature; the U.S. Supreme Court did the same in 1915. When the grafters found that option closed, they moved on to other methods.[27]

Looters found vulnerable Natives in every Indian nation in the state that was rich with timber, coal, asphalt, gas, and oil. Conditions in the oil-rich Seminole Nation were so horrible, federal officials said that the only possible parallel was the White Earth Reservation in Minnesota, where the theft of the Chippewa tribe's pinelands was a recognized tragedy. Stolper represented blatant cases of Indian orphan pillage in the oil-rich Creek Nation and in the Cherokee Nation, but he said that the most troubling and most strongly resisted cases were in the Chickasaw Nation and the

Choctaw Nation. The McCurtain County case in Choctaw Nation was the most infamous. McCurtain County, in the far southeastern portion of the state, was named for a Choctaw family that produced three principal chiefs. The case was particularly important because of the scope of corruption and its ultimate effect on Kate's department.[28]

Kate first heard about problems with Indian estates in McCurtain County in the summer of 1910, when Dana Kelsey wrote her office repeatedly asking what she could and would do about the "very unsatisfactory" probate conditions there. Nothing, she replied, because at the time she had authority only for orphans in public institutions, and "I have been afraid to stretch my authority in so important a case." Kate was cautious about the possibility of failure in the McCurtain County case, making an ominous observation: "I notice that as time goes on, the guardians whom I am trying to displace are making a harder and harder fight, and this admonishes me that I must be sure of my ground." This is when she began planning to extend her power to intervene as next friend in the cases for all orphan children, not just those in state institutions. Reaching for even broader authority, Stolper argued in district court that the term "orphan" applied to any child under eighteen whose mother *or* father was deceased. Kate eventually got authority to protect all Indian orphans, but not all Indian minors, and they "were exploited by the guardians as systematically as the orphans were," Debo said.[29]

Kelsey had discovered business dealings of "a questionable nature" by McCurtain County judge T. J. Barnes in the handling of Indian property deeds, and further investigations unraveled a network of collusion involving the judge, guardians, bankers, doctors, lawyers, "numerous people of lesser prominence," and three lumber companies to defraud the Choctaw Indians. Kelsey's district agents called McCurtain County "the most corrupt county in Oklahoma with wholesale graft of every conceivable kind." More full-blood Indians lived in McCurtain County than in any other county, and the county seat of Idabel was the headquarters of the grafters, where, with the connivance of the county judge, "the stealing of Indian property seemed to be the principal business of a large number of people." Kate sent Stolper and Huson to meet Kelsey and discuss the situation further. U.S. district agents Fred Cook and Grattan McVay provided Stolper with "quite a large number" of affidavits indicating "an unexcusable [sic] misuse of Orphan children's moneys" by Judge Barnes and his friends. The judge, Kelsey's agents concluded, was "a man of very little legal ability or education," but a very shrewd person about acquiring property and money.[30]

It was a dirty, tangled problem.

Kelsey's effective federal protection of minor restricted allottees was limited to counties with cooperative judges; Kate's authority was still limited to orphans; and E. P. Hill and D. C. McCurtain, the two federal attorneys hired by the Choctaw tribe, had been of little help to the thousands of defrauded Indian minors and adults across the eleven counties of the Choctaw Nation. The good news was that McCurtain County attorney J. M. Barrett was cooperative. Kelsey's agency said that Stolper was "the only state official in any manner who assisted us." This tiny team of federal, state, and tribal attorneys faced a sprawling and entrenched criminal conspiracy to seize the rich Indian property. Moreover, Kelsey reported to Washington that it was a difficult situation trying to keep these three independent concerns—tribal, state, and federal—from trampling on each other's toes, "particularly if any of them are sensitive." They all were. Some were not only sensitive but territorial. Kelsey's involvement was further complicated because as he provided essential information, he worked delicately to keep the federal office in the background, to stay out of the newspapers, and to neither solicit nor receive public credit. He tried to keep his federal head down, away from state resentment.[31]

Their plan was to have Judge Barnes removed, through either the district court or a grand jury, and prosecuted for fraud, and only then would they pursue legal action to restore the defrauded orphans' money and cancel all titles obtained wrongfully. However, things got complicated.

No grand jury could be found in the county to indict the judge, and nobody would prosecute him. Most of the county commissioners were his friends and would not accept his resignation. Governor Cruce agreed not to prosecute the judge if he would resign and end his nefarious practices, so Stolper devised a plan of arbitration. Kate was ill and in a Colorado sanitarium, but he kept her apprised by mail: "The whole state of Oklahoma is talking about it and Governor Cruce seems to be very enthusiastic," he wrote. Stolper thought they could "reclaim land and moneys of fifty million dollars or more." Instead of moving smoothly toward resolution, however, the plan ran aground.[32]

The judge decided not to resign, and for some reason the two Choctaw Nation attorneys reversed their position and telegrammed the secretary of the interior that they did not want either Stolper or Kelsey involved in the arbitration. Their telegram followed Stolper's confiding to them that he expected to be rewarded for his work on the case by being named to a post in the state office of attorney general, a position of more prestige and higher pay. After considerable unpleasantness—accusations, quarrels, self-dealing, and some backstabbing—eventually the arbitration went on. Stolper, Huson, and Estelle Blair from Kate's office were at the meetings, but Kate was still ill and did not attend. Moneys began to be returned. The first day, $30,692.24 was recovered for sixty-seven minors. Within a month, $64,000 in actual cash and quitclaim deeds covering 4,113 acres had been saved for the Choctaw allottees, all from transactions through the McCurtain County probate court by the county judge and his associates.[33]

The fight lasted six months, Kelsey reported to Washington. He and his staff were bitterly attacked, "and only those on the ground would ever know what a battle has been waged in investigating frauds perpetrated on the Indian in this county." Going forward, tribal attorney McCurtain played a more active role in restoring properties to Choctaw citizens. The district agents were bitterly criticized by local citizens, and one of them was assaulted. The Union Agency territory was reorganized, and McCurtain County became a separate district. Judge Barnes was forced to resign, several people were indicted, and others were put out of business. Stolper got into a fistfight with Choctaw tribal attorney Hill on a public street, and an attorney in private practice was under such mental stress that he "lost his mind," according to an official report from Kelsey, and "it was necessary to remove him to a sanitarium." Twelve notary commissions were revoked, and the notaries were charged with various offenses from misdemeanors to felonies, including forgery, making a false certificate of acknowledgment to a deed, procuring Indian signatures on blank deeds, assault with intent to kill, selling liquor, and being "too drunk to attend to business." Stolper did not get the position in the attorney general's office he so desired. Instead— and what a bitter cup this must have been—the Choctaw tribal attorney McCurtain was named special representative to the state attorney general to assist in prosecutions before a grand jury. Stolper's only comfort was the proviso that McCurtain receive no extra pay for the work.[34]

Despite his pique, Stolper pressed on with Indian orphan cases. By October 1911, he had represented at least 207 children and recovered $187,991.94. By October 1912, he had represented 1,373 more children and saved them $949,390.70. He accomplished a lot as general attorney for Kate's department: he presented successful cases in twenty-five counties, had guardians removed when he discovered fraud or neglect, and had fraudulent deeds set aside. His self-satisfaction glowed from afar as he wrote U.S. Representative Carter from Oklahoma, "the state [meaning himself] is adequately protecting the Indian children and would be glad to take over the adults." Stolper took it upon himself to speak for Kate's department because she was ill and absent. More modestly, Huson admitted that Kate's department was so understaffed, it took on only the most notorious cases.[35]

Granted, Stolper had no assistants, but his policy was to prosecute only Indian orphan cases where proof was furnished him. Except for McCurtain County, he did most of his Indian orphan work in counties where judges, genuinely distressed by the wholesale robbery, were highly cooperative. He did not prosecute where his assistance was not welcomed. He sought and followed the easy path. He accomplished much because so much was available to be accomplished. For all of Kate's good intentions, the good work of the federal, state, and tribal team left no more dent in the colossal Indian graft than a strider on the surface of a pond.[36]

Further arbitration was planned in McCurtain County, and perhaps more money was recovered, but no further details appeared in Kate's annual reports, because by then her department was no longer printing them. By then Kate's department was under full attack, being assaulted by a hostile state legislature. The Indian Problem happened so fast—such an immense public eruption of criminal avarice and malice—that it engulfed her. And at first, said Barnard researcher Edith Copeland, "all she wanted to do was get the tangles out of [three children's] hair."[37]

CHAPTER ELEVEN

Grim Times

EVERYTHING AROUND KATE was grim—the economy, her health, the grafters, the small-minded politicians, the parsimonious governor, even the weather. The only things flourishing were greed and need.

It was a bad time for her to be the only official prosecuting grafters of Indian properties, and if she hoped to incline the public heart to kindness, it was the worst time for that. Either people were too broke and desperate to care about Indian estates, or they were ambitious speculators anxious to make some real money from Indian properties just begging to be acquired, developed, leased, bought, and looted.

The summer's heat, which Kate so hated, joined forces with a pitiless drought that had stretched into a third year. A grasshopper plague hit in one part of the state, and a smallpox epidemic in another. Crops failed and farmers went bust. Oklahoma was an agricultural state, and when cotton and corn prices crashed, the whole state suffered.[1]

Kate's department saw firsthand the effects of the economy and weather on people living on the margins. Ruined farmers could not feed their families, and poor widows could not care for their children. Some sought the only refuge left to them—state orphanages and mental hospitals. The Oklahoma Children's Home Society reported admissions of "more children during the last two winters to provide for than during any other like period since this work was organized and chartered in 1900." Admissions to the mental hospital in Norman soared as farmers collapsed physically and mentally, and hospital records noted a substantial increase in patients with depression. The mental hospital at Fort Supply saw "a considerable number of deaths," almost all "due to old age or exhaustion."[2]

Kate's departmental inspections revealed state institutions filled with more people than they could handle. The jails were still firetraps with inadequate sewage systems and undrinkable water. Crises erupted spectacularly: a malaria outbreak that affected 443 inmates at the penitentiary; an unaccountably high infant mortality rate at the Home for Erring Girls; the deaths of young inmates from typhoid at the state reformatory; and the insoluble problems reported by the superintendent of the Oklahoma State Home.[3]

The steady bombardment of appalling reports was wearing on Kate, and the administrators' angry denials and resistance were taking a toll. Her physical collapses increased in frequency and duration. She was out of the state more, in hospitals in Missouri, in spas in Oklahoma, or consulting specialists from California to New York. One doctor said her health had been "shattered" by work, and Huson often described her condition as a "nervous collapse." She sought dry air in Arizona and Colorado for the respiratory problems she called hay fever. She was suffering more severely from an undiagnosed skin condition of rashes and blisters so painful she called it "agony," which made public appearances difficult. The rash was a reminder of the mysterious skin disorder that had likely contributed to her father's death. Her health was so bad that in 1911 she was out of the office for six months, and in 1912 she was gone for eight months. This was fruity ammunition in the hands of her opponents.[4]

Huson and Stolper came to the forefront in her department's work when she traveled, and this was unfortunate. They accomplished what Kate wanted them to do—Stolper filing cases in court as Huson kept the department running—but their immense unpopularity reflected badly on her. She knew they were criticized when she was not there to protect them, and she wrote them often when she was away. "If they touch a hair of your heads," she said at one point, "I will put them into the penitentiary, so help me God!"[5]

In April of 1912, Kate went to Arizona, not to celebrate the state's admission to the union or to champion progressive reform as she once had planned, but seeking rest and a health cure in the desert air. Yet, as sick as she was—and she was very sick—she spoke to the press about her theories of prison reform, gave a talk to inmates at the state penitentiary, and addressed a joint session of the Arizona State Legislature. The *Arizona Gazette* identified her as "one of the greatest women in the United States," and the governor said, "a soul like hers can find no rest while sorrow and sin prevail." The legislature's galleries were packed, and a dozen reporters attended. They came to hear what one newspaper reporter called "a woman with an inspired mission," and they listened intently, applauding frequently as she spoke about child labor, children of the poor, jails and prisons, hospitals, and education for the blind, deaf, and mute. When she took on Arizona's death penalty and said the jury that convicted ought to be required to execute the person, she heard thunderous applause.[6]

The difference with her talk in Arizona was her flagging energy. Kate was so ill, she began her address to the Arizona lawmakers by saying, "Excuse me, gentlemen, but I must sit down." In contrast to her ringing campaign speeches, she spoke quietly, almost conversationally, but still her power came though. "There was no wailing, no scolding, no beseeching," a newspaper reported, just "a little woman weighing 92 pounds talking, but it was more—it was the fearful truth speaking through her."[7]

She was slightly stronger when she addressed the Governors' Conference in Richmond, Virginia, in November to deliver what reporters described as "the most effective speech of the conference." The program had been set and was full, but somehow Kate convinced the governors to find a place for her, and in her rapid-fire delivery she pleaded yet again for child labor and compulsory education laws, workmen's compensation, mothers' compensation, public works for the unemployed, and a minimum wage. And then "she preached to them a little" and said "she hoped to be able to congratulate them upon something accomplished when they all stood before the great judgment seat." The conference seemed to welcome this "small dose of religion" based on "the way the governors wiped their eyes and crowded around the tiny Oklahoma commissioner of charities."[8]

She needed this applause more than ever because there was no cheering in Oklahoma these days. What she heard at home was politicians rattling sabers at her with accusations of excessive spending. One rumor was that she spent $50,000 annually in travel, when, she scoffed, "my whole department has but $7,200 a year." But even outrageous rumors can deliver fatal wounds.[9]

The previous legislature had battered her about the position of public defender, and the current one was hammering her about departmental expenditures, but greater forces than these were at work, and they reflected darker intentions. Kate and Stolper had flipped over the rock that hid the thievery of Indian property on a monumental scale. In addition to timber and coal, gas and oil reserves were discovered in eastern Oklahoma, and by 1912 Oklahoma was pumping one-fifth of the nation's oil and had become the United States' number two oil-producing state. Much of it came from Creek and Osage allotments. The values of Indian properties were almost unimaginable, and the grab for leases spread beyond the oil-men in Oklahoma to eastern oil companies and Washington politicians. Their stumbling block, a rock wall barrier, was the legal restrictions on Indian lands.[10]

The Indian Appropriation Bill would come before Congress in December 1912, and with it, the federal government hoped to end once and for all its involvement with the "Indian Affair" that had dragged on for decades. The clarion call from state politicians to the Oklahoma delegation in Washington was: Remove restrictions!

It was a call that had never silenced. White settlers had always opposed restrictions that limited their opportunity to buy surplus Indian land or lease Indian allotments. Even before statehood, a local judge had proclaimed that the hold on Indian land was "literally killing [the Indian Territory] and stifling all business [and] improvement." Remove restrictions, he said, and "this country would blossom like a rose and the material condition of the [white] people would be vastly improved."[11]

The prevalent racism in the state was a contributing factor. Restrictions on the freedmen's surplus was especially galling. Many believed that freedmen were not entitled to Indian land and that the federal government had forced the Indians to divide their property with these governmental "special favorites" in the treaties of 1866 in retaliation for some Indians' support for the Confederate cause.[12]

The Creek leader Chitto Harjo was an Indian who agreed with the whites and who disapproved of the government's "cutting up my land and . . . giving it away to black people." He believed the land was exclusively for Indians. "These black people, who are they? They are negroes that came in here as slaves. They have no right to this land." The federal government came to share the opinion that Blacks were not entitled to Indian land and hastened to withdraw its supervision of this segment of allottees. By then it was too late, and allotments had been made. As Angie Debo said pointedly, "It was unfortunate for the Indians that the United States did not make this discovery earlier." By then the Black population made up a substantial percentage of the state's residents. At statehood, the federal census reported the white population as 538,512 (79.1 percent) and the Negro population (both tribal and immigrant) as 80,649 (11.8 percent). Indians were third, with 61,925 (9.1 percent).[13]

During the 1911–12 congressional session, the Oklahoma delegation fought a pitched battle in Congress to remove restrictions by eliminating Union Agency superintendent Kelsey's district agents who looked after Indian interests. The Oklahoma politicians in Washington took the position that the federal government should withdraw all supervision and the Indians should care for themselves. They were not alone. The Department of the Interior, public sentiment across the country, and President Theodore Roosevelt agreed. Kate never took a public stand on restrictions, but Stolper was not so restrained, and with notable hubris he wrote Oklahoma's U.S. representative Scott Ferris that in the interest of the white man's rights, the Indian segregated land—along with mineral rights—should be sold "without any unnecessary delay." His letter was read to Congress as reflecting the sentiments of the state. It is a curious letter in light of the work he was doing to reclaim Indian orphans' properties.[14]

Other congressmen argued for continued funding of district agents and accused the Oklahomans of bowing to a grafter constituency. It was a heated debate, but the Oklahomans won the day: the district agents were eliminated. The remaining Union Agency employees became field clerks, with administrative duties that did not include probate matters. Federally appointed tribal attorneys were given authority to handle probate issues, but this was small comfort to Kate. Some of the tribal attorneys were of dubious merit. Attorney Hill had been mostly absent from the McCurtain County battle on behalf of the Choctaws, and initially the other tribal attorney, McCurtain, had not been "as energetic in securing information as a man of his ability could have been." Other federal attorneys acquitted themselves honorably: the Cherokees' attorney, William W. Hastings, prosecuted delinquent guardians; William A. Baker handled probate matters effectively for the Chickasaws; district agents praised the Choctaw Nation attorneys Semple, Tucker, and Latham; and James E. Gresham served admirably in his work with the Seminoles.[15]

The tribal attorney who was both most venerated and most hated was M. L. Mott, who had been employed by the Creek Nation for six contracts. Extremely conscientious about his duties, he hired fifteen men to investigate guardianship records in the eight counties of the Creek Nation, and then he compiled all the data in eight volumes of exhibits. His report was not only damning, it was shocking almost beyond belief. He found 6,900 cases involving minors, although there were many more he could not document because only one-third of the cases were complete. Even worse were the exorbitant fees charged by grafters described as "professional guardians" of Indian children in Oklahoma. Statistics from thirty states revealed that the average cost of guardianship was 3 percent of the amount handled. The cost of natural guardianship in Oklahoma was 3.1 percent, which matched the national rate; the costs and fees for professional administrators and guardians, in contrast, were assailed as "robbery unparalleled in American history," and the numbers support the charge: 52.8 percent, 71.2 percent, and as high as 80 percent.[16]

In November 1912, Mott sent his report to Secretary of the Interior Walter Lowrie Fisher, who sent it to Congress, where it caused an uproar both in Washington and in Oklahoma. It was proof of the profitable guardianship business and its corrupting influence in Oklahoma, and it supported Kate's claims that the corruption was extensive. For those men agitating for the removal of restrictions, the timing was disastrous, because the Indian Appropriation Bill was coming before the House in committee immediately. Part of that bill would eliminate the remaining field workers, the few men left to look after Oklahoma's Indians and their properties.[17]

Discussion of Indian affairs in Oklahoma was oily and volatile in the U.S. House of Representatives' Committee on Indian Affairs as some made halfhearted arguments for Indian autonomy, others worried about the Indians' helplessness, and still others resented federal supervision. James R. Mann from Illinois asked, "Why is it that as we go ahead, civilizing the

Indians under our method, making allotments in severalty, we still have to support them, police them, and attend to them in every direction?" Joseph G. Cannon, also from Illinois, was fully in favor of "withdraw[ing] the arm of the Government and . . . the Treasury" from Oklahoma when possible. Clarence B. Miller, the representative from Minnesota, disagreed. He had visited the state a year and a half earlier and was convinced that "if we should to-day remove the protecting care of the Government from the Indians, we would turn the Indians over to those portions of the white race that are rapacious, that are full of greed, [with] no consideration for any human being save themselves." The Indians, "wards of the Government," would be at the mercy of "human wolves in white skin." Not because the people of Oklahoma were worse than people elsewhere, but because the prize was so rich and the incentive to greed so great. "If the Government of the United States does not look after them, does not protect them, nobody will. They are or should be the objects of consideration of this House."[18]

Oklahoma representative James S. Davenport, one of the delegation lobbying to have restrictions removed, argued that keeping the Indians "tied hand and foot" would not teach them to manage their property, and cutting appropriations "will not cause a single Indian to part with his property." Representative Miller argued in favor of funding Indian police everywhere, including Oklahoma, because they were important to hold down the liquor traffic, but when the lawmakers voted $200,000 to fund Indian police for other tribes, the Five Tribes were excluded. Representative Ferris, from western Oklahoma, painted a rosy picture of his state, where the unequal population ratio, 1,500,000 whites to 100,000 Indians, showed "good feeling, good dealing, and wholesome results. . . . It is a beautiful scene to see two races moving side by side in the progressive new State."[19]

The congressmen from Oklahoma were of two minds about funding for the state's tribes. They were sympathetic to some federal support for the poorer tribes from western Oklahoma—Comanche, Apache, Cheyenne, Kiowa, and Arapaho—who had far fewer resources than the rich Five Tribes of the eastern part of the state. While debating a request for the secretary of the interior to withdraw from the funds on deposit for the Kiowa, Comanche, and Apache tribes to build an Indian hospital, Representative Ferris spoke of the need for medical care for the Kiowa Reservation in his district, and how for eleven years he had seen Indians suffering from trachoma and ophthalmia walking the streets whose eyes were "so glued together" that they had to be led. And yet, few of the Kiowa and Comanche were "far enough along with civilization to be readily admitted to the white hospital. They are almost blanket Indians." Representative Charles H. Burke, a Republican from South Dakota, replied with some sarcasm that it was surprising to learn of such deplorable conditions "in view of the lauda-tory speeches which were made earlier [about] the attitude of the people of Oklahoma toward the Indians." He said it demonstrated how dependent Indians of Oklahoma—and elsewhere—were on the federal government.[20]

When the House of Representatives began to debate the appropriation bill in early December of 1912, Burke spoke twice on the floor in earnest support of maintaining appropriations. He read from an article in the *Muskogee Times-Democrat*, which was often anti-Indian and anti-Kate, that clearly linked state and national positions on removing restrictions and supported a proposal "to have the assistant secretary [of the Depart-ment of the Interior] empowered to remove restrictions upon Indian allot-ments." The newspaper article said that Oklahoma's Senator Gore, "who is perhaps closer to the incoming administration than any other living man," was "heartily in favor of the plan and also favors the appointment of an Oklahoma man." And this, the newspaper boasted, would make Muskogee "a little Washington." How happily the no-restriction boosters anticipated more authority coming to the state once the federal hold was loosened. Burke recognized this and referred to the upcoming March inauguration of Woodrow Wilson and resulting new federal appointments. "The Okla-homa congressional delegation look with favor upon the Gore plan, and it is quite likely that soon after March 4 an assistant secretary of the inte-rior will be located in Muskogee with power to act in all Indian matters, such as the sale of lands." He also prophesied that in March "our Demo-cratic friends will cause to be removed the very efficient commissioner [of Indian Affairs], J. George Wright, [as well as] the Union agent, Mr. Kelsey." And then Representative Burke spoke his heart. "Mr. Chairman, in conclu-sion I want to say if that is to be the policy of the incoming administration, then God pity the poor Indians in Oklahoma."[21]

The Mott Report created a furor in Congress. The two Oklahoma senators and three of the Oklahoma congressmen denied having seen it, and the

other three angrily and emphatically denied its claims, furiously condemning both Mott and the Indian Office. They said the report was wholly inac-
curate and merely "a trick to perpetuate Republican appointees, whose
tenure would soon be terminated by the incoming Wilson administration."
But they could not ignore the report because it had been read to the House,
and a summary was published in the *Congressional Record*. The Oklahoma
delegation sent Governor Cruce a summarized copy, demanding an inquiry
to clear the state's good name and, most importantly, "to forestall a Congressional investigation." To have federal eyes looking into Oklahoma's
Indian affairs was the last thing the politicians wanted.[22]

Cruce had the state examiner and inspector's office investigate Mott's
allegations. It validated the report's charge that administrative costs were
"extravagant beyond defense," as the governor told the Fourth Legislature.
Cruce was still eager, "thoroughly convinced," in fact, that the Indian
orphans' cases were better served in the state's courts instead of under
federal jurisdiction. Toward that end, he urged the lawmakers to "prompt
action" to correct the probate abuses. He said laws should be passed making it impossible for the estate of any minor in Oklahoma to be squan-
dered by improvident guardians approved by the state's probate courts.
When he referred to Kate's intervention on behalf of approximately three
thousand orphans whose estates had been exploited or disposed of by
incompetent or grafting guardians, the governor's message "was received
with hoots."[23]

Despite the governor's appeal, the state legislature voted down and
defeated all the proposed remedies. The Oklahoma politicians in Washington considered the situation so dire that Senator Owen traveled to
Oklahoma and addressed the legislators himself, telling them clearly that
if they failed to protect the Indian children, "Congress [will] never take
its hands off the eastern side of the state." His feeble recommendation
involved a law with a penalty for recording a deed against a restricted
homestead, and the state legislators came up with a small recommendation of their own, limiting to five the number of children who might be
wards of one guardian. These two puny actions did not even gild the problem, much less resolve it.[24]

Kate did not talk publicly about the fiery congressional debate in Washington, but when she was in New York in the winter of 1912, she did talk to
the press about the looting of Indian properties in Oklahoma. "The

grafters are fighting [my] department with all their power," she said. Her interviews appeared in the *New York Sun*, the *New York Times*, and the *Literary Digest* and included a recap of her work in Oklahoma. The national press remained intrigued by the young state and this "intense, fiery little person" who was "all alive with enthusiasm, and . . . not afraid either of showing her feelings or confessing that she has 'prayed a great deal' about her work."[25]

As charmed as they were by her, the press did her no favors when they reported her scattershot conversation and her stream-of-consciousness thinking. In one chattering interview, she linked her interest in prison reform with her concern for pure milk for the children of Oklahoma City and a vague plan for putting convicts to work in the dairy business. She made remarks off the top of her head to audiences of young women in New York and Boston, spontaneously proposing that they go on a marriage strike and refuse to marry until an eight-hour labor law was enacted and women's suffrage was adopted. Her marriage strike suggestion captured headlines as an entertaining but outrageous idea. Kate said later that she had spoken without thinking and wished she had not said it.[26]

She did not seem overly concerned about the grafters and said she was proud that the public defender in her office had never lost a case, that her department had restored about $2 million in lands and cash to the Indian children, and that two of the grafters were in the penitentiary. She seemed, or was reported to seem, almost lighthearted about the fight. "It is a wonderful game, politics," she told the reporter. "I am going to write a book one of these days [about] my political experiences. When? Oh, when I give up my office. My term ends two years from now and I think I'll step out then." It was not because of the grafters, she said: "I am tired. I want to write books and to travel."[27]

Others were gravely concerned about the Oklahoma Indian situation and visited the state to make their own assessments: Secretary of the Interior Fisher; Chairman of the Board of Indian Commissioners George Vaux Jr., along with board member Warren K. Moorehead; and J. Weston Allen of Boston's Indian Citizenship Committee. The Board of Indian Commissioners, which would play a key role in Kate's work, was a nonpolitical committee established in 1869 to advise the federal government on Indian policy and to supervise the purchases of goods for tribal use. It was separate from the far more influential Office of Indian Affairs (Indian Office), which became the Bureau of Indian Affairs, a federal agency established in 1824 within the Department of the Interior and responsible for the administration and management of land held in trust by the federal government for Indians. Sometimes the two groups worked in harmony, and at other times they were in conflict. Kate would interact with both groups with varying degrees of success. Moorehead was also a leading force of the Lake Mohonk Conference, a crusading gathering of eastern humanitarians with such a special interest in Indian affairs that they called themselves Friends of the Indian. This group would become important to Kate, too.

Moorehead was shocked by the plunder and exploitation he saw in Oklahoma. "I never dreamed that the famous Five Civilized Tribes, once so prosperous, had sunk into such poverty and distress, until I beheld with my own eyes what our removal of restrictions has brought about.... Force, intimidation and even murders have been resorted to in order that valuable property might be obtained." He issued a report to the Interior Department, but it was watered down to suppress some of the prominent names, so he published and distributed it in pamphlet form at his own expense. He titled it *Our National Problem: The Sad Condition of the Oklahoma Indians*. Its purpose was to arouse the American conscience and to bring pressure on Congress to end an "intolerable condition." He defined this intolerable condition as the virtual wholesale robbery of oil and coal revenues due to removal of restrictions of freedmen and mixed bloods and the violations by court-appointed guardians.[28]

Moorehead believed that "the vast majority of the Indians are totally incompetent to manage their own affairs," and he disdained "the Oklahoma delegation [that] has exerted much influence in Congress in Indian affairs" and had petitioned the federal government to remove all supervision of Indian affairs. Moorehead was very clear in naming the people leading what he considered a misguided policy, "persons who have little or no Indian blood in their veins such as Senator Owen and [Oklahoma] Congressman [Charles D.] Carter, ... and other eminent and educated Indians."[29]

From statehood, members of Oklahoma's earliest national delegation—Senator Owen, Representative Carter, and Representative

Bird S. McGuire—all received appointments on Indian Affairs committees, and all introduced bills to modify the restrictions. Oklahomans in
the House at the time were Republicans McGuire and Dick T. Morgan
and Democrats James S. Davenport, Carter, Ferris, William H. Murray,
Joseph B. Thompson, and Claude Weaver. Senators Owen and Gore were
both Republicans, but as Huson wrote the secretary of the interior on Kate's
behalf, the endeavor to remove restrictions was not political, not a Republican or Democratic interest, but an organized, far-reaching conspiracy.
"[The Oklahoma delegation] are tools of men and interests not confined to
Oklahoma but having far reaching power and influence in many states."[30]

Senator Owen was a veteran in the campaign against restrictions. In
1907 he said that his ultimate purpose was to secure the removal of all
restrictions, and that he would work with the rest of the Oklahoma delegation to persuade the Interior Department to do just that. His position
was well known. He once shared a speakers' platform at an Oklahoma
special event with Creek chief Moty Tiger, among others. When the chief
took the podium to give a welcome address, Owen sat directly behind
him, handsome and radiating professional success. Without mentioning
Owen by name, Tiger said, "The polished and educated man with the
Indian blood in his veins who advocates the removal of restrictions from
the lands of my ignorant people, apart from governmental regulations, is
only reaching for gold to ease his itching palms, and our posterity will
remember him only for his avarice and his treachery." Everybody in attendance knew that he had addressed his remarks to Owen. Owen knew that
they knew. The usually poised senator was so outraged, he leapt up to
defend himself in heated language.[31]

Moorehead's publication praised several men—and one woman—who
were working to protect the Indians: Dana Kelsey of the Union Agency; J.
George Wright, commissioner of the Five Civilized Tribes; the heroic
M. L. Mott, attorney for the Creeks; Patrick J. Hurley, who seemed to perform admirably as attorney for the Choctaws; James E. Gresham,
applauded by district agents for his work as attorney for the Seminoles;
Grant Foreman, a lawyer in Muskogee who became a foremost Oklahoma
historian; and Kate Barnard.[32]

A month before Wilson's March 1913 inauguration, Moorehead ran into
a downcast Mott at a Washington hotel. The attorney was accompanied
by two chiefs of the Creek Nation, Moty Tiger and George Washington

The eloquent Creek chief Moty Tiger pleaded with the federal government not to remove restrictions from his people's land "for gold to ease . . . itching palms," or "our posterity will remember [the white man] only for his avarice and his treachery." Photograph courtesy Muscogee (Creek) Nation.

Grayson. The secretary of the interior had praised Mott for his honesty and fearlessness, but it was not enough to save him from what was described as an honorable defeat. "Moorehead," Mott said, "they are rid of me. The next step will be to force out the Department of Justice men, [tribal attorneys] Gresham and Frost; then Kelsey and Wright will have to go; Kate Barnard must stop protecting minor heirs, or her [department] will be abolished; also your Indian Commissioners. Having cut off the real fighters, then they will remove restrictions. A few years hence—and do not forget this—the Oklahoma Congressmen will ask the American people to support Indian paupers, claiming that . . . the State of Oklahoma must not be called upon to care for these indigents." Within eight months, nearly half of Mott's predictions came true.[33]

Mott's contract with the Creek Nation expired in January 1914, and he and Chief Tiger campaigned vigorously to have it renewed. The chief appealed in person to Commissioner Cato Sells in Washington and then

Creek Nation attorney M. L. Mott (*front row left*) worked heroically and futilely to protect Native estates. The 1908 Creek delegation to Congress included Mott, Principal Chief Moty Tiger (*front row center*), and George Washington Grayson, who succeeded Tiger as federally appointed chief. Standing are Samuel J. Haynes (*left*) and Johnson E. Tiger. Photograph courtesy Muscogee (Creek) Nation.

wrote him wrote earnest and eloquent letters, saying he knew of the pressure on Sells not to renew it, but he thought he should be able to hire whomever he chose (since the tribe paid for the attorney position). He also recapped the good works Mott had accomplished for the tribe since 1904, including a successful case argued before the U.S. Supreme Court. He said Mott was unpopular because of the suits he had won and the indictments he had achieved. "He is a good lawyer, a good man, and a good fighter and is not afraid to do his duty." The chief said, "The papers say that the Oklahoma men in Congress will not let you approve my contract with Mr. Mott without walking over their dead bodies." Chief Tiger said he always heard talk of this kind, and it almost always came from white men and part-Indians "hoping that Congress will make a law to let the Indian sell his land."[34]

The chief's pleas were denied. Secretary of the Interior Franklin K. Lane wrote him that after long consideration, and having heard what "many gentlemen from Oklahoma have had to say," he thought it best for the tribe to retain another attorney besides Mott. "The time has come to put the courts and the juries and the people of Oklahoma to the test to see whether they are anxious and willing to do right by the Indians whose estates are in their care, or whether they are willing to allow bad lawyers and bad guardians to prey upon these estates like carrion birds."[35]

Mott's contract was not renewed, and he was dismissed from his position of Creek tribal attorney. It was all about money, Kate remarked the following year. Mott was removed because it got him out of Creek County, where "the largest oil wells have been discovered—wells flowing from 5,000 to 8,000 barrels a day."[36]

On his way out the door, Mott said that the only relief he could see from the present situation was "an awakening of the public conscience" of respectable citizenship. The one person he believed could do it was Kate Barnard. He said she was "a woman of strength of character and fixedness of purpose and entirely independent of any influence. The people in the rural sections of the state believe in her and would follow her." He shared her confidence in the power of the people. Mott's hope hung suspended as the politicians and oil interests linked arms and marched on.[37]

The demand for Indian properties heightened to a frenzy. To Mott and others sympathetic to the Indians, Kate was their salvation. To the grafters, she was as annoying as a little dog that barks and bites and needed to be removed from the scene.

CHAPTER TWELVE

Bloodhounds

W HEN THE FOURTH LEGISLATURE convened January 31, 1913, it convened with a vengeance. The state legislators were so fixated on economy, they "bayed like bloodhounds," one historian wrote. They had been elected on promises of frugality, and they intended, by God, to cut spending. They so resented the cost of state government that one representative rose to speak in the House, saying, "In Oklahoma every man has to work to support an office holder. I am tired of it."[1]

Throughout this tightfisted legislative session, the Washington congressional delegation battered the Oklahoma governor, the presiding officers of both statehouses, and the chairmen of legislative committees to take action and get some control over the Indian probate issues. Otherwise, said a telegram signed by both senators and all of Oklahoma's representatives, they would not be able to retain state probate jurisdiction and would be helpless in further removal of restrictions on Indian lands.

Governor Cruce assumed office committed to governmental economy and set about trying to reduce spending in state agencies, state institutions, and state colleges. The wise Creek chief Moty Tiger observed, "It seems to cost a lot of money to run the state and the white man who wanted statehood so much does not seem to be willing to pay what it costs but wants the Indian to pay, too." Retrenchment played into the hands of those with darker motives, and the movement took on a life of its own. The governor made other trouble for himself. He tried to abolish public institutions in some districts, and lawmakers from those districts rebelled. He was dismissive of partisan politics and governed more like the president of a private company than the top administrator of a state. He set a high moral tone, adopting "blue laws" to close businesses on Sunday, and he tried to abolish prizefighting, gambling, bootlegging, and horse racing. He appointed close friends to office. All of this set him at odds with the elected officials and weakened his authority. In this leadership vacuum, a mob mentality took over the legislature.[2]

The lawmakers went after Cruce with a tally sheet of grievances. As Oklahoma historian Arrell Gibson wrote, "The legislature got its vengeance on the governor and the executive branch of government by investigating executive departments and impeaching office holders." It investigated in a frenzy.[3]

Leading the pack of bloodhounds was Speaker of the House J. H. Maxey from Muskogee, one of Kate's strongest opponents. He was also chairman of the General Investigating Committee, which vowed to investigate every state official and department. A second member of the committee was a county judge who was especially hostile to both Kate and Stolper, and a third was E. P. Hill, the former attorney for the Choctaw tribe, Stolper's old adversary from the McCurtain County case, and now a state representative. The committee launched a sweeping series of investigations of almost every executive department, looking for fraud, misuse of public funds, bribery, "women in the case," and other abuses of office. They left a path of "wholesale destruction of political and official reputations."[4]

The state auditor, the state insurance commissioner, and the state printer were impeached. The auditor was charged with perjury and arrested; he made bond, and then the case against him was dismissed for lack of evidence. The insurance commissioner resigned. The School Land Commission was censured for extending "very imprudent" oil leases to wildcatter E. W. Marland, who was also chastised.[5]

Fueled by a hysteria akin to the Salem witch trials, the General Investigating Committee and its subcommittees slashed through state offices, condemning the chairman of the State Board of Public Affairs, the secretary of the State Election Board, the warden of the state penitentiary, an assistant examiner and inspector, and the state health commissioner. There were so many investigations that Cruce was forced to call a special session so they could continue into July. The governor himself was not exempt from the furor. When the investigating committee went after him, he escaped impeachment by one vote.[6]

Of course, the committee went after Kate's department, too. It was no surprise to her. Friends had warned her months earlier to expect reprisals for the enemies Stolper had accumulated with his successful prosecutions. Almost six months before the lawmakers of the Fourth Legislature were elected, she had written Stolper urging him to "proceed at once in courts" against the State Board of Education, which had been given authority over the orphans in state orphanages but was doing nothing to protect their estates. "We cannot let the blame rest on us," she wrote. Speed was important. "It will not be long till those who are aspiring to my position will be quietly investigating these institutions." She was right: the investigating committee not only scrutinized her department, it tore through many of the institutions under her jurisdiction, ordering one investigation after another. Her inspections had revealed and reported problems in these institutions for years; now the committee wanted to lay blame at her doorstep.[7]

Grafters lined up against her, and while their point of attack was Stolper, Kate was the real target. Even before they took office, the avenging politicians held secret meetings and mapped out a plan. They "agreed something had to be done about Kate," historian Margaret Truman wrote, but they were "unable to attack her directly" because she was too popular. As votes showed, she was the state's most popular elected official, and the committee itself acknowledged to the House that "the office of Commissioner of Charities and Corrections has been a very popular office in the State." Instead, they took aim at Stolper—and he was so unpopular, they could not miss. Researcher Edith Copeland believed that Stolper's personality marked him for attack: his accent, dress, and mannerisms were foreign, and not of Anglo origin. Bill Murray referred to him publicly as a "curly haired dago." In commonplace Oklahoma, Stolper had a formal bearing in public, and even at home. After a meal, his children pushed their chairs to the table, thanked their mother, and bowed or curtsied to her. His air of superiority was a minor annoyance compared to his major sin: he prosecuted grafters. He was standing between them and fortunes. He had to go.[8]

The investigators launched a whispering campaign, claiming that he took bribes and used his influence with the governor to win pardons and paroles, and then the committee read to the House three affidavits stating that Stolper had solicited money in exchange for influence. Kate made a hard fight to defend him. She explained that what they thought were bribes were fees for his private legal work. They were attacking him, she said quite accurately, because they were afraid to attack her. "Every effort has been made since the first day of the legislature to exterminate my department."[9]

The Efficiency Committee searched Kate's departmental records for evidence of wrongdoing and charged Stolper with using state funds to pay for out-of-state trips to attend conferences and to discuss Indian affairs with federal officials in Washington, D.C. The committee said that at tax-payers' expense he was "running and galloping all over the state and part of the continent on every little pretext of official duty." It criticized Huson, too, citing his excessive travel expenses. He had traveled for a month the previous summer, making trips to Kansas, Missouri, Illinois, and Colorado—"thirty days outside of the state, and at a total cost to the taxpayers of the State of $303.10." This was extreme in a year when the average national annual income was $1,296. Kate defended the trips. They were not junkets, she said; they were undertaken to make her staff better qualified to inspect institutions, and some of the trips were for Huson to consult with her when she was in a hospital or a sanitarium. Her explanations were waved away.[10]

The committee was selective in its research. It was able to track Huson's travel as diligently as a Pinkerton detective, but said it could not find concrete information about Stolper's Indian minor probate cases—cases that he had listed with names, dates, and moneys won in the Department of Charities and Corrections' printed annual reports, which were distributed to each member of the House and Senate.[11]

If the concern was economy, Kate proposed a solution. She had a bill introduced in the House that would help fund her department's legal efforts by assessing each orphan's estate a fee of five dollars for legal services. "The remedy for all these [Indian minor legal] troubles is certainly not to wreck the Department of Charities, but rather to strengthen it," she said. The bill required county judges to report all cases of orphans' estates involved. Kate was sure that thousands of cases had not been reported to her. The problem was so enormous, she would need "five or ten good lawyers." The possibility of putting such resources into her hands must have left the grafters pale and wide eyed.[12]

The bill went nowhere because the fight was not about funding. It was about Kate's threat to the grafters. In February 1913, reporter Frederick S. Barde interviewed Kate for an article in the *St. Louis Post-Dispatch* titled "'Grafters after Me.'" Barde was no starry-eyed devotee of hers. He had covered her career since 1908 and had quoted her critics who called her a "hysterical tear pumper," and he had accused her of inspecting institutions only when political activity boiled in the area. Now, he wrote that "sinister influences" were at work in the Oklahoma legislature to cripple her department and to render her powerless against "a great ring of grafters who robbed children wholesale." Always before, she had been "capable of overcoming all obstacles with the fire of her zeal, unafraid and defiant." For the first time, Barde saw that she was frightened and frail. "To see her in tears and despondency was something strange and new."[13]

There was a real possibility that her work would end in Oklahoma because "she dared to use the power of her department" to protect Indian minors and orphans who were being robbed of their estates by white men in eastern Oklahoma, and now, "Every grafter in Oklahoma hates her 'like the devil hates holy water.'"[14]

Supporters defended Kate on the House floor with oratory and poetry, describing her as a "dewdrop from heaven." Without her, the Indians were common prey, one said, and he pleaded, "For God's sake don't take away their only defender." One legislator who spoke in her defense was Houston B. Teehee, a descendant of Sam Houston and Talihini Rogers, Houston's Cherokee wife when he had lived in Indian Territory. Teehee, considered one of the best-educated men in the House, implored the House to keep "the only safeguard the state has ever given little Indian children."[15]

The opposition got tougher and bolder. Kate was told that "as long as Stolper stayed in the office I would not receive a penny in appropriations from the Legislature." Stolper submitted his resignation. She held the letter for a week, and then, in an attempt to save her department, she accepted it February 18, 1913.[16]

After six weeks of battling with the legislature, Kate got a long-distance telephone call from a man named Frank Montgomery. He told her that if she appointed him as her attorney, he would stop the fight against her department in twenty-four hours, but if she did not hire him, her department would receive no funding. Kate told him there was no vacancy; she had already replaced Stolper with Ross F. Lockridge as departmental attorney. Lockridge was a former county judge and a prominent member of the

Young Men's Christian Association. Montgomery countered with his own credentials as the man in charge of the election machinery in Muskogee, where he had once pulled in eight hundred more Democratic votes than there were Democrats in town. A crooked politician who wanted to be Kate's attorney to fight graft? She was appalled. But there was more. He told her that he and his wife had been married in the Muskogee home of E. P. Hill, Stolper's nemesis and an investigator into her office expenses.[17]

Montgomery called on Kate personally, bringing with him Speaker of the House Maxey and his friend Hill, both from Muskogee County, and Representative J. E. Wyand from neighboring Pittsburg County—a stronghold of her opponents. She persuaded them to put their offer in writing, then took the letter immediately to the county attorney and reminded him that offering to swap votes on appropriation bills in return for an appointment in office was illegal and carried a two-year penitentiary term. She wanted them arrested, and she wanted them arrested on the floor of the House of Representatives the next day. When there were no front-page headlines about their arrest the next morning, she called the county attorney. He had the law, she told him, so "haven't you the backbone?" He told her that the businessmen of Oklahoma City did not want anything done that might jeopardize a pending bill on the location of the new state capital, which was the object of a tug-of-war between Oklahoma City and Muskogee.[18]

Kate refused to hire Montgomery, and in March the Efficiency Committee issued its report to the House. It was not a report; it was a death sentence. It censured Kate "emphatically" for "extravagant expenditure," including "some national convention" in Boston that she, Huson, and Stolper had attended in 1911. It condemned her for criticizing "the various penal, eleemosynary and charitable institutions in the State, together with the hospitals and various county and city jails," and then "notify[ing] the parties in charge to put them in proper condition." It maintained that this expensive work could be done more effectively by others, including sheriffs, county commissioners, mayors, and city officers. It declared that her staffing was excessive and the work of her department could be done with one commissioner and one stenographer. In summary, "Our investigation . . . convinces us that this department could be dispensed with in its entirety, and the duties performed be put upon local authorities, thereby saving a great expense to the State." In short, the lawmakers excoriated her for doing the job she was mandated to do.[19]

The committee did recognize that "something should be done in order to protect the minor Indian's property," but noted, ironically, that too many cases existed to be handled by one attorney.[20]

The committee, led by Maxey and Hill, concluded that Kate's department was a complete failure that should not be a separate branch of state government, and recommended that it be abolished and combined with the offices of the commissioner of labor and the chief mine inspector. One of the legislators who signed this report was Houston Teehee, who had spoken in Kate's defense earlier. Governor Cruce also recommended abolishing the Department of Charities and Corrections. Friends were jumping ship.[21]

Kate was not in Oklahoma City for the humiliation when these charges were read and accepted by the legislature. She knew what was coming. Sick at heart and in body, she had fled to Arizona, where she was the guest first of Governor George W. P. Hunt and his wife and then of the Arizona state prison warden and his wife. This was the trip during which she spoke to the Arizona legislature while seated. But Kate found no respite in Arizona. The desert air did not relieve her respiratory condition. And desert air cannot heal a broken heart. The *Daily Oklahoman* reported that when news reached her sickbed at the governor's mansion that the legislature was about to undo her work and cripple her department with retrenchment and restrictions, "she was completely prostrated." Her Arizona allies were horrified. "Can it be that a state that wrote the first progressive constitution on the American continent be so devoid of chivalry as to strike with a mailed fist the greatest Christian worker for humanity today in the United States?" asked an incredulous Arizona state official.[22]

Nor did she find rest in Arizona. She was harried by letters from the ambitious Montgomery, who still wanted to be hired, and by urgent telegrams telling her to return home and continue the fight for her department. She did return—and immediately checked into the hospital in Oklahoma City. Montgomery called her in the hospital, "just one hour before the appropriation bill came up on the floor," Kate said, and told her again that if she appointed him, the fight would be stopped. Again she refused.[23]

As much as they wanted to do so, the legislators could not abolish an office created by the constitution. What they could do was slash the appropriation for Kate's department and eliminate her assistants. So they did. Her department's appropriation was cut from $14,900 to $5,800. Her contingency fund of $9,900 was reduced to $400. All that was left was her salary of $2,500, the salary for a stenographer, and reduced funds for travel, postage, legal services, and office expenses. She had always spent less than most offices. Her printing bill was $1,075 compared to the insurance commissioner's bill of $6,391. For the coming year, she was allocated $500 for printing. This explains why there were no further annual reports from her office. Salaries were eliminated for an inspector and an assistant commissioner. Without funding for his position, Huson, her stalwart assistant and collaborator, had to go.[24]

As she had so often in the past, Kate pleaded her case before the public. She issued a long statement to the press detailing the sequence of events that had wrecked her department and naming the men responsible: Maxey, Hill, Wyand, and Montgomery. Why did they want control of the Department of Charities and Corrections? she asked rhetorically. She answered her own question: "To control her actions in the prosecution of the Indian orphan grafters on the east side of the state."[25]

And then Kate disappeared from sight. She arranged for the shards of her office—Estelle Blair, attorney Lockridge, and inspector R. C. Meloy—to carry on in her absence, and she left the state to stew in the summer heat and its own sour motives. All three remaining staff members would resign at the end of the year. And thus the Department of Charities and Corrections was bludgeoned to its knees and the bright reform sun of statehood was eclipsed.[26]

To its shame, the Oklahoma press was silent. Kate's valiant friend Roy Stafford, former *Daily Oklahoman* editor and state senator, was gone from the scene. Kate was bitter about the timid press, but she knew the reason for its silence. "I have a barrel of clippings from our home newspapers . . . in which they called me an 'Angel of Mercy,' and all kind of beautiful but impossible things, but since this wrecking of my Department, I have gone to them and begged them to help me to get this news to their readers, but not a word has appeared. The reason is that the railroad and lumber men and coal operators, who want to gobble these Indian lands, are the big advertisers. . . . I have no money to advertise. We will never have freedom and liberty in America . . . until we have a free press."[27]

"From the standpoint of aggressive efficiency," Barde reported in the *St. Louis Post-Dispatch*, "the State Department of Charities and Corrections in Oklahoma has been wiped off the map." The *New York Sun* condemned the state legislature for wrecking a constitutional office and tying the hands of an officer elected by the people, actions "unexampled in the history of nations." Mitigating factors might have been the legislators' personal dislike of Stolper and Kate's own aggressive style, but when Debo wrote her history of this Oklahoma era, her assessment was that "the attack was inspired in the main by the rage of the guardians who had been brought to account by the Department of Charities and Corrections."[28]

That summer, while Kate was away, Governor Cruce asked her department's new attorney, Ross Lockridge, to go to Osage County to investigate the probate court in Pawhuska. The governor was still under pressure to handle the "Indian Problem" with state authority before Congress did. Lockridge reported to Kate that in the Osage Nation he found "a very deplorable condition" with "much waste and mismanagement of probate estates" involving administrators, executors, and guardians of Indian estates. After a short investigation, he could not have known the magnitude of this understatement. The oil-rich Osage reservation was the wealthiest nation in the world from the 1890s through the 1920s, but the oil and mineral rights belonged to tribal members. In the extreme prejudice of the time, white people thought this was against human nature, said Osage scholar Garrick Bailey. Whites resorted to corruption and murder to wrest away the Indian money in a cover-up that involved lawyers, law enforcement, and doctors. Even merchants joined in the exploitation and overcharged the Natives. "There was a carnival of crime in Osage County," Bailey said, while the state's oil tycoons, who knew what was happening, stood silent. "Indian history is not just warfare such as the well-known Battle of the Little Bighorn. The Osage tribe was in a battle; a silent one."[29]

With the Osage now the richest people per capita on earth, they also became the most murdered people per capita, killed for their headrights (allotments) and revenues from the vast oil fields. The story of the Osage Reign of Terror would not be known more fully until the 1920s, when the Bureau of Investigations, which became the Federal Bureau of Investigation, arrived to investigate, and it was not told fully for decades. One of the earliest detailed accounts of the crimes of larceny, embezzlement, fraud, and murder against the Osage was related by C. B. Glasscock in his

1938 book *Then Came Oil*. He wrote of "methods more subtle than murder" in siphoning oil wealth and listed the names of oil and pipeline companies charged in federal court with allegedly chiseling millions of dollars from the tribe: Carter Oil, Sinclair-Prairie Oil, Stanolind Crude Oil, Oklahoma Pipe Line, Stanolind Pipe Line, and Sinclair-Prairie Pipe Line.[30]

In researching his 1994 book *The Deaths of Sybil Bolton*, author Dennis McAuliffe Jr. discovered that 605 Osage died from 1907 to 1923, more than one and a half times the national rate. Even these numbers, he wrote, were undercounted because of the conspiracy with doctors and law enforcement officers who falsified crime reports and death certificates. The Osage murders became the subject of other books, including the best-selling *Killers of the Flower Moon* by David Grann and Linda Hogan's novel *Mean Spirit*, and two movies. The investigation by Kate's department preceded all these accounts.[31]

During Kate's time in office, the subject of the Osage Indian tragedy was just surfacing, and it attracted far less attention than her Five Tribes investigations in other counties. The criminal activity that Stolper had unearthed continued, and Lockridge discovered that the state's Indian problem was more widespread than Kate realized. "These conditions exist to a greater or less degree in a large number of the counties of the state," he told her. He found mismanagement in Tulsa County in the Cherokee Nation and egregious offenses in Garvin County in the Chickasaw Nation. The Garvin County judge under fire there sent a telegram to U.S. Representative Carter: "If you can't abolish the [district agents], for God's sake cut off the appropriations." Eliminating appropriations was becoming the politicians' favorite weapon of destruction.[32]

The next news of Kate came in August. She was at the Neurological Institute of New York for what was described variously as "a critical condition" and a "general nervous breakdown." She was thirty-eight years old, alone, sick, and bereft. Incredibly, she would get up for one last shindy.[33]

CHAPTER THIRTEEN

"The Grafters Are after Me"

THE NEW WILSON ADMINISTRATION brought disappointment to the Oklahomans who had salivated over political spoils. Senator Owen wanted an Oklahoman to be appointed secretary of the interior, but Franklin K. Lane of California was named to the post. Thomas P. Smith of Muskogee, a staunch anti-restrictions man, aspired to commissioner of Indian affairs, but Texan Cato Sells was chosen. These two appointments ended the dream of a Little Washington in Muskogee. The Oklahoma congressmen did succeed in their efforts to have the commissioner to the Five Civilized Tribes, George Wright, transferred and Union Agency superintendent Dana Kelsey's position eliminated. The two jobs were consolidated as superintendent for the Five Civilized Tribes, with Kelsey in the new position. Maybe because he was the survivor, Kelsey was remarkably upbeat about the consolidation and thought others were unduly anxious about the change.[1]

All told, the bitter congressional fight raged for three years between those who were determined to eliminate the federal protection given to the Five Tribes allottees and those who were trying to retain it. One of the first casualties of the battle was Kate and her Department of Charities and Corrections. Creek attorney Mott, as he himself had prophesied, was fired. So it was that some of the most active agencies and fearless individuals working to protect the Indians were destroyed. Their voices were extinguished one by one, like candles. Mott wrote a little book tracing the problem back to the Act of 1908, which had placed Oklahoma Indian jurisdiction in probate courts. It was, as Mott said in the subtitle, "a national blunder."

His assailed Mott Report had resulted in at least one attempt to ameliorate the damage. Oklahoma's congressional Democrats changed their minds about federal appointees, and in an effort to compensate for the loss of the district agents, in June 1913 they voted to appropriate a generous $85,000 for the secretary of the interior to hire attorneys to deal with probate matters of individual allottees of the Five Tribes. Hundreds applied, and Kate called the ones chosen "twenty-nine little lawyers given political jobs."[2]

She vehemently opposed the new policy of politically appointed probate attorneys because they were vulnerable to self-interest and corruption. To her horror, one of the first to be appointed was Frank Montgomery, the man who had angled to replace Stolper in her office by bragging about tinkering with a local election in Muskogee. The foxes were now guarding the henhouse. Kate fired off telegrams and letters to Washington saying the policy was simply an effort to appease the public and that some of the appointees were "grafters in the guise of probate attorneys."[3]

She beseeched Sells, the new commissioner of Indian affairs, to let her furnish him with facts about the candidates' "unsavory records in Indian matters." She protested particularly three federal appointments: Judge S. F. Parks for the Cherokees, whose ruling had turned over an Indian orphan's estate to a person not his legal guardian; and W. M. B. Mitchell and E. P. Hill, one of whom had been indicted and the other of whom had a case pending in court for transgressions in Indian orphan estates. Hill, proposed as attorney for the Choctaws, had joined Maxey in trying to railroad Montgomery into Kate's department. As for Mitchell, who had sought appointment as probate attorney for the Chickasaws, a Chickasaw tribal lawyer said, "The English language does not contain sufficient language strong enough to condemn [Mitchell's] nefarious work in permitting the wholesale robbery of minor children."[4]

Kate was ignored.

Oklahoma politicians both at home and in Washington scurried to quiet the uproar surrounding the probate scandal involving Indian minors. The real sorrow amid their letters, telegrams, and speeches—as Debo pointed out—is that nowhere in this flurry of communication was there one single word of "condemnation or concern over the exploitation of the children."

Instead, state lawmakers destroyed "the only agency of the state that had any right to intervene to protect some of the children from the rapacity of their guardians." Debo denounced this as one of the state's darkest periods in history, and none has stood to say nay.[5]

Without funds for a departmental attorney to defend Indian orphans' estates, Kate was helpless, but as unlikely as it seemed at the time, a second chance would soon come her way. It was attorney Mott who set in motion a series of events that immersed Kate in her last great shindy.

The odds were against her, but Kate was a good Catholic who knew her Bible and the story of David and Goliath. She believed that even a small person, if armed with courage and right, could defeat a giant. She once said, "I often wondered why nature had made no more of me so far as size goes. I've concluded it was a deep-laid plan of Providence to leave me so small that nobody would ever suspect me of being dangerous."[6]

In the fall of 1913 she returned to Oklahoma, still unwell but with fire in her eyes. She came home with three goals: (1) to do her job as best she could with a skeleton staff, (2) to fight in some way for what she now called "the Indian Question," and (3) to settle scores with the Oklahoma politicians who had gutted her department.

She still had state institutions to investigate, and new crises were erupting in several of them. First were the revelations of cruelty at the Cornish Orphans Home, and then major setbacks at the McAlester penitentiary, where seven men were shot during a prison break and Kate discovered repeats of the horrors of the Lansing prison—dungeons, beatings, and the water cure. The press had praised her for her Lansing prison reports. Now the *Muskogee Daily Phoenix*, hometown newspaper of Hill and Maxey, said it had had enough of her "silly sob stuff."[7]

Attendants at the Fort Supply mental hospital killed a patient—stomped him to death, Kate said. The governor's office investigated, and she attended the resulting public meeting, which drew an overflow crowd in the district courtroom at Woodward, where she spoke in a rage of frustration and helplessness. Such things had not happened when her office had funds for travel, inspections, and investigations, she railed. The Fourth Legislature

had destroyed her department, and now "the orphans and the unfortunates are neglected all over the state." She was so distraught that one of
the investigators reported her "disconcerted" behavior to Governor Cruce,
who replied kindly, "We will have to attribute her indiscretions to her
wretched state of health."[8]

She headed to Muskogee, where J. E. Wyand was campaigning for
mayor. Kate had first met Wyand on a Muskogee platform when she campaigned *for* him at the request of Haskell in exchange for the governor's
signature on her child labor bill. Despite her support, Wyand had been
defeated. The last time she had seen him had been more fractious; he was
one of the Maxey-Hill-Wyand trio trying to strong-arm her into hiring
Montgomery. Now she met Wyand in the district courtroom, where the
local newspaper described a "howling crowd" that "filled the room, the
galleries and the hallways." What happened next, the reporter wrote, was
"one of the most turbulent political gatherings ever held in Muskogee and
a woman led it."[9]

Kate was almost out of control as she attacked Wyand for ruining her
department and depriving the state's most vulnerable citizens of her help
and protection. "I'll get you and your whole gang; I'll teach you that I have
some power in this state; I'll camp on your trail and hound you till I get
you."[10]

Wyand thundered back that she could not find two members of the
legislature who would be willing to swear he had said one word against
her department. His supporters roared with voluminous cheering.

Kate rose angrily and shouted, "You are a liar and you know it."[11]

Wyand's supporters jeered her, but the union men rallied behind her at
the polls, and Wyand lost the March election. That night, Kate wired Governor Cruce, "I am sure God has helped me win this victory over this
enemy of the poor."[12]

In May she returned to Muskogee, determined to defeat Maxey in his
bid for election to the U.S. House of Representatives. "Mr. Maxey's interest is in money," she told the crowd. "He doesn't care anything about the
helpless, poor, deaf, mute, the blind, the orphans or the insane." Again
Kate prevailed, and Maxey lost the August primary to Cherokee tribal
attorney William W. Hastings. When the elections were over, Kate could
boast that "every one of my enemies" in the Fourth Legislature who were

candidates had been defeated. It was "the wildest session I have ever known in Oklahoma politics, but I defeated these men."[13]

Kate intended to campaign for reelection and believed she could win "provided this Indian question is kept in the background," but that was against her nature. She did not run from fights; she ran toward them. And then, out of the blue, a big gun came to her aid—former secretary of the interior Walter Lowrie Fisher. What happened next changed her life.[14]

Fisher had not forgotten a quick trip he had made to Oklahoma and a meeting there with Kate when she told him that her department was destroyed because it defended Indian minor children from the grafters. Neither had he forgotten the Mott Report, which he himself had sent to Congress, and the effect it had there. Fisher was no longer in office, but the Indian Question in Oklahoma was unfinished business he wanted to settle. In May of 1914, Fisher asked Frederick H. Abbott, secretary of the Board of Indian Commissioners, and Mott to go to Oklahoma City and meet with Kate. She invited Huson to join them.[15]

They agreed that the situation was a disaster. As Mott summed it up, Secretary of the Interior Lane had turned over to Commissioner of Indian Affairs Sells full and complete control of all matters affecting the Five Tribes, and the commissioner had turned it all over to the Oklahoma delegation: "They are dictating and controlling the entire policy and dictating all appointments of the numerous probate attorneys and all others in the Indian [Office] service in this state." They were not acting alone, Mott said. Their constituents were the ones committing the frauds against the Indians, and they were "a powerful part of the electorate sending these men to Congress." Consequently, "the looters of the Indians are, through the delegation, dictating policy." Mott and Abbott believed the sole hope for Oklahoma's Indians was Kate's Department of Charities and Corrections, "the only branch of government clothed with legal authority to enter the courts and protect helpless Indian minors."[16]

Speaking for former secretary of the interior Fisher, the two men implored Kate to help. What a group they were, as battered as four flood survivors washed up on dry land. Abbott, a precise man who parted his hair in the middle, had been either assistant commissioner or acting commissioner of the Board of Indian Affairs since 1909, dealing with formidable issues of lumber and liquor on reservations in Wisconsin and Minnesota. He was thoroughly knowledgeable about Oklahoma's problems with allotment and the federal government's Indian education program in the state. Mott had been ravaged by the Oklahoma delegation in Washington, where he had made a futile death stand on behalf of the Five Tribes. Both Kate and Huson had been pilloried by the Fourth Legislature, and both Mott and Huson had been drummed out of a job. They all understood that the Oklahoma lawmakers in Washington were winning the day in Congress and were supported by politicians, businessmen, oilmen, and investors in the state and beyond. Time was running out. The Indian Question in Oklahoma had lingered on for decades, and everyone was tired of it, even eastern friends of the Indians.[17]

Everybody in that room realized that Kate had the charisma for the goal of awakening the public conscience through speeches and the press and making the Indian Question not just a state issue but a national one. What she needed was sufficient funding. Fisher was willing to provide it, in the amount of $10,000, the current equivalent of $250,000. Abbott and Mott encouraged Kate, almost pleaded with her, to continue her work for the Indian cause in a new, bigger campaign beyond state borders. Only Kate and Huson knew what a personal toll that would demand of her.[18]

Two agendas were on the table: Mott and Abbott had their sights set on influencing Congress; Kate was running for reelection. As Abbott explained it, Fisher's fundraising appeal would be for "an unselfish, patriotic, non-partisan campaign of publicity on behalf of the unprotected Indians in her state." Unselfish and patriotic—what powerful words. And yet, the professional risk to her was immense. Kate assessed the situation and came to a startling decision. She thought she would be more effective if she made the fight not as an elected official, but as a private citizen, so if the Indian campaign were to be funded, she would not stand for reelection but would aim for a larger audience.[19]

Mott and Abbott were ecstatic. They sent Fisher enthusiastic letters and telegrams congratulating him for selecting this "brave and patriotic little woman" to campaign for the Indians of Oklahoma and the nation. They urged him to act quickly, because the state primary was coming up August 3. If Kate changed her mind and decided to run for reelection, she would have to file for office in June, barely a month away. They needed her commitment as soon as possible, and to get it, they needed Fisher's promise of $10,000 in funding.[20]

Abbott reminded Fisher of the immense value of Indian estates at risk, the upcoming distribution of millions of dollars of tribal funds plus the valuable timber, coal, oil, and gas leases. The numbers were staggering. Tribal funds amounted to approximately $5 million ready for distribution among approximately 60,000 Creeks, Cherokees, and Seminoles, plus about $30 million when the remaining property of the Choctaws and Chickasaws was disposed of. The Choctaw and Chickasaw Nations' land included 870,000 acres of timberlands; 430,000 acres of surface of segregated coal and asphalt lands, which would amount to about $250,000 annually in leases; and approximately 2,500 town lots. "The volume of work connected with these deeds, interest, supervision of per capita payments to 100,000 Indians," Abbott explained, "and the work of handling funds deposited in 170 Oklahoma banks, along with the appointment of guardians for thousands of minors who will receive their final per capital payments during the new few years is immense." Yet Congress had reduced appropriations for administrative expenses instead of increasing them. It was a catastrophic combination: more tempting money and less supervision.[21]

Kate wrote Fisher of the damage that had already been done. "Fully two-thirds of the adult Indians' lands are now in the hands of white owners, and only about one-third of the allotments remain in the hands of the Indians. Nearly all inherited lands have already been taken from the Indian minor children. However, a large proportion of the minor children's allotments are still intact and these can be saved."[22]

Fisher was a Republican and a lawyer, with the lean looks of a patrician. He was also a social reformer from Chicago who was noted for his work with that city's public transportation. He had been appointed secretary of the interior in 1911 by President William H. Taft and spent much of his term concerned with Alaska's railroads, coal leases, and emerging status as a territory. The Indian Office (Bureau of Indian Affairs) was under his jurisdiction, and it was in that capacity that he visited Oklahoma, met Kate, and learned firsthand about her battles for Indian orphan estates. He would raise most of the

$10,000 from wealthy Chicago-based businessmen and philanthropists: Cyrus H. McCormick of the International Harvesting Company and other members of the McCormick family, including Mrs. Emmons Blaine (Anita McCormick before her marriage) and Mrs. M. J. McCormick; Julius Rosenwald of Sears, Roebuck & Company; Charles R. Crane, a manufacturer of plumbing fittings; Edward E. Ayer, who was in the railroad commission business; David B. Jones, one of the founders of the zinc industry; and six more donors. Fisher, who donated $125 personally, referred to it as the "Oklahoma Indian Fund" because some of the donors had a special interest in Indian current affairs, history, and art. The donors must be kept secret, he told Kate, because many of the men were supporters of President Wilson, although they realized that "a mistake is being made with regard to the Indians." This meant the actions of Secretary Lane and Commissioner Sells. He assured her that the mistakes were due to "misinformation or misunderstanding of actual conditions," and neither official should be treated with "anything but the greatest consideration and without the slightest imputation upon their motives." Kate's campaign must never breathe a word of criticism against the administrations of either Wilson or Taft.[23]

Discretion was a condition of Fisher's funding. He wanted to win, but he wanted to win as a gentleman, playing nicely. It was a hard thing to ask of Kate, who was a street fighter accustomed to rough Oklahoma politics. She did not capitulate easily, but she agreed not to attack the national administration or any political party "except the present plan of probate attorneys." She spoke plainly. "I am fully of the opinion that the appointment of nineteen federal probate attorneys is but the development of a conspiracy by which the Indian is to be despoiled of all he possesses in the shortest time possible"; and what is more, "I could not agree to have my hands tied nor my lips closed" in saying as much about them and even "men higher up in politics" involved in the scheme. "I hear this talked among the leaders of our party and I know what is in the wind."[24]

She spelled out to Fisher what she hoped to accomplish in her Indian campaign: reinvest the Department of Charities and Corrections with the power to intervene on behalf of Indian orphan minors, retain and strengthen the offices of the commissioner of the Five Civilized Tribes and the superintendent of the Union Agency, increase the number of field officers under Kelsey's supervision, and expand the duties of tribal attorneys to aid the cases of individual Indians instead of tribal matters exclusively. "I am against the winding up of Indian affairs at this time because I know that the grafters are only waiting to get their hands on the money now held by the government."[25]

It is fascinating to see how these two personalities worked out their differences to come to an agreement. His letters are smooth; hers often vibrate with emotion. Huson was part of the communication, too, usually attempting to bridge the differences between them and writing on Kate's behalf when she was on the road making speeches.[26]

However carefully Kate evaluated the proposal from Mott, Abbott, and Fisher, it is unlikely that she asked important questions such as: Could she count on their financial support after the November elections? Could they help her in other ways—with the press, for example? What would happen if they did not succeed with the upcoming Congress? If she did ask these questions, and if Abbott and Mott gave her reassuring answers, that part of their communications was not recorded. Kate announced that spring that she would not seek reelection, attributing her decision to her poor health. The Indian campaign would be separate but concurrent with her departmental work until the November election, when her term of office ended.[27]

Kate began to separate herself from her role of commissioner, but she and Fisher were anxious that the Department of Charities and Corrections continue after she left office, and they looked around for a successor. Kate's first choice was Estelle Blair, the young woman who had begun work in the department as a stenographer, but who, Kate admitted, was "worn down and her health is in pretty bad condition just as mine is, all brought about by worry and hard work." Fisher was cool to the suggestion and to Kate's other proposal that Huson return as assistant commissioner, so she offered another candidate: "There is a Mrs. Mabel Bassett, a woman strong in mind and body who has given us valuable aid and who has the breadth of mind and the vigor to carry out anything she undertakes." Bassett did not run for the office, however, and a Methodist minister named William D. Matthews was elected. He served as a bland commissioner until 1923, when he was succeeded by Bassett, who served with distinction until 1947.[28]

---— ∞ —·—

Initially, Kate and Fisher corresponded frequently—sometimes several letters a day—until he stepped away from active involvement in the campaign and delegated Chicago colleagues to send payments to Kate. From this point on, Abbott and Warren K. Moorehead were the driving force in Kate's new Indian campaign, orbiting her with help in raising funds and cheering her on.

She could not have had better allies than Moorehead and Abbott. She was not experienced with the national knot of Indian agencies, committees, and politics she was entering, but those two men were experts in the field. Both had considerable experience with Indian affairs, and Kate needed that. They had worked with the Board of Commissioners of Indian Affairs and the Indian Office. In fact, Abbott was instrumental in securing the congressional appropriation that kept the Indian Office alive when some wanted to abolish it. Both men also were familiar with the Friends of the Indian, the Society of American Indians, the Indian Rights Association, and other well-meaning Indian support groups. Relationships ranging from uneasy, to contentious, to hostile existed among the Board of Indian Commissioners, the Indian Office, and congressional committees on Indian affairs, and it was in part to avoid conflicting loyalties that Fisher wanted his donors kept anonymous. Unknowingly, Kate was entering treacherous territory when she launched her Indian campaign.[29]

Abbott knew very well that the state's reduced appropriation "to strangle the Department of Charities and Corrections came from the business interests of Oklahoma." He despaired "of inducing Congress to extend federal jurisdiction any further in this state and thereby undo the permanent harm which has been done by Congress . . . as long as the Oklahoma Delegation in Congress wields the tremendous influence which it now exercises in shaping Indian legislation." He saw even more to fear from "the same poisonous political influence" that had destroyed Mott, Wright, and Gresham, and which was now attacking the Five Tribes' school service. "Unless the friends of the Indians in Oklahoma and elsewhere will help Miss Barnard to preserve the Department of Charities and Corrections, the sole remaining legal protection to the minor children in Oklahoma, I shrink from trying to predict the future of these Indians."[30]

Moorehead was an archaeologist, anthropologist, author, and museum curator at the Smithsonian Institution and elsewhere, a humanitarian who was sincere about protecting Indians, and he knew all about politicians who wrangled policies counter to the interest of Indians. As chairman of the Board of Indian Commissioners, he had reorganized the

Indian Office and investigated the White Earth Reservation in Minnesota, where the Chippewa (Ojibwe) were swindled out of millions of dollars from their land allotments and white pine timber. The headwaters of the Minnesota theft was a 1906 law that removed restrictions held by mixed-blood Indians in the reservation, a bill sponsored by U.S. senator Moses Clapp, chairman of the Senate Committee on Indian Affairs. It was a mirror image of the situation in Oklahoma. Moorehead had experience in uncovering fraud perpetrated on Indians by individuals, companies, and elected officials, so when he toured Oklahoma, he knew what he was seeing. He knew that when restrictions on Indian land were removed, what resulted was fraud and graft. Moorehead had seen the effects of inadequate federal funding for education and health care for the Indians of White Earth as the tribe was ravaged by trachoma, tuberculosis, and scrofula; he witnessed the same conditions among the Five Tribes in Oklahoma. His considerable influence caused the Board of Indian Commissioners and the Lake Mohonk Conference of 1912 and 1913 to focus attention on the wrongs suffered by Oklahoma Indians, and Kate was invited to address the Lake Mohonk group in 1914. This would be the keynote speech in her Indian campaign.[31]

Kate opened the headquarters for her Indian campaign in two rooms of the Bristol Hotel in Oklahoma City June 28, 1914. She named it the People's Civic Welfare League. It was an informational campaign, but she also intended it to be a permanent nonpartisan organization with chapters in every school district of the state dedicated to ensuring honest government. Huson was the campaign manager, as he had been for all of Kate's political campaigns. The first campaign publication was a fireball of a pamphlet titled *Kate Barnard Says, "Wake Up and Defend the Honor of the State,"* which detailed the history of her involvement with protecting Indian minors and the resulting assault by the Fourth Legislature. She attacked both the acts and the actors who ruined her department, leaving thousands of Indian children hapless prey for "human buzzards" looting their estates. As for the majority of the legislature, it was nothing but "rabble," a group "indulging in rowdyism by day and resorting to gambling places, boot-legger joints, and immoral places at night."[32]

With the initial funds from Fisher, Huson sent 56,000 copies of their blazing pamphlet to "ministers, laboring men, and societies"; paid his own salary and that of R. C. Meloy, who was hired to check probate records in Creek and Okmulgee Counties; and gave a stipend to Stolper, who was checking records in Muskogee County. He hired people to give speeches and to organize groups. By the end of September, he had spent almost $6,000 of their $10,000 budget. Much of the money had gone for printing and mailing. None of it had gone to Kate directly. The funds came to her in dribs and drabs from Chicago, and almost every report she sent to Fisher asked for payment of overdue funding.[33]

That October, Kate launched a rigorous speaking campaign, addressing "overflow crowds across the state." Although her health was tenuous, she assured Fisher that she was feeling strong and could hold up under the strain. The campaign was scheduled to end November 3, election night for both the state and federal races, but she told him she wanted to extend it until the state legislature met the first week of January. Then, she planned on holding "a large convention of farmers, ministers, and others to pass resolutions in favor of bills they have discussed." All of this depended on funding, she reminded him. "Until I receive more money, I am at a standstill."[34]

She was enthusiastic about adding what she called a "very catchy plan"—a People's Lobby. This unexpected addition so startled Fisher that Huson had to assuage his concerns. The Indian Question would still be uppermost, Huson promised. The People's Lobby would address local issues of good roads, school land leases, school matters, and economy of state and county government. Since the new legislature would have a "large number of new and untried men," Kate's goal was to keep it true and straightforward. The campaign might appear out of the ordinary in a political way, Huson explained, "but Miss Barnard's methods are always different and her manner of attack unexpected." Also, he added, "She has been out of funds for some weeks. She needs $2,500 to ensure success."[35]

Kate's People's Lobby was one of her bursts of inspiration, as enthusiastic as it was spontaneous, the kind of unexpected action that exasperated Huson and her staff. To Kate, it was logical. "What we are fighting for now is to control the Legislature, and we are organizing the State by counties," she said. They hoped to organize thousands of men to join by giving "what I call, 'the pennies of the poor'—not more than twenty-five or fifty cents apiece, because I want it to be a movement of the masses." The People's Lobby was a mixed bag of intentions. She intended to pressure the next legislature to make an appropriation to the Department of Charities and restore a lawyer to her staff. Also, it would be a legislature watchdog with her at the helm. Kate was still traumatized by the political destruction of her department and disillusioned by lawmakers in a body, but she had faith in the common people and an abundance of confidence in herself. She would examine every bill introduced in the legislature to be sure there were no "jokers" in it "intended to kill the Child Labor or Compulsory Education laws, or any other of the people's laws." This was something new in politics, she admitted. Government watchdog agencies would one day be commonplace, but at the time the notion was startling, the inspiration of the fertile mind of a woman ahead of her time. It was also breathtaking in its ambition and far more than any one person could do, yet no bolder than her original idea of a department of charities and corrections to investigate every state charitable and penal institution. An unspoken *raison d'être* for the People's Lobby was that once she was out of office, she would need a job, and more than a job, she would need a cause.[36]

Kate began her Indian campaign speaking tour in Oklahoma, then traveled to the Lake Mohonk Conference in upstate New York, before concluding in New York City for lectures and press interviews. Huson accompanied her on the eastern trip.[37]

The Mohonk mountain resort was a sprawling Victorian castle in the forested Hudson Valley, ninety miles north of New York City. It had been the summer home of Albert K. Smiley, a member of the Board of Indian Commissioners, who opened it in 1883 to annual meetings of Friends of the Indian, a group of influential people and philanthropists who met to confer about Indian policies and interests. William "Alfalfa Bill" Murray, now a U.S. representative, had spoken at Lake Mohonk the year before in a show of solidarity with the rest of the Oklahoma delegation. He lamented the theft of Indian minor estates, but he advocated relaxing the controls on Indian land, and he supported leasing. This was in direct opposition to Indian advocates such as Moorehead, who believed that under the guise of leasing, Indians were duped into signing mortgages and deeds and lost their property.

Kate was at the Lake Mohonk Conference October 14 and 15, 1914, to give the last big speech of her career. "It seems fitting that here I should bring the message of my own broken life and crushed efforts," she told the audience, spooling out her tale as skillfully as Scheherazade: first this happened, and then this, and then that. The Department of Charities and Corrections had "made enemies when we took the children out of the mills and factories and got them into schools through the Child Labor and Compulsory Education laws. These laws made for us bitter enemies of the coal and railroad corporations, also those interested in using the children in manufactories." Despite this—and it was a big hurdle to overcome—"we were still able to maintain our integrity and keep our Department going until we stepped into this fight for the Indians of our State. It was then that all of our enemies massed themselves against us, and we went down to defeat." Quite simply, her work for the protection of the Indians of the state had led to the destruction of her department.[38]

"Some sinister motive" had influenced the Oklahoma delegation in Congress in 1907 to demand that Congress abdicate its jurisdiction over the Indians of the Five Tribes and their estates and vest that jurisdiction in the probate courts of Oklahoma. She explained her department's work in prosecuting grafters and exposing corrupt county judges, she told them about the assault by the Fourth Legislature, and then she leveled her deadliest accusation: "We did not know at that time what we now believe is a fact; namely, that a national conspiracy exists all the way from Oklahoma to Washington, to get rid of every individual who is in authority, and who is known to be friendly to the Indians." The Oklahoma delegation, she said, "voted for it, and fought for it, and finally succeeded in getting the measure through." This was a determined effort to "take charge of all the offices and Governmental agencies maintained for the purpose of protecting the Indians, to then and there rob the 101,000 Indians of Oklahoma and leave them penniless paupers." She rebuked the press for not reporting the abuses. As she had written Fisher at the beginning of her campaign, "I am practically barred out of the press in Oklahoma and have been for the past year or more as all of our papers are owned and controlled by certain interests."[39]

This was a seasoned audience accustomed to hearing egregious wrongs against the Indians, but Kate held her listeners enthralled with her drama. She built to an emotional crescendo about how this had affected her. "Then followed a period in which I almost lost my religion,—a time when I said: 'There is no God; Chaos rules this world.'" Finally, she offered the audience a wisp of hope. She listed her years of political successes in Oklahoma and said, "In spite of this, the Democrats are saying to me, 'Kate, you are ruining your political future by this fight.' My answer is: 'I can't ruin it. The youth of Oklahoma, seeing the fight that I am making, will, when I am dead, take up the banner where I drop it and march upward toward the heights. No battle for justice was ever lost.'"[40]

Kate was not the only one who spoke at the conference about the crisis in Oklahoma. After her address, several people rose to affirm what she had said. In his address, the Right Reverend Theodore Payne Thurston, Oklahoma's Episcopal bishop, called the grafters "wolves." Representative J. Weston Allen of Massachusetts, who had visited Oklahoma as a member of Boston's Indian Citizenship Committee, referenced repeated reports about the needs of Oklahoma's Indians from Five Tribes expert Dana Kelsey. Allen reminded the audience that in 1913 James E. Gresham, a special assistant to the U.S. attorney general, had detailed the plight of the Seminole Indians in Oklahoma and referred to the Lake Mohonk Conference as "the court of last resort for the dependent American Indian." *Collier's Weekly* financial editor John Oskison said, "If Miss Barnard had told you the whole story of why the Oklahoma newspapers did not publish her story, it would have involved the names of some whom even you would not like to have mentioned."[41]

After hearing these testimonials, the Lake Mohonk Conference adopted a platform that said, "In the event that the Oklahoma legislature shall fail to give early and adequate protection to these Indians, we see no alternative but that the Federal Government should resume full jurisdiction over all of the 'restricted' Indians of that State." The Board of Indian Commissioners supported the call for increased federal protection of the Five Tribes. This was exactly the response that Kate's Indian campaign team had hoped for.[42]

She went from Lake Mohonk to New York, where she gave speeches in churches and clubs and before "a packed house in Carnegie Hall"; shared the stage with Carrie Chapman Catt ("one of the world's best known women," Kate said) at the Hudson Theater, sponsored by the League for Political Education; and gave interviews to the press. It was about this time that Moorehead called Kate the "Joan of Arc of Oklahoma." She was not a French maid leading an army, but she was a single earnest young woman carrying the banner in what seemed to be a noble, almost lost, cause. Could she marshal public opinion enough to stir congressional hearts and change federal policy and appropriations?[43]

Kate had promised to tell the story to the national press, and she did so effectively. In November the *New York Sun*, the *Survey*, the *Literary Digest*, and the *New York Herald* ran interviews with her describing "what is perhaps the most unparalleled campaign in the interest of humanity to confront the biggest plot to rob and plunder ever contemplated in American history, a plot which reaches all way from Oklahoma to Washington, D. C.," and the collusion behind it.[44]

The press was startled at Kate's charges of conspiracy, but Commissioner Sells acknowledged that they were "in the main true." The Philadelphia *Public Ledger* wrote, "It was freely admitted at the Indian Office that a systematic robbing of Indians in Oklahoma had been going on for a long time and the office was at work trying to get at the bottom of the criminality." The *Survey*, a magazine published in New York about social and political issues, wrote an editorial praising the work of "the girl commissioner of charities" and lamenting, "Never has *The Survey* staff felt more keenly our financial limitations than in our inability to send a competent investigator to Oklahoma to make a searching and disinterested portrayal of the situation."[45]

And yet, for all the applause, something went wrong during the Lake Mohonk Conference. Kate realized it at once. She said she was appalled to find some with Indian missionary interests allied with the officials in the Indian Office and more interested to know whether her fight would affect those officials than how it would benefit the Indians. Moorehead and Abbott were appalled, too. She had been too bold in her accusations. She had splashed mud on the Taft and Wilson administrations, and she had hinted at funding sources associated with the Board of Commissioners of Indian Affairs and the Interior Department (Fisher). This opened rifts among Indian interest groups and violated the secrecy Fisher required.[46]

Calling public attention to the Indian Problem in Oklahoma was one thing, but implicating prominent people in reaping the spoils and federal officials in ignoring the criminality crossed the line of discretion. As Oskison said, some of the names were so big, nobody wanted to say them aloud. J. D. Rockefeller Jr. was one of those names. Moorehead almost secured a donation from Rockefeller, but he said the philanthropist backed away when he heard "the cry against his oil company in Oklahoma." Moorehead was careful not to mention Rockefeller's name to Kate lest she attempt to appeal to him personally, which she surely would have done. "He is a very sedate and proper man and he would not be taken with her emotional speech."[47]

Kate was winning with the press but failing in her fundraising efforts. She had hoped to raise $5,000 in the East but was unable to raise more than $300. She felt helpless against the vast and invisible opponent of Standard Oil, as if she were "caught in mid ocean and drawn under by some powerful undertow, sucked under, and swallowed alive." This was a force with influence in "every newspaper, every bank, every State house, pulpit and corn row, for even mortgaged farmers must eat out of its banker's hand." Beyond that, she said, "Everybody in New York is busy contributing to, and making clothes for the distressed and dying in Belgium and elsewhere, and in taking care of the tremendous unemployment problem in New York City due to the closing down of so many American industries." Without funding for travel, printing, and mailing, her campaign to generate public support was stalled. She sensed that she was losing Fisher's interest, but she kept writing him, saying she had booked fifteen more speaking dates that would take her campaign through January 10. She signed a letter to him "sincerely, hurriedly, and anxiously."[48]

The only good news she had was the Oklahoma election results. Her campaign against her political enemies was successful, and forty-two members of the Fourth Legislature were defeated. There were only ninety-seven state legislators, so this was almost half of them. Very few county judges were reelected.[49]

Abbott and Moorehead were in deep dismay. "Oklahoma affairs have reached a crisis," Abbott said. The newly minted probate attorneys had wreaked havoc by dismissing indictments and allowing other flagrant probate matters. The situation was so grave, it intensified their belief that the only hope was for the next Congress to rescue the situation, and only "Miss Barnard can lead that victory."[50]

Moorehead and Abbott continued to try to raise funds for her campaign, and so did Kate with fees from her lectures, but there were bigger problems. Public tastes had changed, and Kate's oratorical style seemed dated, especially in the East. Moorehead broached the subject gingerly with Abbott, saying that several people had written him about her rhetorical style, and he wondered whether Huson might influence her "not to put so much in her speeches on sociology and religion, etc." It was a delicate matter, he realized, but "she is not a real sociologist and a good deal of her appeal along religious lines is not understood." This was not a new observation. Two years earlier, the *New York Sun* had written that her oratory sounded quaint and provincial to New York ears. The newspaper said she spoke with "the naïve sentimentality of a schoolgirl and an old-fashioned piety reminiscent of the mourner's bench at a revival."[51]

Moorehead and Abbott consoled and commiserated with one another, anguishing over Kate's haphazard work style. She was waging a remarkable fight, but "the girl really needs someone to keep her balanced." Still, they felt that success was near. "The Indian Office is thoroughly scared," Abbott said. "They are now really sorry for their boldness in attacking civil service, not through conscience, but fear." It was important not to lose their advantage, he said: "We must push them over the breastwork while they are on the run. We cannot win by sitting at dignified attention. We shall have to peel our coats and deliver blow for blow with the Indian Office officials, Congressmen, everybody who is on the wrong side. It is a great victory for Indians if we win and victory is within our reach. We *must* win."[52]

Moorehead was losing hope. He did his part to publicize the story of the Oklahoma Indians by writing about it in his new book on Indians in the United States, but that would not be off the press for a month, too late to help Kate's campaign. His fundraising efforts fared even worse. "I have exhausted every channel in her behalf, have contributed what money I could [and] this is no time to 'beg' in view of the dreadful situation in Europe, but unless this woman is supported in the next two or three weeks, we shall lose all that every one of us have been fighting for the past seven years in Oklahoma." He said that Kate was discouraged and depressed and had every reason to be. The enemy was powerful, he wrote a potential donor. "If you can do anything for this heroic woman," he pleaded, "please heed the call for help from this modern Joan d'Arc." He himself was giving up. "It is utterly impossible for me to raise any money for her."[53]

The "dreadful situation in Europe" was a major reason Kate was having trouble raising funds and getting more press coverage of her Indian campaign. Another reason, according to Oskison, was that times had changed along with the interest of the reading public. "Miss Barnard is a muckraker," he said at the Lake Mohonk Conference, "one of the purest and finest types we have ever developed," but a muckraking story was out of fashion. The national press had a more important wrong to address, and that was the escalating war in Europe that would become known as World War I.[54]

Moorehead consoled Kate. "Not that the people have no interest in your fight, but you in Oklahoma cannot realize that everybody is sending money abroad. The suffering in Belgium, France, and Germany passes belief. Returning travelers tell stories of death from gangrene, starvation, etc. For this reason, every possible dollar is sent abroad." He assured her that her Indian campaign was not lost totally because she had all of the following year to raise funds. "As soon as the war is over, money can be raised for you." He was wrong, because 1915 would be far from the end of the war. As Winston Churchill wrote, "Hereafter the fire roared on till it burned itself out." World War I would not be over for four more years. The battlefields of Ypres, Gallipoli, Verdun, and the Somme drowned out the quiet laments from Pawhuska, Tulsa, Sapulpa, Vinita, Wewoka, and other Oklahoma towns where Indians were being killed and their estates were being plundered. Amid this worldwide conflagration, news about Oklahoma's Indians did not spark even a flicker of interest in the press.[55]

As the year came to an end, Kate pleaded with Fisher, asking for $1,700 still owed her. "I hope you will not allow a woman of my position and record to be pushed out into a fight where she has engendered the hatred of the whole democratic machine and then be left without funds."[56]

He did allow it.

Fisher's colleagues sent her no more money, and he stopped communicating with her. He had honored his agreement regarding the Indians of Oklahoma, and then he sailed for Europe to see the war situation for himself. He returned to Chicago to his wealthy friends and family, concerned with the war and his law practice. Oklahoma and the Indian Question were behind him.

Abbott and Moorehead moved on, too. Abbott rolled off the Board of Indian Commissioners and became an advocate of progressive farming. Moorehead continued his prolific writing about Indians and archaeology while curating the archaeology department and museum at the Phillips Academy in Andover, Massachusetts.[57]

Kate went back to Oklahoma. Oklahoma was her only interest.

Progressive social reform was yesterday's roses. Interest had peaked and wilted—too expensive, too difficult, too complicated. The nation's attention had shifted to the conflagration in Europe and the heart-stopping fear that if war escalated in Europe, the United States might be drawn into it—which it was.

Congress would convene in January without fear of a powerful confrontation defending Indian estates, and Kate's Indian campaign died, not because she was ineffective, but because of a lack of funding and a lack of national interest. For seven years her career had been in the ascendancy. She said with justifiable pride that she was never defeated, but she was defeated now by forces beyond her influence or control. Her Indian campaign was a brief but epic battle and a quiet yet resounding defeat.

As 1914 came to an end, Kate was out of funds for her Indian campaign, out of office, out of power, and out of favor. She had been abandoned by Fisher, Abbott, Moorehead, and her beloved Democratic Party. The wounded, bleeding earth collapsed under her feet, and Kate began to fall. She fell and fell and fell.

CHAPTER FOURTEEN

Celtic Twilight

O N THE STATE'S FIRST INAUGURATION DAY, in 1907, when Kate ascended the ceremonial stage bedecked with chrysanthemum garlands, the exultant crowd cheered her.

On the state's second Inauguration Day, in 1911, the governor served buttermilk, Kate wore a plain dark taffeta dress, and again the crowd cheered her.

On the morning of the state's third Inauguration Day, January 12, 1915, while Robert Lee Williams, a former Oklahoma Supreme Court justice from Durant was being sworn in as governor, Kate packed her personal items and walked out of her office for the last time. Nobody cheered her.[1]

During the campaign, Williams had told her that her People's Lobby might jeopardize his success, so she canceled her speaking dates ten days before the election lest her speeches be damaging to him. She wrote the governor-elect a few days before the inauguration reminding him that she had been his friend in the primaries. She reminded him also of his written assurance—a letter dated September 29, 1914, she noted—that she could absolutely count on him to recommend and approve all appropriations to maintain the Department of Charities. She was not doubting his word, she said diplomatically, but just writing him "so the subject won't be overlooked." The Indian orphans of Oklahoma needed an attorney in the Department of Charities.[2]

After her East Coast speeches, Kate returned to the state weary and disgusted, saying she would travel no more for the Indian campaign at her own expense and would not seek a third term: "I would not have the office and suffer the heartbreak and nervous strain again for twenty thousand a

Kate was ferocious and fearless in her official investigations and
political battles, but the conspiracy of grafters she faced in the "Indian
Question" left her, for the first time in her career, frightened and frail.
Photograph courtesy Oklahoma Historical Society.

year." She was determined to continue her fight on behalf of Indian orphans and to clean up the legislature with pressure from her People's Civic Welfare League, but she came home to an inhospitable climate in which much of the press either ignored her or ridiculed her. Humor can be a devastating weapon. When the influential *Harlow's Weekly* reported that she might have a prominent role to play in the upcoming Fifth Legislature, another publication responded, "Not on your tin type. 'A people's lobby' under petticoat leadership will mighty soon be invited to go away 'back and sit down.'" The *Hugo Husonian* jumped on the laughingstock bandwagon, mocking "a red-hot, straight off the fire communication from Katherine, the Great Champion of the down trodden, the poor Indian and Dr. Stolper," and adding, "If 'twere not for Kate the gayety of Oklahoma would diminish." Even the *Daily Oklahoman*, her staunch ally since pre-statehood days, deserted her and wrote that her work for the Indian had gone awry.[3]

Harlow's Weekly did not often ridicule Kate. The nonpartisan publication run by Victor E. Harlow was dedicated to "logical thinking and accurate information," and despite reprinting the crack about "the Great Champion," it was not part of the state press that dismissed her. Quite the contrary. In a more earnest tone it wrote, "The tendency in Oklahoma in the last few years, especially among the politicians, has been to consider Kate Barnard a joke, perhaps at times a bitter kind of joke, but nevertheless not to be taken seriously. . . . It is time that this attitude should be changed." Especially beyond state borders, it considered her "an extremely potent factor in all matters pertaining to the Oklahoma Indians." She had reform connections, the publication said, which made her "undoubtedly the most powerful single influence upon public opinion in the east." Oklahoma officials dealing with Indian affairs should recognize this, resolve the Indian affairs, and restore the state's reputation.[4]

Others took her seriously, too. A year earlier, an uneasy Governor Cruce wrote Robert Lee Williams, then still a judge, urging him to get a certain senator "in line for Miss Kate" and to "assist us in calling halt to the onslaught of grafters." Her proposed People's Lobby was a statewide campaign, Cruce explained, and "would call attention to the misdeeds and questionable behavior of the Fourth Legislature and its inactiveness to impede grafter's activities." If she does this, the governor said, "it will stir up things [and] there is no telling what will come of it. If she tells the truth about the rotten bunch in the legislature, you know it will bring on a hornet's nest."[5]

No longer the commissioner of charities and corrections in 1915, Kate, as a private citizen and lobbyist, rented an office in a bank building and continued her one-woman campaign. When the Fifth Legislature convened January 8, Kate was there handing each lawmaker an open letter titled "What Are You Going to Do about the Robbing of Indian Orphan Children in Oklahoma?" She did, indeed, bust open a hornet's nest, denouncing twelve bills and one joint resolution before the legislature, saying, "every one will promote graft and robbery of Indian orphan children." She lobbied to have these removed, and she went a step farther and tried, unsuccessfully, to have a Senate bill introduced to expand protection of Indian minors.[6]

In the Senate, she went from seat to seat to speak with each senator individually. It was uphill work. Despite the considerable turnover after the elections, a sizable number of the lawmakers were entrenched in opposing Kate's work for Indian minors. The Democratic Party that she had been so instrumental in bringing into state power had shifted alliances, and now some Democrats went so far as to say that Kate was "an unpleasant presence" in their midst. The conflict came to a head in the House in mid-March in a final monumental public clash between Kate and Murray. Now a U.S. congressman, Murray arrived to speak to the House on the Indian question at, he claimed, the special request of Indian Commissioner Sells. Murray said that Oklahomans could convince Congress and the East that it was the state's desire to protect the Indian wards and that "these stories about robbing the Indians are lies." The state's probate courts were capable of handling the issue; it was certainly beyond the capabilities of "a commissioner of charities and a curly haired dago."[7]

The clamor that arose in response was so loud, it was hard to hear a legislator's request that Kate be allowed to rebut Murray's remarks. All of the Republicans and some Democrats supported the proposal, and so when order was restored, Kate, "almost too angry to speak," stood before the House chamber and delivered a scorching reply: "I am glad to see that the southern democracy is gallant enough to hear a woman who has been attacked by a man who has come all the way from Washington" to do it. She said she had Sells's endorsement on behalf of Indians, but if Murray's statement about representing Sells was true, "Either I have been double crossed or Bill Murray lied."[8]

Kate was justifiably almost too angry to speak, and her rage was understandable. Frederick Abbott agreed with her and wrote the secretary of the Lake Mohonk Conference that Sells was "playing both sides of the game in Oklahoma." Abbott said that the Oklahoma Supreme Court ruling left the federal attorneys "without standing in the courts, pretenders to power they have not, and a real menace because of the false pretense of protection." Sells knew this, but "he has not displayed the courage to tell the truth to Congress nor to the public." Kate managed to have all thirteen bills either stricken or weakened. It was a small victory.[9]

Kate's ordeal was a tragedy for her and a tragedy for Oklahoma, but apparently it was not a unique tragedy, as Ben Lindsey wrote years later. Judge Lindsey was the social reformer from Denver who pioneered the juvenile court system and traveled to Oklahoma to help Kate with juvenile court legislation for the state. He was a judge with the California Supreme Court in 1940 when he reminisced about his admiration for the "frail, courageous, wonderful little woman [who] carried on her battle for humanity and justice." His letter could stand as a definitive treatise on privilege and patriotism in politics. Lindsey wrote that he fully understood why Kate had been deserted by some of her Democratic allies. "In such legislative battles there are always privileged interests and reactional individuals who are opposed to all liberalism and all progress. They are devoted mostly to property rights without any consideration for human rights. They make themselves powerful in legislatures, city councils, city government, state government, and even in courts. It is a subtle but forceful and dangerous power that rises in opposition to just such work as Miss Kate pioneered and championed.[10]

"I have encountered it all through my public life," Lindsey added, the "eternal problem of envy and jealousy in the hearts of the mediocrities who become frightened at the strength of leadership focused in one person." And they had reason to fear. In Kate's battle for humanity, it was inevitable that she would become "a marked woman." He had warned her of this and told her to be prepared. "It is a real compliment to her work and the strength and power that came to her from the people because of her championship of their rights" and was sure to make her "a dangerous obstacle in the way of privileged and selfish interests in politics who are constantly usurping the powers of government." Kate's purposes were unselfish, with a statesmanship that was all too rare. "Miss Kate did become hated by [privileged interests] and it was their purpose to drive her from public life simply because they feared her," the judge said. "She was the state's greatest leader and greatest citizen."[11]

Governor Williams could not keep his promise to Kate. The Fifth Legislature refused to provide funds for an attorney for the Department of Charities and Corrections, removed many safeguards related to Indian property, and increased the power of county judges for probate cases. Kate failed in her work as a lobbyist. She realized that seeking any state help was futile. The Democrats in the state had thoroughly suppressed support for the Indians and convinced her that there was "no hope for the Indian in Oklahoma." As 1915 came to an end, she wrote Walter Lowrie Fisher a final letter of despair, telling him that she had no support from the state's Democratic Party, no press support, and no support from the Indian officials who had been fired or transferred. "What in the name of God is the use?"[12]

Her only recourse was Washington and increased federal authority. Without Fisher's donors, her fundraising was limited to the disappearing help from Abbott and Moorehead. Moorehead's new book, *The American Indian in the United States*, was off the press at last, and he sent a copy to Joseph P. Tumulty, President Wilson's White House chief of staff, telling him that Kate intended to be in Washington in late March to "lay the cause of the Indian minors and orphans of Oklahoma before the committees of the House and Senate." He said she would like to meet with the president for ten minutes to state her case, and he asked Tumulty's help in arranging the interview. Neither meeting happened, not with the congressional committees or with the president.[13]

The closest Kate came to President Wilson was the following year when she sent him a letter with a detailed account of her last two years' work on the Indian Question. No reply was found in the archives. It was too late. She was broken in spirit and in body. "This battle is too much for me. It would kill a strong man." She left public life, and she left Oklahoma in search of doctors, hospitals, sanitariums, or sanctuary that might restore her health. It would be a long, long search.[14]

———— ∞ ————

Kate was not the only one from her department who wandered in the wilderness. Hobart Huson's health had worsened after another unsuccessful surgery for his old leg injury. After his job with Kate's People's Lobby dried up, his life went into a tumble. Kate tried to help him with his dream of devoting himself to literature and agriculture and turned over to him the management and income of her homesteaded Newalla farm. It was a mistake. "He was no farmer and almost ruined it by bad management. I had to take it back to save it," she wrote. He and Kate had a falling-out, and in 1918 she charged him with embezzlement and sought recovery of $3,000 with interest from an oil and gas lease connected to a school land commission. The jury found for the defense, and although Kate considered appealing to the Oklahoma Supreme Court, she did not. Out of office, she became consumed with two things: her health and her properties. She kept minutely detailed records of the former and filed lawsuits involving the latter.[15]

Huson wrote his son that he had been offered jobs managing the campaigns of several candidates, but refused them. "I am completely disgusted with politics—its eternal bickering, backbiting, and double crossing." He intended to "eke out a living by writing for magazines." Then Huson vanished. He left Kate with a storage ticket for his worldly possessions: his library of books. It was only after he was gone that Kate discovered he was married and had an estranged family in Texas. She rushed to Texas to meet his sons—"fine young lawyers in San Antonio," she described them—and learned there that their mother had died three years before. Almost six decades later, Hobart Huson Jr. politely said that he and his brother, both of whom were personally acquainted with Kate, considered her an exceptional woman. Less favorably, he remembered how she had "barged in" to see him, "a masculine outfit" who looked like "any other old maid," barking orders and demanding to know Huson's whereabouts. Kate tried to find Huson but could not. After his death, she learned that he had died "aged, penniless, sick, alone, forgotten in the Salvation Army of New York City. What a tragic end for one who had served Oklahoma so nobly."[16]

Huson's sons spent nine years trying to find him and finally located him in New York City. They wrote offering assistance, but he died with the unanswered letter in his pocket. Huson's sons, like Kate, romanticized him, and said that his life ended miserably: he was living in "a squalid little cubbyhole of a room, his only friends from the Salvation Army." His sister Martha, a doctor who lived at the fashionable Hotel Grenoble near

Carnegie Hall in New York City, contradicted this account and said he had not died of starvation or want of bare necessities and was welcome in the home of their sister Clara, "but he probably had enough decency not to trouble them after the way he behaved and probably felt the same way to you and your brother. I am truly sorry that a man of so much capability and personality should have made so little of his life." Huson died June 12, 1925, in the Hospital of St. Barnabas in Newark, New Jersey. Martha took charge of the arrangements, and at his sons' expense, the man who was such a scholar of the Civil War and a proclaimed supporter of the South was buried at the historic Mount Olivet Cemetery in Queens, a garden cemetery with a tall monument honoring Union soldiers. The official cause of death was bronchitis. He was sixty-nine years old. The space on the death certificate for occupation was left empty.[17]

Dr. J. H. Stolper had been out of Kate's life since his resignation under fire from the Fourth Legislature when he was accused of extorting money from convicted bootleggers in return for procuring pardons for them. The House Investigating Committee recommended his prosecution, but no action was taken. Researcher Edith Copeland concluded that Stolper, "one of Kate's greatest problems," was likely inserted into Kate's department at the insistence of incoming governor Charles Haskell. University of Oklahoma professor Jerome Dowd knew Stolper and described him as a "rascal" and a "blatherskite," an old-fashioned term meaning someone who talks a lot but says nothing. Dr. D. W. Griffin, the superintendent of the Norman mental hospital, considered Stolper "very vain" and remembered when he had "paraded down the aisle in a Prince Albert [frock coat], white gloves, and carrying a top hat" at the Boston meeting over which Jane Addams presided.[18]

In Kate's employ, Stolper and Huson allied themselves as friends and learned men. Their correspondence with one another was dotted with references to the Roman generals Hannibal and Marius and winks at the state's prohibition. Huson called Stolper "one of the most faithful men I have ever met although somewhat busy and nervous in his methods." Stolper said that Huson was "a gentleman of elderly age" who wanted nothing more than "to keep away from official life and be allowed to devote [himself] to literature and agriculture." Stolper described Huson as "a brick and like a real true man, ready at a minute's notice either for a fight or frolic." Kate admired both men. They were condescending toward her, alternately exasperated and amused. Stolper's daughter remembered that Stolper and Huson both thought of Kate as "a pretty little bit of fluff" and believed that the two men did the thinking and convinced her it was what she wanted to do. It was Estelle Blair, she said, who was so organized: "She's the one who really kept the office going." Stolper referred to Kate as "big hearted Miss Kate," and in letters he addressed her occasionally as "Miss Kate, dear." He wrote more sarcastically to Huson, "What is Miss Kate doing and is the world getting better?"[19]

After the first of their five children was born, Stolper moved the family from Krebs to Muskogee, living in a neighborhood near that of the friend he called "Charlie" Haskell. He practiced medicine, with brief absences for teaching appointments at a college in New York. He never sent his patients bills, saying, "I did not go into the practice of medicine to get rich," although some times were so lean that the family lived on oatmeal. He was also engaged in legal work, often handling veterans' cases, and one of those cases was his downfall. In 1935, he and his law clerk were charged with conspiracy to defraud a veteran's estate by charging exorbitant fees. He pleaded guilty and was convicted of violating the World War Veterans' Act of 1924, fined one dollar, and sentenced to a year and a day at the federal prison in El Reno, Oklahoma. Some suspected the charges were fabricated by old political foes. Stolper died January 13, 1942, at his home in Muskogee after a second stroke. He was buried at Oklahoma's Fort Gibson National Cemetery, a privilege afforded him as a retired medical corps officer of honorable service in the United States armed forces. He was sixty-six years old.[20]

Estelle Blair, the third member of Kate's core team, never ran for the office of commissioner of charities and corrections. She married a man named Hartwig O. Bjerg and moved to Flagstaff, Arizona.[21]

Kate disappeared not only from public life but, for a while, from public view in Oklahoma. Sometime in 1915 she moved to Denver, near the sheltering friendship of her friend and colleague Judge Lindsey. She lived in an apartment near the state capitol and worked for the judge in his juvenile court until her failing health made that impossible. Kate had burned herself out helping other people, but had nobody close by to help her when she needed help herself. In addition to her worsening physical ailments, her emotional state was deteriorating. Her loyal supporter Warren Moorehead said, "Due to her experiences, she has become a nervous wreck."[22]

She was depressed, brooding about victims and penal reform, when she talked to a newspaper reporter about her friend Henry Starr, whom she said she had known for many years. Starr was the notorious Oklahoman bank robber who had gone to Hollywood between bank heists and prison sentences to make silent western movies. Known sometimes as the Cherokee Bad Boy, he claimed to have robbed more banks than any man in America, more than both the James-Younger Gang and the Doolin-Dalton Gang put together. Kate saw him as a victim and sympathized with him. She loaned him money and said that he had been "forced back into a life of crime" when a motion picture company did not pay him for filming his life story, and he was fatally shot during another bank robbery. What his life proved to Kate, always the reformer, was "the need of a state agency to help back to a straight path those who have strayed." She criticized the present attitude toward criminals: "once a man has taken a false step he is forever afterward a criminal." Kate was feeling like a victim herself. "I feel quite discouraged with life. It seems useless to try and help any one in this greedy world."[23]

By the fall of 1922, she was so ill that she had to be hospitalized. Lindsey telegraphed the *Daily Oklahoman* in Oklahoma City on September 18, saying that Kate had been admitted to Mercy Hospital weighing only seventy-two pounds and was in critical condition. "Her life is despaired of unless she undergoes [a] delicate operation which to be successful, must be done at Mayo's hospital [the Mayo Clinic]. She is without funds for this purpose." He asked her friends to send donations to him, and the newspaper coordinated the collections. People contributed several hundred dollars, and the news so cheered Kate that her condition improved and she sent a message to the newspaper: "Tell my friends in Oklahoma that their kind interest in my behalf has served to make life more worth living."[24]

The painful, blistering skin rash that had tormented her for decades continued to get worse. Despite it, by 1925 Kate was recuperated enough to return to Oklahoma City, where she rented a room at the residential Egbert Hotel, traveling back and forth to Denver. She attended to details of her properties, supervised repairs made to the Newalla homestead, fussed with a neighbor of her Reno Street house in Oklahoma City who sued her for slander after she claimed that he was operating a whiskey still on the property, leased out some of her land, and sold some royalties and mineral rights. She lived frugally and worried about money because of her medical expenses. A doctor made frequent house calls—sometimes twice a day—to treat her, and she planned on going east for extensive treatment.[25]

She began writing her memoir, a book about her career and the men who had created the state of Oklahoma. She typed so far into the night that other hotel residents complained, so she moved to the fifth floor. She was a terror to the hotel maids, who considered her "unusually eccentric" and not always rational. The hotel manager said she was a "shrew" and that the maids and other employees tried to avoid her. She ranted about her treatment in the press. Even her old friend Jerome Dowd said she was insane near the end of her life and talked of visions. A woman who knew her well said Kate was odd in her last few years, talked constantly, and was "demanding, exacting, and selfish," so difficult that she lost most of her friends. In fact, she was gravely ill and angry. Kate was always impatient and had a short temper, and these characteristics would have been worsened by her medical condition—burning blisters on her hands, lip, nose, and scalp—but we might wonder if the treatments she was prescribed, especially arsenic and kerosene, exacerbated her neurological functions and moods.[26]

At least one researcher saw Kate's last days as a tragedy and relates a sad story about her reliving her rural life as a child by walking along the city streets looking at gardens. Sometimes she would ask the owner, "May I weed your strawberry bed?" Everybody knew her and said yes, and occasionally she took off her shoes and stockings and worked barefoot. Then again, maybe she was following doctor's orders. One physician had recommended "out-door hard work in field." She was desperate to find a cure for her skin condition, and perhaps an urban garden was the only outdoor work she could do.[27]

She was in agony because of the skin condition and spent a lot of time taking long soaks in very hot Lysol baths. Her room was as untidy as ever, with clothes in piles and tossed behind the radiator. It was the messy way she had always lived. Now, however, the bedsheets and some of her clothes were filled with sand. To ease the maddening—literally maddening—itch of the spreading skin disease, occasionally she rode a streetcar to the end of the line, where she would find a mound of coarse builder's sand from construction and in the darkness roll in it to scratch her skin.[28]

In May of 1925, Oklahoma politicians were calling for a new constitutional convention, an action that threatened to undo the last vestiges of Kate's social reform work. She believed it was an attempt to repeal the eight-hour workday and the child labor plank and characterized it, in her colorful way, as an effort by "selfish interests" to "tear the child labor plank out of the constitution and fling the children of the poor into the sweat and grind of stifling cotton mills." She rallied for yet another final shindy and said publicly that if necessary, she would "stump the state from a stretcher in defense of the humanitarian sections of the constitution." She did not have to resort to that because the proposed constitutional convention did not materialize.[29]

People muttered that Kate had become irrational as she aged, but a reporter noted that she had explained in "calm, reasoned detail" how legislative action or an initiated bill could correct any defects in Oklahoma's basic law without a constitutional convention being called. Reasons given for a new constitutional convention included issues with the appellate court, the corporation commission chairman, redistricting, and revenue and taxation. Kate dismissed these. "The legislature and the people, by initiation, under the present constitution can do anything they see fit. If the people cannot elect a legislature to do these things, how can they hope to elect convention delegates to do them?" A newspaper article described her as "old, worn, and grayed by illness, but still fired by the indomitable zeal and firmness of purpose."[30]

At the Egbert Hotel, nobody saw her all day Saturday, February 22, 1930, but the hotel manager said that was not unusual. She often stayed in her room for days at a time typing. Sunday afternoon about four o'clock, a hotel maid found her dead, sitting in the bathtub. A physician was called, and the acting coroner attributed her death to "heart trouble." She was fifty-five years old. Authorities had some difficulty locating relatives or anyone to make funeral arrangements.[31]

If Kate was mentally unstable the last couple of years of her life, the papers she left behind are not proof. They were disorganized and rambling, but classified into three parts. One section was a directory listing addresses of friends, professional associates (attorneys, bankers), members of the press, workmen (plumbers, carpenters), businesses (dressmakers, jewelers, bootmakers), renters and lessees of her properties, and storage locations of her personal property. It is the sort of list that any responsible person might keep.

The section of notes for her book is fragmented but typical for a writer. She listed possible titles for her memoir: *Daughter of Destiny, Builders of Human Destiny, The Game of Life.* She wrote profiles of men she had worked with at statehood: Hobart Huson, Stump Ashby, Charles Haskell, Pat Nagle, Eugene Debs, and S. O. Daws, noting how many of them died poor, disappointed, or even of suicide. She wrote about her humiliating carriage ride on Statehood Day and her triumph at the Minneapolis convention. She captured memories from her youth, her father, and her favorite music.

The third section contained meticulous information under the heading "Physicians and Prescriptions." She documented the diagnoses and treatments she had sought over the years for her recurring skin problems. She suffered from respiratory problems, which she called hay fever, and nervous collapses, likely brought about by stress and overwork, which drove her to sanitariums for quiet retreats, but it was the burning skin condition that troubled her the most as she grew older, and rightly so. It is what killed her.

Various doctors she consulted had diagnosed her with actinomycosis, a rare and infectious bacterial disease; trichinosis, a parasitical disease caused by roundworms; streptococci bacteria, which are associated with strep throat, scarlet fever, and acute infectious skin rashes; pneumococci bacteria, which can cause a bloodstream infection that often results in inner-ear infection; an "animal parasite"; chilomastix, an intestinal protozoan parasite; and spirochetes, a bacterium associated with infections from Lyme disease to leprosy, syphilis, and rabbit fever. The exhaustive list she kept is typical of Kate. In her social reform work, she sought out the best experts she could find, and she did the same with her health. She sought doctors around the country, including in Denver; in Hot Springs, Arkansas; in Baltimore at Johns Hopkins Hospital; in New York City; and at the University of Oklahoma hospital, trying to identify the cause of the rash. Kate was convinced that it was a parasite. In outbreaks every three or four weeks, "tiny white blisters" spread, breaking out in "a thick gum" that affected her scalp, throat, mouth, hands, and genitals; it sent her seeking treatment in "hysterical agony."[32]

She tried special diets of vegetables and herbs, vitamins, enemas, and medications including arsenic, Lysol baths, peroxide, copper, Campho-Phenique, turpentine, and castor oil. The skin condition seemed worse in bright sunlight, so she stayed in dark rooms. Then she was advised to sit in the sun for three hours and drink potassium permanganate on an empty stomach. She tried salves, special shampoos, mange medication, cold baths, douches, massage, and calisthenics. Nothing worked.[33]

Although some have diagnosed Kate's skin condition as a herpes virus, physician G. Pete Dosser says she almost certainly suffered from not one but two conditions: delusions of parasitosis and pemphigus vulgaris.

Her fixation with trying to locate "the parasite" reads like a textbook case of delusions of parasitosis, a false belief that the patient is affected with parasites, worms, or other organisms. Medical dictionaries say it often afflicts "a lonely woman in middle life" and is associated with paranoid schizophrenia or depressive disorder.[34]

Unfortunately, she had a second and very real dermatological condition: pemphigus vulgaris, a serious blistering disease. Today it can be treated effectively with corticosteroids, but neither the diagnosis nor the treatment was known in Kate's time. In that era, the condition was fatal. Soaking in a Lysol bath gave her some temporary relief. That was what she was doing when she died. She was obsessive about her health because she was not only ill, she was a dying woman, and she knew it. Dying did not make her saintly; it made her irascible and angry.[35]

Reading Kate's medical diary, it is easy to dismiss her as obsessive, and she probably was. At least one doctor, pediatrician Robert J. Hudson, sees something particularly significant in her memoir notes: the repeated references to the wintry death of her mother when she was so young. The death of a mother, he said, "is the most devastating thing that can happen to a child." It haunted Kate. She once wrote a twelve-year-old boy who kept running away from the grandparents raising him, "My mother died when I was a few months old and I was brought up by strangers." Her mother's death followed by her father's abandonment shaped Kate's whole life. She devoted herself to rescuing (a child, prisoners, anyone in need) as she hoped to be rescued.[36]

In 1913, when she was under siege for her work with Indian orphans, a disheartened Kate told a reporter that she was "sick and tired of it all." She summarized her career: "My whole life work has been for the conservation of the home. My child labor bill and my compulsory education bill . . . my appeal for a shorter work day, all were to allow families to have better health and some hours of energy and leisure together. . . . The home is the keystone of the nation and the greatest of all American institutions." That was the home of her longing.[37]

Kate rescued many people, but she was fated to be abandoned again and again: by Haskell and the other Democrats who solicited her to bring West Side support to the constitution; by Abbott, Mott, Moorehead, and Fisher, who persuaded her to fight for the Indian Question; by her loyal helpmate Huson; and even by Oklahoma itself. Pioneer Elva Ferguson, a newspaperwoman and the wife of territorial governor Thomas B. Ferguson, understood the dream that swept up Kate. "Perhaps we were in love with an ideal created in our own minds of the greater privileges we would enjoy under statehood, without realizing that greater problems would surely follow."[38]

A few days after Kate died, someone—not a relative—was found to help with the final arrangements, and her funeral was held in Oklahoma City at 9 A.M. Thursday, February 27, 1930. It was the kind of weather that Kate loved—not summer with its heat and pollen, but a clear day, with a temperature of 51 degrees and a gentle breeze. Governor William J. Holloway ordered the flag at the state capitol lowered to half-mast in her honor and issued a proclamation praising Kate as "one who served well and faithfully in the cause of human welfare, and one who committed this commonwealth in its infancy to the call of the unfortunate and afflicted." Some 1,400 people—men, women, and children—gathered for a solemn funeral mass in St. Joseph's Cathedral. She was "eulogized as dedicated to suffering humanity" and as "devoid of self-interest."[39]

Governor Holloway and the seven former governors who had served since statehood acted as honorary pallbearers. The active pallbearers were Oklahoma Supreme Court justices Thomas H. Doyle and J. W. Clark; Professor Dowd from the University of Oklahoma; Dr. R. C. Meloy, the former inspector with her department; Dr. D. W. Griffin from the Norman mental hospital; and Kate's former departmental attorney, Dr. Stolper. Some of these men who had known her well spoke about her tiny size, rapid speech, and beautiful eyes. Dowd said he grieved for "a very great woman" who had fired his students "with vibrant words" to adopt a life of studious work for the improvement of social conditions. He expressed the hope that the Rotary Club of Norman would erect a statue of her on state capitol grounds.[40]

The press recapped her place in history, describing her as "an advocate of the labor cause always" and "a creator of the first farmer-labor bloc in Oklahoma, the original bloc [in the] west and perhaps in the entire United States." This farmer-labor bloc "controlled the destinies of Oklahoma absolutely, made W. H. 'Alfalfa' Bill Murray president of the [constitutional] convention, resulted in Charles N. Haskell being named first governor . . . and made Kate Barnard the first woman to be elected to office in Oklahoma." No stronger political alliance ever prevailed in Oklahoma. "She recognized it as her opportunity and she seized it by both horns."

A eulogistic article in the *Lincoln (Nebraska) Sunday Star* summarized her career in a lyrical style that Kate would have liked. "Her real history will be written in the hearts of those whom she helped. The underpaid and overworked, the hungry and ill-clothed, the sick and the weary, orphans, derelicts, poor renters. Perhaps the worthless, for Kate Barnard was a visionary, and she turned from no one."[41]

Her work with Indian grafters was barely mentioned in her obituaries. At the bottom of one newspaper story, the reporter wrote that after her early prison work, "the champion of the needy threw herself wholeheartedly into a fight to prevent abuse of Indians and illegal seizure of their lands."[42]

She died full of dreams of more political fights. Oil had been discovered on her Newalla farm, and she had begun to receive royalties, which gave her some financial security, but she did not live long enough to enjoy it. She said she wanted to establish her farm as the Kate Barnard Home for the Unfortunates. Only three days before her death, she told friends she intended to go east for a year to regain her health, then launch a vigorous campaign for the U.S. Senate. Kate was buried at Fairlawn, Oklahoma City's oldest cemetery, next to her father. Once the most celebrated woman in the state, she lay for fifty years in an unmarked grave. In 1982, a group of women raised funds to install a headstone that reads:

KATE BARNARD, 1875–1930, INTREPID PIONEER LEADER FOR SOCIAL ETHICS IN OKLAHOMA.[43]

————∞————

It is not surprising, considering Kate's erratic personality, that her estate of approximately $30,000, almost $500,000 in today's currency, was a muddle. Ironically, just as the subject of probate had so plagued her professional life, now it troubled her in death. She had made a will, but altered it with so many handwritten changes, none legally witnessed, that the document was declared invalid. She wanted to leave her Reno Street home to the Catholic diocese for a Barnard Home for the Friendless, stocked with the 1,500 books in her library as the Hobart Huson Library, and she intended some assets, including the Newalla homestead farm, to go to her father's Trainor family in Michigan. It was not to be.[44]

Her half-brother in Kansas contested the will, and her two half-brothers in California joined the fray. When the probate was settled, her estate was divided among the three half-brothers: Frank Krohlow in Kansas, the son of her father and his second wife; and John and Robert Mason in California, the sons from her mother's first marriage. Krohlow got the larger portion, real property and Kate's personal property.[45]

Hobart Huson Jr. remembered his father's library: "two big things like coffins. Wherever he went, they went with him." He and his brother Frank tracked down Krohlow and bought the nearly five hundred books that had been among Kate's possessions. It was a lucky thing for history that they did, because with that library they also acquired the notes Kate had been working on at her death and photographs of her during her years as commissioner. Huson Jr. had Kate's notes typed and titled "Reference of Her Life Work." Years later, he gave the typescript to Edith Copeland, one of Kate's earliest researchers. Julee Short referred to it for her master's thesis, and ultimately the document found its way from the Oklahoma Department of Libraries into the archives at the University of Oklahoma. In 2017, the Oklahoma Historical Society acquired Kate's original diary, which included some materials not included in "Reference."[46]

Kate would have hated the final disposition of her estate. The Catholic Church got nothing. She had close, tender feelings for her father's Trainor relatives and for her mother's Mason sons, and she had kept in touch with them. She had no such feelings for Krohlow.[47]

One bequest in Kate's will could not be contested. In the opening paragraph, she wrote, "I give my soul to God and I bequeath the example of my public life to the youth of the world."[48]

Epilogue

ANGIE DEBO DESERVES A FINAL WORD on what she called Kate Barnard's "work and failure." This is what she wrote in 1974, not as polished prose for print, but in an informational private letter to Kate's researcher Julia Short:

Nobody admires Miss B. more than I do, but I concede that she was emotional and exaggerated things and feelings. . . .

There was every indication that Oklahoma would start out on its career as a leader among the states in its humane policy towards unfortunate and helpless people and criminals. [Kate] would have lost some of the reforms she advocated, but she could have achieved them gradually except that she stirred up the Indian exploiters. They were in control of politics, the press, public sentiment, everything. And they destroyed the department [of Charities and Corrections], rendered it innocuous. [Her successors in that office] meant well but there was nothing [they] could do. The harmless office was finally abolished by public mandate on July 22[, 1975]. The reform in mental health has finally been accomplished somewhat, but very slowly. As for the penal situation, it was an open scandal that finally erupted in the riot of 1973 and a sane penal system has not yet been put in operation. There is a stirring of reform, but its success is not assured. All this is what the destruction of her office has done to Oklahoma.

As for the Indian children she sought to protect and was prevented from doing it, they grew up in poverty and degradation. The sodden, hopeless poverty of the fullblood settlements in the mountains and timber of eastern Oklahoma is the result, a problem still unsolved.[1]

———⟨∞⟩———

Kate was proud to see the new United States flag raised June 30, 1908, at the temporary capitol in Guthrie, because she had been instrumental in creating the forty-sixth state, and she was one of ninety-two prominent Oklahoma women chosen to sew the enormous flag (12 × 20 feet) with its new forty-sixth star. How dismayed she would be to see the current state of two institutions she cherished, the public K–12 school system (which is underfunded and poorly rated) and the penal system (which is over-crowded and has the highest rate of female incarceration in the nation). By contrast, the Five Tribes and the Osage Nation have flourished under responsible tribal governments that mastered white bureaucracy and law, and with resources from gaming and casinos.[2]

How ruefully both Kate Barnard and Angie Debo would have viewed the 2020 landmark ruling of the U.S. Supreme Court that determined that Congress never disestablished the borders of the permanent home of the Creek Nation. Justice Neil M. Gorsuch, writing for the majority in *McGirt v. Oklahoma*, held: "On the far end of the Trail of Tears was a promise." The Creek Nation was assured that their new lands in the West would be secure forever, and no state or territory had the right to pass laws govern-ing them. "Because Congress has not said otherwise, we hold the govern-ment to its word."[3]

How interested Kate Barnard and Angie Debo would be to see a Native American woman chosen in 2021 to be secretary of the interior. They would watch closely to see if Deb Haaland, a citizen of the Laguna Pueblo, could shift the agency's historical Indian policy of assimilation or extinction.[4]

In 1906, as Kate was campaigning for statehood, a committee of the U.S. Senate held hearings throughout Indian Territory, and a group of full-blood Indians attended the hearing held in Tulsa on November 23 to plead for their sovereign nation. Their spokesman Chitto Harjo (Crazy Snake) spoke through his interpreter with "desperate earnestness" about the relations between the white men and his people through the centuries, the treaties made and broken. "I am here and stand before you to-day," he said, "as a man of misery." He appealed to them to keep "these ancient promises," and he held up a copy of the treaty at the time of Removal, which promised them that their lands in the West would always remain theirs in perpetuity, as long as grass grows. He spoke in vain. The senators explained that the treaty had been abrogated and that "Congress and the President wanted all the Indians to give up and take their allotments."[5]

The issue of Indian properties destroyed Kate's career and her life. That can never be put right. Although her position was correct in her Indian crusade, she did not live to see the wheel of justice grind exceedingly fine, at least in principle. She had been dead ninety years by the time the Supreme Court determined that much of eastern Oklahoma remains Indian land. With some bitterness, she would have appreciated the prophecy attributed to writer D. H. Lawrence, "that the Indian will again rule America—or, rather, his ghost will."[6]

Acknowledgments

A NGIE DEBO DID THE RESEARCH for her books before copy machines existed, so she wrote her notes in longhand, usually finding the information in documents stored in dark basements and dusty archives. Then she typed her manuscripts on a manual typewriter. When I visited her in her little white house in Marshall, Oklahoma, the second bedroom was her office. She showed me her filing cabinet filled with notes on half sheets of typing paper, a system I emulated. She wrote on a manual typewriter.

I began researching this book about Kate Barnard before the internet, personal computers, or smart phones were available. That is why I am indebted to the generosity of people—genealogists, librarians, journalists, local historians, plain folk—who helped me with legwork in Kansas, Michigan, Missouri, Nebraska, Oklahoma, and Texas. Some individuals searched their memories to give me personal recollections. These included the Oklahoma City newspaperman Irvin Hurst, who reported Kate's death, and the woman who owned Kate's Newalla homestead and invited me to visit and to sit alone inside in the room with the wide plank floors that Kate had swept and beside the big open fireplace. It was such an emotional experience, I wept.

———∞———

I am particularly grateful for the diligent work of genealogist John E. McInerney, who scoured original documents and records in Washington, D.C., and Ontario. A woman in Phillipsburg, Kansas, and a man in Topeka, Kansas, searched early Kansas newspapers for details about Kate's childhood, her schooling, her mother's death, and a scandal involving her father. A man in Kirwin, Kansas, found Kate's mother's grave and took a Polaroid photograph of its distinctive headstone. The president of the Fillmore County Heritage Genealogical Society in Geneva, Nebraska, sent me information about homesteading there. Nebraska's first female veterinarian described the landscape of her state, and a librarian in Sandusky, Michigan, told me about the timber business in that region. Tulsa journalist Julie DelCour appeared out of the blue to give me a document invaluable to my research. All of these hands and more helped build this book.

Freda Stolper Gold and Hobart Huson Jr. were so helpful, I wish I could have written only favorably about their fathers, who were important in Kate's career.

Historians Anne Hodges Morgan, Rennard Strickland, and Garrick Bailey were encouraging all along the way. Alexandria L. Gough provided valuable citation and research assistance. Physicians Robert J. Hudson and G. Pete Dosser contributed medical insight into Kate's health. Rodger A. Randle explained the Oklahoma legislature.

I am particularly grateful to the University of Tulsa (librarians Andra J. Lupardus and especially Guy Logsdon, professors Paul Alworth and Patrick J. Blessing, and the faculty grants committee); Oklahoma State University librarians; the University of Oklahoma (Jack Haley and staff of the Western History Collections, especially Jacquelyn D. Reese); the Oklahoma Department of Libraries (Carol Guilliams, Jan Davis); the Oklahoma Historical Society (Mary Moran, Jeffrey M. Moore, Laura Martin, Rachel Mosman, Mallory Covington); the Nebraska State Historical Society; the St. Joseph Public Library in Missouri; the Tulsa Historical Society; the Muscogee (Creek) Nation (Cherrah Giles, Odette Freeman, RaeLynn Butler); and Jay Cronley, who piloted many of my road trips.

I thank the University of Oklahoma Press, especially Kathleen Kelly, the editor who solicited the manuscript, and Alessandra Jacobi Tamulevich, the supremely patient editor who shepherded it through to publication; senior editor Stephanie Attia Evans; and copyeditor Jane Lyle for her sharp eye and skill.

My apologies for all the others I have failed to name here by oversight and forgetfulness, not for lack of appreciation.

My deepest gratitude to Angie Debo, who wanted Kate's story told, and to Edith Copeland and Julee Short, who did trailblazing research. They paid homage to Pauline (Polly) Jamerson, who went before them in collecting information about Kate. What a chain of women all pointing to Kate.

Many of these people are gone from my life—retired, relocated, or dead—but my gratitude to them will live as long as I do.

Notes

Preface

1. A. J. McKelway, "'Kate,' the 'Good Angel' of Oklahoma," *American Magazine*, October 1908, 587–93.

2. Joseph B. Thoburn, "Kate Barnard," in *A Standard History of Oklahoma*, vol. 3 (Chicago: American Historical Society, 1916), 1329–33, quotes from 1329.

3. Samuel J. Barrows to Kate Barnard, January 11, 1908, Box 2, Folder 14, Julia (Julee) A. Short Collection, MS 24, Oklahoma Department of Libraries, Oklahoma City (hereafter Short Collection); Edith Copeland, Manuscript, 240, Box 1, Folder 2, Short Collection (hereafter Edith Copeland Manuscript).

4. Edith Copeland Manuscript, 240; McKelway, "'Kate'"; Thoburn, "Kate Barnard," 1333.

5. Nell Bracken, "90 Pounds of Human Dynamite," *Orbit Magazine, Sunday Oklahoman*, December 10, 1972, 10, 12–14; "End of Fair Will Bring Cry for Aid," *St. Louis Post-Dispatch*, November 11, 1904; Edith Copeland Manuscript, 162; Kate Barnard to Roland B. Molineux, June 23, 1908, Box 20, Folder 1, Department of Charities and Corrections Records, Record Group 36, Oklahoma State Archives, Oklahoma Department of Libraries, Oklahoma City (hereafter DOCC Records); Kate Barnard to John Glenn, June 27, 1908, Box 20, Folder 1, DOCC Records. The Oxford dictionary at lexico.com defines a shindy as "a noisy disturbance or quarrel."

6. Kate Barnard, "For the Orphans of Oklahoma: Children of the Disinherited," *Survey*, November 7, 1914, 154. The word "civilized" was used at the time to distinguish these five tribes on the basis of their adoption of European American norms such as practicing Christianity, attaining literacy, and establishing a tribal government. The term is no longer used. In modern usage, the Creek tribe is now known as the Muscogee (Creek) Nation; the tribe's spoken language is spelled Mvskoke; the city in Oklahoma is spelled Muskogee. Muscogee (Creek) Nation, *Oklahoma Tribal Nation Education Resource Guide*, March 2018, *Oklahoma State*

Department of Education, https://sde.ok.gov/sites/default/files/OSDE_OIER _MCN_032018.pdf (accessed January 31, 2021); Ben B. Lindsey to Pauline Jamerson, July 16, 1940, Box 2, Folder 14, Short Collection.

7. "Death Claims Kate Barnard in City Hotel," *Daily Oklahoman*, February 24, 1930; "Death Takes Pioneer Woman Leader," *Oklahoma City Times*, February 24, 1930.

8. Angie Debo, Marshall, Oklahoma, interviews with author, April and May 1981.

9. Thoburn, "Kate Barnard," 1333.

10. Shirley A. Leckie, *Angie Debo: Pioneering Historian* (Norman: University of Oklahoma Press, 2000), 215.

Chapter 1

1. George J. Abbot, United States Commercial Agency, Goderich, Ontario, to Hon. F. W. Seward, Assistant Secretary of State, Washington, D.C., December 17, 1877, and November 18, 1878, Dispatches from U.S. Consuls in Goderich, Canada, 1865–1906, microcopy T-468, Archives of Ontario, Toronto.

2. 1861 Canada West Census, Enumeration District 1, Ward 4, Wawanosh Township, Huron County, 45, Ministry of Citizenship and Culture, Archives of Ontario.

3. Huron County Marriage Register, 1858–1909, Microfilm MS 248, reel 8, Archives of Ontario, Toronto.

4. Robert Shiell, patent application no. 4198, May 11, 1870, final patent certificate no. 3049, July 2, 1877, *U.S. Land Office at Beatrice, Nebraska, U.S. Department of the Interior, Bureau of Land Management, General Land Office Records*, https://glorecords.blm.gov/ (accessed January 31, 2021); Evelyn Mersch to author, January 31, 1986; Provincial Archives Land Records Index, 1797–1913, Genealogical Research Library, London, Ontario; Noel Montgomery Elliot, *People of Ontario, 1600–1900: Alphabetized Directory of the People, Places and Vital Dates* (London, Ont.: Genealogical Research Library, 1984), 769, 770, 1158, 1161; Canada West Census, 1851, District No. 1, Ashfield Township, Huron County, 13; Canada West Census, 1861, Ward 2, Wawanosh Township, Huron County, 18; Nebraska Territory Census, 1854, 1855, and 1860; U.S. Census, 1880; Federal Writers' Project of the Work Projects Administration for the State of Kansas, *Kansas: A Guide to the Sunflower State* (New York: Viking Press, 1939), 56.

5. Ordella Geisler Hoffman to author, August 20, 1987.

6. Federal Writers' Project of the Works Progress Administration for the State of Nebraska, comp., *Nebraska: A Guide to the Cornhusker State* (New York: Viking Press, 1939), 379–81, 403; Federal Writers' Project, *Kansas*, 33–40, 59–60.

7. Federal Writers' Project, *Nebraska*, 60, 290.

8. Kate Barnard to J. H. Stolper, March 2, 1908, Box 2, Folder 19, DOCC Records.

9. U.S. Census, 1900; "Child Labor Conference," *New Orleans Times-Picayune*, March 30, 1909; Kate Barnard, "Reference of Her Life Work," typescript, 29, Box 4, Folder 7, Fayette Copeland Jr. Collection, Western History Collections, University of Oklahoma Libraries, Norman (hereafter Copeland Collection). The 1880 Kansas Census (Soundex) lists John Barnard's birthplace as Tennessee, the 1885 Kansas Census says Iowa, and the 1900 Oklahoma Census says Mississippi. Census records were not always accurate. The 1880 Kansas Census lists Rachel's birthplace as Scotland, but that information was likely provided by James Gillis, with whose family five-year-old Kate was boarding.

10. U.S. Census, 1900 and 1910; Ontario Census, 1852; Sharron Merritt, Sandusky Public Library, Sandusky, Michigan, to author, September 7, 1985; Mrs. Russell (Carol) Rose, Agra, Kansas, to author, September 3, 1985. Barnard and Trainor are both traditional North Irish names, although so is Shiell. "The native turf of these families puts them in the ranks of the fighting Irish; fighting for Catholic freedom of worship for centuries; in most centuries, against the British; and in their spare time, among themselves." Edward MacLysaght, *Irish Families: Their Names, Arms and Origins* (Dublin: Hodges Figgis & Company, 1957), 269, 278, 317.

11. Phillips County, Kansas, Marriage License Records, Book A, 239, and St. James (Sacred Heart Parish), Crete, Nebraska, Holy Sacrament of Baptism, June 29, 1875, both Box 1, Folder 52, Short Collection.

12. "Judge Barnard Is Laid to Rest," *Daily Oklahoman*, May 12, 1909.

13. Helen Winter Stauffer, *Mari Sandoz: Story Catcher of the Plains* (Lincoln: University of Nebraska Press, 1982), 177, 178.

14. Edith Copeland Manuscript, 29; J. P. Barnard, Real Estate Dealer, *Daily Kirwin (Kans.) Chief*, September 30, 1885, and September 14, 1886; *Independent* (Kirwin, Kans.), October 1, 1885.

15. U.S. Census, 1880.

16. "Local Items," *Kirwin (Kans.) Progress*, January 25, 1877, and *Chief* (Phillipsburg, Kans.), January 20, 1877; also *Kirwin (Kans.) Progress*, January 18, 1877.

17. Kate Barnard, "Working for the Friendless," *Independent* 63, no. 3078 (November 28, 1907): 1307–8.

18. Rachel Barnard and her infant are buried in space 9 of block 19 in the Kirwin Cemetery. D. Harvey Atchison, Kirwin, Kansas, to author, February 3 and 25, 1982.

19. District Magistrate Judge Decision in the Matter of the Estate of Rachel Barnard, case no. A-14, Phillips County, Kansas; Register of Deeds, Phillips County, Phillipsburg, Kansas.

20. "An Appeal for the Poor," *Oklahoma City Times Journal*, October 29, 1905; Thoburn, "Kate Barnard," 1332.

21. Barnard, "Reference of Her Life Work," 30; Edith Copeland Manuscript, 22; marriage license, J. P. Barnard and Anna T. Rose, April 30, 1881, and divorce filed August 7, 1883 (case no. 541), District Court Clerk, Phillipsburg, Phillips County, Kansas; *Phillips County Review*, August 31, 1972.

22. Thoburn, "Kate Barnard," 1332; "A Dirty Trick—Rawlins County Racket Repeated," *Independent* (Kirwin, Kans.), April 29, 1886.

23. Barnard, "Reference of Her Life Work," 29, 30; "A Dirty Trick—Rawlins County Racket Repeated," *Independent* (Kirwin, Kans.), April 29, 1886; untitled clipping from *Kirwin (Kans.) Progress*, July 12, 1877; "Local Items," *Kirwin (Kans.) Republican*, August 15, 1885 ("vague rumor afloat"); Register of Deeds, Phillips County, Phillipsburg, Kansas; Thoburn, "Kate Barnard," 1332; George W. P. Hunt, "An Appreciation of Miss Barnard," *Good Housekeeping*, November 1912, 606–7.

24. Stauffer, *Mari Sandoz*, 126; Hunt, "An Appreciation of Miss Barnard," 606; Barnard, "Reference of Her Life Work," 29.

25. Angie Debo, *Oklahoma: Foot-Loose and Fancy-Free* (Norman: University of Oklahoma Press, 1949), 26–29; John W. Morris, Charles R. Goins, and Edwin G. McReynolds, *Historical Atlas of Oklahoma*, 2nd ed. (Norman: University of Oklahoma Press, 1976), v.

26. John P. Barnard, final patent certificate no. 1350, August 9, 1895, *U.S. Land Office at Oklahoma, Oklahoma Territory, U.S. Department of the Interior, Bureau of Land Management, General Land Office Records*, https://glorecords.blm.gov/ (accessed January 31, 2021); Morris, Goins, and McReynolds, *Historical Atlas of Oklahoma*, 2nd ed., 48; Dianna Everett, "Kingfisher County," *Encyclopedia of Oklahoma History and Culture*, https://www.okhistory.org/publications/enc/entry.php?entry=KI012 (accessed January 31, 2021); "Judge Barnard Is Laid to Rest," *Daily Oklahoman*, May 12, 1909; Danney Goble, *Progressive Oklahoma: The Making of a New Kind of State* (Norman: University of Oklahoma Press, 1980), 118–19.

27. Thoburn, "Kate Barnard," 1332; Glenn Shirley, "Oklahoma Kate—Woman of Destiny," *West*, March 1968, 19–21, 56–58.

28. *Independent* (Kirwin, Kans.), September 3, 4, and 17, and October 1, 1890, courtesy Katie Davis, genealogist, Phillipsburg, Kansas.

29. *Independent* (Kirwin, Kans.), November 22, 1889, and November 26, 1870; Katie Davis, Philipsburg, Kansas, to author, November 2, 1987, and February 26 and March 11, 1988.

30. O. Gene Clanton, *A Common Humanity: Kansas Populism and the Battle for Justice and Equality, 1854–1903* (Manhattan, Kans.: Sunflower University Press, 2004), 117.

31. "Miss Kate Barnard," *Kirwin Kansan*, November 1, 1916.

32. Thoburn, "Kate Barnard," 1332.

33. Debo, *Oklahoma*, 28–30.

34. Kate Barnard to Hon. R. Roddie, December 14, 1910, Box 22, Folder 28, DOCC Records; Kate Barnard to unnamed woman in Oklahoma City, 1908, Box 12, Folder 1, DOCC Records.

35. Edith Copeland Manuscript, 23.

36. Julia A. Short, "Kate Barnard: Liberated Woman" (master's thesis, University of Oklahoma, 1972), chap. 1, pp. 16, 17.

37. Bracken, "90 Pounds of Human Dynamite," 14; Short, "Kate Barnard," 19.

38. Elma Childers, "Elma Childers from Her Homestead near Deer Creek," *Edmond (Okla.) Booster,* May 21, 1939; Barnard, "Reference of Her Life Work," 76.

39. According to the homestead certificate, the Barnard property is "the North East quarter of Section twenty-five in Township eleven North of Range One East of Indian Meridian in Oklahoma Territory," which places it at the corner of Southeast 59th Street and Harrah Road. *U.S. Department of the Interior, Bureau of Land Management, General Land Office Records,* https://glorecords.blm.gov/ (accessed January 31, 2021); Thoburn, "Kate Barnard," 1332.

40. John P. Barnard, original homestead application no. 7287, final patent certificate no. 1350, August 9, 1895, *U.S. Land Office at Oklahoma, Oklahoma Territory, U.S. Department of the Interior, Bureau of Land Management, General Land Office Records,* https://glorecords.blm.gov/ (accessed January 31, 2021).

41. Myrtle Ownbey to author, June 13, 1986; Angie Debo, interviews with author, 1976–85.

42. Mont Highley to Julee Short, n.d., Box 1, Folder 47, Short Collection; Hobart Huson Jr., conversations with author, April 24–26, 1981.

43. Barnard, "Reference of Her Life Work," 9, 45, 46; Angie Debo, interviews with author, 1976–85; Kate Barnard to Nell A. Snider, June 7, 1909, Box 17, Folder 1, DOCC Records; Mabel Bassett, interview, Oklahoma City, January 25, 1950, Box 2, Folder 54, Short Collection. In 1923 Ms. Bassett became the commissioner of Oklahoma's Department of Charities and Corrections.

44. Barnard, "Reference of Her Life Work," 63.

Chapter 2

1. Angie Debo to author, May 4, 1982.

2. Edith Copeland Manuscript, 20; *Bulletin of the United States Bureau of Labor* 5, no. 26 (1900): 805.

3. Edith Copeland to Edward T. James, November 8, 1961, Box 2, Folder 1, Copeland Collection.

4. Short, "Kate Barnard," chap. 1, pp. 22, 23.

5. Albert McRill, *And Satan Came Also: An Inside Story of a City's Social and Political History* (Oklahoma City: Britton, 1955), 116; Goble, *Progressive Oklahoma,* 184; Short, "Kate Barnard," chap. 3, p. 4.

6. Edith Copeland Manuscript, 30, 52, 59.

7. Edith Copeland Manuscript, 47; "Territorial Legislature," *Daily Oklahoman,* October 1, 1927; Barnard, "Reference of Her Life Work," 62.

8. Barnard, "Reference of Her Life Work," 63; Carl Resek, *The Progressives* (Indianapolis: Bobbs-Merrill, 1967), xix; Goble, *Progressive Oklahoma,* 109–10, 195, quote from 109; H. Wayne Morgan and Anne Hodges Morgan, *Oklahoma: A Bicentennial History* (New York: W. W. Norton and Company, 1977), 81, 82; Irvin Hurst, *The 46th Star: A History of Oklahoma's Constitutional Convention and Early Statehood* (Oklahoma City: Semco Color Press, 1957), 3; Linda D. Wilson, "Asp, Henry E.,"

Encyclopedia of Oklahoma History and Culture, https://www.okhistory.org/publications/enc/entry.php?entry=AS007 (accessed January 31, 2021).

9. Edith Copeland Manuscript, 36.

10. Patricia Barley and Joan Woods, "The Greatest of Expositions," *Missouri Life Magazine*, May–August 1979, 12–17; James W. Buel, *Louisiana and the Fair: An Exposition of the World, Its People and Their Achievements* (St. Louis: World's Progress, 1904), 4:1387.

11. Catherine Barnard, "An Oklahoma City Girl Writes of the Exposition," *Daily Oklahoman*, May 1, 1904; Kate Barnard, "At World's Fair," *Daily Oklahoman*, May 10, 1904; Kate Barnard, "At the World's Fair," *Daily Oklahoman*, May 1, 1904.

12. Official Guide Company, *World's Fair Authentic Guide: Complete Reference Book to St. Louis and the Louisiana Purchase Exposition* (St. Louis: Official Guide Company, 1904), 136, 2341, 2343; H. Merle Woods, "Historical Preservation Which Occurred in El Reno and St. Louis 75 Years Ago," *Chronicles of Oklahoma* 57, no. 4 (Winter 1979–80): 446–50; Catherine Barnard, "An Oklahoma City Girl Writes of the Exposition," *Daily Oklahoman*, May 1, 1904; Kate Barnard, "At World's Fair," *Daily Oklahoman*, May 10, 1904.

13. Fred Wenner, interview, Guthrie, Oklahoma, May 18, 1950, Box 2, Folder 1, Short Collection. Charles Reeves was also the night editor of the *St. Louis Globe-Democrat* and political editor of the *St. Louis Post-Dispatch*, and it was probably he who assigned a reporter to give Kate a tour and then told her to go home and look at Reno Street if she wanted to see poverty. Edith Copeland Manuscript, 36.

14. Kate Barnard, "At World's Fair," *Daily Oklahoman*, May 10, 1904; Henry S. Iglauer, "The Demolition of the Louisiana Purchase Exposition of 1904," *Bulletin of the Missouri Historical Society* 22, no. 4, pt. 1 (July 1966): 457–67; Ruth Schueler, "My Mother, the Photographer," *Missouri Life Magazine*, May–August 1979, 12, 25–27; Buel, *Louisiana and the Fair*, 8:2853; Barley and Woods, "The Greatest of Expositions," 17; Edith Copeland Manuscript, 36.

15. Catherine Barnard, "An Oklahoma City Girl Writes of the Exposition," *Daily Oklahoman*, May 1, 1904.

16. Resek, *Progressives*, xviii, xix, xx.

17. Edith Copeland Manuscript, 68; Resek, *Progressives*, xvii.

18. "Oklahoma's Attractive Pavilion," in Buel, *Louisiana and the Fair*, 6:2338–40.

19. Jane Addams, "Problems of Municipal Administration," in Howard J. Rogers, ed., *Congress of Arts and Science: Universal Exposition*, vol. 7: *Economics, Politics, Jurisprudence, Social Science* (Boston: Houghton, Mifflin and Company, 1906), 435, 436, 439; Editorial, *St. Louis Republic*, September 18, 1904.

20. Barnard, "Reference of Her Life Work," 24.

21. Thoburn, "Kate Barnard," 1330; "Economic Nationalism and Collective Memory," *Economist*, March 17, 1990, 28; T. M. Finney, "Provident Association," in William Hyde and Howard Conrad, *Encyclopedia of the History of St. Louis: A Compendium of History and Biography for Ready Reference* (New York: Southern

History Company, 1899), 3:1830; "St. Louis Provident Association," *Inland Monthly Magazine*, April 1872, 49–55; W. H. McClain to Kate Barnard, March 13, 1909, Box 24, Folder 2, DOCC Records; "William H. McClain, Social Expert, Dies," *St. Louis Globe-Democrat*, December 8, 1911; "W. H. McClain Must Rest," *St. Louis Globe-Democrat*, May 17, 1911.

22. Helen Christine Bennett, "Kate Barnard," in *American Women in Civic Work* (New York: Dodd, Mead and Company, 1915), 96; Kate Barnard to Isabel Clingensmith, March 26, 1909, Box 17, Folder 4, DOCC Records.

23. Bennett, "Kate Barnard," 96; Kate Barnard to Isabel Clingensmith, March 26, 1909, Box 17, Folder 4, DOCC Records.

24. Kate Barnard to Isabel Clingensmith, March 26, 1909, Box 17, Folder 4, DOCC Records.

25. Kate Barnard to Hedwig Wiess, March 20, 1909, Box 34, Folder 3, DOCC Records.

26. "Resources of Carmen, Okla.," *Frisco System Magazine*, August 1904, 38; "Empire Building in the Frisco System Field," *Frisco System Magazine*, February 1904, 31, 39; "Second Annual Southwestern Tour of the Frisco System Land and Immigration System," *Frisco System Magazine*, March 1904, 62; "Red Fork, Indian Territory," *Frisco System Magazine*, April 1904, 29.

27. W. F. Kerr and Ina Gainer, *The Story of Oklahoma City, Oklahoma: "The Biggest Little City in the World"* (Oklahoma City: S. J. Clarke, 1922), 1:269, 270; McRill, *And Satan Came Also*, 114.

28. Kerr and Gainer, *The Story of Oklahoma City*, 1:270; Bracken, "90 Pounds of Human Dynamite," 12; Leonard Brown to Kate Barnard, December 12, 1908, Box 23, Folder 1, Short Collection.

29. Barnard, "Working for the Friendless"; Kate Barnard, "Progress with Poor in Charitable Work," *Daily Oklahoman*, November 5 and 18, 1905; Kate Barnard, "The Poor House," *Daily Oklahoman*, November 26, 1905; Kate Barnard, "An Appeal for the Poor," *Oklahoma Daily Times-Journal*, October 29, 1905.

30. Kate Barnard, "The Poor House," *Daily Oklahoman*, November 26, 1905; Linda Williams Reese, *Women of Oklahoma, 1890–1920* (Norman: University of Oklahoma Press, 1997), 185; Barnard, "An Appeal for the Poor," *Oklahoma Daily Times-Journal*, October 29, 1905.

31. Kate Barnard to Mrs. S. B. Wilke, November 20, 1909, Box 15, Folder 19, DOCC Records; Edith Copeland Manuscript, 55; Barnard, "Progress with Poor in Charitable Work," *Daily Oklahoman*, November 5, 1905.

32. Kate Barnard to Eliza Egan, December 6, 1909, Box 15, Folder 19, DOCC Records.

33. Kate Barnard to Mrs. S. B. Wilke, November 20, 1909, Box 15, Folder 19, DOCC Records; Edith Copeland Manuscript, 55.

34. Edith Copeland Manuscript, 38, 58. The Provident Association grew into modern Oklahoma City's Community Chest, Organized Charities, and United Drive. Bennett, "Kate Barnard," 99.

35. Barnard, "The Poor House," *Daily Oklahoman*, November 26, 1905; *St. Louis Post-Dispatch*, August 12, 13, and 16, 1904.

36. Edith Copeland Manuscript, 63, 74; Kate Barnard to Eliza Egan, December 6, 1909, Box 15, Folder 19, DOCC Records; Kate Barnard, "The Poor House," *Daily Oklahoman*, December 10, 1905; Kate Barnard to Lilah Lindsay, March 26, 1909, Box 34, Folder 7, DOCC Records.

37. Kate Barnard, letter of reply to query from New Orleans about social work, November 14, 1909, Box 24, Folder 4, DOCC Records; Bob Burke and Glenda Carlile, *Kate Barnard: Oklahoma's Good Angel* (Edmond: University of Central Oklahoma Press, 2001), 16.

38. Edith Copeland Manuscript, 73.

39. Edith Copeland Manuscript, 23, 73.

40. Kate Barnard, "Oklahoma's Child Labor Laws," *Sturm's Oklahoma Magazine*, February 1908, 42.

41. Keith L. Bryant Jr., "Kate Barnard, Organized Labor, and Social Justice in Oklahoma during the Progressive Era," *Journal of Southern History* 35, no. 2 (May 1969): 149, 151; "Woman's Union Label League," *Daily Oklahoman*, December 20, 1905; "Barnard, Kate, Philanthropist," in *National Cyclopedia of American Biography* (New York: James T. White and Company, 1915), 15:110–11; Keith L. Bryant Jr., "Labor in Politics: The Oklahoma State Federation of Labor during the Age of Reform," *Labor History* 11, no. 3 (Summer 1970): 265; Short, "Kate Barnard," chap. 2, p. 12.

42. Fred S. Clinton, "Some Red Cross History," *Chronicles of Oklahoma* 21, no. 2 (March 1943): 184; Short, "Kate Barnard," chap. 3, p. 8.

43. Barnard, "Through the Windows of Destiny," 600.

44. Goble, *Progressive Oklahoma*, 184; Kate Barnard, "Human Ideals in Government," *Survey*, October 2, 1907, 17.

Chapter 3

1. Kate Barnard, "Shaping the Destinies of the New State," in *Proceedings of the National Conference of Charities and Correction, at the Thirty-Fifth Annual Session Held in the City of Richmond, Va., May 6th to 13th, 1908*, ed. Alexander Johnson (Fort Wayne, Ind.: Press of Fort Wayne Printing Company, 1909), 36; Barnard, "Reference of Her Life Work," 66.

2. Barnard, "Shaping the Destinies," 36, 37; Barnard, "Human Ideals in Government," 17; "Achievements of an Oklahoma Editor," *Sturm's Oklahoma Magazine*, January 1907, 5–6.

3. Barnard, "Shaping the Destinies," 37.

4. Kate Barnard to Mrs. Deroos Bailey, November 9, 1909, Box 46, Folder 23, DOCC Records; Kate Barnard, "Address by Miss Kate Barnard," in *Transactions of the Sixth International Congress on Tuberculosis, Washington, September 28 to*

October 5, 1908 (Philadelphia: William F. Fell, 1908), 801; Barnard, "Shaping the Destinies."

5. Barnard, "Address by Miss Kate Barnard," 802–3; Kate Barnard to Mrs. Deroos Bailey, November 9, 1909, Box 46, Folder 23, DOCC Records.

6. E.g., Barnard, "Address by Miss Kate Barnard," 803.

7. Barnard, "Address by Miss Kate Barnard," 807, 805, 808.

8. Barnard, "Shaping the Destinies," 37.

9. Bryant, "Kate Barnard," 148; Edith Copeland Manuscript, 83; Kate Barnard, "'Stump' Ashby Saves the Day," *Journal of the West* 12 (April 1973): 298; Short, "Kate Barnard," chap. 4, p. 6; Barnard, "Shaping the Destinies," 37.

10. Short, "Kate Barnard," chap. 4, p. 6; Barnard, "Shaping the Destinies," 39; Edith Copeland, "Miss Kate of Oklahoma," 83, Box 4, Folders 1 and 2, Copeland Collection.

11. Jerome Dowd, interview with Julee Short, March 1950, Box 2, Folder 54, Short Collection.

12. Edith Copeland to Edward T. James, November 8, 1961, Box 2, Folder 1, Copeland Collection.

13. Kate Barnard to Ethel M. Adams, May 29, 1909, Box 34, Folder 5, DOCC Records; Mary Harris Jones, *Autobiography of Mother Jones* (Chicago: Charles H. Kerr and Company, 1925), 41; McKelway, "'Kate,'" 589–91; Copeland, "Miss Kate of Oklahoma," 88; Morgan and Morgan, *Oklahoma*, 76, 77.

14. McKelway, "'Kate,'" 589–91.

15. Barnard, "Reference of Her Life Work," 278.

16. Barnard, "Reference of Her Life Work," 28.

17. Copeland, "Miss Kate of Oklahoma," 114. Kate also wrote impassioned articles for the October 1906 issues of *Oklahoma State Labor News*. Coralee Paul to author, January 20, 1987, regarding railroad transportation in 1904–14; Nell Snider, interview with Edith Copeland, January 25, 1950, Box 2, Folder 2, Short Collection.

18. Kate Barnard to Mrs. O. A. Robbins, August 20, 1910, Box 23, Folder 7, DOCC Records.

19. "Kate Barnard Eulogizes Work of Convention and Defends against Critics," *Daily Oklahoman*, March 14, 1907; "The Minneapolis Conference," *Charities and the Commons*, July 6, 1907, 391; *Oklahoma State Capital* (Guthrie), September 12, 1907; Bryant, "Kate Barnard," 151; Barnard, "Reference of Her Life Work," 389.

20. "Program of Speeches," *Daily Ardmoreite* (Ardmore, Okla.), September 4, 1906.

21. Angie Debo to Julee Short, May 21, 1973, Box 1, Folder 59, Short Collection; "Kate Barnard Eulogizes Work of Convention and Defends against Critics," *Daily Oklahoman*, March 14, 1907.

22. Angie Debo to Julee Short, May 21, 1973, Box 1, Folder 59, Short Collection.

23. Barnard, "Reference of Her Life Work," 63; Copeland, "Miss Kate of Oklahoma," 90.

24. J. H. Stolper letterhead, Box 21, Folder 19, DOCC Records; J. H. Stolper to Hon. A. O. Bacon, U.S. Senate, May 4, 1912, Box 30, Folder 10, DOCC Records; Dr. D. W. Griffin, interview with Julee Short, February 1, 1950, Box 2, Folder 54, Short Collection; Copeland, "Miss Kate of Oklahoma," 156; Freda Stolper Gold, interview with author, Tulsa, Oklahoma, January 5, 1983; Mrs. Arnold Mignery, archivist, University of the South, to author, January 29, 1985; Angie Debo to Julee Short, n.d. but likely 1975, Box 1, Folder 2, Short Collection.

25. Kate Barnard to Ethel M. Adams, Box 34, Folder 5, DOCC Records. It turned out to be ninety-nine Democrats, twelve Republicans, and one Independent. Goble, *Progressive Oklahoma*, 201; Hurst, *The 46th Star*, 8.

26. Frederick Upham Adams, "A Twentieth-Century State Constitution," *Saturday Evening Post*, November 16, 1907, 3–4, 25.

27. Constitutional Convention notes, Box 2, Folder 1, Short Collection; Burke and Carlile, *Kate Barnard*, 19.

28. "Kate Barnard Rode into Oklahoma with First Farmer-Labor Bloc," *Daily Oklahoman*, October 1, 1922; Copeland, "Miss Kate of Oklahoma," 98.

29. Bertha Baker to Mabel Porter, August 12, 1952, Box 1, Folder 1, Short Collection.

30. Adams, "Twentieth-Century State Constitution," 4.

31. Hurst, *The 46th Star*, 8.

32. Hurst, *The 46th Star*, 3–4, 10; Robert L. Dorman, *Alfalfa Bill: A Life in Politics* (Norman: University of Oklahoma Press, 2018), 46, 47; Burke and Carlile, *Kate Barnard*, 56; Short, "Kate Barnard," chap. 4, p. 14; Bertha Baker to Mabel Porter, August 12, 1952, Box 1, Folder 1, Short Collection.

33. Hurst, *The 46th Star*, 7; Adams, "Twentieth-Century State Constitution," 4; Franklin, *Blacks in Oklahoma*, v; Goble, *Progressive Oklahoma*, 140; Kate Barnard to S. Douglas Russell, June 17, 1908, Box 21, Folder 28, DOCC Records.

34. Hurst, *The 46th Star*, 13, 14; Barnard, "Reference of Her Life Work," 63.

35. Kate Barnard to Mrs. L. B. Snider, June 19, 1908, Box 12, Folder 1, DOCC Records; "Little Big 'Miss Kate' Made a Constitution," *New York Sun*, November 30, 1912; Julee Short to Patrick Blessing, February 9, 1980, Box 2, Folder 27, Short Collection; Short, "Kate Barnard," chap. 4, p. 21.

36. Bennett, "Kate Barnard," 105–6.

37. Kate Barnard to John Fulton, August 26, 1908, Box 25, Folder 3, DOCC Records.

38. Oklahoma Constitutional Convention, *Proceedings of the Constitutional Convention of the Proposed State of Oklahoma, Held at Guthrie, Oklahoma, November 20, 1906 to November 16, 1907* (Muskogee, Okla.: Muskogee Printing Company, 1907), 86; Henry S. Johnston, interview with Edith Copeland, August 1951, Box 1, Folder 44, Short Collection; Short, "Kate Barnard," chap. 4, p. 20.

39. Copeland, "Miss Kate of Oklahoma," 100.

40. Copeland, "Miss Kate of Oklahoma," 100.

41. Barnard, "Reference of Her Life Work," 36, 74; Copeland, "Miss Kate of Oklahoma," 100.

42. "The Bitter Cry of the Children," *Daily Oklahoman*, October 21, 1906; "Need Factory Inspector and Child Labor Laws," *Daily Oklahoman*, October 28, 1906; "The Constitution and Child Labor," *Daily Oklahoman*, November 11, 1906; "Child Legislation Necessary for Greatest Industrial Efficiency," *Daily Oklahoman*, December 16, 1906; "Burbank Would Train Children as Plants," *Daily Oklahoman*, January 27, 1907.

43. "Letters from the People: Mrs. Woodworth's Statement," *Daily Oklahoman*, November 18, 1906; Mabel Bassett, interview, Oklahoma City, January 25, 1950, Box 2, Folder 54, Short Collection; Edith Copeland Manuscript, 151; Kate Barnard to Mrs. Mary Wilkes Glenn, March 23, 1909, Julee Short Notes/Women/United Provident, DOCC Records.

44. Hurst, *The 46th Star*, 9; Barnard, "Reference of Her Life Work," 75; Kate Barnard to Mrs. Deroos Bailey, November 9, 1909, Box 46, Folder 23, DOCC Records; Copeland, "Miss Kate of Oklahoma," 102.

45. Bryant, "Kate Barnard," 152; "Kate Bernard [*sic*] to Be Here: Famous Anti-Child Labor Advocate Will Visit the Convention," *Oklahoma State Capital* (Guthrie), December 6, 1906.

46. Kate Barnard to Hon. W. B. Riley, April 10, 1908, Box 20, Folder 1, Short Collection; Barnard, "Reference of Her Life Work," 64; Barnard, "Shaping the Destinies," 39.

47. Kate Barnard, remarks in "Discussion on Child Labor," in *Proceedings of the National Conference of Charities and Correction, at the Thirty-Fourth Annual Session Held in the City of Minneapolis, Minn., June 12th to 19th, 1907*, ed. Alexander Johnson (Indianapolis: Wm. B. Burford, 1907), 207; Barnard, "Reference of Her Life Work," 65.

48. Barnard, "Reference of Her Life Work," 64.

49. Barnard, "Reference of Her Life Work," 65; "Oklahoma Delegate Better Known Now," *Minneapolis Journal*, June 14, 1907.

50. "The Minneapolis Conference," 389; "Oklahoma Delegate Better Known Now," *Minneapolis Journal*, June 14, 1907; "Miss Barnard Unique Figure in Charities Conference," *Minneapolis Tribune*, June 14, 1907.

51. Hurst, *The 46th Star*, 97; Victor Harlow, *Oklahoma, Its Origins and Development: A History* (Oklahoma City: Harlow, 1935), 310; Copeland, "Miss Kate of Oklahoma," 104.

52. Hurst, *The 46th Star*, 97; "Kate Barnard Eulogizes Work of Convention and Defends against Critics," *Daily Oklahoman*, March 14, 1907; Kate Barnard to Ethel M. Adams, May 25, 1909, Box 34, Folder 5, DOCC Records.

53. "Barnard, Kate, Philanthropist"; Adams, "Twentieth-Century State Constitution," 3; Barnard, "Reference of Her Life Work," 601; Shirley, "Oklahoma

Kate," 21; Ellis, *History of the Constitutional Convention*, 129. Some attribute the "zoological" description to Secretary of War William H. Taft; Morgan and Morgan, *Oklahoma*, 87.

54. Barnard, "Reference of Her Life Work," 59, 60, 61.

55. *Oklahoma State Capital* (Guthrie), September 12, 1907; Charles Robert Goins and Danney Goble, *Historical Atlas of Oklahoma*, 4th ed. (Norman: University of Oklahoma Press, 2006), 190, 191, 158, 159; Copeland, "Miss Kate of Oklahoma," 30.

56. Copeland, "Miss Kate of Oklahoma," 111; Bryant, "Labor in Politics," 271.

57. Ellis, *History of the Constitutional Convention*, 174; *Tulsa World*, December 31, 1907.

58. Kate Barnard to Guthrie Trades Assembly, n.d., Box 16, Folder 3, DOCC Records; Kate Barnard to Mrs. C. H. Fuller, January 25, 1909, Box 18, Folder 4, DOCC Records; "Statistics of Railways for the Year Ended June 30, 1905," *Railway Age*, September 28, 1906, 382.

59. Kate Barnard to C. Leonard Brown, December 17, 1908, Box 23, Folder 1, DOCC Records.

60. Barnard, "Reference of Her Life Work," 27, 28.

61. Barnard, "Through the Windows of Destiny," 600.

62. Barnard, "Through the Windows of Destiny," 601.

63. Bennett, "Kate Barnard," 100; Barnard, "Reference of Her Life Work," 49.

64. "Bryan Speaks to Fully 10,000 People Here," *Daily Oklahoman*, September 6, 1907.

65. "Little Woman Campaigner Will Make a Speech Here," *Daily Oklahoman*, September 15, 1907; "Department of Charities and Corrections," in *The Oklahoma Red Book*, vol. 2, comp. W. B. Richards (Oklahoma City: n.p., 1912), 26.

66. "Kate Barnard Eulogizes Work of Convention and Defends against Critics," *Daily Oklahoman*, March 14, 1907; "Barnard, Kate, Philanthropist"; Barnard, "Reference of Her Life Work," 49.

67. Barnard, "Reference of Her Life Work," 27, 28; S. W. Hayes to Pauline Jamerson, July 13, 1940, Box 1, Folder 1, Short Collection; Kate Barnard to Governor of Kansas, February 15, 1910, Box 13, Folder 16, DOCC Records; Hobart Huson to William Allen White, July 13, 1910, Box 13, Folder 16, DOCC Records.

Chapter 4

1. Hurst, *The 46th Star*, 32.

2. Hurst, *The 46th Star*, 38; Connie Cronley, "Much Love Lost," *Oklahoma Monthly*, February 1977, 10–19, 54–58.

3. Barnard, "Reference of Her Life Work," 48.

4. Barnard, "Reference of Her Life Work," 48, 49; McKelway, "'Kate,'" 591.

5. Helen F. Holmes, correspondence with author, May 15–19, 1984; unidentified clippings, Box 45, Folder 15, DOCC Records; Edith Copeland Manuscript, 127.

6. Kate Barnard to Carter's Ink Company, Boston, July 21, 1908, Box 18, Folder 7, DOCC Records; Kate Barnard to Oklahoma Publishing Company, Oklahoma City, January 1, 1908, Box 20, Folder 1, DOCC Records.

7. Hurst, *The 46th Star*, 46; Kate Barnard to Singer Company, Publishers, New York, March 25, 1908, Box 34, Folder 8, DOCC Records; Kate Barnard to Samuel J. Barrows, April 14, 1908, Box 18, Folder 8, DOCC Records.

8. Harlow, *Oklahoma*, 315; Oklahoma Constitution, Article VI, Sections 27–30; Bryant, "Labor in Politics," 272; Kate Barnard, *First Annual Report of the Commissioner of Charities and Corrections of the State of Oklahoma, for the Year Ending December 31, 1908* (Guthrie, Okla.: Leader Printing Company, 1908), 73–84. The compulsory education bill required at least three months' school attendance a year for all healthy children ages eight to sixteen.

9. Harlow, *Oklahoma*, 312; Edith Copeland Manuscript, 220; State Board of Charities and Corrections to Kate Barnard, December 22, 1907, Box 17, Folder 29, Short Collection. In 1909, the Commission of Charities and Corrections' appropriation of $12,950 for office expenses was the smallest in the state, compared to $38,000 for the state mine inspector and $20,362 for the state library.

10. Thoburn, "Kate Barnard," 1331.

11. Edith Copeland Manuscript, 131. Angie Debo wrote to Julee Short about the allegations of Barnard's affair with Huson, "I suppose you know that she had an affair with Huson, whom she made her assistant in the department. But I think that never got out; her enemies would certainly have used it if they had known. I never knew until Edith Copeland told me a few years ago. It began when Huson was at the Constitutional Convention and she was in Guthrie doing some private lobbying to get a place for a commissioner of Charities and Corrections in the state offices, also labor legislation." Angie Debo to Julee Short, May 21, 1973, Box 1, Folder 59, Short Collection. Debo continued, "Edith Copeland told me that Kate and Huson had an affair that began in Guthrie during the Constitutional Convention and continued during the years. She told it as an established fact. It is possible that it was not firmly proved. Edith talked with Huson's son and he regarded it as an established fact. And Edith told me that during Kate's last sad years she became disillusioned with Huson." Angie Debo to Julee Short, n.d., Box 1, Folder 2, Short Collection; Barnard, "Reference of Her Life Work," 69, 74. Huson's great-granddaughter said the family did "not much appreciate Kate Barnard" and considered her the "other woman" in Huson's life; Mary Ann Maxwell to author, August 11, 2020.

12. Edith Copeland Manuscript, 98; Hobart Huson Jr., conversations with author, April 24–26, 1981; Hobart Huson to Lilah Lindsey, April 17, 1909, Box 24, Folder 7, DOCC Records.

13. Barnard, "Reference of Her Life Work," 74; Kate Barnard to Thomas Graham, August 11, 1908, Box 34, Folder 8, DOCC Records; Hobart Huson to Carl Kelsey, January 17, 1910, Box 12, Folder 3, DOCC Records; Hobart Huson to H. Greenhow, June 2, 1910, Box 33, Folder 6, DOCC Records.

14. Barnard, "Reference of Her Life Work," 36; Jerome Dowd, interview with Julee Short, March 1950, Box 2, Folder 54, Short Collection. One person who did like Huson was J. H. Stolper, whose classical education and tastes set him apart from many rough-and-ready Oklahomans. Stolper named a daughter after Huson, Freda Hobarta. Hobart Huson Jr., conversations with author, April 24–26, 1981; Freda Stolper Gold, interview with author, Tulsa, Oklahoma, January 5, 1985; Edith Copeland Manuscript, 138; Hobart Huson to Jerome Dowd, May 18, 1909, Box 20, Folder 10, DOCC Records; Kate Barnard to Dr. E. G. Newell, [Fort] Supply, September 12, 1908, Box 24, Folder 25, DOCC Records.

15. Hobart Huson to Hobart Huson Jr., n.d., Box 2, Folder 47, Short Collection; Alfred Ely, *Journal of Alfred Ely, a Prisoner of War in Richmond* (New York: D. Appleton and Company, 1862), 9–17, 37–41, 157–63; Hobart Huson Jr., conversations with author, April 24–26, 1981; Hobart Huson to Hobart Huson Jr., October 6, 1912, and September 24, 1909, Box 3, Folder 20, Short Collection.

16. Unsigned letter to Hobart Huson Jr. with salutation "Dear Cousin," July 8, 1925, Box 2, Folder 29, Short Collection; "In Supreme Court—The Death of Mr. Huson," *Rochester (N.Y.) Union and Advertiser*, October 19 and December 3, 1861, and August 6, 1862. Legal documents and newspaper articles found through genealogical research confirm this story: John Edward McInerney to author, September 10, 1984; *Julia H. Robinson v. Hobart Huson*, Supreme Court of the State of New York in Monroe County, February 8, 1879; *Rochester Daily Union and Advertiser*, February 12, 1879.

17. Edith Copeland Manuscript, 98; Hobart Huson Jr., conversations with author, April 24–26, 1981; Nellie Cregler to "My Dear Mrs. [Hobart] Huson [Sr.]," July 1903, given to author by Hobart Huson Jr.

18. Barnard, "Reference of Her Life Work," 74; Kate Barnard to T. P. Gore, March 13, 1909, Box 10, Folder 8, DOCC Records; Kate Barnard to Senator Owen, March 18, 1909, Box 10, Folder 8, DOCC Records; Kate Barnard to Hon. James Gibbons, March 13, 1909, Box 23, Folder 9, DOCC Records.

19. Kate Barnard to Mrs. Clarence Burns, March 19, 1908, Box 34, Folder 8, DOCC Records.

20. McKelway, "'Kate,'" 593; Barnard, "Oklahoma's Child Labor Laws," 44; Ben B. Lindsey to Pauline Jamerson, July 16, 1940, Box 2, Folder 14, Short Collection.

21. Kate Barnard to Samuel J. Barrows, December 23, 1909, Box 18, Folder 19, DOCC Records; Samuel J. Barrows to Kate Barnard, January 11, 1908, Box 2, Folder 14, Short Collection; Edith Copeland Manuscript, 240.

22. Kate Barnard to Owen Lovejoy, January 11, 1908, Box 18, Folder 11, DOCC Records.

23. Elizabeth H. Davidson, *Child Labor Legislation in the Southern Textile States* (Chapel Hill: University of North Carolina Press, 1939), 1–2, 56, 126–29.

24. William H. Murray, "The Constitutional Convention," *Chronicles of Oklahoma* 9, no. 2 (June 1931): 133.

25. Kate Barnard to unnamed recipient, October 7, 1908, Box 19, Folder 10, DOCC Records; Barnard, "Reference of Her Life Work," 72–73; Bryant, "Kate Barnard," 157–58.

26. Barnard, "Reference of Her Life Work," 72, 73.

27. Kate Barnard to William Franklin, June 11, 1908, Box 24, Folder 4, DOCC Records; Kate Barnard to Samuel J. Barrows, June 23, 1908, Box 19, Folder 23, DOCC Records; Samuel J. Barrows to Paul Kellogg, director of *Pittsburg Survey*, n.d., in Edith Copeland Manuscript, 162.

28. Edith Copeland Manuscript, 162; Kate Barnard to Roland B. Molineux, June 23, 1908, Box 20, Folder 1, DOCC Records.

29. Kate Barnard to Laura M. Corder, June 18, 1908, Box 19, Folder 23, DOCC Records.

30. Kate Barnard to J. N. Hackler, March 2, 1909, Box 14, Folder 5, Short Collection; Harlow, *Oklahoma*, 388.

31. Barnard, "Reference of Her Life Work," 73.

32. Kate Barnard to Roland B. Molineux, June 23, 1908, Box 20, Folder 1, DOCC Records; Kate Barnard to John Glenn, June 27, 1908, Box 20, Folder 1, DOCC Records; Edith Copeland Manuscript, 162.

33. Samuel J. Barrows to Kate Barnard, June 15, 1908, Box 24, Folder 4, DOCC Records; Ben B. Lindsey to Pauline Jamerson, July 16, 1940, Box 2, Folder 14, Short Collection; John Glenn to Kate Barnard, June 24, 1908, Box 11, Folder 5, DOCC Records; Edith Copeland Manuscript, 133.

34. Edith Copeland Manuscript, 151, 182; Helen F. Holmes to author, May 15, 1984.

35. Hobart Huson to P. E. Martin, July 23, 1910, Box 25, Folder 4, DOCC Records.

36. Keith L. Bryant Jr., *Alfalfa Bill Murray* (Norman: University of Oklahoma Press, 1968), 81; McKelway, "'Kate,'" 592; Kate Barnard to Roland B. Molineux, February 20, 1908, Box 18, Folder 8, DOCC Records.

37. Kate Barnard to Roland B. Molineux, February 20, 1908, Box 18, Folder 8, DOCC Records; McKelway, "'Kate,'" 593.

38. Kate Barnard to William Franklin, June 17, 1908, Box 24, Folder 4, DOCC Records.

39. Barnard, "Reference of Her Life Work," 36.

40. Kate Barnard to Samuel J. Barrows, June 8, 1908, Box 24, Folder 4, DOCC Records; Kate Barnard to Hon. Scott Ferris, September 24, 1910, Box 22, Folder 30, Short Collection; Barnard, "Reference of Her Life Work," 11.

41. Kate Barnard to Hon. J. A. West, August 1, 1908, Box 17, Folder 1, DOCC Records; Hobart Huson to William Franklin, July 18, 1908, Box 24, Folder 4, DOCC Records; Hobart Huson to Hon. Howell Smith, August 3, 1908, Box 24, Folder 6, DOCC Records; Kate Barnard to Hon. Scott Ferris, September 24, 1910, Box 22, Folder 30, DOCC Records.

42. McKelway, "'Kate,'" 591; "The Day Si (Silas H. Reid) Met Kate in Oklahoma," *Tanana Miner* (Chena, Alaska), November 9, 1908.

43. A. J. Sellers to Kate Barnard, November 24, 1908, Box 24, Folder 8, DOCC Records.

44. F. W. Skillern to Kate Barnard, July 14, 1908, Box 24, Folder 6, DOCC Records; Kate Barnard to E. A. Bowerman, August 10, 1908, Box 24, Folder 1, DOCC Records; Kate Barnard to Hon. J. A. West, August 1, 1908, Box 17, Folder 1, DOCC Records; James R. Scales and Danney Goble, *Oklahoma Politics: A History* (Norman: University of Oklahoma Press, 1982), 41–58; Hobart Huson to Hon. Howell Smith, August 3, 1908, Box 24, Folder 6, DOCC Records; Edith Copeland Manuscript, 272.

45. Kate Barnard to William Franklin, August 8, 1908, Box 24, Folder 1, DOCC Records; William Franklin to Kate Barnard, August 7, 1908, Box 20, Folder 1, DOCC Records.

46. Hobart Huson to W. B. Alexander, July 26, 1908, Box 23, Folder 11, DOCC Records; Edith Copeland Manuscript, 272.

47. Bryant, "Kate Barnard," 157; Kate Barnard, "The New State and Its Children," in National Child Labor Committee, *Child Labor and Social Progress: Proceedings of the Fourth Annual Meeting of the National Child Labor Committee* (Philadelphia: American Academy of Political and Social Science, 1908), 174.

48. Kate Barnard to Hon. H. P. Hanson, May 26, 1910, Box 34, Folder 13, DOCC Records; Kate Barnard, speech to National Conference of Charities and Correction, Richmond, Virginia, May 1908, Box 3, Folder 4, Short Collection.

49. Kate Barnard to Edward T. Devine, July 21, 1908, Box 34, Folder 8, DOCC Records; Kate Barnard to J. H. Stolper, May 2, 1908, Box 21, Folder 19, DOCC Records.

50. Barnard, "Address by Miss Kate Barnard"; Barnard, "Reference of Her Life Work," 69. Some of Kate's speeches and articles, along with excerpts from her diary, are reprinted in Burke and Carlile, *Kate Barnard*.

51. Kate Barnard to Robert Henderson Pope, October 12, 1908, Box 18, Folder 7, DOCC Records; Kate Barnard to unidentified recipient, October 13, 1908, Box 24, Folder 2, DOCC Records; Kate Barnard to Samuel Gompers, September 23, 1908, Box 25, Folder 3, DOCC Records. When Woodrow Wilson ran for president in 1912, McKelway suggested that he seek Kate's help with his campaign because "she was 'the most consummate politician' in Oklahoma." Bryant, "Kate Barnard," 163; A. J. McKelway to Woodrow Wilson, February 8, 1912, Box 1, Alexander Jeffrey McKelway Papers, Library of Congress, Manuscript Division, Washington, D.C.

52. For example, on October 21, she was in Mounds; on October 22, in Kiefer and Sapulpa; on October 23, in Bartlesville; on October 24, in Stigler; on October 29, in Bartlesville; on October 30, in Bartlesville and Nowata; on October 31, in Kiefer and Okmulgee; on November 2, in Muskogee; and on November 5, in Guthrie.

53. Kate Barnard notes, October 15, 1908, Box 24, Folder 1, DOCC Records; Hobart Huson notes, October 18, 1908, Box 17, Folder 27, DOCC Records.

54. Kate Barnard to W. J. Bryan, November 7, 1908, Box 34, Folder 7, DOCC Records.

55. Kate Barnard to Hon. Thomas P. Gore, November 7, 1908, Box 22, Folder 21, DOCC Records; Kate Barnard to Federation of Labor, November 9, 1908, Box 25, Folder 3, DOCC Records.

Chapter 5

1. Kate Barnard to Dr. E. G. Newell, [Fort] Supply, September 12, 1908, Box 34, Folder 14, DOCC Records.

2. Shirley, "Oklahoma Kate," 56; Hurst, *The 46th Star*, 70–71.

3. Kate Barnard to D. F. Sutherland, January 5, 1910, Box 34, Folder 24, Short Collection; Barnard, *First Annual Report*, 28.

4. Lucretta Forston to Kate Barnard, January 14, 1910, Box 9, Folder 2, DOCC Records; Yukon Justice of the Peace to Kate Barnard, January 13, 1910, Box 9, Folder 2, DOCC Records; unnamed woman in Canadian County to Kate Barnard, January 14, 1910, Box 9, Folder 2, DOCC Records.

5. Anonymous attendant to Kate Barnard, January 27, 1910, Box 9, Folder 1, DOCC Records; Affidavit of Cruelty by Hugh Devine, December 20, 1909, Box 9, Folder 1, DOCC Records.

6. Kate Barnard to J. E. Wolfe, December 23, 1909, Box 9, Folder 1, DOCC Records; Kate Barnard to Dr. D. W. Griffin, December 8, 1910, Box 11, Folder 2, DOCC Records.

7. Barnard, "Through the Windows of Destiny," 604; Kate Barnard to Sarah Knott, January 12, 1910, Box 9, Folder 1, DOCC Records.

8. Kate Barnard to Rev. C. H. Holland, January 9, 1910, Box 9, Folder 1, DOCC Records.

9. Barnard, "Through the Windows of Destiny," 604; Kate Barnard to J. E. Wolfe, December 17, 1909, Box 9, Folder 1, DOCC Records; Kate Barnard to Dr. D. W. Griffin, n.d., Box 11, Folder 2, DOCC Records; Kate Barnard to D. F. Sutherland, January 5, 1910, Box 34, Folder 14, DOCC Records.

10. Barnard, *First Annual Report*, 23, 26, 27.

11. Barnard, *First Annual Report*, 27; E. B. Egbert to Hon. Lee Cruce, November 5, 1913, Box 41, Folder 4, DOCC Records.

12. Kate Barnard to Hon. C. N. Haskell, December 18, 1909, Box 17, Folder 30, DOCC Records; E. B. Egbert to Hon. Lee Cruce, November 5, 1913, Box 41, Folder 4, DOCC Records.

13. Kate Barnard to Hon. Charles West, December 18, 1909, Box 17, Folder 30, DOCC Records.

14. Kate Barnard to Hon. Charles West, December 18, 1909, Box 17, Folder 30, DOCC Records; Kate Barnard to Dr. E. G. Newell, December 6, 1909, Box 17, Folder 30, DOCC Records.

15. Kate Barnard to Dr. E. G. Newell, December 6, 1909, Box 17, Folder 30, DOCC Records.

16. Barnard, *First Annual Report*, 24; Barnard, "Through the Windows of Destiny," 604.

17. Barnard, *First Annual Report*, 30; Kate Barnard to Dr. E. G. Newell, January 21, 1910, Box 10, Folder 5, DOCC Records; Dr. E. G. Newell to Kate Barnard, January 21, 1910, Box 10, Folder 5, DOCC Records.

18. Edith Copeland Manuscript, 251.

19. Kate Barnard to Dr. E. G. Newell, December 5, 1910, Box 10, Folder 5, DOCC Records; Kate Barnard to New York Hospital for the Insane, November 16, 1909, Box 11, Folder 1, DOCC Records.

20. Barnard, *First Annual Report*, 28, 30, 31.

21. Dr. D. W. Griffin, interview with Julee Short, February 1, 1950, Box 2, Folder 54, Short Collection; Jerome Dowd, interview with Julee Short, March 1950, Box 2, Folder 54, Short Collection. Dowd said he recommended Dr. Griffin to replace Superintendent Clark. Edith Copeland Manuscript, 255; Kate Barnard to Dr. A. T. Clark, December 3, 1909, Box 11, Folder 2, DOCC Records.

22. Kate Barnard to Dr. E. G. Newell, December 21, 1909, Box 17, Folder 30, DOCC Records.

23. Kate Barnard to Dr. A. T. Clark, December 3, 1909, Box 11, Folder 2, DOCC Records.

24. Kate Barnard to Dr. A. T. Clark, December 3, 1909, Box 11, Folder 2, DOCC Records.

25. Kate Barnard to Dr. A. T. Clark, December 3, 1909, Box 11, Folder 2, DOCC Records.

26. Kate Barnard to Dr. A. T. Clark, n.d., 1909, Box 14, Folder 3, DOCC Records.

27. Hobart Huson to unnamed recipient, January 22, 1910, Box 18, Folder 13, DOCC Records; Kate Barnard to Dr. D. W. Griffin, December 4, 1909, Box 36, Folder 2, DOCC Records; Edith Copeland Manuscript, 252; Kate Barnard to Dr. A. T. Clark, January 11, 1910, Box 11, Folder 2, DOCC Records; Kate Barnard to L. H. Selsor, January 15, 1910, Box 11, Folder 2, DOCC Records.

28. Edith Copeland Manuscript, 255; Kate Barnard to Dr. A. T. Clark, January 11, 1910, Box 11, Folder 2, DOCC Records; Hobart Huson to unnamed recipient, January 22, 1910, Box 18, Folder 13, DOCC Records; Kate Barnard to unnamed woman in Hobart, n.d., 1910, Box 9, Folder 2, DOCC Records.

29. Kate Barnard to Hon. C. L. Long, October 19, 1909, Box 16, Folder 1, DOCC Records.

30. Kate Barnard to Dr. F. M. Adams, January 2, 1913, Box 45, Folder 1, DOCC Records.

31. Kate Barnard to Governor Haskell, October 19, 1909, Box 10, Folder 9, DOCC Records; Felix M. Adams to Kate Barnard, January 2, 1913, Box 45, Folder 1, DOCC Records; Kate Barnard to Robert Dunlop, October 19, 1909, Box 16,

Folder 1, DOCC Records; "Vinta [*sic*] State Hospital," updated September 12, 2018, *Asylum Projects*, https://www.asylumprojects.org/index.php/Vinta_State _Hospital (accessed January 31, 2021); Felix M. Adams to Kate Barnard, June 19, 1913, Box 2, Folder 10, DOCC Records.

32. Hobart Huson to unnamed recipient, January 22, 1910, Box 18, Folder 13, DOCC Records; Kate Barnard to Dr. D. W. Griffin, January 2, 1910, Box 11, Folder 2, DOCC Records; Edith Copeland Manuscript, 259; Kate Barnard to Rev. Lydia M. Herrick, January 15, 1910, Box 16, Folder 1, DOCC Records.

33. Unnamed sender to Kate Barnard, February 12, 1909, Box 16, Folder 24, DOCC Records; unnamed sender to Kate Barnard, January 4, 1909, Box 10, Folder 5, DOCC Records; unnamed sender to Kate Barnard, June 10, 1910, Box 10, Folder 5, DOCC Records; Kate Barnard to McAlester County Attorney, November 25, 1910, Box 29, Folder 6, DOCC Records; Kate Barnard to unnamed man in Ponca City, Oklahoma, July 25, 1910, Box 16, Folder 12, DOCC Records; Kate Barnard to Sister Aloysia, September 13, 1910, Box 22, Folder 30, DOCC Records.

34. Edith Copeland Manuscript, 219.

35. Kate Barnard to Hon. A. J. Jennings, March 30, 1910, Box 22, Folder 3, DOCC Records; Hobart Huson to unnamed father, June 10, 1910, Box 22, Folder 3, DOCC Records; Kate Barnard to unnamed father, December 8, 1910, Box 22, Folder 3, DOCC Records; Jon D. May, "Jennings, Alphonso J.," *Encyclopedia of Oklahoma History and Culture*, https://www.okhistory.org/publications/enc /entry.php?entry=JE006 (accessed January 31, 2021).

36. George Damon to Kate Barnard, August 25, 1910, Box 12, Folder 1, DOCC Records; Kate Barnard to George Damon, September 15, 1910, Box 12, Folder 1, DOCC Records; Kate Barnard to Pete Hanraty, October 19, 1910, Box 34, Folder 15, DOCC Records; Edith Copeland Manuscript, 219.

37. Hobart Huson to H. H. Hart, October 19, 1910, Box 18, Folder 16, DOCC Records; Kate Barnard to Nell Snider, June 7, 1909, Box 12, Folder 1, DOCC Records; Kate Barnard to Mrs. W. E. Carter, July 20, 1910, Box 24, Folder 4, DOCC Records; Kate Barnard to Dr. W. E. Settle, July 12, 1910, Box 29, Folder 11, DOCC Records.

38. Kate Barnard to James O'Neil, November 12, 1909, Box 33, Folder 12, DOCC Records.

39. Kate Barnard to Claremore County Judge, June 3, 1909, Box 12, Folder 8, DOCC Records; Barnard, *First Annual Report*, 43, 44.

40. Barnard, *First Annual Report*, 43; Barnard, "Through the Windows of Destiny," 604.

41. Barnard, *First Annual Report*, 52.

42. Barnard, *First Annual Report*, 44.

43. Kate Barnard to Claremore County Judge, June 3, 1909, Box 12, Folder 8, DOCC Records.

44. Unnamed Chickasaw man to Kate Barnard, April 14, 1909, Box 12, Folder 8, DOCC Records.

45. Barnard, *First Annual Report*, 49; Shirley, "Oklahoma Kate," 57.

46. Barnard, *First Annual Report*, 50, 51.

47. Barnard, *First Annual Report*, 45, 50, 52.

48. Barnard, *First Annual Report*, 53; Edith Copeland Manuscript, 139; Kate Barnard to Hon. Chairman and Board of County Commissioners, Enid, October 30, 1909, Box 17, Folder 6, DOCC Records; Kate Barnard to W. H. Roberts, February 26, 1910, Box 15, Folder 16, DOCC Records; Kate Barnard to Samuel J. Barrows, February 8, 1909, Box 18, Folder 19, DOCC Records.

49. Barnard, *First Annual Report*, 43.

50. Barnard, *First Annual Report*, 45.

51. Kate Barnard to Will Penny, August 10, 1908, Box 24, Folder 6, DOCC Records; Will Penny to Kate Barnard, August 12, 1908, Box 24, Folder 6, DOCC Records.

52. Barnard, *First Annual Report*, 63.

53. Kate Barnard to C. H. Holland, January 12, 1910, Box 9, Folder 1, DOCC Records; Kate Barnard to Sarah Knott, January 12, 1910, Box 9, Folder 1, DOCC Records; Kate Barnard to unnamed former patient, January 20, 1910, Box 14, Folder 3, DOCC Records; H. H. Hart to Hobart Huson, October 22, 1910, Box 18, Folder 16, DOCC Records; Kate Barnard to unnamed recipient, July 13, 1909, Box 13, Folder 1, DOCC Records.

Chapter 6

1. Barnard, *First Annual Report*, 16; Barnard to Association Women's Board of Charities, Denver, February 11, 1909, Box 13, Folder 11, DOCC Records; Harvey Hougen, "Kate Barnard and the Kansas Penitentiary Scandal, 1908–1909," *Journal of the West* 17, no. 1 (January 1978): 9.

2. Short, "Kate Barnard," chap. 8, p. 5; Barnard, *First Annual Report*, 4, 5; Edith Copeland Manuscript, 193.

3. The prison's Board of Directors is sometimes referred to as the Board of Control in Barnard's second annual report, among other sources. Kate Barnard, *Second Report of the Commissioner of Charities and Corrections, from October 1, 1909 to October 1, 1910* (Oklahoma City: Warden Printing Company, 1910), 134; Barnard, *First Annual Report*, 5.

4. Barnard, *First Annual Report*, 8.

5. Barnard, *First Annual Report*, 7, 8, 14, 15.

6. Barnard, *First Annual Report*, 9, 10, 7, 6; Kate Barnard to Dr. D. S. Ashby, April 1908, Box 24, Folder 8, DOCC Records; Kate Barnard to Frank Thompson, July 12, 1910, Box 10, Folder 4, DOCC Records.

7. Barnard, *First Annual Report*, 17–18.

8. Kate Barnard to Dr. D. S. Ashby, December 26, 1908, Box 24, Folder 8, DOCC Records; Kate Barnard to I. H. Jennings, March 21, 1910, Box 34, Folder 5, DOCC Records; Governor Haskell quoted in Hougen, "Kate Barnard," 11; Hurst, *The 46th Star*, 101; Edith Copeland Manuscript, 199.

9. Hougen, "Kate Barnard," 12.

10. Kate Barnard to William A. White, *Emporia Gazette*, December 14, 1908, Box 46, Folder 23, DOCC Records. "I have seen your paper quoted in which I was termed a muck-raker by you. I keep a scrapbook and would like to have the original article. I am very much interested in seeing the various estimates of my work." Kate Barnard to William A. White, December 23, 1908, Box 46, Folder 23, DOCC Records.

11. Edith Copeland Manuscript, 199; William A. White to Kate Barnard, December 21, 1908, Box 45, Folder 23, DOCC Records.

12. Edith Copeland Manuscript, 201; Kate Barnard to Dr. D. S. Ashby, December 28, 1908, Box 24, Folder 8, DOCC Records; Kate Barnard to William A. White, December 28, 1908, Box 46, Folder 23, DOCC Records; Edith Copeland Manuscript, 201, 203.

13. Edith Copeland Manuscript, 201–3; Barnard, *Second Report*, 12–13; J. H. Stolper and Hobart Huson correspondence, January 1909, Box 29, Folder 4, DOCC Records; Edith Copeland Manuscript, 221. According to a *Daily Oklahoman* news story, when Stolper told the joint committee that Governor Haskell had appointed him to make an investigation of the penitentiary, "Attorney General West refused to recognize Dr. Stolper and declared that they would have nothing to do with him [but] Dr. Stolper was permitted by the prison officials to make an inspection of the institution." "Kate Barnard Tells of Prison Horror," *Daily Oklahoman*, January 8, 1909.

14. Barnard, *Second Report*, 12, 139, 141; "Convicts in Cell-House Cheer 'Kate,'" *Daily Oklahoman*, January 3, 1909.

15. Short, "Kate Barnard," chap. 8, p. 12; Barnard, *Second Report*, 12.

16. Barnard, *Second Report*, 102–3, 132.

17. Barnard, *Second Report*, 112–13, 115.

18. Oklahoma committee report on Lansing investigation, in Barnard, *Second Report*, 115.

19. Barnard, *Second Report*, 130–31, quotes from 131.

20. Barnard, *Second Report*, 130, 125.

21. Barnard, *Second Report*, 118, 133–35; "Kate Barnard Tells of Prison Horror," *Daily Oklahoman*, January 8, 1909.

22. Barnard, *Second Report*, 105, 116, 125, 128, 129, 162.

23. Kate Barnard to William A. White, December 21, 1908, Box 46, Folder 9, DOCC Records; Barnard, *Second Report*, 134, 135, 137, 138, 140, 141.

24. Barnard, *Second Report*, 139, 140.

25. Barnard, *Second Report*, 133, 141, 146.

26. Barnard, *Second Report*, 143–44, 146, 141.

27. Barnard, *Second Report*, 141–45, 148.

28. Barnard, *Second Report*, 147, 149.

29. Barnard, *Second Report*, 149, 152, 153, 155, quotes from 152, 151.

30. Barnard, *Second Report*, 155; Kate Barnard to Dr. D. S. Ashby, December 30, 1908, Box 24, Folder 8, DOCC Records; Barnard, *Second Report*, 157.

31. Kate Barnard to Samuel J. Barrows, January 13, 1909, Box 24, Folder 4, DOCC Records; Barnard, *Second Report*, 13.

32. Kate Barnard to William A. White, January 12, 1909, Box 25, Folder 5, DOCC Records; "Governor Haskell's Twelfth Special Message to the Legislature," in Barnard, *Second Report*, 101–6, quotes from 105, 106, 101; William A. White to Kate Barnard, January 18, 1909, Box 46, Folder 23, DOCC Records; Barnard, *Second Report*, 14; Short, "Kate Barnard," chap. 8, p. 13; Hougen, "Kate Barnard," 16.

33. Short, "Kate Barnard," chap. 9, p. 2; Kate Barnard to Ethel M. Adams, May 29, 1909, Box 34, Folder 5, DOCC Records; Hurst, *The 46th Star*, 103.

Chapter 7

1. Kate Barnard to J. K. Turner, December 20, 1909, Box 12, Folder 2, DOCC Records; Oklahoma Constitution, Article VI, Section 27.

2. "Statement of Kate Barnard," Box 42, Folder 17, DOCC Records.

3. Oklahoma Constitution, Article VI, Sections 27, 20, 22, 25, 31, 19, 33.

4. Barnard, *First Annual Report*, 43, 42.

5. Kate Barnard to Superintendent Steward, December 6, 1913, Box 41, Folder 15, DOCC Records.

6. Kate Barnard, *Third Report of the Commissioner of Charities and Corrections, from October 1, 1910 to October 1, 1911* (Oklahoma City: Oklahoma Engraving and Printing Company, 1911), 8, 321, 326, 332; Edith Copeland Manuscript, 185.

7. Barnard, *Third Report*, 5, 8.

8. Barnard, *First Annual Report*, 42, 43, 3.

9. The counties that had sent the most inmates were Muskogee (103), Oklahoma (80), Wagoner (67), and Pittsburg (66). There were none from Ellis County. In contrast, the Oklahoma State Reformatory said that the state's most populous counties, Oklahoma and Muskogee, had never sent a prisoner to the institution. Barnard, *Fourth Report of the Commissioner of Charities and Corrections, from October 1, 1911 to October 1, 1912* (Oklahoma City: Oklahoma Engraving and Printing Company, 1912), 374–77, 383.

10. Barnard, *Second Report*, 35–38.

11. Barnard, *First Annual Report*, 49; Barnard, *Second Report*, 96.

12. Barnard, *First Annual Report*, 30, 28.

13. Barnard, *Fourth Report*, 367.

14. Barnard, *Second Report*, 83–85.

15. Barnard, *First Annual Report*, 60, 61.

16. Examples from Barnard, *Second Report*, 41, 42, 46, 47.

17. Kate Barnard to A. L. Churchill, December 12, 1910, Box 11, Folder 12, DOCC Records; Report from Oklahoma School for the Deaf in Sulphur, 1913, Box 3, Folder 1, DOCC Records; Kate Barnard to Nazarene Home, 1913, Box 2, Folder 10, DOCC Records; Barnard, *Third Report*, 212.

18. Barnard, *First Annual Report*, 39, 49; Barnard, *Second Report*, 86–87; Barnard, *Fourth Report*, 446; Barnard, *First Annual Report*, 62.

19. Barnard, *First Annual Report*, 55, 54–55; U.S. Census data for 1910 from Harlow, *Oklahoma*, 326; Barnard, *Second Report*, 32, 78.

20. Barnard, *First Annual Report*, 49. She commended the poor farms in Kingfisher, Pottawatomie, and Oklahoma Counties; she was discreet about the others. Kate Barnard to Roland B. Molineux, May 29, 1909, Box 11, Folder 8, DOCC Records.

21. Barnard, *Second Report*, 82; Barnard, *Fourth Report*, 289.

22. Barnard, *Fourth Report*, 350; Barnard, *Second Report*, 39.

23. Barnard, *Fourth Report*, 285, 346; Barnard, *Second Report*, 30.

24. Barnard, *Fourth Report*, 343.

Chapter 8

1. Short, "Kate Barnard," chap. 9, p. 6, and chap. 12, p. 8; notes in Kate Barnard file, March 2, 1909, Box 41, Folder 7, DOCC Records; Kate Barnard to Mrs. C. C. Guy, c/o *Enid Wave* newspaper, October 28, 1909, Box 17, Folder 6, DOCC Records.

2. Ida Tarbell to Kate Barnard, February 27, 1908, Box 34, Folder 8, DOCC Records; "Ida Tarbell," *Encyclopedia Britannica*, updated January 2, 2021, https://www.britannica.com/biography/Ida-Tarbell (accessed January 31, 2021); Andy Piascik, "Ida Tarbell: The Woman Who Took On Standard Oil," January 6, 2020, *Connecticut History*, https://connecticuthistory.org/ida-tarbell-the-woman-who -took-on-standard-oil/ (accessed January 31, 2021).

3. Moorehead, *The American Indian*, 151; Kate Barnard to Ben Oliver, November 6, 1908, Box 24, Folder 8, DOCC Records.

4. "Kate Barnard, Unsung Hero," *Daily Oklahoman*, February 23, 1941; itemized travel expenses for Kate's department from statehood to January 1911 and for 1912–13, Box 3, Folder 1, DOCC Records; Thoburn, "Kate Barnard," 1333. She was asked to address the National Editorial Association in New Orleans and a national labor meeting (the Brotherhood of Carpenters and Joiners) in Des Moines.

5. Kate Barnard to Mrs. R. M. Haynes, November 17, 1909, Box 12, Folder 7, DOCC Records.

6. Keith L. Bryant Jr., "The Juvenile Court Movement: Oklahoma as a Case Study," *Social Science Quarterly* 49, no. 2 (September 1968): 368; Juvenile Court of the City and County of Denver, *The Problem of the Children and How the State of Colorado Cares for Them: A Report of the Juvenile Court of Denver* (Denver: Merchants, 1904), 34, 12; "Ben B. Lindsey," *Encyclopedia Britannica*, updated November 21, 2020, https://www.britannica.com/biography/Ben-B-Lindsey (accessed January 31, 2021); Kate Barnard to Effie Andrews, November 6, 1909, Box 46, Folder 25, DOCC Records.

7. Bryant, "The Juvenile Court Movement," 370; Hobart Huson to unnamed recipient, December 27, 1909, Box 24, Folder 4, DOCC Records.

8. Bryant, "The Juvenile Court Movement," 371.

9. Kate Barnard to Roy Stafford, January 14 and February 17, 1909, Box 11, Folder 4, DOCC Records; Roy Stafford to Kate Barnard, January 22, 1909, Box 11, Folder 4, DOCC Records.

10. Kate Barnard to Mrs. Finis Bentley, May 10, 1910, Box 33, Folder 4, DOCC Records; Kate Barnard to Roy Stafford, February 17, 1909, Box 11, Folder 4, DOCC Records. The five normal schools were located at Edmond, Ardmore, Alva, Weatherford, and Tonkawa. The universities were the University of Oklahoma in Norman and Epworth University, which became Oklahoma City University.

11. Kate Barnard to Assistant Editor, *The Commoner*, Lincoln, Nebraska, December 21, 1908, Box 34, Folder 7, DOCC Records; Roy Stafford to Kate Barnard, March 17, 1909, Box 14, Folder 30, DOCC Records; Kate Barnard to Roy Stafford, March 8, 1909, Box 11, Folder 4, DOCC Records.

12. Edith Copeland Manuscript, 222.

13. Kate Barnard to unnamed recipient, June 25, 1909, Box 24, Folder 4, DOCC Records; Rodger Randle to author, January 18, 2019; Kate Barnard to Effie Andrews, November 6, 1909, Box 46, Folder 25, DOCC Records; Kate Barnard to unnamed recipient, June 25, 1909, Box 24, Folder 4, DOCC Records; Kate Barnard to Roy Stafford, March 8, 1909, Box 11, Folder 4, DOCC Records; Short, "Kate Barnard," chap. 9, p. 11. The juvenile bill, Senate Bill 88, was titled "An Act to Define Dependent, Neglected and Delinquent Children and to Regulate the Treatment, Control and Custody Thereof by County Courts." It specified that a child under the age of sixteen who violated a law would be designated a delinquent, a dependent, or a neglected child, but not a criminal; the jurisdiction for these youths was a county juvenile court; no child under the age of twelve was to be kept in any jail with adult criminals; and the maximum penalty was to send the child to the State Training School until the age of twenty-one "unless sooner reformed." See Hobart Huson, "Oklahoma's Juvenile Court Law Most Effective of All," *Daily Oklahoman*, January 28, 1912.

14. Kate Barnard to Samuel J. Barrows, May 3, 1909, Box 18, Folder 19, DOCC Records.

15. Barnard, *Second Report*, 53; Bryant, "The Juvenile Court Movement," 375.

16. Barnard, *Second Report*, 54–64.

17. Barnard, *Second Report*, 65–68, quote from 65.

18. Bennett, "Kate Barnard," 107; Edith Copeland Manuscript, 266.

19. Kate Barnard to Charles Walker, May 3, 1909, Box 13, Folder 1, DOCC Records; Kate Barnard to Mrs. D. E. Emerson, June 29, 1909, Box 13, Folder 1, DOCC Records; *State of Oklahoma v. County Commissioners of Garfield County*, Box 44, Folder 2, DOCC Records; Barnard, *Second Report*, 31; Edith Copeland Manuscript, 292; Ross Lockridge, report to Kate Barnard, July 1, 1913, Box 44, Folder 2, DOCC Records.

20. Edith Copeland Manuscript, 214; Kate Barnard to Warden Henry Wolfer, March 20, 1909, Box 34, Folder 5, DOCC Records; Barnard, *Second Report*, 29; Kate Barnard to Lucy P. Berry, January 21, 1910, Box 13, Folder 4, DOCC Records.

21. Warden Henry Wolfer to Kate Barnard, March 17, 1909, Box 34, Folder 5, DOCC Records; Hobart Huson to Walter Bennett, October 15, 1908, Box 34, Folder 8, DOCC Records; Kate Barnard to Emma Rose, January 28, 1909, Box 34, Folder 3, DOCC Records.

22. Kate Barnard to Warden Henry Wolfer, March 13, 1909, Box 34, Folder 5, DOCC Records.

23. Edith Copeland Manuscript, 214; Kate Barnard to Samuel J. Barrows, February 8, 1909, Box 18, Folder 19, DOCC Records; Kate Barnard to Warden Henry Wolfer, March 20, 1909, Box 34, Folder 5, DOCC Records.

24. Kate Barnard to Samuel J. Barrows, February 8, 1909, Box 18, Folder 9, DOCC Records; Kate Barnard to A. Cornelius, March 2, 1909, Box 33, Folder 12, DOCC Records.

25. Kate Barnard to Y. M. Yoder, September 1909, Box 33, Folder 12, DOCC Records; Kate Barnard to Ethyl Lowder, October 14, 1909, Box 33, Folder 12, DOCC Records.

26. Kate Barnard to Warden Dick, December 9, 1909, Box 33, Folder 12, DOCC Records.

27. Kate Barnard to Benjamin Offutt, March 2, 1909, Box 33, Folder 12, DOCC Records; Kate Barnard to Joe Brasier, April 19, 1909, Box 33, Folder 12, DOCC Records; Kate Barnard to prisoner, October 15, 1909, Box 33, Folder 12, DOCC Records; Kate Barnard to J. C. Woods, October 26, 1909, Box 33, Folder 12, DOCC Records.

28. Kate Barnard to James O'Neil, November 12, 1909, Box 33, Folder 12, DOCC Records; John C. Barber to Kate Barnard, January 21, 1909, Box 33, Folder 12, DOCC Records.

29. Kate Barnard to J. Scott Stanley, November 1, 1909, Box 30, Folder 3, DOCC Records.

30. Frederick L. Ryan, *A History of Labor Legislation in Oklahoma* (Norman: University of Oklahoma Press, 1932), 85. The law prohibited children under the age of fourteen from working in factories, workshops, theaters, bowling alleys, pool halls, and steam laundries, or in any occupation injurious to health or morals. Children under sixteen could not work around machinery, where dangerous or poisonous acids were used, in the manufacture of paints, in dipping or dyeing, or around explosives. Women and children were prohibited from working in mines.

31. Kate Barnard to Governor Haskell, February 23, 1909, Box 25, Folder 5, DOCC Records; Edith Copeland Manuscript, 213; "Child Labor Bill Now on Way to Governor," *Daily Oklahoman*, February 24, 1909; Kate Barnard to J. Scott Stanley, November 1, 1909, Box 30, Folder 3, DOCC Records.

32. Barnard, *Second Report*, 31.

33. Edith Copeland Manuscript, 185.

34. Barnard, *First Annual Report*, 68.

35. Barnard, *First Annual Report*, 63.

36. Barnard, *First Annual Report*, 63.

37. Barnard, *First Annual Report*, 64.

38. Barnard, *First Annual Report*, 65.

39. Kate Barnard to Samuel J. Barrows, February 8, 1909, Box 18, Folder 19, DOCC Records.

40. Kate Barnard to Samuel J. Barrows, February 8, 1909, Box 18, Folder 19, DOCC Records. After Kate left office, the reformative emphasis at the Granite institution weakened and the emphasis shifted to generating revenue. Barnard, *Second Report*, 31–33, 34; *Oklahoma Department of Corrections History: The 20th Century* (Oklahoma City: Oklahoma Department of Corrections, 2003).

41. Kate Barnard to Hon. James E. Gibbons, October 12, 1910, Box 23, Folder 9, DOCC Records; Kate Barnard to D. F. Sutherland, September 3, 1910, Box 34, Folder 14, DOCC Records; Kate Barnard to E. B. Nelson, December 10, 1910, Box 20, Folder 30, DOCC Records; Short, "Kate Barnard," chap. 9, p. 12; Edith Copeland Manuscript, 29.

42. Hobart Huson to Hon L. K. Taylor, April 8, 1909, Box 12, Folder 8, DOCC Records; Kate Barnard to Hon. J. T. Highley, June 13, 1909, Box 18, Folder 3, DOCC Records.

43. Kate Barnard to H. H. Hart, n.d., Box 11, Folder 1, DOCC Records; "Investigation of Wrongful Conditions Alleged in Oklahoma State Training School for Boys," October–November 1912, Box 27, Folder 5, DOCC Records; "Investigation of Boys Training School, Pauls Valley," October 31, 1912, Box 41, Folder 13, DOCC Records.

44. Kate Barnard to Mrs. R. M. Haynes, November 17, 1909, Box 12, Folder 7, DOCC Records; Edith Copeland Manuscript, 295.

45. Kate Barnard to J. M. Glenn, March 13, 1909, Box 14, Folder 5, DOCC Records; Kate Barnard to Mrs. R. M. Haynes, November 17, 1909, Box 12, Folder 7, DOCC Records.

46. Barnard, *Second Report*, 6–7; Edith Copeland Manuscript, 321; Kate Barnard to J. M. Glenn, March 13, 1909, Box 14, Folder 5, DOCC Records.

47. Kate Barnard to Lilah Lindsay, March 29, 1909, Box 24, Folder 7, DOCC Records.

48. Edith Copeland Manuscript, 163, 190.

49. Edith Copeland Manuscript, 190; Kate Barnard to Oklahoma City Democratic Campaign, April 22, 1909, Box 14, Folder 9, DOCC Records.

50. Short, "Kate Barnard," chap. 9, p. 18; Hobart Huson to Ben B. Lindsey, June 3, 1909, Box 13, Folder 11, DOCC Records; "Judge Barnard Is Laid to Rest," *Daily Oklahoman*, May 12, 1909.

51. Kate Barnard to unnamed recipient, October 4, 1909, Box 24, Folder 3, DOCC Records; Kate Barnard to Eva Perry Moore, May 20, 1909, Box 10, Folder 8, DOCC Records.

52. Short, "Kate Barnard," chap. 10, p. 1; Edith Copeland to Julee Short, n.d., Box 1, Folder 2, DOCC Records.

53. Short, "Kate Barnard," chap. 10, p. 2; John P. Barnard, probate no. 1119, Oklahoma County Court, Oklahoma City; Edith Copeland, letter to Julee Short, n.d., Box 1, Folder 2, Short Collection; Barnard, "Reference of Her Life Work," 29.

54. Kate Barnard to Dr. A. T. Clark, June 4, 1909, Box 17, Folder 32, DOCC Records; Kate Barnard to C. W. Bull, May 19 1909, Box 24, Folder 7, DOCC Records; Short, "Kate Barnard," chap. 10, p. 3.

55. Kate Barnard to Lillian Wald, October 12, 1908, Box 22, Folder 10, DOCC Records; Adam Hochschild, *Rebel Cinderella: From Rags to Riches to Radical, the Epic Journey of Rose Pastor Stokes* (Boston: Houghton Mifflin Harcourt, 2020), 39, 48; John M. Oskison, "A Tale of the Old I. T.," 109, unpublished memoir, Box O-8, Folder 6, John M. Oskison Collection, Western History Collections, University of Oklahoma Libraries, Norman; Kate Barnard to C. W. Bull, May 19 1909, Box 24, Folder 7, DOCC Records.

56. Edith Copeland Manuscript, 240; Short, "Kate Barnard," chap. 10, pp. 5, 12.

57. Edith Copeland Manuscript, 185.

Chapter 9

1. Kate Barnard, "The Crisis in Oklahoma Indian Affairs: A Challenge to Our National Honor," in Lake Mohonk Conference of Friends of the Indian and Other Dependent Peoples, *Report of the Thirty-Second Annual Lake Mohonk Conference on the Indian and Other Dependent Peoples, October 14th, 15th and 16th, 1914* (New York: Lake Mohonk Conference, 1914), 18. Another version of this story dates Kate's discovery of "Cherokee 'elf children'" to the spring of 1909 near Tahlequah. Edith Copeland Manuscript, 268. Kate wrote Dana Kelsey that it was one of his field men who first told her about neglected Indian orphan children. Kate Barnard to Dana H. Kelsey, April 15, 1910, Box 30, Folder 6, DOCC Records; Barnard, "For the Orphans of Oklahoma," 155.

2. Barnard, "The Crisis in Oklahoma Indian Affairs," 18.

3. Barnard, *First Annual Report*, 34, 55, 58. These homes included the Baptist Orphan Home near Oklahoma City, the Receiving Home run by the Oklahoma Children's Home Society near Guthrie, and others sponsored by fraternal orders such as the Masonic Home at Atoka, the IOOF home at Checotah, and the Oklahoma Odd Fellows home at Carmen.

4. "Program of Speeches," *Daily Ardmoreite*, November 19, 1903; John D. Benedict, *Muskogee and Northeastern Oklahoma, Including the Counties of Muskogee, McIntosh, Wagoner, Cherokee, Sequoyah, Adair, Delaware, Mayes, Rogers, Washington, Nowata, Craig, and Ottawa* (Chicago: S. J. Clarke, 1922), 1:586–87; Edith Copeland Manuscript, 185; Oklahoma Constitution, Article XXIII, Section 11; Barnard, *Fourth Report*, 269; Barnard, *Second Report*, 202; Barnard, *First Annual Report*, 37.

5. Barnard, *First Annual Report*, 34.

6. Barnard, *Second Report*, 94; "Oklahoma Man Built a Town for Widows," *New York Times*, September 12, 1915; Barnard, *Second Report*, 94–95, quote from 94.

7. Kate Barnard to M. E. Harris, January 24, 1913, Box 3, Folder 1, DOCC Records.

8. Affidavit by Mrs. B. Stevens, Jefferson County, March 2, 1914, Box 41, Folder 14, DOCC Records.

9. 1913–14 Annual Report, Box 2, Folder 9, DOCC Records. These rescue homes included the Pentecostal Mission of Oklahoma City, the Holmes Home and Hospital at Guthrie, and the Home of Redeeming Love at Enid. Barnard, *First Annual Report*, 59, 60; Barnard, *Fourth Report*, 331–36.

10. Barnard, *Third Report*, 275, 274; "Report of the Oklahoma State Home Conditions," May 1, 1910–February 1, 1912, Box 3, Folder 1, DOCC Records; "Report of Oklahoma State Home at Pryor Creek," March 1, 1912, Box 31, Folder 7, DOCC Records.

11. Unnamed man in Atoka to Kate Barnard, January 8, 1910, Box 9, Folder 3, DOCC Records.

12. "My Dear Miss Kate . . . My little daughter's name is Sheina Freida and to amuse our friend Mr. Huson, we also call her Hobarta." J. H. Stolper to Kate Barnard, May 29, 1912, Box 31, Folder 2, DOCC Records.

13. A. L. Malone to Kate Barnard, November 26, 1910, Box 9, Folder 3, DOCC Records.

14. A. L. Malone to Kate Barnard, November 26, 1910, Box 9, Folder 3, DOCC Records.

15. Edith Copeland Manuscript, 274; Barnard, *Third Report*, 212–13; Barnard, *Second Report*, 52–53.

16. B. F. Lee to Kate Barnard, February 23, 1910, Box 9, Folder 3 DOCC Records; Kate Barnard to Dana H. Kelsey, replying to his letter asking her to assist in behalf of Indian orphans, April 15, 1910, Box 30, Folder 6, DOCC Records; James E. Gresham to Kate Barnard, October 21, 1910, Box 29, Folder 11, DOCC Records; Grattan G. McVay and Dana H. Kelsey to Commissioner of Indian Affairs, September 26, 1911, Records of the Bureau of Indian Affairs, Record Group 75, U.S. National Archives and Records Administration (hereafter RG 75, NARA); Angie Debo, *And Still the Waters Run: The Betrayal of the Five Civilized Tribes* (New York: Gordian Press, 1966), 195.

17. Barnard, *Second Report* 40, 49.

18. A. L. Malone to Kate Barnard, November 26, 1910, Box 9, Folder 3, DOCC Records; Kate Barnard to Hon. Ben LaFayette, December 6, 1910, Box 9, Folder 3, DOCC Records; Edith Copeland Manuscript, 275; Kate Barnard to A. L. Malone, December 5, 1910, Box 9, Folder 3, DOCC Records.

19. Barnard, "The Crisis in Oklahoma Indian Affairs," 18, 19; Edith Copeland Manuscript, 283.

20. Kate Barnard to Dana H. Kelsey, April 8 and May 8, 1910, Box 30, Folder 6, DOCC Records; Kate Barnard to Thomas Ryan, April 15, 1910, Box 30, Folder 6, DOCC Records; Debo, *And Still the Waters Run*, 63.

21. Copy memo from Dana H. Kelsey, May 18, 1910, Box 46, Folder 26, DOCC Records. Section 28 of Article VI of the Oklahoma State Constitution gives the commissioner of charities and corrections "power to appear as 'next friend' for all minor orphans, defectives, dependents, and delinquents who are inmates of any public institution . . . , and also to intervene where it appears that the estates of such minors are being mismanaged or dishonestly administered." "Department of Charities and Corrections," in Richards, *Oklahoma Red Book*, 2:26; "Statement of Kate Barnard," 1913, Box 2, Folder 9, DOCC Records; Kate Barnard to D. W. Matthews, February 26, 1915, Box 46, Folder 26, DOCC Records; Kate Barnard to Dana H. Kelsey, April 15, 1910, Box 30, Folder 6, DOCC Records.

22. Moorehead, *The American Indian*, 160; Kate Barnard to Charles Inglish, February 17, 1910, Box 30, Folder 5, DOCC Records.

23. Debo, *And Still the Waters Run*, 5–6; Angie Debo, *A History of the Indians of the United States* (Norman: University of Oklahoma Press, 1970), 120, 124; J. David Hacker and Michael R. Haines, "American Indian Mortality in the Late Nineteenth Century: The Impact of Federal Assimilation Policies on a Vulnerable Population," *Annales de démographie historique* 110, no. 2 (2005): 17–29; McFarlin Fellows Featuring Joy Harjo (literary evening), University of Tulsa, Tulsa, Oklahoma, April 16, 2019.

24. The Osage Nation's reservation became a separate county in the former Oklahoma Territory. The wealthy Osage suffered a history equally as painful and violent as the Five Civilized Tribes, but Kate worked primarily with the Five Tribes. For more information about the Osage, see John Joseph Mathews, *The Osages: Children of the Middle Waters* (Norman: University of Oklahoma Press, 1961); and Debo, *And Still the Waters Run*, 5–6, 34–36.

25. Debo, *And Still the Waters Run*, 90.

26. Debo, *And Still the Waters Run*, 179–80; M. L. Mott to Secretary of the Interior, November 27, 1912, Box 2, Folder 50, Short Collection; Kate Barnard to D. W. Matthews, February 26, 1915, Box 46, Folder 26, DOCC Records; Edith Copeland Manuscript, 314. The Oklahoma delegation in Washington in 1907–9 consisted of Senators Robert L. Owen (D) and Thomas P. Gore (D) and Representatives Bird S. McGuire (R), Elmer L. Fulton (D), and James S. Davenport (D).

27. Barnard, "The Crisis in Oklahoma Indian Affairs," 19.

28. Debo, *And Still the Waters Run*, 91. This thumbnail summary is better told in shelves of history books, especially Debo's *And Still the Waters Run*, which is devoted entirely to documenting the spoliation of the Five Civilized Tribes.

29. Kate Barnard to D. W. Matthews, February 26, 1915, Box 46, Folder 26, DOCC Records; Debo, *And Still the Waters Run*, 178–79, 113.

30. Excerpt from attorney general's brief in *State ex rel. West, Atty. Gen., v. Cobb, County Judge*, 24 Okla. 662 (Okla. 1909), Box 22, Walter L. Fisher Papers, Library of Congress, Manuscript Division, Washington, D.C.

31. Barnard, *Third Report*, 96–101, quote from 101.

32. Barnard, *Second Report*, 6; Edith Copeland Manuscript, 274; Conway Barton to J. H. Stolper, February 16, 1912, Box 31, Folder 2, DOCC Records; J. H. Stolper to Hon. James Davenport, February 5, 1912, Box 25, Folder 8, DOCC Records.

33. Debo, *And Still the Waters Run*, 191; Robert L. Owen to Kate Barnard, December 5, 1910, Box 34, Folder 16, DOCC Records.

34. Debo, *And Still the Waters Run*, 98–99, 104–7.

35. Samuel J. Barrows to Roland B. Molineux, January 19, 1909, Box 19, Folder 2, DOCC Records; Samuel J. Barrows to Kate Barnard, January 11, 1908, Box 28, Folder 8, DOCC Records; Edith Copeland Manuscript, 223.

36. Kate Barnard to D. F. Sutherland, February 3, 1910, Box 34, Folder 14, DOCC Records.

37. Edith Copeland Manuscript, 260; Kate Barnard to Anna Garry, April 9, 1910, Box 14, Folder 5, DOCC Records; Kate Barnard to Henry Hanson, April 18, 1910, Box 34, Folder 13, DOCC Records; untitled Hobart Huson document, February 12, 1910, Box 19, Folder 5, DOCC Records; Kate Barnard to unnamed recipient, March 8, 1910, Box 14, Folder 11, DOCC Records.

38. Kate Barnard to unnamed recipient, July 13, 1909, Box 34, Folder 6, DOCC Records; "Corresponding Secretary" of Department of Charities and Corrections to Jerome Dowd, April 14, 1910, Box 9, Folder 7, DOCC Records; Edith Copeland Manuscript, 261, 162; Kate Barnard to Robert S. Sievally, March 22, 1910, Box 9, Folder 7, DOCC Records.

39. Lynn Musslewhite and Suzanne Jones Crawford, *One Woman's Political Journey: Kate Barnard and Social Reform, 1875–1930* (Norman: University of Oklahoma Press, 2003), 140; Debo, *And Still the Waters Run*, 202–3; Short, "Kate Barnard," chap. 13, pp. 1, 2, 3, 6, 8, 9; Edith Copeland Manuscript, 277, 280.

40. Kate Barnard to unnamed recipient, July 13, 1909, Box 34, Folder 6, DOCC Records; Kate Barnard to Pete Hanraty, October 19, 1910, Box 34, Folder 15, DOCC Records.

41. Kate Barnard to Pete Hanraty, October 19, 1910, Box 34, Folder 15, DOCC Records; Edith Copeland Manuscript, 277; Hobart Huson to Anna Garry, October 13, 1910, Box 15, Folder 28, DOCC Records; Edith Copeland Manuscript, 297; Debo, *And Still the Waters Run*, 186.

42. Kate Barnard to Chickasaw Governor Johnson, November 28, 1910, Box 25, Folder 4, DOCC Records.

43. Debo, *Oklahoma*, 42, 43, 53.

44. Edith Copeland Manuscript, 277, 280; Short, "Kate Barnard," chap. 13, pp. 1, 3, 9.

45. James Shannon Buchanan and Edward Everett Dale, *A History of Oklahoma* (Evanston, Ill.: Row, Peterson and Company, 1939), 296–97; Harlow,

Oklahoma, 322; Edith Copeland Manuscript, 280; Hobart Huson to unnamed recipient, July 27, 1910, Box 30, Folder 6, DOCC Records; Short, "Kate Barnard," chap. 14, p. 2.

Chapter 10

1. Barnard, *Third Report*, 12–14; "Woman's Fight for Indians," *New York Sun*, November 1, 1914; Edith Copeland Manuscript, 286; Barnard, "The Crisis in Oklahoma Indian Affairs," 18. Kate's "public defender bill" was H.R. 419, 62nd Cong. (1911).

2. Edith Copeland Manuscript, 287; Oklahoma Climatological Survey, http://climate.ok.gov/(accessed January 31, 2021); Barnard, *Fourth Report*, 283–84.

3. Barnard, *Third Report*, 105.

4. Edith Copeland Manuscript, 300.

5. Senator J. B. Thompson quoted in Short, "Kate Barnard," chap. 14, p. 6; Barnard, *Third Report*, 104; Dana H. Kelsey, "Status and Needs of the Five Civilized Tribes," in Lake Mohonk Conference of Friends of the Indian and Other Dependent Peoples, *Report of the Thirty-First Annual Lake Mohonk Conference of Friends of the Indian and Other Dependent Peoples, October 22d, 23d and 24th, 1913* (New York: Lake Mohonk Conference, 1913), 22; *Report of the Commissioner to the Five Civilized Tribes to the Secretary of the Interior for the Fiscal Year Ended June 30, 1913* (Washington: GPO, 1913), 56; Debo, *And Still the Waters Run*, 183; Vaux, "Some Observations of Conditions in the Five Civilized Tribes," 39.

6. Senator E. M. Landrum quoted in Short, "Kate Barnard," chap. 14, p. 7; Edith Copeland Manuscript, 284; Barnard, *Third Report*, 104–5.

7. "Indian Bill Is Riddled," *Daily Oklahoman*, February 7, 1911; Barnard, *Third Report*, 12; "Woman's Fight for Indians," *New York Sun*, November 1, 1914; Barnard, "The Crisis in Oklahoma Indian Affairs," 18; Kate Barnard to G. A. Warfield, December 17, 1910, Box 9, Folder 3, DOCC Records.

8. Edith Copeland Manuscript, 287; Bennett, "Kate Barnard," 108–11; "Dr. Potter Thrown Bodily from Meeting," *Daily Oklahoman*, February 14, 1911; "Dr. Potter Sues Kate Barnard," *Daily Oklahoman*, February 14, 1911. The slander suit against Kate commenced February 13, 1911, and was dismissed September 30, 1911. Stolper wrote to her in Kirksville, Missouri, where she was hospitalized, to tell her that "the case has been thrown out from the court. We had a mighty close call, but it is all over." Official files, September 30, 1911, Box 3, Folder 19, Short Collection.

9. Jim Edwards and Hal Ottaway, *The Vanished Splendor: Postcard Views of Early Oklahoma City* (Oklahoma City: Abalache Book Shop, 1982), 115–17; Charles Francis Colcord, *The Autobiography of Charles Francis Colcord, 1859–1934* (Tulsa, Okla.: C. C. Helmerich, 1970), chap. 25.

10. Kate Barnard to Samuel Gompers, October 11, 1909, Box 3, Folder 2, DOCC Records.

11. Warren K. Moorehead, *Our National Problem: The Sad Condition of the Oklahoma Indians* (n.p., 1913), 22, 28; Kelsey, "Status and Needs of the Five Civilized Tribes," 19; Vaux, "Some Observations of Conditions in the Five Civilized Tribes," 30–31; Barnard, *Second Report*, 68–69.

12. Grattan G. McVay and Dana H. Kelsey to Commissioner of Indian Affairs, September 26, 1911, RG 75, NARA; Kelsey, "Status and Needs of the Five Civilized Tribes," 17–18; Vaux, "Some Observations of Conditions in the Five Civilized Tribes," 38–39; Debo, *And Still the Waters Run*, 194–96.

13. Debo, *And Still the Waters Run*, 183, 195, 196; Vaux, "Some Observations of Conditions in the Five Civilized Tribes," 38–39; Barnard, *Third Report*, 85.

14. Debo, *And Still the Waters Run*, 93, 183; Rt. Rev. Theodore Payne Thurston, "Promotion of Industry among the Indians of Oklahoma," in Lake Mohonk Conference, *Report of the Thirty-Second Annual Lake Mohonk Conference*, 29; Kelsey, "Status and Needs of the Five Civilized Tribes," 23; Moorehead, *The American Indian*, 137.

15. Kelsey, "Status and Needs of the Five Civilized Tribes," 21; Debo, *Oklahoma*, 55, 60; Edith Copeland Manuscript, 270; Kate Barnard to Dr. Thomas C. Beeler, July 14, 1914, Box 2, Folder 7, DOCC Records; Warren K. Moorehead, "The Situation in Oklahoma," *Andover Townsman*, October 19, 1923, Box 2, Folder 52, Short Collection; Debo, *And Still the Waters Run*, 109–10.

16. Moorehead, *The American Indian*, 150, 155–56; Angie Debo to Julee Short, Box 1, Folder 2, Short Collection; Debo, *And Still the Waters Run*, 235. Alexander Johnson, secretary of the National Conference of Charities and Correction, discusses the *Fourth Report* in "The Commissioner of Charities in Oklahoma," *Survey*, April 26, 1913, 138–39.

17. "Choctaw Lands by Poison Plot: Officers Arrest Two," *Nowata Weekly Star*, May 2, 1913; Edith Copeland Manuscript, 299; Warren K. Moorehead, "The Lesson of White Earth," in Lake Mohonk Conference of Friends of the Indian and Other Dependent Peoples, *Report of the Thirtieth Annual Lake Mohonk Conference of Friends of the Indian and Other Dependent Peoples, October 23rd, 24th and 25th, 1912* (New York: Lake Mohonk Conference, 1912), 58; Attorney William O. Beall to Dana H. Kelsey, May 29, 1911, RG 75, NARA.

18. Debo, *And Still the Waters Run*, 198.

19. Acting Commissioner, Five Civilized Tribes, to Kate Barnard, April 23, 1912, Box 28, Folder 2, DOCC Records; statement by Malinda Davis Higgs in office of Fred S. Cook, April 15, 1911, Box 28, Folder 2, DOCC Records.

20. Moorehead, *Our National Problem*, 22; Debo, *And Still the Waters Run*, 198.

21. Russell Cobb, *The Great Oklahoma Swindle: Race, Religion, and Lies in America's Weirdest State* (Lincoln: University of Nebraska Press, 2020), 60–64; C. B. Glasscock, *Then Came Oil: The Story of the Last Frontier* (New York: Grosset and Dunlap, 1938), 182.

22. Rennard Strickland to author, April 16, 2020.

23. Garrick Bailey to author, August 20, 2020; J. D. Colbert to author, December 14, 2020.

24. Barnard, "The Crisis in Oklahoma Indian Affairs," 20.

25. Barnard, *Third Report*, 180, 174, 176, 178.

26. Department of Commissioner to the Five Civilized Tribes to J. H. Stolper, October 14, 1911, Box 31, Folder 1, DOCC Records.

27. Debo, *And Still the Waters Run*, 197.

28. Barnard, *Fourth Report*, 218; Louis Coleman, "McCurtain County," *Encyclopedia of Oklahoma History and Culture*, https://www.okhistory.org/publications /enc/entry.php?entry=MC017 (accessed January 31, 2021); "Suggestions and Recommendations Regarding Five Civilized Tribes' Matters," 1913, RG 75, NARA. The Chickasaw Nation is Grady County, and the Choctaw Nation includes Pushmataha, Pittsburg, Hughes, and McCurtain Counties.

29. District Agent Fred S. Cook and Dana H. Kelsey to Commissioner of Indian Affairs, September 26, 1911, RG 75, NARA; Grattan G. McVay and Dana H. Kelsey to Commissioner of Indian Affairs, September 26, 1911, RG 75, NARA; Dana H. Kelsey, Kate Barnard, and J. H. Stolper correspondence, August 4–December 10, 1910, RG 75, NARA; Kate Barnard to Dana H. Kelsey, December 9, 1910, Box 46, Folder 26, DOCC Records; Barnard, *Fourth Report*, 200–206; Angie Debo to Julee Short, n.d., Box 24, Folder 2, Short Collection.

30. Barnard, *Third Report*, 117; Fred S. Cook to Dana H. Kelsey, September 16, 1911, RG 75, NARA; Dana H. Kelsey to Commissioner of Indian Affairs, September 26, 1911, RG 75, NARA; Barnard, *Third Report*, 122.

31. District Agent Fred S. Cook to Commissioner of Indian Affairs, September 26, 1911, RG 75, NARA; Debo, *And Still the Waters Run*, 196.

32. Barnard, *Third Report*, 130, 131; Short, "Kate Barnard," chap. 14, p. 12; Grattan G. McVay to Dana H. Kelsey, August 7, 1911, RG 75, NARA; Kate Barnard to Secretary of the Interior, August 4, 1911, RG 75, NARA; J. H. Stolper to Kate Barnard, August 4, 1911, Box 9, Folder 3, DOCC Records.

33. District Agent Cook and Dana H. Kelsey to Commissioner of Indian Affairs, September 26, December 16, and December 26, 1911, RG 75, NARA; Barnard, "The Crisis in Oklahoma Indian Affairs," 20; Agreement of Submission to Arbitration re: T. J. Barnes, Pittsburg County, July 31, 1911, Box 3, Folder 1, DOCC Records; Barnard, *Third Report*, 140, 154; "Transaction of the Kate Barnard–McCurtain Land Cases," Board of Arbitration, September 5, 1911, Box 28, Folder 1, DOCC Records.

34. Dana H. Kelsey to Commissioner Valentine, December 26, 1911, RG 75, NARA; Report of C. F. Hawke, Second Assistant Commissioner of Indian Affairs, to Secretary of the Interior, September 21, 1911, RG 75, NARA; Dana H. Kelsey to Commissioner of Indian Affairs, Report on Conditions in McCurtain County, August 16, 1911, RG 75, NARA; Barnard, *Fourth Report*, 56–60, quote from 58.

35. J. H. Stolper to Hon. Charles D. Carter, January 10, 1913, Box 30, Folder 11, DOCC Records; Barnard, *Fourth Report*, 140–54; Debo, *And Still the Waters Run*, 191–92.

36. J. H. Stolper to Charles Buzart, August 16, 1910, Box 16, Folder 15, DOCC Records; Debo, *And Still the Waters Run*, 187–88; Barnard, *Fourth Report*, 137.

37. Barnard, "The Crisis in Oklahoma Indian Affairs," 18; Kate Barnard to A. L. Churchill, December 12, 1910, Box 11, Folder 2, DOCC Records; B. F. Lee to Kate Barnard, February 23, 1910, Box 9, Folder 3, DOCC Records; "Department of Charities and Corrections," 26; Short, "Kate Barnard," chap. 14, p. 14; Edith Copeland to Polly Jamerson, May 7, 1951, Box 2, Folder 1, Copeland Collection.

Chapter 11

1. Goins and Goble, *Historical Atlas of Oklahoma*, 4th ed., 170; *Yearbook of the United States Department of Agriculture, 1908* (Washington: GPO, 1909), 151; *Yearbook of the United States Department of Agriculture, 1912* (Washington: GPO, 1913), 562.

2. Barnard, *Fourth Report*, 442; Barnard, *Third Report*, 250, 264.

3. Kate Barnard to A. L. Churchill, December 12, 1910, Box 11, Folder 12, DOCC Records; Report from Oklahoma School for the Deaf in Sulphur, 1913, Box 3, Folder 1, DOCC Records; Kate Barnard to Nazarene Home, 1913, Box 2, Folder 10, DOCC Records; Barnard, *Third Report*, 214, 244, 212, 275; "Report of the Oklahoma State Home Conditions," May 1, 1910–February 1, 1912, Box 3, Folder 1, DOCC Records.

4. Edith Copeland Manuscript, 291; "Kate Barnard in Quest of Health," *Daily Oklahoman*, April 9, 1913; "Politicians Seek to Wreck Office, Says Miss Kate," *Daily Oklahoman*, May 8, 1913.

5. Bennett, "Kate Barnard," 113.

6. "Kate Barnard in Quest of Health," *Daily Oklahoman*, April 9, 1913; "Kate Barnard Captures Arizona Salons," *Arizona Gazette*, April 27, 1912.

7. Short, "Kate Barnard," chap. 15, pp. 6, 7; "Kate Barnard Captures Arizona Salons," *Arizona Gazette*, April 27, 1912.

8. A. J. McKelway, "The Governors' Conference," *Survey*, December 21, 1912, 348.

9. "Politicians Seek to Wreck Office, Says Miss Kate," *Daily Oklahoman*, May 8, 1913.

10. Geological Survey (U.S.), *Mineral Resources of the United States, 1914*, vol. 2: *Nonmetals* (Washington: GPO, 1916), 900.

11. Debo, *And Still the Waters Run*, 136.

12. Debo, *And Still the Waters Run*, 135.

13. Debo, *And Still the Waters Run*, 133, 135.

14. M. L. Mott, *The Act of May 27, 1908, Placing in the Probate Courts of Oklahoma Indian Jurisdiction: A National Blunder* (Washington: n.p., 1925), 48; J. H. Stolper to Scott Ferris, January 3, 1912, Box 31, Folder 3, DOCC Records; Debo, *And Still the Waters Run*, 231.

15. Debo, *And Still the Waters Run*, 232; Thos. Cook to Dana Kelsey, September 16, 1911, RG 75, NARA.

16. Debo, *And Still the Waters Run*, 232, 233; Moorehead, *The American Indian*, 155.

17. Debo, *And Still the Waters Run*, 234.

18. Discussion on H.R. 20728, Indian Appropriation Bill, House of Representatives, April 5, 1912, 62nd Cong., 2nd sess., *Congressional Record*, vol. 48, pt. 5, 4342, 4346.

19. *Congressional Record*, vol. 48, pt. 5, 4347, 4346, 4345.

20. *Congressional Record*, vol. 48, pt. 5, 4358, 4360.

21. Indian Appropriation Bill speech of Hon. Charles H. Burke in the House of Representatives, December 13, 1912, 62nd Cong., 3rd sess., *Congressional Record*, vol. 49, pt. 1, 602. Burke became the commissioner of Indian affairs in the 1920s.

22. Debo, *And Still the Waters Run*, 234, 235. The three congressmen who were vocal in their condemnation were James S. Davenport, Scott Ferris, and Charles D. Carter.

23. Debo, *And Still the Waters Run*, 235, 236; M. L. Mott to Walter L. Fisher, May 22, 1914, Box 2, Fisher Papers; Moorehead, *Our National Problem*, 17; M. L. Mott to Secretary of the Interior, July 1, 1913, RG 75, NARA; Hobart Huson to W. L. Fisher, November 21, 1914, Box 2, Fisher Papers.

24. M. L. Mott to Walter L. Fisher, May 22, 1914, Box 2, Fisher Papers; Debo, *And Still the Waters Run*, 236; Edith Copeland Manuscript, 310.

25. "Little Big Miss Kate Made a Constitution," *New York Sun*, November 30, 1912; "She Is 'Uplifting' Oklahoma," *Literary Digest*, January 11, 1913, 108.

26. Short, "Kate Barnard," chap. 15, p. 10; Musslewhite and Crawford, *One Woman's Political Journey*, 159.

27. "Little Big 'Miss Kate' Made a Constitution," *New York Sun*, November 30, 1912.

28. Moorehead, *Our National Problem*, 3, 12, 13, 16, 18, quotes from 5, 12.

29. Moorehead, *Our National Problem*, 32.

30. Moorehead, *Our National Problem*, 32; Debo, *And Still the Waters Run*, 174–77; Hobart Huson to W. L. Fisher, November 21, 1914, Box 2, Fisher Papers.

31. Debo, *And Still the Waters Run*, 172.

32. Patrick J. Hurley became secretary of war under President Herbert Hoover. Short, "Kate Barnard," chap. 16, p. 3.

33. Moorehead, *The American Indian*, 162, 163.

34. Chief Moty Tiger to Cato Sells, December 30, 1913, RG 75, NARA.

35. Franklin K. Lane to Chief Moty Tiger, February 11, 1913, RG 75, NARA.

36. Kate Barnard, remarks in First Session discussion, in Lake Mohonk Conference, *Report of the Thirty-Second Annual Lake Mohonk Conference*, 40; M. L. Mott to Walter L. Fisher, May 22, 1914, Box 2, Fisher Papers.

37. M. L. Mott to Walter L. Fisher, May 22, 1914, Box 2, Fisher Papers.

Chapter 12

1. Short, "Kate Barnard," chap. 16, p. 1; Edith Copeland Manuscript, 309; Musslewhite and Crawford, *One Woman's Political Journey*, 163.

2. Chief Moty Tiger to Cato Sells, December 30, 1913, RG 75, NARA. The Third Legislature had appropriated $9 million for state operations, an amount that had more than doubled since the First Legislature appropriated $4 million for state operations. Edwin C. McReynolds, *Oklahoma: A History of the Sooner State* (Norman: University of Oklahoma Press, 1954), 325; Arrell M. Gibson, *Harlow's Oklahoma History*, 6th ed. (Norman, Okla.: Harlow, 1972), 113–14; Harlow, *Oklahoma*, 322.

3. Gibson, *Harlow's Oklahoma History*, 113–14; Harlow, *Oklahoma*, 324–25.

4. Edith Copeland Manuscript, 305, 306; Short, "Kate Barnard," chap. 16, p. 1; Harlow, *Oklahoma*, 324–25.

5. Edith Copeland Manuscript, 306, 309; H. H. Smith, General Investigating Committee, report on "the so-called Marland gas and oil leases," March 2, 1913, *Journal of the House of Representatives of the Extraordinary Session of the Fourth Legislature of the State of Oklahoma, Session Opened March 18, 1913, Closed July 5, 1913*, 133–51, quote from 143; Robert Gregory, *Oil in Oklahoma* (Muskogee, Okla.: Leake Industries, 1976), 33–41; John Joseph Mathews, *Life and Death of an Oilman: The Career of E. W. Marland* (Norman: University of Oklahoma Press, 1951). Marland, thirty-nine years old at the time, had come to the state five years earlier, broke after losing a fortune in West Virginia oil wells, and was scrambling to regain his wealth. He succeeded and became one of the state's legendary oil millionaires, transforming the little town of Ponca City into a polo-playing and foxhunting mecca on the Osage prairie. Eventually, he lost that fortune, too. He then went into politics and defeated Alfalfa Bill Murray to become the tenth governor of the state.

6. Harlow, *Oklahoma*, 324–25; Edith Copeland Manuscript, 310, 305; Gibson, *Harlow's Oklahoma History*, 114.

7. Kate Barnard to J. H. Stolper, June 1, 1912, Box 31, Folder 3, DOCC Records; Edith Copeland Manuscript, 303, 312.

8. Margaret Truman, "The Good Angel of Oklahoma," in *Women of Courage from Revolutionary Times to the Present* (New York: William Morrow and Company, 1976), 195; "Barnard and 'Bill' Murray Clash Again," *St. Louis Post-Dispatch*, March 17, 1915; General Investigating Committee, report on Commissioner of Charities and Corrections, *Journal of the House of Representatives of the Extraordinary Session of the Fourth Legislature*, 1079–87, quote from 1083; Debo, *And Still the Waters Run*, 327–28; Edith Copeland Manuscript, 306.

9. Edith Copeland Manuscript, 306; unidentified newspaper clipping dated February 14, 1913, Box 2, Folder 55, Short Collection.

10. General Investigating Committee, report on Commissioner of Charities and Corrections, *Journal of the House of Representatives of the Extraordinary Session of*

the Fourth Legislature, 1083, 1084; Debo, *And Still the Waters Run,* 238; Kate Barnard to Hon. Gid Graham, May 1, 1913, Box 46, Folder 26, DOCC Records.

11. General Investigating Committee, report on Commissioner of Charities and Corrections, Box 2, Folder 55, Short Collection; Kate Barnard to Hon. Gid Graham, May 1, 1913, Box 46, Folder 26, DOCC Records.

12. "Politicians Seek to Wreck Office, Says Miss Kate," *Daily Oklahoman,* May 8, 1913; House Bill no. 355, February 6, 1913, Box 44, Folder 8, DOCC Records; "Kate Barnard Statement," Box 42, Folder 17, DOCC Records.

13. "'Grafters after Me,' Says Kate Barnard: Oklahoma's Guardian Angel Hits Foes Appeals to Legislature for Hearing," *St. Louis Post-Dispatch,* February 16, 1913; Short, "Kate Barnard," chap. 16, p. 5; Burke and Carlile, *Kate Barnard,* 67, 68, 118–20.

14. "'Grafters after Me,' Says Kate Barnard: Oklahoma's Guardian Angel Hits Foes Appeals to Legislature for Hearing," *St. Louis Post-Dispatch,* February 16, 1913; Edith Copeland Manuscript, 307.

15. Edith Copeland Manuscript, 308.

16. Barnard, "The Crisis in Oklahoma Indian Affairs," 16; Short, "Kate Barnard," chap. 16, p. 7; Edith Copeland Manuscript, 306; Barnard, "The Crisis in Oklahoma Indian Affairs," 20.

17. Barnard, "The Crisis in Oklahoma Indian Affairs," 20, 22; untitled newspaper article, February 22, 1913, Box 2, Folder 55, Short Collection.

18. Barnard, "The Crisis in Oklahoma Indian Affairs," 22; "Woman's Fight for Indians," *New York Sun,* November 1, 1914. This article says the letter from Wyand, Hill, and Maxey was dated February 25, 1913.

19. General Investigating Committee, report on Commissioner of Charities and Corrections, *Journal of the House of Representatives of the Extraordinary Session of the Fourth Legislature,* 1081, 1082, 1083.

20. General Investigating Committee, report on Commissioner of Charities and Corrections, *Journal of the House of Representatives of the Extraordinary Session of the Fourth Legislature,* 1082, 1083.

21. General Investigating Committee, report on Commissioner of Charities and Corrections, *Journal of the House of Representatives of the Extraordinary Session of the Fourth Legislature,* 1087; J. H. Stolper to Kate Barnard in Kirksville, Missouri, June 22, 1912, Box 30, Folder 10, DOCC Records.

22. Edith Copeland Manuscript, 310; "Kate Barnard Very Ill in Arizona," *Daily Oklahoman,* April 9, 1913.

23. Short, "Kate Barnard," chap. 16, p. 11; "Politicians Seek to Wreck Office, Says Miss Kate," *Daily Oklahoman,* May 8, 1913.

24. Debo, *And Still the Waters Run,* 238; Edith Copeland Manuscript, 310; Short, "Kate Barnard," chap. 16, p. 11.

25. "Politicians Seek to Wreck Office, Says Miss Kate," *Daily Oklahoman,* May 8, 1913.

26. Edith Copeland Manuscript, 310.

27. Barnard, "The Crisis in Oklahoma Indian Affairs," 22, 25.

28. Short, "Kate Barnard," chap. 16, p. 3, quoting the *St. Louis Post-Dispatch*, January 18, 1914; "Woman's Fight for Indians," *New York Sun*, November 1, 1914; Debo, *And Still the Waters Run*, 237.

29. Ross Lockridge, report to Kate Barnard, July 1, 1913, Box 44, Folder 2, DOCC Records; "[University of Tulsa] Professor Bailey's Work Assists *New York Times*' Best-Selling Author David Grann," October 18, 2019, *University of Tulsa*, https://utulsa.edu/david-grann-garrick-bailey/ (accessed January 31, 2021).

30. Glasscock, *Then Came Oil*, 272.

31. The Osage murders were an open secret to oilmen of Tulsa and Osage Counties, according to Osage historian Dr. Garrick Bailey. Bailey, interview with author, July 9, 2019. The libraries of the *Tulsa Tribune* and *Tulsa World* are the source of a long article the author wrote about the murders: Connie Cronley, "Osage Reign of Terror," *Oklahoma Monthly*, July 1976, 41–44.

32. William A. Baker to George D. Rodgers, May 31, 1913, RG 75, NARA; Ross Lockridge to Kate Barnard, July 1, 1913, Box 44, Folder 2, DOCC Records.

33. Short, "Kate Barnard," chap. 16, p. 12.

Chapter 13

1. Debo, *And Still the Waters Run*, 253–54; Moorehead, *The American Indian*, 161–62.

2. Debo, *And Still the Waters Run*, 230–32, 240–41; *Kate Barnard Says "Wake Up and Defend the Honor of the State"* (Oklahoma City: Warden Company, 1914), Box 2, Fisher Papers; Mott, *The Act of May 27, 1908*; U.S. Senate, *Indian Appropriation Bill: Hearings before the Committee on Indian Affairs, United States Senate, Sixty-Third Congress, First Session, on H.R. 1917* (Washington: GPO, 1913); Warren K. Moorehead to Walter L. Fisher, February 17, 1913, Box 2, Fisher Papers; Kate Barnard to Walter L. Fisher, May 19, 1914, Box 2, Fisher Papers.

3. Barnard, "The Crisis in Oklahoma Indian Affairs," 24–25; Kate Barnard to Walter L. Fisher, May 18, 1914, Box 2, Fisher Papers; "Background of the Indian Situation," signed by Hobart Huson, 1914, Box 2, Fisher Papers; Kate Barnard to Walter L. Fisher, May 19, 1914, Box 2, Fisher Papers.

4. Kate Barnard to Cato Sells, December 29, 1913, RG 75, NARA; "Background of the Indian Situation," signed by Hobart Huson, 1914, Box 2, Fisher Papers; William A. Baker to George D. Rodgers, May 31, 1913, RG 75, NARA.

5. Debo, *And Still the Waters Run*, 236, 237.

6. Musslewhite and Crawford, *One Woman's Political Journey*, 158.

7. Kate Barnard to R. W. Dick, December 8, 1913, Box 41, Folder 15, DOCC Records; Short, "Kate Barnard," chap. 16, p. 3; "Kate Barnard—Sob Sister," *Muskogee Daily Phoenix*, January 27, 1914.

8. Edith Copeland Manuscript, 313; Short, "Kate Barnard," chap. 16, pp. 13–14; "Orphans Home to Be Investigated," *Daily Oklahoman*, March 13, 1914.

9. "Shouts of 'Liar' Greet Wyand and Kate Barnard," *Muskogee Daily Phoenix*, March 17, 1914; Short, "Kate Barnard," chap. 17, p. 1.

10. "Shouts of 'Liar' Greet Wyand and Kate Barnard," *Muskogee Daily Phoenix*, March 17, 1914; Short, "Kate Barnard," chap. 17, p. 1.

11. "Shouts of 'Liar' Greet Wyand and Kate Barnard," *Muskogee Daily Phoenix*, March 17, 1914; Short, "Kate Barnard," chap. 17, p. 2.

12. "Kate Wires Cruce of 'Her' Victory," *Muskogee Daily Phoenix*, March 18, 1914; Short, "Kate Barnard," chap. 17, p. 2.

13. "Now Kate Barnard Sounds Battlecry to J. Harve Maxey," *Muskogee Daily Phoenix*, May 9, 1914; Short, "Kate Barnard," chap. 17, pp. 3, 10; Barnard, "The Crisis in Oklahoma Indian Affairs," 25.

14. Kate Barnard to Walter L. Fisher, May 19, 1913, Box 2, Fisher Papers.

15. M. L. Mott to Walter L. Fisher, May 22, 1914, Box 2, Fisher Papers.

16. "Background of the Indian Situation," signed by Hobart Huson, 1914, Box 2, Fisher Papers; Kate Barnard to Walter L. Fisher, May 19, 1913, Box 2, Fisher Papers; M. L. Mott to Walter L. Fisher, May 22, 1914, Box 2, Fisher Papers.

17. "Assistant Commissioner Abbott Starts on Tour of Southwest and Northwest," *Evening Star* (Washington, D.C.), October 31, 1910.

18. Frederick H. Abbott to Walter L. Fisher, May 18, 1914, Box 2, Fisher Papers; M. L. Mott to Walter L. Fisher, May 22, 1914, Box 2, Fisher Papers; Short, "Kate Barnard," chap. 17, p. 4.

19. Frederick H. Abbott to Walter L. Fisher, May 18, 1914, Box 2, Fisher Papers; Kate Barnard to Walter L. Fisher, May 19 and June 2, 1914, Box 2, Fisher Papers.

20. Short, "Kate Barnard," chap. 17, p. 5; Frederick H. Abbott to Walter L. Fisher, May 18, 1914, Box 2, Fisher Papers.

21. Frederick H. Abbott to Walter L. Fisher, May 18, 1914, and accompanying memorandum, Box 2, Fisher Papers.

22. Kate Barnard to Walter L. Fisher, June 9, 1913, Box 2, Fisher Papers.

23. Walter L. Fisher to Kate Barnard, June 11, 13, and 14, 1914, Box 2, Fisher Papers; Robert S. La Forte, "Fisher, Walter Lowrie," *American National Biography*, online February 2000, https://www.anb.org/view/10.1093/anb/9780198606697.001 .0001/anb-9780198606697-e-0600186 (accessed January 31, 2021).

24. Kate Barnard to Walter L. Fisher, June 8 and 9, 1913, Box 2, Fisher Papers; Walter L. Fisher, telegrams to Kate Barnard, June 2 and 4, 1913, Box 2, Fisher Papers.

25. Kate Barnard to Walter L. Fisher, June 8, 1913, and June 13, 1914, Box 2, Fisher Papers.

26. Hobart Huson to Walter L. Fisher, October 9, 1914, Box 2, Fisher Papers.

27. Kate Barnard to Walter L. Fisher, June 2 and 9, 1914, Box 2, Fisher Papers; Walter L. Fisher to Kate Barnard, June 10, 1914, Box 2, Fisher Papers.

28. Kate Barnard to Walter L. Fisher, May 19, 1914, Box 2, Fisher Papers; Tobie A. Cunningham, "Bassett, Mabel Luella Bourne," *Encyclopedia of Oklahoma History*

and Culture, https://www.okhistory.org/publications/enc/entry.php?entry=BA035 (accessed January 31, 2021).

29. Henry E. Fritz, "The Last Hurrah of Christian Humanitarian Indian Reform: The Board of Indian Commissioners, 1909–1918," *Western Historical Quarterly* 16, no. 2 (April 1985): 151.

30. Frederick H. Abbott to Warren K. Moorehead, June 5, 1914, Box 2, Folder 52, Short Collection; M. L. Mott to Walter L. Fisher, May 22, 1914, Box 2, Fisher Papers.

31. Fritz, "The Last Hurrah," 155–62; Debo, *And Still the Waters Run*, 240.

32. "Organize Now. Join the People's Civic Welfare League," campaign flyer, Box 2, Fisher Papers; *Kate Barnard Says, "Wake Up and Defend the Honor of the State"* (Oklahoma City: Warden Company, 1914), Box 2, Fisher Papers; Musslewhite and Crawford, *One Woman's Political Journey*, 172–73.

33. Hobart Huson to Kate Barnard, August 3 and September 1 and 21, 1914, Box 2, Fisher Papers; Kate Barnard to Dr. Henry Baird Favill, September 11, 1914, Box 2, Fisher Papers.

34. Kate Barnard to Walter L. Fisher, September 21 and October 9, 1914, Box 2, Fisher Papers.

35. Hobart Huson to Walter L. Fisher, November 9 and 21, 1914, Box 2, Fisher Papers.

36. Barnard, "The Crisis in Oklahoma Indian Affairs," 25, 23.

37. Kate Barnard to Walter L. Fisher, October 9, 1914, Box 2, Fisher Papers.

38. Barnard, "The Crisis in Oklahoma Indian Affairs," 16–17, 17–18; Short, "Kate Barnard," chap. 17, p. 10; Fritz, "The Last Hurrah," 150.

39. Barnard, "The Crisis in Oklahoma Indian Affairs," 18, 19, 25; Kate Barnard to Walter L. Fisher, June 9, 1914, Box 2, Fisher Papers.

40. Barnard, "The Crisis in Oklahoma Indian Affairs," 22.

41. Barnard, "The Crisis in Oklahoma Indian Affairs," 23; Thurston, "Promotion of Industry," 29; J. E. Gresham, "The Status of the Seminole Indians," in Lake Mohonk Conference, *Report of the Thirtieth Annual Lake Mohonk Conference*, 244–49; John M. Oskison, remarks in First Session discussion, in Lake Mohonk Conference, *Report of the Thirty-Second Annual Lake Mohonk Conference*, 39.

42. "Platform of the Thirty-Second Annual Lake Mohonk Conference on the Indian and Other Dependent Peoples, 1914," in Lake Mohonk Conference, *Report of the Thirty-Second Annual Lake Mohonk Conference*, 7; "Woman's Fight for Indians," *New York Sun*, November 1, 1914; Debo, *And Still the Waters Run*, 240.

43. Kate Barnard to Walter L. Fisher, December 29, 1914, Box 2, Fisher Papers; Moorehead, *The American Indian*, 151.

44. Untitled *New York Herald* clipping datelined Oklahoma City, November 1, 1914, Box 2, Folder 52, Short Collection; Barnard, "Reference of Her Life Work," 17, 33–37; "Woman's Fight for Indians," *New York Sun*, November 1, 1914.

45. "Stealing $200,000,000 from the Oklahoma Indians," *Literary Digest*, November 28, 1914, 1054, 1055; Barnard, "For the Orphans of Oklahoma," 154.

46. "Woman's Fight for Indians," *New York Sun*, November 1, 1914; Kate Barnard to Walter L. Fisher, October 27, 1914, Box 2, Fisher Papers; Barnard, "The Crisis in Oklahoma Indian Affairs," 23; Warren K. Moorehead to Frederick H. Abbott, October 30, 1914, Box 2, Folder 52, Short Collection.

47. Warren K. Moorehead to Frederick H. Abbott, November 27, 1914, Box 2, Folder 53, Short Collection. Moorehead said he was forwarding Kate's letter of appeal to a few wealthy people he knew, including George F. Kunz, a mineralogist who curated the Morgan-Tiffany gem collection for the American Museum of Natural History, and George G. Heye, who collected Native American artifacts and whose collection would become the core of the National Museum of the American Indian.

48. Kate Barnard to Walter L. Fisher, October 9, 1914, Box 2, Fisher Papers; Barnard, "Reference of Her Life Work," 317; Kate Barnard to Walter L. Fisher, November 16 and December 29, 1914, Box 2, Fisher Papers.

49. Hobart Huson to Walter L. Fisher, November 21, 1914, Box 2, Fisher Papers.

50. Frederick H. Abbott to Warren K. Moorehead, November 28 and December 4, 1914, Box 2, Folder 52, Short Collection.

51. Barnard, "Reference of Her Life Work," 281, 181; Warren K. Moorehead to Frederick H. Abbott, November 27, 1914, Box 2, Folder 53, Short Collection; *New York Sun* quoted in Musslewhite and Crawford, *One Woman's Political Journey*, 158.

52. Frederick H. Abbott to Warren K. Moorehead, November 28, 1914, Box 2, Folder 52, Short Collection.

53. Frederick H. Abbott to Warren K. Moorehead, November 28, 1914, Box 2, Folder 52, Short Collection; Warren K. Moorehead to Frederick H. Abbott, November 27, 1914, Box 2, Folder 52, Short Collection; Warren K. Moorehead to unidentified recipient, n.d. but probably November 1914, Box 2, Folder 53, Short Collection.

54. Oskison, remarks in First Session discussion, in Lake Mohonk Conference, *Report of the Thirty-Second Annual Lake Mohonk Conference*, 39. John Milton Oskison was born near Vinita in the Cherokee Nation, Indian Territory, to a white father and a one-quarter Cherokee mother. He was a close friend of Will Rogers, a Stanford graduate, a magazine writer and editor, and a novelist. In 1941, he and Angie Debo were coeditors of *Oklahoma: A Guide to the Sooner State*, part of the WPA-funded American Guide Series.

55. Warren K. Moorehead to Kate Barnard, November 19 and 24, 1914, Box 2, Folder 52, Short Collection; Winston Churchill, *The World Crisis* (New York: C. Scribner's Sons, 1923), 17; Ian F. W. Beckett, *The Great War, 1914–1918* (Harlow: Pearson/Longman, 2007), xx–xxv.

56. Kate Barnard to Walter L. Fisher, November 16, 1914, Box 2, Fisher Papers.

57. "Abbott, Frederick H.," in *Who Was Who in America*, vol. 1 (Chicago: A. N. Marquis Company, 1943); "Funeral in Waycross for Fred. H. Abbott," *Atlanta Constitution*, August 29, 1932; "Moorehead, Warren King, 1866–1939," *Robert S.*

Peabody Museum of Archaeology, https://peabody.pastperfectonline.com/archive /C3D0F053-16A7-43E8-A099-474507159554 (accessed January 31, 2021).

Chapter 14

1. Musslewhite and Crawford, *One Woman's Political Journey,* 177; Buchanan and Dale, *A History of Oklahoma,* 298–300.

2. Kate Barnard to Hon. R. L. Williams, January 9, 1915, Box 46, Folder 26, DOCC Records.

3. Barnard, "The Crisis in Oklahoma Indian Affairs," 23; "About Politics and Politicians," *Harlow's Weekly,* December 19, 1914, 196; "Kittenish Kitty," *Hugo (Okla.) Husonian,* March 4, 1915; "Kate Barnard," *Daily Oklahoman,* March 20, 1915; "Kate Barnard Charges Conspiracy to Rob Exists," *Harlow's Weekly,* March 27, 1915, 216.

4. "Kate Barnard Charges Conspiracy to Rob Exists," *Harlow's Weekly,* March 27, 1915, 215.

5. Gov. Lee Cruce to Judge Robert L. Williams, n.d., Box 45, Folder 20, DOCC Records.

6. Kate Barnard to Rev. D. W. Matthews, February 26, 1915, Box 46, Folder 26, DOCC Records.

7. Short, "Kate Barnard," chap. 18, pp. 2, 4; Kate Barnard to Rev. D. W. Matthews, February 26, 1915, Box 46, Folder 26, DOCC Records; "'Liar' Is Hurled at 'Alfalfa Bill' by Kate Barnard," *Muskogee Daily Phoenix,* March 18, 1915.

8. "Barnard and 'Bill' Murray Clash Again," *St. Louis Post-Dispatch,* March 17, 1915; "'Liar' Is Hurled at 'Alfalfa Bill' by Kate Barnard," *Muskogee Daily Phoenix,* March 18, 1915.

9. Musslewhite and Crawford, *One Woman's Political Journey,* 179; "Barnard and 'Bill' Murray Clash Again," *St. Louis Post-Dispatch,* March 17, 1915; Short, "Kate Barnard," chap. 18, p. 7.

10. Ben B. Lindsey to Pauline Jamerson, July 16, 1940, Box 2, Folder 14, Short Collection.

11. Ben B. Lindsey to Pauline Jamerson, July 16, 1940, Box 2, Folder 14, Short Collection.

12. Edith Copeland Manuscript, 322; Musslewhite and Crawford, *One Woman's Political Journey,* 180.

13. Warren K. Moorehead to J. P. Tulmulty, March 1, 1915, Box 2, Folder 52, Short Collection.

14. Musslewhite and Crawford, *One Woman's Political Journey,* 180, 182; Warren K. Moorehead to J. P. Tulmulty, March 1, 1915, Box 2, Folder 52, Short Collection; Short, "Kate Barnard," chap. 18, p. 8.

15. Barnard, "Reference of Her Life Work," 127; Edith Copeland Manuscript, 325; Hobart Huson to Hobart Huson Jr., October 6, 1912, Box 2, Folder 47, Short Collection.

16. Hobart Huson to Hobart Huson Jr., June 11, 1913, private collection of Hobart Huson Jr.; William D. Matthews to Hobart Huson Jr., July 10, 1916, private collection of Hobart Huson Jr.; Kathleen Huson Maxwell to author, February 5, April 30, May 5, and June 17, 1981; Barnard, "Reference of Her Life Work," 8, 9, 30.

When I visited Hobart Huson Jr. at his home in Refugio, Texas, in 1981, he remembered how Kate had visited him two or three times when he lived in San Antonio, always looking for Huson Sr. She was "energetic and overpowering," he said kindly, and advised him on his diet. She was on a special diet herself, in an effort to improve her health, and wanted to share her expertise. If the son knew of Huson's whereabouts, he did not tell her: "I was afraid she might want to hurt the old man." He believed Kate was motivated by infatuation with Huson, and said she thought he might be ill or might need help. He did not believe they had an affair, or it would have had to be extremely discreet, because Kate was under constant scrutiny from her political opposition.

Huson Jr. was an old man himself when I met him, a retired attorney and a polite southern gentleman. He had a special interest in history and the Greek philosopher Pythagoras. He wanted me to know that he loved his father and was proud of him, and he was anxious that I present his father with a "kind and fair treatment." If Huson Sr. had "stooped to anything less than platonic with Kate, there still was far more to him than Kate's part." He shared with me some of his father's wooing letters from the 1880s to Kitty, his mother, a red-headed piano teacher. They are erudite, charming letters that flirt, tease, and sparkle with literary references to the English critic John Ruskin, for example, and Ouida, the pen name of an English novelist. Reading those letters, it is easy to see how women were attracted to Huson, so eloquent and learned. Like his father, Huson Jr. had an extensive private library, including some of his father's leather-bound sets of Voltaire, Tolstoy, and Civil War histories. In personal conversation he might describe Kate's aggression, but he wrote graciously about her. "She did much that was worthwhile and lasting," he told me.

17. Hobart Huson Jr. to Hattie Mason, June 13, 1925, Box 2, Folder 29, DOCC Records; Harriet H. Mason to Hobart Huson Jr., July 13, 1925, Box 2, Folder 29, DOCC Records; Certificate of Death, record no. 2453, New Jersey State Department of Health; Mount Olivet Cemetery, Maspeth, Borough of Queens, New York, to John E. McInerney, May 18, 1984; petition, Surrogate of the County of Essex, New Jersey, July 7, 1925; phone conversation between author and Mount Olivet Cemetery, August 2, 2019.

18. "Oklahoma Printer Charged with Forgery," *Eufaula (Okla.) Indian Journal*, February 28, 1913; Edith Copeland Manuscript, 156; Jerome Dowd, interview with Julee Short, March 1950, Box 2, Folder 54, Short Collection; Dr. D. W. Griffin, interview with Julee Short, February 1, 1950, Box 2, Folder 54, Short Collection.

19. Hobart Huson to J. H. Stolper, July 21, 1908, Box 21, Folder 19, DOCC Records; Hobart Huson to Henry Wolfer, June 28, 1909, Box 34, Folder 5, DOCC

Records; J. H. Stolper to Hon. Charles D. Carter, January 10, 1913, Box 30, Folder 11, DOCC Records; Freda Stolper Gold, interview with author, Tulsa, Oklahoma, January 5, 1985; J. H. Stolper to Hobart Huson, May 23, 1908, Box 21, Folder 19, DOCC Records; J. H. Stolper to Kate Barnard, May 29, 1912, Box 31, Folder 2, DOCC Records; J. H. Stolper to Hobart Huson, June 29, 1908, Box 21, Folder 19, DOCC Records.

20. U.S. Department of Justice/Federal Prison System, El Reno, Oklahoma, to author, January 19, 1985; "Dr. Stolper, Local Attorney, Escapes Felony County by Action," *Muskogee Times-Democrat*, January 9, 1935; Helen A. Petry and Elizabeth Nickinson Chitty, *Sewanee Centennial Alumni Directory* (Sewanee, Tenn.: University Press, 1954); "Dr. J. H. Stolper, 66, Dies at Home," *Muskogee Times-Democrat*, January 13, 1942.

21. Barnard, "Reference of Her Life Work," 36; U.S. Census, 1940.

22. Bryant, "The Juvenile Court Movement," 376; *Ballenger & Richards Denver Directory*, vol. 52 (Denver: Gazetteer Publishing and Printing Company, 1924); Warren K. Moorehead, "The Situation in Oklahoma," *Andover Townsman*, October 19, 1923, Box 2, Folder 52, Short Collection.

23. Kathy Weiser, "Henry Starr—The Cherokee Bad Boy," updated November 2019, *Legends of America*, http://www.legendsofamerica.com/we-henrystarr/ (accessed January 31, 2021); Jon D. May, "Starr, Henry," *Encyclopedia of Oklahoma History and Culture*, https://www.okhistory.org/publications/enc/entry.php?entry=ST060 (accessed January 31, 2021); "Kate Barnard Grieves for Henry Starr," *Daily Oklahoman*, February 23, 1921.

24. Musslewhite and Crawford, *One Woman's Political Journey*, 181; "Judge Lindsey Seeks Aid for Kate Barnard," *Daily Oklahoman*, September 19, 1922; "Miss Barnard Gets Cheer from Friends," *Daily Oklahoman*, September 23, 1922.

25. Edith Copeland Manuscript, 325, 328.

26. Musslewhite and Crawford, *One Woman's Political Journey*, 182–83, quote from 183; Edith Copeland Manuscript, 325; Jerome Dowd, interview with Julee Short, March 1950, Box 2, Folder 54, Short Collection; Nell Snider, interview, January 25, 1950, Box 2, Folder 47, Short Collection; Irvin Hurst to author, July 18, 1985; Kate Barnard, Diary, Kate Barnard Collection, Oklahoma Historical Society Research Division, Oklahoma City, 58, 74, 83.

27. Edith Copeland Manuscript, 327; Barnard, Diary, 78.

28. Edith Copeland Manuscript, 328.

29. "Kate Barnard Flays Change in Basic Law," *Daily Oklahoman*, May 24, 1925; Short, "Kate Barnard," chap. 18, p. 9.

30. Unidentified clippings, Box 45, Folder 15, DOCC Records; "Kate Barnard Flays Change in Basic Law," *Daily Oklahoman*, May 24, 1925.

31. Edith Copeland Manuscript, 328; "Death Claims Kate Barnard in City Hotel," *Daily Oklahoman*, February 24, 1930.

32. Barnard, "Reference of Her Life Work," 13, 14.

33. Barnard, "Reference of Her Life Work," 14–17, 19, 20, 23, 29.

34. Joseph D. Demis, *Clinical Dermatology*, 18th rev. ed. (Philadelphia: J. P. Lippincott, 1991), 4:837.

35. G. Pete Dosser, M.D., interview with author, Tulsa, Oklahoma, September 14, 2018; Rona M. Mackie, *Clinical Dermatology: An Illustrated Textbook* (Oxford: Oxford University Press, 1991), 2:2–17.

36. Robert J. Hudson, M.D., interview with author, Tulsa, Oklahoma, July 6, 1987; Kate Barnard to Gorden Light, January 13, 1909, Box 12, Folder 6, DOCC Records.

37. Burke and Carlile, *Kate Barnard*, 119.

38. Robert J. Hudson, M.D., interview with author, Tulsa, Oklahoma, July 6, 1987; Mrs. Tom B. Ferguson, *They Carried the Torch: The Story of Oklahoma's Pioneer Newspapers* (Kansas City, Mo.: Burton Publishing Company, 1937), 128; Reese, *Women of Oklahoma*, 188.

39. "Kate Barnard to Be Honored," *Daily Oklahoman*, February 25, 1930; "Good Morning," *Daily Oklahoman*, February 27, 1955; "'Kate of Oklahoma' They Called Her," *Lincoln Sunday Star*, March 2, 1930.

40. The other honorary pallbearers were former governors Charles N. Haskell, Lee Cruce, Robert L. Williams, James B. A. Robertson, Jack C. Walton, Martin E. Trapp, and Henry S. Johnston. Burke and Carlile, *Kate Barnard*, 78; unidentified newspaper clippings from the time of Kate's death, Box 45, Folder 15, DOCC Records.

41. "'Kate of Oklahoma' They Called Her," *Lincoln Sunday Star*, March 2, 1930; Short, "Kate Barnard," chap. 18, p. 14.

42. "Death Takes Pioneer Woman Leader," *Oklahoma City Times*, February 24, 1930; "Death Claims Kate Barnard," *Daily Oklahoman*, February 24, 1930.

43. Julee Short notes, Box 3, Folder 11, Short Collection; Edith Copeland Manuscript, 328; unidentified newspaper clippings from the time of Kate's death, Box 45, Folder 15, DOCC Records; Burke and Carlile, *Kate Barnard*, 81.

44. Hurst, *The 46th Star*, 171; In the Matter of the Estate of Kate Barnard, Deceased, probate no. 9311, County Court, Oklahoma County, Oklahoma, Box 45, Folder 14, DOCC Records; "Kate Barnard, Unsung Hero," *Daily Oklahoman*, February 23, 1941.

45. Hurst, *The 46th Star*, 171; Edith Copeland Manuscript, 330; Petition for Contest of Will, Barnard, probate no. 9311, Box 45, Folder 14, DOCC Records.

46. Hobart Huson Jr., conversations with author, April 24–26, 1981; author to Kathleen Maxwell, August 13, 1983; Short, "Kate Barnard," chap. 1, pp. 3–4. Copeland acknowledged that "Col. Hobart Huson, lawyer, philosopher, and historian of Refugio, Texas," was responsible for the preservation of Barnard's personal papers.

47. Petition for Contest of Will, and Final Decree, Box 45, Folder 15, DOCC Records. Kate's diary lists the locations of other trunks, boxes, and the contents of a bank safety deposit box containing family photographs (father, mother, grandparents) and historic letters and pictures. It is unlikely that these were recovered, and that is a loss to history.

48. Hurst, *The 46th Star*, 171.

Epilogue

1. Angie Debo to Julee Short, n.d., 1975, Box 1, Folder 2, Short Collection.

2. Hurst, *The 46th Star*, 74, 75; David Blatt, former executive director of the Oklahoma Policy Institute, to author, August 25, 2020; Garrick Bailey to author, August 20, 2020.

3. *McGirt v. Oklahoma*, Supreme Court of the United States, July 9, 2020.

4. Timothy Egan, "After Five Centuries, a Native American with Real Power," *New York Times*, January 2, 2021.

5. Angie Debo, *Tulsa: From Creek Town to Oil Capital* (Norman: University of Oklahoma Press, 1943), 91–96, quotes from 96; *Report of the Select Committee to Investigate Matters Connected with Affairs in the Indian Territory, with Hearings, November 11, 1906–January 9, 1907* (Washington: GPO, 1907), 2:1253.

6. Rennard Strickland, *Fire and the Spirits: Cherokee Law from Clan to Court* (Norman: University of Oklahoma Press, 1975), 9.

Bibliography

Archival Sources

Barde, Frederick S. Collection. Oklahoma Historical Society Research Division, Oklahoma City, Okla.

Barnard, Kate. Collection. M2013.037. Oklahoma Historical Society Research Division, Oklahoma City, Okla.

———. Diary. Kate Barnard Collection, M2013.037, Oklahoma Historical Society Research Division, Oklahoma City, Okla.

———. "Reference of Her Life Work." Typescript. Box 4, Folder 7, Fayette Copeland Jr. Collection. Western History Collections, University of Oklahoma Libraries, Norman, Okla.

Carlisle Indian School Digital Resource Center. Archives and Special Collections, Waidner-Spahr Library, Dickinson College, Carlisle, Pa.

Copeland, Edith. Manuscript. Box 1, File 2, Julia (Julee) A. Short Collection, MS 24. Oklahoma Department of Libraries, Oklahoma City, Okla.

———. "Miss Kate of Oklahoma." Box 4, Folders 1 and 2, Fayette Copeland Jr. Collection. Western History Collections, University of Oklahoma Libraries, Norman, Okla.

Copeland, Fayette, Jr. Collection. Western History Collections, University of Oklahoma Libraries, Norman, Okla.

Department of Charities and Corrections Records. Record Group 36. Oklahoma State Archives, Oklahoma Department of Libraries, Oklahoma City, Okla.

Fisher, Walter L. Papers. Library of Congress, Manuscript Division, Washington, D.C.

Johnson, Edith Cherry. Papers. Western History Collections, University of Oklahoma Libraries, Norman, Okla.

McKelway, Alexander Jeffrey. Papers. Library of Congress, Manuscript Division, Washington, D.C.

Records of the Bureau of Indian Affairs (BIA). Record Group 75. U.S. National Archives and Records Administration, various locations.

Short, Julia (Julee) A. Collection. MS 24. Oklahoma Department of Libraries, Oklahoma City, Okla.

Thoburn, Joseph. Collection. Oklahoma Historical Society Research Division, Oklahoma City, Okla.

Newspapers

Alva Review and Courier (Alva, Oka.)
Cherokee Republican (Sallisaw, Okla.)
Chief (Phillipsburg, Kans.)
Daily Ardmoreite (Ardmore, Okla.)
Daily Kirwin Chief (Kirwin, Kans.)
Daily Oklahoman (Oklahoma City, Okla.)
Edmond Booster (Edmond, Okla.)
Eufaula Indian Journal (Eufaula, Okla.)
Harlow's Weekly (Oklahoma City, Okla.)
Independent (Kirwin, Kans.)
Indian Country Today (digital platform)
Kiowa County Democrat (Snyder, Okla.)
Kirwin Kansan (Kirwin, Kans.)
Kirwin Progress (Kirwin, Kans.)
Kirwin Republican (Kirwin, Kans.)
Muskogee Daily Phoenix (Muskogee, Okla.)
Muskogee Times-Democrat (Muskogee, Okla.)
New York Herald (New York, N.Y.)
New York Sun (New York, N.Y.)
New York Times (New York, N.Y.)
Nowata Weekly Star (Nowata, Okla.)
Oklahoma Daily Times-Journal (Oklahoma City, Okla.)
Oklahoma Labor Unit (Oklahoma City, Okla.)
Oklahoma State Capital (Guthrie, Okla.)
Rochester Union and Advertiser (Rochester, N.Y.)
St. Louis Globe-Democrat (St. Louis, Mo.)
St. Louis Post-Dispatch (St. Louis, Mo.)
St. Louis Republic (St. Louis, Mo.)
Tanana Miner (Chena, Alaska)
Washington Post (Washington, D.C.)

Books and Theses

Andreas, A. T. *History of the State of Nebraska*. Chicago: Western Historical Company, 1882.

Barnard, Kate. *First Annual Report of the Commissioner of Charities and Corrections of the State of Oklahoma, for the Year Ending December 31, 1908*. Guthrie, Okla.: Leader Printing Company, 1908.

———. *Second Report of the Commissioner of Charities and Corrections, from October 1, 1909 to October 1, 1910*. Oklahoma City: Warden Printing Company, 1910.

———. *Third Report of the Commissioner of Charities and Corrections, from October 1, 1910 to October 1, 1911*. Oklahoma City: Oklahoma Engraving and Printing Company, 1911.

———. *Fourth Report of the Commissioner of Charities and Corrections, from October 1, 1911 to October 1, 1912*. Oklahoma City: Oklahoma Engraving and Printing Company, 1912.

Beckett, Ian F. W. *The Great War, 1914–1918*. Harlow: Pearson/Longman, 2007.

Bernard, Richard M. *The Poles in Oklahoma*. Norman: University of Oklahoma Press, 1980.

Bicha, Karel D. *The Czechs in Oklahoma*. Norman: University of Oklahoma Press, 1980.

Blessing, Patrick J. *The British and Irish in Oklahoma*. Norman: University of Oklahoma Press, 1980.

Brown, Kenny L. *The Italians in Oklahoma*. Norman: University of Oklahoma Press, 1980.

Bryant, Keith L., Jr. *Alfalfa Bill Murray*. Norman: University of Oklahoma Press, 1968.

Buchanan, James Shannon, and Edward Everett Dale. *A History of Oklahoma*. Evanston, Ill.: Row, Peterson and Company, 1939.

Buel, James W. *Louisiana and the Fair: An Exposition of the World, Its People and Their Achievements*. St. Louis: World's Progress, 1904.

Burke, Bob, and Glenda Carlile. *Kate Barnard: Oklahoma's Good Angel*. Edmond: University of Central Oklahoma Press, 2001.

Churchill, Winston. *The World Crisis*. New York: C. Scribner's Sons, 1923.

Clanton, O. Gene. *A Common Humanity: Kansas Populism and the Battle for Justice and Equality, 1854–1903*. Manhattan, Kans.: Sunflower University Press, 2004.

Colcord, Charles Francis. *The Autobiography of Charles Francis Colcord, 1859–1934*. Tulsa, Okla.: C. C. Helmerich, 1970.

Coleman, Thelma, and James Anderson. *The Canada Company*. Stratford, Ont.: Perth County Historical Board, 1978.

Davidson, Elizabeth H. *Child Labor Legislation in the Southern Textile States*. Chapel Hill: University of North Carolina Press, 1939.

Debo, Angie. *And Still the Waters Run: The Betrayal of the Five Civilized Tribes.* New York: Gordian Press, 1966.

————. *A History of the Indians of the United States.* Norman: University of Oklahoma Press, 1970.

————. *Oklahoma: Foot-Loose and Fancy-Free.* Norman: University of Oklahoma Press, 1949.

————. *Tulsa: From Creek Town to Oil Capital.* Norman: University of Oklahoma Press, 1943.

Demis, Joseph D. *Clinical Dermatology.* 18th rev. ed. Philadelphia: J. P. Lippincott, 1991.

Dorman, Robert L. *Alfalfa Bill: A Life in Politics.* Norman: University of Oklahoma Press, 2018.

Edwards, Jim, and Hal Ottaway. *The Vanished Splendor: Postcard Views of Early Oklahoma City.* Oklahoma City: Abalache Book Shop, 1982.

Elliot, Noel Montgomery. *People of Ontario, 1600–1900: Alphabetized Directory of the People, Places and Vital Dates.* London, Ont.: Genealogical Research Library, 1984.

Ellis, Albert H. *History of the Constitutional Convention of the State of Oklahoma.* Muskogee, Okla.: Economy Printing Company, 1923.

Ely, Alfred. *Journal of Alfred Ely, a Prisoner of War in Richmond.* New York: D. Appleton and Company, 1862.

Federal Writers' Project of the Work Projects Administration for the State of Kansas, comp. *Kansas: A Guide to the Sunflower State.* American Guide Series. New York: Viking Press, 1939.

Federal Writers' Project of the Works Progress Administration for the State of Nebraska, comp. *Nebraska: A Guide to the Cornhusker State.* American Guide Series. New York: Viking Press, 1939.

Francis, David R. *The Universal Exposition of 1904.* St. Louis: Louisiana Purchase Exposition, 1913.

Franklin, Jimmy Lewis. *The Blacks in Oklahoma.* Norman: University of Oklahoma Press, 1980.

Gaffney, Wilbur. *The Fillmore County Story.* Geneva, Nebr.: Geneva Community Grange No. 403, 1968.

Gibson, Arrell M. *Harlow's Oklahoma History.* 6th ed. Norman, Okla.: Harlow, 1972.

Glasscock, C. B. *Then Came Oil: The Story of the Last Frontier.* New York: Grosset and Dunlap, 1938.

Goble, Danney. *Progressive Oklahoma: The Making of a New Kind of State.* Norman: University of Oklahoma Press, 1980.

Goins, Charles Robert, and Danney Goble. *Historical Atlas of Oklahoma.* 4th ed. Norman: University of Oklahoma Press, 2006.

Grann, David. *Killers of the Flower Moon: The Osage Murders and the Birth of the FBI.* New York: Doubleday, 2017.

Gregory, Robert. *Oil in Oklahoma*. Muskogee, Okla.: Leake Industries, 1976.

Hale, Douglas. *The Germans from Russia in Oklahoma*. Norman: University of Oklahoma Press, 1980.

Harlow, Victor E. *Oklahoma, Its Origins and Development: A History*. Oklahoma City: Harlow, 1935.

Hofstadter, Richard. *The Age of Reform: From Bryan to F.D.R.* New York: Alfred A. Knopf, 1955.

Hogan, Linda. *Mean Spirit*. New York: Ivy Books, 1990.

Hurst, Irvin. *The 46th Star: A History of Oklahoma's Constitutional Convention and Early Statehood*. Oklahoma City: Semco Color Press, 1957.

Hyde, William, and Howard Conrad. *Encyclopedia of the History of St. Louis: A Compendium of History and Biography for Ready Reference*. Vol. 3. New York: Southern History Company, 1899.

Johnson, Alexander, ed. *Proceedings of the National Conference of Charities and Correction, at the Thirty-Fourth Annual Session Held in the City of Minneapolis, Minn., June 12th to 19th, 1907*. Indianapolis: Wm. B. Burford, 1907.

Jones, Mary Harris. *Autobiography of Mother Jones*. Chicago: Charles H. Kerr and Company, 1925.

Juvenile Court of the City and County of Denver. *The Problem of the Children and How the State of Colorado Cares for Them: A Report of the Juvenile Court of Denver*. Denver: Merchants, 1904.

Kansas Pacific Railway Company. *Emigrants' Guide to the Kansas Pacific Railway Lands*. Lawrence, Kans.: Land Department, Kansas Pacific Railway Company, 1871.

Kay, John, and Kathleen Fimple. *Nebraska Historic Buildings Survey: Reconnaissance Survey Final Report of Thayer County, Nebraska*. Lincoln: Nebraska State Historical Society, State Historic Preservation Office, 1991.

Kerr, W. F., and Ina Gainer. *The Story of Oklahoma City, Oklahoma: "The Biggest Little City in the World."* 3 vols. Oklahoma City: S. J. Clarke, 1922.

Lake Mohonk Conference of Friends of the Indian and Other Dependent Peoples. *Report of the Thirtieth Annual Lake Mohonk Conference of Friends of the Indian and Other Dependent Peoples, October 23rd, 24th and 25th, 1912*. New York: Lake Mohonk Conference, 1912.

———. *Report of the Thirty-First Annual Lake Mohonk Conference of Friends of the Indian and Other Dependent Peoples, October 22d, 23d and 24th, 1913*. New York: Lake Mohonk Conference, 1913.

———. *Report of the Thirty-Second Annual Lake Mohonk Conference on the Indian and Other Dependent Peoples, October 14th, 15th and 16th, 1914*. New York: Lake Mohonk Conference, 1914.

Larsen, Charles. *The Good Fight: The Life and Times of Ben B. Lindsey*. Chicago: Quadrangle Books, 1972.

Leckie, Shirley A. *Angie Debo: Pioneering Historian*. Norman: University of Oklahoma Press, 2000.

Litton, Gaston. *History of Oklahoma at the Golden Anniversary of Statehood*. 2 vols. New York: Lewis Historical Publishing Company, 1957.

Mackie, Rona M. *Clinical Dermatology: An Illustrated Textbook*. Oxford: Oxford University Press, 1991.

March, David D. *The History of Missouri*. New York: Lewis Historical Publishing Company, 1967.

Mathews, John Joseph. *Life and Death of an Oilman: The Career of E. W. Marland*. Norman: University of Oklahoma Press, 1951.

———. *The Osages: Children of the Middle Waters*. Norman: University of Oklahoma Press, 1961.

McAuliffe, Dennis, Jr. *The Deaths of Sybil Bolton: An American History*. New York: Times Books, 1994.

McReynolds, Edwin C. *Oklahoma: A History of the Sooner State*. Norman: University of Oklahoma Press, 1954.

McRill, Albert. *And Satan Came Also: An Inside Story of a City's Social and Political History*. Oklahoma City: Britton, 1955.

Monahan, David F. *One Family, One Century: A Photographic History of the Catholic Church in Oklahoma, 1875–1975*. Oklahoma City: Archdiocese of Oklahoma City, 1977.

Moorehead, Warren K. *The American Indian in the United States, Period 1850–1914*. Andover, Mass.: Andover Press, 1914.

———. *Our National Problem: The Sad Condition of the Oklahoma Indians*. N.p., 1913.

Morgan, H. Wayne, and Anne Hodges Morgan. *Oklahoma: A Bicentennial History*. New York: W. W. Norton and Company, 1977.

Morris, John W., Charles R. Goins, and Edwin G. McReynolds. *Historical Atlas of Oklahoma*. 2nd ed. Norman: University of Oklahoma Press, 1976.

Mott, M. L. *The Act of May 27, 1908, Placing in the Probate Courts of Oklahoma Indian Jurisdiction: A National Blunder*. Washington, D.C.: n.p., 1925.

Mowry, George E. *The Progressive Movement, 1900–1920: Recent Ideas and New Literature*. Washington, D.C.: Service Center for Teachers of History, 1958.

Musslewhite, Lynn, and Suzanne Jones Crawford. *One Woman's Political Journey: Kate Barnard and Social Reform, 1875–1930*. Norman: University of Oklahoma Press, 2003.

National Child Labor Committee. *Child Labor and Social Progress: Proceedings of the Fourth Annual Meeting of the National Child Labor Committee*. Philadelphia: American Academy of Political and Social Science, 1908.

Noble, David W. *The Progressive Mind, 1890–1917*. Minneapolis: Burgess Publishing Company, 1981.

Official Guide Company. *World's Fair Authentic Guide: Complete Reference Book to St. Louis and the Louisiana Purchase Exposition*. St. Louis: Official Guide Company, 1904.

Oklahoma Constitutional Convention. *Proceedings of the Constitutional Convention of the Proposed State of Oklahoma, Held at Guthrie, Oklahoma, November 20, 1906 to November 16, 1907.* Muskogee, Okla.: Muskogee Printing Company, 1907.

Reese, Linda Williams. *Women of Oklahoma, 1890–1920.* Norman: University of Oklahoma Press, 1997.

Resek, Carl. *The Progressives.* Indianapolis: Bobbs-Merrill, 1967.

Richards, W. B., comp., under the Supervision of Benjamin F. Harrison, Secretary of State. *The Oklahoma Red Book.* Vol. 2. Oklahoma City: n.p., 1912.

Rohrs, Richard C. *The Germans in Oklahoma.* Norman: University of Oklahoma Press, 1980.

Ruth, Kent, and the Staff of the University of Oklahoma Press, comps. *Oklahoma: A Guide to the Sooner State.* American Guide Series, compiled by the Writers' Program of the Work Projects Administration in the State of Oklahoma. Norman: University of Oklahoma Press, 1941.

Ryerson, Ellen. *The Best-Laid Plans: America's Juvenile Court Experiment.* New York: Hill and Wang, 1978.

Scales, James R., and Danney Goble. *Oklahoma Politics: A History.* Norman: University of Oklahoma Press, 1982.

Schechter, Harold. *The Devil's Gentleman: Privilege, Poison, and the Trial That Ushered In the Twentieth Century.* New York: Ballantine Books, 2007.

Short, Julia A. "Kate Barnard: Liberated Woman." Master's thesis, University of Oklahoma, 1972.

Stauffer, Helen Winter. *Mari Sandoz: Story Catcher of the Plains.* Lincoln: University of Nebraska Press, 1982.

Stevens, Walter B. *Centennial History of Missouri (the Center State): One Hundred Years in the Union, 1820–1921.* Vol. 1. St. Louis: S. J. Clarke, 1921.

Strickland, Rennard. *Fire and the Spirits: Cherokee Law from Clan to Court.* Norman: University of Oklahoma Press, 1975.

Thoburn, Joseph B. *A Standard History of Oklahoma.* Vol. 3. Chicago: American Historical Society, 1916.

Thoburn, Joseph B., and Isaac M. Holcomb. *A History of Oklahoma.* Oklahoma City: Warden Company, 1914.

Thoburn, Joseph B., and Muriel H. Wright. *Oklahoma: A History of the State and Its People.* Vol. 3. New York: Lewis Historical Publishing Company, 1929.

Weiss, Elaine. *The Woman's Hour: The Great Fight to Win the Vote.* New York: Viking Press, 2018.

Wetmore, Claude H. *Out of a Fleur-de-lis: The History, Romance, and Biography of the Louisiana Purchase Exposition.* Boston: W. A. Wilde, 1903.

Zellner, William W., and Ruth L. Laird, eds. *Nebraska: The First Hundred Years.* Ada, Okla.: Galaxy, 1985.

Articles, Chapters, and Addresses

"About Politics and Politicians." *Harlow's Weekly*, December 19, 1914, 194–97.

"Achievements of an Oklahoma Editor." *Sturm's Oklahoma Magazine*, January 1907, 5–6.

Adams, Frederick Upham. "A Twentieth-Century State Constitution." *Saturday Evening Post*, November 16, 1907, 3–4, 25.

Addams, Jane. "Problems of Municipal Administration." In *Congress of Arts and Science: Universal Exposition*, vol. 7: *Economics, Politics, Jurisprudence, Social Science*, ed. Howard J. Rogers, 434–50. Boston: Houghton, Mifflin and Company, 1906.

Barde, Charles M. "Oklahoma City's Press Club." *Sturm's Oklahoma Magazine*, July 1909, 76–78.

Barley, Patricia, and Joan Woods. "The Greatest of Expositions." *Missouri Life Magazine*, May–August 1979, 12–17.

Barnard, Kate. "Address by Miss Kate Barnard." In *Transactions of the Sixth International Congress on Tuberculosis, Washington, September 28 to October 5, 1908*, vol. 3, 800–808. Philadelphia: William F. Fell, 1908.

———. "The Crisis in Oklahoma Indian Affairs: A Challenge to Our National Honor." In Lake Mohonk Conference of Friends of the Indian and Other Dependent Peoples, *Report of the Thirty-Second Annual Lake Mohonk Conference on the Indian and Other Dependent Peoples, October 14th, 15th, and 16th, 1914*, 16–26. New York: Lake Mohonk Conference, 1914.

———. "Fighting the Lease Systems with Pardons." *Survey*, January 4, 1913, 457–58.

———. "For the Orphans of Oklahoma: Children of the Disinherited." *Survey*, November 7, 1914, 154–55, 161–64.

———. "Human Ideals in Government." *Survey*, October 2, 1909, 17–20.

———. "The New State and Its Children." In *Child Labor and Social Progress: Proceedings of the Fourth Annual Meeting of the National Child Labor Committee*, 173–75. Philadelphia: American Academy of Political and Social Science, 1908.

———. "Oklahoma's Child Labor Laws." *Sturm's Oklahoma Magazine*, February 1908, 42–44.

———. "Remarks on Child Labor, Hours of Labor for Women and Wage for Women." In *Proceedings of the Fifth Meeting of the Governors of the States of the Union, Held at Richmond, Virginia, December 3–7, 1912*, 151–54. N.p., 1912.

———. "Shaping the Destinies of the New State." In *Proceedings of the National Conference of Charities and Correction, at the Thirty-Fifth Annual Session Held in the City of Richmond, Va., May 6th to 13th, 1908*, edited by Alexander Johnson, 36–42. Fort Wayne, Ind.: Press of Fort Wayne Printing Company, 1909.

———. "'Stump' Ashby Saves the Day." Edited and introduced by Julee Short. *Journal of the West* 12 (April 1973): 296–306.

———. "Through the Windows of Destiny: How I Visualized My Life Work." *Good Housekeeping*, November 1912, 600–606.

———. "Working for the Friendless." *Independent*, November 28, 1907, 1307–8.

"Barnard, Kate." In *Who's Who in America: A Biographical Dictionary of Notable Living Men and Women of the United States*, edited by Albert Nelson Marquis, 8:121. New York: A. N. Marquis and Company, 1914.

"Barnard, Kate, Philanthropist." In *The National Cyclopaedia of American Biography*, 15:110–11. New York: James T. White and Company, 1915.

Bennett, Helen Christine. "Kate Barnard." In *American Women in Civic Work*, 92–113. New York: Dodd, Mead and Company, 1915.

Bracken, Nell. "90 Lbs. of Human Dynamite." *Orbit Magazine, Sunday Oklahoman*, December 10, 1972, 10, 12–14.

Bryant, Keith L., Jr. "The Juvenile Court Movement: Oklahoma as a Case Study." *Social Science Quarterly* 49, no. 2 (September 1968): 368–76.

———. "Kate Barnard, Organized Labor, and Social Justice in Oklahoma during the Progressive Era." *Journal of Southern History* 35, no. 2 (May 1969): 145–64.

———. "Labor in Politics: The Oklahoma State Federation of Labor during the Age of Reform." *Labor History* 11, no. 3 (Summer 1970): 259–76.

Clinton, Fred S. "Some Red Cross History." *Chronicles of Oklahoma* 21, no. 2 (March 1943): 183–86.

Cobb, Russell. *The Great Oklahoma Swindle: Race, Religion, and Lies in America's Weirdest State*. Lincoln: University of Nebraska Press, 2020.

Copeland, Edith. "Barnard, Kate." In *Notable American Women, 1607–1950: A Biographical Dictionary*, edited by Edward T. James, Janet Wilson James, and Paul S. Boyer, 1:90–92. Cambridge, Mass.: Belknap Press, 1971.

Cronley, Connie. "Much Love Lost." *Oklahoma Monthly*, February 1977, 10–19, 54–58.

"Department of Charities and Corrections." In *The Oklahoma Red Book*, vol. 2, compiled by W. B. Richards, 26. Oklahoma City: n.p., 1912.

Doyle, Thomas H. "Single versus Double Statehood." Pts. 1–3. *Chronicles of Oklahoma* 5, nos. 1, 2, and 3 (1927): 18–41, 117–48, 266–86.

Fritz, Henry E. "The Last Hurrah of Christian Humanitarian Indian Reform: The Board of Indian Commissioners, 1909–1918." *Western Historical Quarterly* 16, no. 2 (April 1985): 147–62.

Hacker, J. David, and Michael R. Haines. "American Indian Mortality in the Late Nineteenth Century: The Impact of Federal Assimilation Policies on a Vulnerable Population." *Annales de démographie historique* 110, no. 2 (2005): 17–29.

Hougen, Harvey R. "The Impact of Politics and Prison Industry on the General Management of the Kansas State Penitentiary, 1883–1909." *Kansas History: A Journal of the Central Plains* 43, no. 3 (1977): 297–318.

———. "Kate Barnard and the Kansas Penitentiary Scandal, 1908–1909." *Journal of the West* 17, no. 1 (January 1978): 9–18.

Hunt, George W. P. "An Appreciation of Miss Barnard." *Good Housekeeping*, November 1912, 606–7.

Iglauer, Henry S. "The Demolition of the Louisiana Purchase Exposition of 1904." *Bulletin of the Missouri Historical Society* 22, no. 4, pt. 1 (July 1966): 457–67.

Johnson, Alexander. "The Commissioner of Charities in Oklahoma." *Survey*, April 26, 1913, 138–39.

"Kate Barnard Charges Conspiracy to Rob Exists." *Harlow's Weekly*, March 27, 1915, 214–16.

Kelsey, Dana H. "Status and Needs of the Five Civilized Tribes." In Lake Mohonk Conference of Friends of the Indian and Other Dependent Peoples, *Report of the Thirty-First Annual Lake Mohonk Conference of Friends of the Indian and Other Dependent Peoples, October 22d, 23d and 24th, 1913*, 16–24. New York: Lake Mohonk Conference, 1913.

Mangold, George B. "Social Reform in Missouri, 1820–1920." *Missouri Historical Review* 15, no. 1 (October 1920): 191–213.

McKelway, A. J. "'Kate,' the 'Good Angel' of Oklahoma." *American Magazine*, October 1908, 587–93.

Meriweather, Lee. "Labor and Industry in Missouri during the Last Century." *Missouri Historical Review* 15, no. 1 (October 1920): 163–75.

"The Minneapolis Conference." *Charities and the Commons*, July 6, 1907, 382–91 (Kate Barnard sketch on 389–91).

Moorehead, Warren K. "The Lesson of White Earth." In Lake Mohonk Conference of Friends of the Indian and Other Dependent Peoples, *Report of the Thirtieth Annual Meeting of the Lake Mohonk Conference of Friends of the Indians and Other Dependent Peoples*, 53–61. New York: Lake Mohonk Conference, 1912.

Murray, William H. "The Constitutional Convention." *Chronicles of Oklahoma* 9, no. 2 (June 1931): 126–38.

"The National Conference in Buffalo." *Survey*, June 26, 1909, 451–65.

Peterson, Ken. "Ransom Powell and the Tragedy of White Earth." *Minnesota History*, Fall 2012, 89–101.

"Program of the Buffalo Conference." *Survey*, May 29, 1909, 318–20.

"She Is 'Uplifting' Oklahoma." *Literary Digest*, January 11, 1913, 108–9.

Sherr, Lynn, and Jurate Kazickas. "Grave of Kate Barnard." In *The American Woman's Gazetteer*, 191. New York: Bantam Books, 1976.

Shirley, Glenn. "Oklahoma Kate—Woman of Destiny." *West*, March 1968, 19–21, 56–58.

"Southern Child Labor Conference." *Survey*, April 17, 1909, 107–9.

Steffens, Lincoln. "The Least of These: A Fact Story." *Everybody's Magazine*, January 1909, 57–62.

Thoburn, Joseph B. "Kate Barnard." In *A Standard History of Oklahoma*, 3:1329–33. Chicago: American Historical Society, 1916.

Thurston, Rt. Rev. Theodore Payne. "Promotion of Industry among the Indians of Oklahoma." In Lake Mohonk Conference of Friends of the Indian and Other Dependent Peoples, *Report of the Thirty-Second Annual Lake Mohonk Conference on the Indian and Other Dependent Peoples, October 14th, 15th and 16th, 1914*, 26–29. New York: Lake Mohonk Conference, 1914.

Truman, Margaret. "The Good Angel of Oklahoma." In *Women of Courage from Revolutionary Times to the Present*, 183–99. New York: William Morrow and Company, 1976.

Vaux, George, Jr. "Some Observations of Conditions in the Five Civilized Tribes." In Lake Mohonk Conference of Friends of the Indian and Other Dependent Peoples, *Report of the Thirtieth Annual Lake Mohonk Conference of Friends of the Indian and Other Dependent Peoples, October 23rd, 24th and 25th, 1912*, 29–42. New York: Lake Mohonk Conference, 1912.

Woods, H. Merle, "Historical Preservation Which Occurred in El Reno and St. Louis 75 Years Ago." *Chronicles of Oklahoma* 57, no. 4 (Winter 1979–80): 446–50.

Zueblin, Charles. "The Day of the Woman: It Is Here Politically and Socially, in Business and in the Home." *The Delineator*, May 1910, 411.

Index

Printed in the USA
CPSIA information can be obtained
at www.ICGtesting.com
LVHW051414241123
764784LV00002B/201